Calm Abiding & Special Insight

Calm Abiding & Special Insight

Achieving Spiritual Transformation Through Meditation

Geshe Gedün Lodrö

Translated and edited by Jeffrey Hopkins
Co-edited by Anne C. Klein and Leah Zahler

Snow Lion Publications
Ithaca, New York USA

Snow Lion Publications
P.O. Box 6483
Ithaca, New York 14851 USA
607-273-8519

Printed in Canada on recycled paper

ISBN 1-55939-110-3

Library of Congress Cataloging-in-Publication Data

Lodrö, Geshe Gedün, 1924-1979

Calm abiding & special insight: achieving spiritual transformation through meditation / Geshe Gedün Lodrö; translated and edited by Jeffrey Hopkins; co-edited by Anne C. Klein and Leah Zahler.

p. cm. -- (Textual studies and translations in Indo-Tibetan Buddhism)

Includes bibliographical references and index.

ISBN 1-55939-110-3 (alk. paper)

1. Meditation--Buddhism. 2. Śamatha (Buddhism) 3. Vipaśyanā (Buddhism) 4. Buddhism--China--Tibet--Doctrines. I. Hopkins, Jeffrey. II. Zahler, Leah. III. Klein, Anne C., 1947- . IV. Series.

BQ7805.L63 1998

294.3'443--dc21 98-34493

CIP

CONTENTS

CHARTS AND LISTS

PREFACE

This book vividly presents an intimate and detailed picture of the intricacies of meditation such that the reader is drawn into a Tibetan world-view of spiritual transformation. In a series of lectures at the University of Virginia during the spring and summer of 1979, Geshe Gedün Lodrö gradually unfolded for a group of advanced students of Tibetan language and Tibetan Buddhism the perspective of the Tibetan landscape of mental development. The environment for meditative change is comprised by the jungle of beings' afflicted states but with hidden potential for change. The restoration of the landscape to its pristine state is wrought by techniques that are built from inner potentialities for stability, clarity, and calm, but these very techniques are fraught with pitfalls from inner habitual weaknesses. The dangers of not recognizing the actual causes of deprivation and distortion are great, and the possibilities of implementing the wrong antidote or of over-extending an appropriate one until it becomes counterproductive are many. Subtle distinctions between types of interfering factors are needed; there is seldom a simple way to coax the mind back to its natural state. The very measures taken to purify it can exacerbate old problems and introduce new ones. Through such detail Geshe Gedün Lodrö makes vividly clear a Tibetan approach to meditative therapy.

Scholastic Buddhism is often thought to be dry, numerically oriented listings of mental and physical phenomena that fail to capture the vibrancy, the force, of life. In this series of lectures Geshe Gedün Lodrö shows that the heritage of Indian and Tibetan meditative lore that he embodied lives and breathes in a relevant and realistic atmosphere of intimately interwoven nuance. By constantly placing techniques of meditation in their larger Buddhist cultural context—a culture whose *raison d'être* is spiritual development—he reveals a living world of mental practices replete with resources for describing, facing, and counteracting both superficial and systemic disorders.

Born in the capital of Tibet, Hla-s̄a, in 1924, Geshe Gedün Lodrö entered Dre-b̄ung Monastic University (Ham-dong House in Go-mang

College) on the outskirts of Hla-s̄a at the age of nine as a novice monk. He took basic examinations in 1940, received full ordination in 1947, and gained the degree of ge-s̄hay in 1961 in exile in India as the first among three scholars who were awarded the number one ranking in the highest class. He was a scholar of prodigious learning, keeping in active memory 1,800 folios of basic texts, which in English would be at least 3,600 pages. He told me that he accomplished this by using all spare time (such as in walking from one place to another!) to recite texts to himself. Even more, he was famed for his ability in debate; by his own account he was the equal of others when taking the position of challenger but was at his best when answering others' challenges. This undoubtedly was why he was chosen to become a faculty member at Go-mang College before graduation.

He told me that when the Chinese began shelling in Hla-s̄a, he climbed the steep hill above Dre-b̄ung and looked down on the unfolding scene, realizing that the type of life and opportunity for study he had had until 1959 would never occur again. He knew he was seeing the end of an era.

In exile in India, he took his ge-s̄hay degree with top honors and later when the Dalai Lama conducted interviews of all the ge-s̄hays who had escaped, Geshe Gedün Lodrö was declared to be the top scholar. The Dalai Lama sent him to teach at the University of Hamburg in 1967, where he learned German fluently and eventually became a tenured member of the faculty. I first met him in 1970 when he visited his main teacher and my mentor, Kensur Ngawang Lekden, in Madison, Wisconsin. Kensur Lekden spoke very highly of his student, and thus I wrote into a Fulbright grant proposal three months of study with him in Hamburg while I was on my way to India at the end of 1971. His fluid treatment of many philosophical issues during my stay in Hamburg led to my inviting him to the University of Virginia in 1979, when I translated the lectures that comprise this book. He returned to Hamburg at the beginning of August of that year, and suddenly passed away in November, slumping to the floor outside the door of his apartment. We had many plans to work on various texts and systems, and indeed the world lost one of its most learned persons.

These lectures were originally edited by Anne C. Klein (then a graduate student at the University of Virginia and now a Professor of Religious Studies at Rice University). A second editing (including identification of Sanskrit equivalents and construction of a glossary and an index) was done by Leah Zahler, then a graduate student at the University of Virginia who wrote a Ph.D. dissertation on related topics; we regret her untimely death and acknowledge that this book would never have reached publication without her great effort. Geshe Gedün Lodrö went through the entire first editing in English, as I have done at each stage of the manuscript.

Jeffrey Hopkins
University of Virginia

TECHNICAL NOTE

- For the names of Indian scholars and systems used in the body of the text, *ch*, *sh*, and *ṣh* are used instead of the more usual *c*, *ś*, and *ṣ* for the sake of easy pronunciation by non-specialists; however, *chchh* is not used for *cch*. In the notes the usual transliteration system for Sanskrit is used.
- The names of Indian Buddhist schools of thought are translated into English in an effort to increase accessibility for non-specialists.
- Transliteration of Tibetan is done in accordance with a system devised by Turrell Wylie, et al.; see "A Standard System of Tibetan Transcription," *Harvard Journal of Asiatic Studies*, vol. 22, 1959, 261-67.
- The names of Tibetan authors and religious orders are given in "essay phonetics" for the sake of easy pronunciation; for a discussion of the system used, see the Technical Note at the beginning of my *Meditation on Emptiness* (London: Wisdom Publications, 1983; rev. ed. Boston: Wisdom Publications, 1996), 19-22.
- Endnotes are marked with "1, 2, 3..."; footnotes are marked with "a, b, c...."
- For translations and editions of texts cited, see the Bibliography.
- A list of technical terms in English, Tibetan, and Sanskrit is provided in the Glossary at the end of the book.

PART ONE:
CALM ABIDING

INTRODUCTION

The focus of the topics to be discussed here are calm abiding[1] and special insight.[2] As the Bodhisattva Shāntideva says in his *Engaging in the Bodhisattva Deeds*:[3]

> Knowing that special insight endowed with calm abiding
> Thoroughly destroys the afflictive emotions,
> One must initially seek calm abiding.
> It is achieved by those liking non-attachment to the world.

Therefore, I will present an explanation of the means for attaining both liberation[4] from cyclic existence[5] and omniscience, based on achieving calm abiding and special insight. The means for achieving calm abiding and special insight are of two types—those depending on sūtra and on tantra. Sūtra itself explains two ways of achieving calm abiding and special insight—the way of the Hīnayāna, or Lower Vehicle, and the way of the Mahāyāna, or Great Vehicle.[6] In Tibet, Tantra also has two methods, that of the New Translation Schools[7] and that of the Old Translation School;[8] the latter method is known as the Great Completeness.[9]

My emphasis here will be on the achievement of liberation and omniscience in dependence on the paths of calm abiding and special insight.

---

1 *zhi gnas, śamatha.*

2 *lhag mthong, vipaśyanā.*

3 *byang chub sems dpa'i spyod pa la 'jug pa, bodhicaryāvatāra;* VIII.4. The Sanskrit is:

śamathena vipaśyanāsuyuktaḥ kurute kleśavināśamityavetya
śamathaḥ prathamaṃ gaveṣaṇīyaḥ sa ca loke nirapekṣayābhiratyā

See Vidhushekara Bhattacharya, ed., *Bodhicaryāvatāra*, Bibliotheca Indica vol. 280 (Calcutta: the Asiatic Society, 1960), 136.

4 *thar pa, mokṣa.*

5 *'khor ba, saṃsāra.*

6 For a discussion of the terms "Hīnayāna" and "Mahāyāna," see p. 152ff.

7 S̄a-ḡya-b̄a (*sa skya pa*), Ḡa-gyu-b̄a (*bka' brgyud pa*), and Ge-luk-b̄a (*dge lugs pa*).

8 N̄ying-ma-b̄a (*rnying ma pa*).

9 *rdzogs chen.*

Most texts discuss the achievement of liberation, and so forth, in terms of a presentation of the five paths[1] and the ten Bodhisattva grounds,[2] it being less common to explain these in terms of calm abiding and special insight. This latter type of presentation is done through a discussion of four topics:

1 the entity or nature of calm abiding and special insight individually
2 the objects of observation and subjective aspects of these
3 the mental factors conjoined with calm abiding and special insight
4 how to develop calm abiding and special insight.

It is rare for all these topics to be collected into a single explanation. Although the great Indian texts discuss them, generally any single text will explain only some but not all of these topics. For example, some texts completely set forth the objects of observation of calm abiding and special insight from within a Hīnayāna system but not in terms of the Mahāyāna.

Also, there are two systems of Manifest Knowledge,[3] lower and higher. The term "lower Manifest Knowledge" refers to the system of Vasubandhu's *Treasury of Manifest Knowledge*,[4] and the term "higher Manifest Knowledge," to the system of Asaṅga's *Summary of Manifest Knowledge*.[5] A text that extensively sets forth the lower system's mode of procedure does not extensively explain that of the higher system, and vice versa. For example, the sixth chapter of Vasubandhu's *Treasury of Manifest Knowledge* sets forth the mode of procedure of a Hīnayānist who, in dependence on a Hīnayāna path, cultivates calm abiding. Similarly, Asaṅga's Five Treatises on the Grounds[6] and Two Summaries [the *Summary of Manifest Knowledge* and the *Summary of the Great Vehicle*[7]] set forth the Mahāyāna mode of achieving calm abiding and special insight. Here, however, *all* of them will be explained under one heading. My hope is to present the entire structure of the path, beginning with the procedure for achieving calm abiding and ranging through the stage of its union with special insight. I will present both the upper and lower systems' assertions on these topics.

There is a mode of procedure for achieving calm abiding and special in-

---

1 *lam, mārga.*

2 *sa, bhūmi.*

3 *chos mngon pa, abhidharma.*

4 *chos mngon pa'i mdzod, abhidharmakośa;* P5590, vol. 115.

5 *chos mngon pa kun btus, abhidharmasamuccaya;* P5550, vol. 112.

6 See the Bibliography for a listing of these.

7 *theg pa chen po bsdus pa, mahāyānasaṃgraha;* P5549, vol. 112.

sight that is common to the sūtra vehicles. This, again, is different from the system of either the higher or lower Manifest Knowledge. Further, the mode of procedure for achieving calm abiding and special insight in the three lower tantra sets is also a little different from those of the sūtra system. In Highest Yoga Tantra not much is said directly about achieving calm abiding and special insight; however, in practicing the four tantra sets, these are achieved along the way. Thus, it is possible to explain the procedure for doing so even in Highest Yoga Tantra, which also differs to some extent from those of the lower tantra sets.

I will try to present the path to omniscience in terms of calm abiding and special insight without quoting the many different texts in which these topics appear. Rather, I will try to explain the *meaning* of these topics. It is important that the general mode of procedure of the paths of calm abiding and special insight be understood not only by proponents of tenet systems[1] but also by ordinary beings, since the latter can benefit from knowing about similitudes of calm abiding and special insight. This is because the technical name "calm abiding" refers to a means of setting, placing, or stabilizing the mind, and similarly although "special insight" is a technical name, it refers simply to the mind's analyzing an object. Calm abiding is a technique for setting the mind, without fluctuation, on a single object of observation. Special insight is a mind that not only remains on its object but analyzes it within clarity and intensity. Thus, I feel that these are very important topics not just for practitioners of systems but for ordinary persons, since anyone can benefit from engaging in analysis of them.

OUTLINE OF TOPICS

Here is a complete outline of the topics relating to calm abiding and special insight that I intend to discuss:

Calm Abiding

Prerequisites for cultivating it

The physical posture

- coarse
- subtle: meditation on the breath

The physical basis: beings who can achieve calm abiding

Mental bases

---

[1] *grub mtha', siddhānta.*

Objects of observation

others' assertions

our own school's assertion

Benefits of cultivating calm abiding and special insight

The order of cultivating calm abiding and special insight

How to achieve calm abiding based on abandoning the five faults by means of the eight antidotes, as taught in Maitreya's *Differentiation of the Middle and the Extremes*[1]

How to achieve calm abiding based on the nine mental abidings, as taught in Asaṅga's *Grounds of Hearers*[2] and *Summary of Manifest Knowledge*

The measure of having achieved calm abiding

The signs of having achieved calm abiding

The mode of rising from meditative equipoise.

Special Insight

Why special insight is necessarily achieved in dependence on calm abiding

How to achieve special insight in dependence on calm abiding

The mode of the mundane path[3]

The mode of the supramundane path

How to differentiate Buddhist and non-Buddhist forms of calm abiding and special insight

The need to achieve the special insight that observes emptiness as asserted by the Mādhyamika and the Chittamātra systems

The mode of seeking the view

seeking meditation from within the view

seeking the view from within meditation

actual mode of seeking the view based on a reasoning such as dependent-arising or the lack of being one or many, as well as the identification of the object of negation[4]

---

1 *dbus dang mtha' rnam par 'byed pa, madhyāntavibhaṅga;* P5522, vol. 108.

2 *nyan sa, śrāvakabhūmi;* P 5537, vol. 110, 35-130.

3 Gedün Lodrö's stay at the University of Virginia ended during his treatment of this topic. He and Jeffrey Hopkins intended to continue working on the remaining topics in the ensuing years, but Gedün Lodrö's unfortunate death prevented these plans. Thus, the book ends in the midst of this topic but with a summary and conclusion that Gedün Lodrö provided at the conclusion of the course.

4 See Jeffrey Hopkins, *Meditation on Emptiness,* 43-66, 127-96, 625-97. For an extensive treatment of the object of negation, see Elizabeth Napper, *Dependent-Arising and Emptiness* (London: Wisdom Publications, 1988).

The measure of having achieved calm abiding and special insight observing emptiness

The stages of the path from the attainment of a union of calm abiding and special insight observing emptiness through to the tenth ground, according to the Prāsaṅgika system

Analysis of whether a final uninterrupted path can be generated by means of the sūtra path alone and if not, why not

Analysis of whether a final uninterrupted path can be generated based on the three lower tantra sets

If the final uninterrupted path cannot be generated based on the three lower tantra sets, the difference between these and the sūtra path

Then, an analysis of whether there is a special meditative stabilization which is a union of calm abiding and special insight in dependence on which the final uninterrupted path can be generated

Then, if Buddhahood cannot be achieved through sūtra or the three lower tantric paths alone, from what viewpoint it is said that one can progress to the final uninterrupted path by Highest Yoga Tantra—whether it is from the viewpoint of obstructions or antidotes

Subsidiarily, a presentation of the mode of abandoning obstructions in the sūtra and tantra Mahāyānas

Since it is in dependence on Highest Yoga Tantra that one can progress to Buddhahood, a presentation of that tantra's assertions on calm abiding and special insight

Elimination of qualms with respect to whether the three lower tantra sets have a method for achieving calm abiding and special insight which is separate from that of the sūtra systems

The mode of progress on the five paths according to the *Guhyasamāja Tantra* from within Highest Yoga Tantra.

This is essentially a complete outline; however, there will be some additional subtopics within these headings. Certain topics may also be condensed and discussed in relation to another topic. I have presented this outline for the sake of giving you a rough idea of what will be discussed; we will not necessarily proceed exactly this way.

SOURCES

The basic source for the order of the topics in the table of contents given just above, from the physical basis through the end of the discussion on calm abiding, is Jam-ȳang-shay-b̄a's[1] *Great Exposition of the Concentrations and Formless Absorptions.*[2] However, Jam-ȳang-shay-b̄a is not necessarily the main source for each individual topic. Within Tibetan commentaries, Jam-ȳang-shay-b̄a's presentation of the concentrations[3] and the formless absorptions[4] is the best. Although, indeed, there are other texts that give brief presentations of similar topics, he presents the topic and its sources at great length, whereby his work on the subject is unexcelled. This is why the arrangement of the order of the topics is taken from his text.

Jam-ȳang-shay-b̄a was innovative in this respect since his ordering of the topics does not accord with the explanations in his own sources. The topics themselves come from Asaṅga's *Grounds of Hearers* and the *Sūtra Unraveling the Thought,*[5] among others, but the ordering in these texts varies with the result that Jam-ȳang-shay-b̄a's ordering is his own. With regard to the topics preceding the discussion of the physical basis of calm abiding, I gathered my points from many different sources. The order of my presentation is not based on a particular text.

Earlier I said I would explain how calm abiding is cultivated in the lower, or Hīnayāna, systems also; although this does not appear in the present outline, it will be included within the topic of objects of observation.

Indian textual sources for the discussion of calm abiding

Maitreya's *Ornament for the Mahāyāna Sūtras*[6]
Maitreya's *Differentiation of the Middle and the Extremes*
The *Sūtra Unraveling the Thought* and Wonch'uk's[7] commentary[8] on it
Asaṅga's *Grounds of Hearers*
Asaṅga's *Summary of Manifest Knowledge*
Vasubandhu's *Treasury of Manifest Knowledge*

---

1 *'jam dbyangs bzhad pa,* 1648-1721.

2 *bsam gzugs chen mo.* The longer title is *Treatise on the Presentations of the Concentrations and Formless Absorptions, Adornment Beautifying the Subduer's Teaching, Ocean of Scripture and Reasoning, Delighting the Fortunate* (*bsam gzugs kyi snyoms 'jug rnams kyi rnam par bzhag pa'i bstan bcos thub bstan mdzes rgyan lung dang rigs pa'i rgya mtsho skal bzang dga' byed*).

3 *bsam gtan, dhyāna.*

4 *gzugs med kyi snyoms 'jug, ārūpyasamāpatti.*

5 *dgongs pa nges par 'grel pa'i mdo, saṃdhinirmocanasūtra;* P774, vol. 29; Toh 106, Dharma vol. 18.

6 *theg pa chen po'i mdo sde'i rgyan, mahāyānasūtrālaṃkāra;* P5521, vol. 108, 1-19.

7 Tib. *Wen tshig,* Chin. *Yüan-ts'e,* 613-696.

8 P5517, vol. 106.

Bhāvaviveka's *Heart of the Middle*[1] and his own commentary on it known as the *Blaze of Reasoning*[2]

Kamalashīla's *Stages of Meditation*.[3]

---

[1] *dbu ma snying po, madhyamakahṛdaya;* P5255

[2] *rtog ge 'bar ba, tarkajvālā;* P5256.

[3] *sgom pa'i rim pa, bhāvanākrama;* P5310-12, vol. 102; Toh 3915-17, Dharma vol. 73, Tokyo *sde dge* vol. 15.

1 PREREQUISITES

The six prerequisites[1] for achieving calm abiding are:

1 staying in an agreeable place[2]
2 having few desires[3]
3 knowing satisfaction[4]
4 not having many activities[5]
5 pure ethics[6]
6 thoroughly abandoning thoughts.[7]

Most of these are readily understandable, but a little commentary is useful for some of them. The fourth, not having many activities, means that when one begins to cultivate calm abiding and special insight it is unsuitable to initiate types of activities that discord with the activity of cultivation. As to the fifth, pure ethics, it is not necessary to have assumed the vows[8] of a monastic[9] or novice,[10] but if one has taken either of these vows and broken them it is necessary to engage in confession[11] and the intention to restrain from such activity in the future. This process is known as purification and renewal,[12] and anyone who has broken vows must engage in it before cultivating calm abiding. Even a person who does not have vows must, if he or she has engaged in non-virtuous[13] activities, confess them

---

1 *tshogs bsten pa.*
2 *mthun pa'i yul na gnas pa.*
3 *'dod pa chung ba.*
4 *chog shes pa.*
5 *bya ba mang po'i 'du 'dzi yong su spang ba.*
6 *tshul khrims dag pa.*
7 *rnam rtog yong su spang ba.*
8 *sdom pa, saṃvara.*
9 *dge slong, bhikṣu.*
10 *dge tshul, śramaṇera.*
11 *bshags pa, deśanā.*
12 *gso sbyong.*
13 *mi dge ba, akuśala.*

and develop an intention to restrain from them in the future and should then consider that these non-virtues have been purified. This is because, if one seeks to improve oneself from within a state of having committed non-virtuous actions, one's basis[1] is defiled to begin with, and it is difficult to generate any improvement. The point here is that pure ethics, as a prerequisite of calm abiding, does not necessarily involve having taken vows.

The sixth prerequisite, thoroughly abandoning thoughts, means that one should abandon coarse non-virtuous thoughts such as a wish to kill or steal, and also thoughts whose motivation is neutral[2] but might involve the generation of fright or fear.

The agreeable place mentioned as the first prerequisite should have four qualities:

1 Nourishment should be easily attainable.
2 The area should be free of wild animals.
3 The place should be one that does not harm.
4 One should be accompanied by friends who do not have different views.[3]

In the first quality, that nourishment should be easily attainable, "nourishment"[4] refers to the coarsest of the four types of nourishment, food. People of the Desire Realm[5] cannot live without depending on food and sleep. The four types of nourishment are (1) coarse food,[6] (2) mental nourishment,[7] (3) nourishment of intention,[8] and (4) nourishment of consciousness.[9] The sense of mental satisfaction that comes when a desire is fulfilled is called mental nourishment. Just as coarse food nourishes the body, so satisfaction nourishes or replenishes the mind upon fulfillment of a desire. The third type, nourishment of intention, is an action[10] that projects the next lifetime. Since it generates or produces the next lifetime, it is called a nourisher, or nourishment; it is the second link of the twelve-

[1] *rten, āśraya.*
[2] *lung du ma bstan pa, avyākṛta.*
[3] *lta ba, dṛṣṭi.*
[4] *zas, āhāra.*
[5] *'dod khams, kāmadhātu.*
[6] *kham gyi zas, kavaḍaṃkāra-āhāra.*
[7] *yid kyi zas.*
[8] *sems pa'i zas, manaḥsaṃcetanāhāra.*
[9] *rnam shes kyi zas, vijñāna-āhāra.*
[10] *las, karma.*

linked dependent-arising.[1] Similarly, the third link, which is called consciousness,[2] is known as the food of consciousness. Just as the action that projects, or impels, a future lifetime is called a nourisher, so the consciousness which is imprinted with that action and which will at the time of the effect of that action in the future life be imprinted with other karmas is called a nourisher, or nourishment. Why is [the first link of dependent-arising,] ignorance,[3] not called a nourisher? It is because ignorance is the agent that pervades everything; thus, it is not singled out as a nourisher.

There is still another type of nourishment, that of meditative stabilization.[4] Persons who have achieved calm abiding and special insight and have proceeded to high levels of the path do not need to use coarse food; they have the nourishment of meditative stabilization. If you should wish to investigate this topic, the nourishment of meditative stabilization is discussed in the context of the four developing causes which replenish or increase the body: sleep, meditative stabilization, massage, and coarse food. The sources here are Kamalashīla's *Stages of Meditation* and Maitreya's *Ornament for the Mahāyāna Sūtras* and, in addition, the *Sūtra Unraveling the Thought* and Wonch'uk's commentary on it.

The second quality of an agreeable place is that the area should be free of wild animals. For example, people go to remote areas to meditate, but it should not be where ferocious animals abide.

The third quality is that the place should be one that does not harm—for example, a region without earthquakes. This may at first seem to be of little purpose, or as if you are making yourself too important. It is not so, however, because based on the type of physical life-support that we now have, although we can indeed waste our lives, we can also achieve calm abiding, special insight, and so forth; therefore, it is absolutely necessary to take care of this body. Similarly, in tantra it is a basic infraction to disregard one's body or to feel that "whatever happens, happens," that it does not make any difference.

The fourth quality is that one should be accompanied by friends who do not have different views. There are many views—Mādhyamika,[5] Chit-

---

1 *rten 'byung, pratītyasamutpāda.*

2 *rnam shes, vijñāna.*

3 *ma rig pa, avidyā.*

4 *ting nge 'dzin, samādhi.*

5 *dbu ma pa.*

tamātra,[1] and so forth. There is the view of the transitory collection [as a real I and mine];[2] there are extreme[3] views [of permanence[4] and annihilation,[5]] and so forth. Also, in general, there are two types of views, natural and adventitious. A person newly achieving calm abiding needs to do so with some associates. Ideally, these associates would be people who have already achieved calm abiding; if not, they should have some familiarity with the process. There would not necessarily be any fault in one's associates' having a different natural view—for example, if one person were of a very peaceful type and the other, very excitable. However, if their adventitious views were discordant, they probably could not serve as associates to one another in achieving calm abiding. A difference in adventitious view means that people have different systems of tenets or have an interest in different treatises[6] or in different people.

The area should also have all the pleasant articles of yoga.[7]

What other prerequisites are there? Asaṅga's *Grounds of Hearers* mentions the ten discriminations[8] that are concordant in quality with the three trainings.[9] They can all be included within the trainings in higher ethics,[10] higher meditative stabilization,[11] and higher wisdom.[12]

There are ten practices that are concordant with the trainings, but I will not discuss them here.

The prerequisites of calm abiding are of two types: excellent and abso-

---

[1] *sems tsam pa.*

[2] *'jig tshogs la lta ba, satkāyadṛṣṭi.*

[3] *mtha', anta.*

[4] *rtag pa, śaśvata.*

[5] *chad pa, uccheda.*

[6] *bstan bcos, śāstra.*

[7] *rnal 'byor.* "The pleasant articles of yoga" refers to having done the hearing and thinking necessary to eliminate false ideas with respect to the object of meditation and to become skilled in the essentials of practice (Jeffrey Hopkins, *Meditation on Emptiness,* 68). See also Lati Rinbochay, Denma Lochö Rinbochay, Leah Zahler, and Jeffrey Hopkins, *Meditative States in Tibetan Buddhism: The Concentrations and Formless Absorptions* (London: Wisdom Publications, 1983), 76.

[8] *'du shes, saṃjñā.*

[9] *bslab pa, śikṣā.*

[10] *lhag pa'i tshul khrims, adhiśīla.*

[11] *lhag pa'i sems, adhicitta.*

[12] *lhag pa'i shes rab, adhiprajñā.* For a brief description of the three trainings, see Tenzin Gyatso, the Fourteenth Dalai Lama, *Opening the Eye of New Awareness,* trans. Donald S. Lopez, Jr., with Jeffrey Hopkins (London: Wisdom Publications, 1985), 53-85.

lutely necessary. If you are without the former, it does not matter much, but if you lack the absolutely necessary prerequisites, the possibility of achieving calm abiding is interrupted; you cannot achieve it. As Atīsha's *Lamp for the Path to Enlightenment*[1] says:

> If the prerequisites for calm abiding deteriorate,
> Then, even if you meditate for a thousand years
> In order to achieve calm abiding, there is no time
> When you can attain meditative stabilization.

Therefore, a yogic practitioner who wishes to achieve calm abiding must be able to distinguish between the excellent and absolutely essential prerequisites. The essential ones involve giving up non-virtuous conceptions and neutral ones causing fright. With regard to pure ethics, it is particularly important for someone who has committed murder to engage in the process of purification, involving confession and the intention of future restraint. Otherwise, it would be impossible for that person to achieve calm abiding. The other prerequisites, such as knowing satisfaction and having few activities, are not essential because there are some people who can engage in activities and also in the meantime achieve calm abiding.

---

1 *byang chub lam gyi sgron ma, bodhipathapradīpa;* P5343, vol. 103. This is stanza 39; see Richard Sherbourne, S. J., *A Lamp for the Path and Commentary* (London: George Allen & Unwin, 1983), 9 and 119.

2 PHYSICAL POSTURE

SEVEN FEATURES OF THE PHYSICAL POSTURE

Let us assume that all the external prerequisites have been fulfilled. The meditator should then sit comfortably on a cushion, set the legs in the cross-legged posture, and put the hands in the position of meditative equipoise[1] about four finger-widths below the navel, with the left hand under the right and the two thumbs just touching; the fingers, rather than the thumbs, are four finger-widths below the navel. The cushion itself should be something that is naturally higher in the rear and lower in front.

Straighten the backbone, and bend the neck a little. Leave your lips and teeth as usual, according to your nature. Do not force them wide open or closed. Some Tibetan commentaries say to open the mouth, and some say to close it, but Asaṅga's *Grounds of Hearers* says to leave it as usual. It is fine for those who like to have their mouths open to meditate in that way. If, because of how the winds[2] course in the body, one likes or finds it necessary to have the mouth closed, that is also fine. The reliable texts all say to leave the lips and teeth as usual.

Join the tongue to the roof of the mouth—that is, touch the tip of the tongue to the area just above the upper teeth. This helps reduce the flow of saliva during deep meditative equipoise. Putting the tongue in this position naturally prevents the saliva from falling.

Set the head and shoulders straight, and partially close the eyes. There are some meditative stabilizations in which it is necessary to shut the eyes completely, but this is not such. Setting the shoulders straight means that there should be no difference in height between the two shoulders. The reason for doing this is that channels[3] exist throughout the body, and when the body is straightened, the channels are straightened. This, in turn, straightens the winds that course in the channels, and because the winds

---

[1] *mnyam bzhag, samāhita.*

[2] *rlung, prāṇa.*

[3] *rtsa, nāḍi.*

and mind[1] operate together, by straightening the winds one can concentrate the mind, or set it on whatever one wants. Because the body, channels, and mind do not exist self-sufficiently but are in a dependent relationship, when one is straightened all are straightened, and when one goes bad all follow. The sources for this explanation are Kamalashīla's *Stages of Meditation* and Haribhadra's *Illumination of (Maitreya's) "Ornament for Clear Realization,"*[2] as well as the *Vajra Garland*,[3] which is one of the four or five explanatory tantras of the *Guhyasamāja Tantra*,[4] and the first section of the *Compendium of the Principles of All Ones Gone Thus Tantra*.[5]

There are two purposes in assuming the meditative posture, common and uncommon. Regarding the former, because the body is straightened well, it is easy to generate pliancy.[6] Although it is difficult for someone not used to this posture to remain in it even for a few minutes, once you are accustomed to it, it is easy to remain this way for a long time. It is much more difficult to proceed if you have not straightened the body. Yet another purpose for this posture is to make known that this mode of behavior is different from others. Furthermore, this posture was recommended by Buddha and the Hearers.[7] The source for this is Asaṅga's *Grounds of Hearers*.

As to the uncommon purposes of sitting in the cross-legged posture, the downward-voiding wind is straightened and caused to enter the central channel.[8] Thus, this posture has the purpose of causing winds to enter the central channel. Coarse mental factors[9] such as jealousy,[10] hatred,[11] and so

---

1 *sems, citta.*

2 *shes rab kyi pha rol tu phyin pa'i man ngag gi bstan bcos mngon par rtogs pa'i rgyan ces bya ba'i 'grel pa, abhisamayālaṃkārnāmaprajñāpāramitopadeśasāstravṛtti;* P5191 vol. 90.

3 *vajramālā, rdo rje phreng ba; śrīvajramālābhidhānamahāyogatantrasarvatantrahṛdayarahasyavibhaṅga, rnal 'byor chen po'i rgyud dpal rdo rje phreng ba mngon par brjod pa rgyud thams cad kyi snying po gsang ba rnam par phye ba,* P82, vol. 3.

4 *de bzhin gshegs pa thams cad kyi sku gsung thugs kyi gsang chen gsang ba 'dus pa zhes bya ba brtag pa'i rgyal po chen po, sarvatathāgatakāyavākcittarahasyaguhyasamājanāmamahākalparāja;* P81, vol. 3.

5 *de bzhin gshegs pa thams cad kyi de kho na nyid bsdus pa zhes bya ba theg pa chen po'i mdo, sarvatathāgatatattvasaṃgrahanāmamahāyānasūtra;* P112, vol. 4 (Toh. 479).

6 *shin tu sbyangs pa, praśrabdhi.*

7 *nyan thos, śrāvaka.*

8 *rtsa dbu ma, avadhūtī.*

9 *sems byung, caitta.*

10 *phrag dog, irṣyā.*

11 *zhe sdang, dveṣa.*

forth, are pacified because this posture causes the winds serving as the mounts[1] of such coarse minds to be pacified. The purpose of placing the hands in the posture of meditative equipoise four finger-widths below the navel is to cause the water wind—from among the earth,[2] water,[3] fire,[4] and wind[5] winds—to enter the central channel. Why should one cause the water wind to enter the central channel? Mainly to pacify hatred, and so forth. The reason for straightening the spine and shoulders is to cause the earth wind to enter the central channel; this, in turn, pacifies obscuration[6] from among the three root poisons—desire,[7] hatred, and obscuration. What is the uncommon purpose of placing the tip of the tongue behind the ridge of the upper teeth? This is to pacify the wind wind; it causes the suppression or pacification of the coarse winds that serve as the mount of desire. It is important to set the eyes in a natural manner because most of the important channels are involved with the eyes.

Question: In Hindu systems, it is suggested that one do *haṭha* yoga to get physical flexibility in order to sit for a long time. Is there anything like this in the Buddhist systems?

Answer: There is a breath meditation known as the pot-like[8] which is set forth in both Hindu and Buddhist systems. There are not too many physical exercises in Buddhism, although there are many varieties of the posture that I have explained. The external body is not the most important factor; the main concern is the internal winds.

SETTLING DOWN OF THE WINDS

There are three stages regarding the settling down of the winds. These are three different systems, or sets of quintessential instructions,[9] on how to settle the winds.

1 A yogi initially seeking to achieve calm abiding meditates on just the ex-

---

[1] *bzhon pa.*

[2] *sa, pṛthivī.*

[3] *chu, āp.*

[4] *me, tejas.*

[5] *rlung, vāyu.*

[6] *gti mug, moha.*

[7] *'dod chags, rāga.*

[8] *bum pa can.*

[9] *man ngag, upadeśa.*

halation and inhalation of the breath[1] without keeping count of the exhalations and inhalations, without paying attention to *how* she or he exhales and inhales but only to the fact that he or she is doing so, thinking, "I am exhaling; I am inhaling." Such a meditative stabilization has as its object of observation[2] only the exhalation and inhalation of the breath.

2 The yogic practitioner keeps count of the inhalations and exhalations, mentally repeating the number only once for each cycle of breathing in and breathing out. The count begins with the inhalation. One does not force the breath in or out but breathes naturally. This practice is known as the twenty-one cycles because the practitioner counts to twenty-one.

3 The yogi breathes in through the left nostril and out through the right three times and then reverses this, breathing in through the right nostril and out through the left three times. The count begins with the inhalation. Then the yogi inhales through both nostrils and exhales through both, doing this also three times. For those who have not trained in this practice, it is suitable to press closed the nostril temporarily not being used, but for a trained practitioner such pressure is unnecessary. Some texts say to use the fingers in this way, but such advice is directed to beginners. This practice does not mainly rely on the exhalation and inhalation of the breath but on imagination of it. This third system is called "the nine-cycled dispelling of wind-corpses" [that is, bad winds]. It is as though the coarse winds that serve as the mounts of impure motivations and coarse thoughts are expelled with them.

There are two types of instruction, textual[3] and experiential.[4] The latter means that a yogic practitioner gives instruction on how to achieve calm abiding based on his or her own experience. Within the latter type, there are two sets of quintessential instructions regarding the purification of bad motivation. Persons who initially want to achieve calm abiding set up their motivation, which is that they are meditating in order to attain calm abiding. Then, before assuming the formal physical posture, they cleanse impure motivation. Having done this, they assume the formal posture. If, at this time, no other coarse thought appears, there is no need to purify motivation and the practice of meditating on the breath is begun immediately, but if, between the time of assuming the formal posture and begin-

---

1 *dbugs 'byung rngub, ānāpāna.*

2 *dmigs pa, ālaṃbana.*

3 *gzhung khrid.*

4 *myong khrid.*

ning observation of the breath, coarse thoughts interfere, then, together with meditating on the breath, the practitioner again purifies the motivation. This is one mode of instruction from experience. According to the other instruction, the person thinks, "I wish to achieve calm abiding," sits down in the formal posture, and, just before beginning the cultivation of meditative stabilization on the breath, purifies the motivation.

In order to purify bad motivation, it is necessary to make it manifest. This is another mode of instruction from experience. However, with regard to instructions from texts, there is no certainty that a given text will explain one person's practice, beginning at the beginning and going through to the end. Also, there is no definiteness regarding the order; a text may explain special insight first, or emptiness,[1] or calm abiding. Therefore, when texts mention how to act when sustaining objects of observation and subjective aspects,[2] such statements detail the mode of procedure for practical application of the teachings, which can be presented variously in the texts.

There is both a reason and a purpose for cultivating the meditative stabilization observing exhalation and inhalation of the breath. The reason is mainly to purify impure motivations. What exactly is to be purified? The main of these are the three poisons—desire, hatred, and obscuration. Even though we have these at all times and even though the meditator will still retain them, she or he is seeking to suppress their manifest functioning at that time. The specific purpose for cleansing impure motivations before meditation is to dispel bad motivations connected with this lifetime, such as having hatred toward enemies, attachment to friends, and so forth. In terms of the practice I am explaining here, even the thought of a religious practitioner of small capacity is included within impure motivations; such a person engages in practice mainly for the sake of a good future lifetime. Similarly, if on this occasion one has the motivation of a religious practitioner of middling capacity—that of only oneself escaping from cyclic existence, this is also impure.

What is a pure motivation? To take as one's aim the welfare[3] of all sentient beings.[4] This is the motivation of a religious practitioner of great capacity. Meditators should imagine or manifest their own impure motiva-

---

1 *stong pa nyid, śūnyatā.*

2 *dmigs rnam skyong ba'i skabs.*

3 *don, artha.*

4 *sems can, sattva.*

tion in the form of smoke, and with the exhalation of breath should expel all bad motivation. When inhaling, they should imagine that all the blessings and good qualities of Buddhas and Bodhisattvas, in the form of bright light, are inhaled into them. This practice is called purification by way of the descent of ambrosia.[1] There are many forms of this purification, but the essence of the practice is as just indicated.

The above has been a discussion of the reasons for cultivating meditative stabilization observing exhalation and inhalation; its purpose involves the seven features of the physical posture and an eighth point, the settling down of the winds. These establish predispositions[2] for oneself achieving the body, speech, and mind of a Buddha. There are two types of refuge,[3] causal refuge and effect refuge; the latter is the body, speech, and mind of the Buddha into which one will be transformed. How does this practice establish predispositions for achieving a Buddha's type of body, speech, and mind? In assuming the physical posture, one is engaging in a virtuous[4] physical deed; the virtue of dispelling the three physical non-virtues establishes predispositions in the mental continuum that will later produce the body of a Buddha. The settling down of the breath establishes predispositions for later achieving a Buddha's speech. This is because speech primarily depends upon wind. There are many different types of winds, coarse[5] and subtle,[6] but here we can consider only the coarse winds mentioned in sūtra; by training or purifying them one establishes predispositions that eventually create the speech of a Buddha. Since wind serves as the mount of consciousness, purifying the winds also purifies the mind. Through this purification of coarse conceptuality,[7] one establishes predispositions for developing the mind of a Buddha. This is how the predispositions for the body, speech, and mind of a Buddha are established in one's own mind. Great texts such as Ḏzong-ka-ḇa's *Great Exposition of the Stages of the Path*[8] usually refer to the seven features of the posture and to that of settling

---

1 *bdud rtsi 'bebs sbyang.*

2 *bags chags, vāsanā.*

3 *skyabs, śaraṇa.*

4 *dge ba, kuśala.*

5 *rags pa, audārika.*

6 *phra mo, sūkṣma.*

7 *rnam rtog, vikalpa.*

8 *tsong kha pa blo bzang grags pa* (1357-1419), *lam rim chen mo/ skyes bu gsum gyi rnyams su blang ba'i rim pa thams cad tshang bar ston pa'i byang chub lam gyi rim pa;* P6001, vol. 152.

down the winds as the eight features of Vairochana's[1] posture. When there is reference to only seven features of Vairochana, the final one, settling down the winds, has not been included.

What are the purposes of the seven features of Vairochana's posture? Vairochana is the factor of purification of the form aggregate[2] of all Buddhas. From another viewpoint, Vairochana is the factor of purification of the pervasive wind. The function of the pervasive wind, which abides in all the important places in the body—joints, and so forth—is to cause the movement of the limbs.

There is still another reason for training in observing the breath. It is impossible to have meditative stabilization and, for example, to be angry at the same time. Thus, in order to pacify the winds of anger, and so forth, one engages in meditation on the breath. When you think on the winds, anger naturally diminishes and becomes pacified. You might think that if the meditative stabilization observing the breath reduces a mind of hatred, it is, therefore, suitable to serve as an antidote[3] to such a mind. However, these are not in a relationship of harmer and harmed. When one contemplates the breath, minds of hatred, and so forth, are merely diminished. As Dharmakīrti says in the second chapter of his *Commentary on (Dignāga's) "Compilation of [Teachings on] Valid Cognition"*:[4]

> Even if desire and hatred are mutually different,
> They do not harm each other.

Nevertheless, when strong desire manifests, hatred will not manifest and vice versa because hatred and desire are two different conceptions, and it is impossible for different conceptions of a similar type—they are both mental consciousnesses—to operate in the continuum[5] of any one sentient being at the same time. Sūtra says that the consciousnesses of similar type in one sentient being are single during any given moment. This is why concentration on the breath is important for the pacification of all other types of minds at the time of practicing meditative stabilization. Since all other minds settle down into a neutral state, it becomes easy to develop a virtuous attitude. This practice is called a quintessential instruction in a

---

[1] *rnam par snang mdzad, vairocana.*

[2] *gzugs kyi phung po, rūpaskandha.*

[3] *gnyen po, pratipakṣa.*

[4] *tshad ma rnam 'grel gyi tshig le'ur byas pa, pramāṇavartikakārikā;* P5709, vol. 130. This is II.193ab.

[5] *rgyud, saṃtāna.*

forceful technique.

Is the cultivation of meditative stabilization observing the breath something that only Buddhists can have? Not at all, for non-Buddhists can achieve calm abiding, as well as the four concentrations and the four formless absorptions. However, the instructions for achieving meditative stabilization observing the breath which are adorned with these other quintessential instructions, such as of purification through the descent of ambrosia, are unique to Buddhists.

Question: Why is it impossible for two different conceptions of similar type to operate at the same time?

Answer: It can be said there is no such thing as two mental consciousnesses[1] operating at the same time. There are systems which assert eight consciousnesses, but here we are talking from the viewpoint of systems which assert six consciousnesses. There will not be two conceptions of similar type which are different substantial entities[2] operating simultaneously. "Similar type" refers to a second mental consciousness operating at the same time as the first. For instance, with regard to the eye consciousness,[3] "of similar type" would mean to have a second eye consciousness operating at the same time as the first. Still, in one of the Chittamātra systems, the example of the eye consciousness does not fit since they are willing to say that more than one type of eye consciousness can be generated at the same time.

DISCUSSION

Question: It was said that in practicing the nine-cycled dispelling of bad winds one relies not so much on the breath itself as on the imagination of inhalation and exhalation. Why is this?

Answer: This is because you are mainly cleansing your own motivation after making manifest your impure motivation. Thus, the main point is the imagination. As much as you are able to withdraw the mind during this period of meditative stabilization on the breath, so great will be your ability to do as you wish in meditative stabilization.

Question: It is said that calm abiding cannot be achieved with the eye consciousness. However, in watching the breath you are using the body con-

---

[1] *yid kyi rnam shes, manovijñāna.*

[2] *rdzas, dravya.*

[3] *mig gi rnam shes, cakṣurvijñāna.*

sciousness[1] to achieve calm abiding. Is there anything contradictory in this?

Answer: It would probably be suitable to stop all coarse forms of the body consciousness during this practice. We are talking about a phase preparatory to calm abiding during which, indeed, you have to use your body consciousness to know whether you are exhaling or inhaling. During calm abiding itself, the sense consciousnesses[2] will cease. Here we are speaking only of the preparatory stages. We refute those who say that calm abiding can be achieved with the eye consciousness or body consciousness. Calm abiding must be attained with the mental consciousness.

Question: Why is it impossible to achieve calm abiding with the eye consciousness?

Answer: The basic nature[3] or entity[4] of a mind of calm abiding is a withdrawn, serviceable mind. The uncommon function of the sense consciousnesses is to know external objects. The only person who can remain in a state of deep meditative equipoise while sense consciousnesses operate is a Buddha. This is because the sense consciousnesses are factors of distraction[5] or scattering to external objects. From the eighth of the nine mental abidings[6] that precede calm abiding, all scattering to external objects has ceased. There are some texts that relate calm abiding to the eye consciousness, but only because they do not distinguish between the preparatory stages and actual calm abiding. That is the reason in brief. [For a detailed discussion of this topic, see 34-35 and 40-41.]

Question: How long would you recommend meditative sessions on the breath to be?

Answer: I will talk about this later. The texts do not give any definite statements on how long sessions should be. They set forth the mode of meditation, the object of observation, the order, and so forth, but not a definite length of time because that mainly depends on instruction given from experience. A person—not a text—points out what has to be done. For instance, when two people are meditating on, for example, imperma-

---

1 *lus kyi rnam shes, kāyavijñāna.*

2 *dbang shes, indriyajñāna.*

3 *rang bzhin, svābhāva.*

4 *ngo bo, vastu.*

5 *rnam par g.yeng ba, vikṣepa.*

6 *sems gnas dgu, navākārā cittasthiti.*

nence,[1] their progress depends on such things as their previous familiarity with the topic and the activation of certain predispositions. Thus, texts do not say, "Meditate for one hour," or, "Meditate for two hours." When meditation goes clearly, one should extend the session, but if, for example, you are to meditate on something white and only blackness appears, it is necessary to leave the session immediately. It is not that the length of the session is not explained in texts at all; rather, it is explained in reference to specific situations.

Question: Does the practice of the twenty-one cycles mean counting to twenty-one and then going back to one and beginning again?

Answer: Doing it up to twenty-one once is sufficient if it succeeds. If, however, one is still beset by coarse conceptions, one should leave the session and come back again later. It is in the nature of this process that if you succeed in keeping your mind on the twenty-one breaths the mind will settle down somewhat. If thoughts settle down even a little, that is fine. Tomorrow and the next day they can settle down a little more.

Question: Are the three different types of instruction on watching the breath to be practiced sequentially by one person?

Answer: They can apply to one person, and they can also apply to different persons. In the former case, the person progresses from one to the next as he or she increases in capacity. The person would begin with just watching the breath, then go to counting it, then take up the nine cycles of dispelling bad winds, later working in the purification through the descent of ambrosia. There are some people who naturally have little discursiveness, or coarse conceptuality; such people can even from the very beginning take up the nine-cycled practice, and their winds will easily settle down. On the other hand, for some people it is both confusing and harmful to begin with counting the breath; initially they should simply watch it.

---

1 *mi rtag pa, anitya.*

3 OBJECTS OF OBSERVATION

I have already explained the preliminaries to calm abiding—the physical and mental bases, and so forth. Now we have reached the point of discussing calm abiding itself. The Tibetan commentaries are sometimes not very explicit in dealing with these topics, whereas the Indian texts elaborate on them greatly. From time to time I will give word commentaries on statements from these texts.

Calm abiding's objects of observation are sometimes referred to as object-of-observation supports,[1] or object-of-observation bases. They are also said to be the supports, or bases, which are the object of observation.[2] Some say that the support which is the object of observation of calm abiding is something perceived by the eye consciousness. This is not so because it is impossible to withdraw the mind inside unless the sense consciousnesses are stopped. Except by withdrawing the mind inside, one cannot achieve calm abiding. Thus, it is utterly incorrect to say that the object of observation of calm abiding is an object of observation of the eye consciousness. This error arises because, when the objects of observation of calm abiding are discussed, there is reference to something that we have seen, such as a picture of a Buddha. Nevertheless, an object of the eye consciousness is not a basis that is the object of observation of calm abiding, for, when the mind is withdrawn inside in the development of calm abiding, the sense consciousnesses necessarily cease. It is impossible to cause the mental consciousness to become stronger by developing the eye consciousness. Only after the sense consciousnesses have ceased can one cause the mental consciousness to become one-pointed and achieve calm abiding.

The sense consciousnesses are by their very nature distracted to external objects. Until their activity ceases, it is impossible to stop the distraction of scattering[3] and excitement.[4] One cannot achieve even the fifth through

---

1 *dmigs rten.*

2 *dmigs pa'i rten.*

3 *'phro ba.*

4 *rgod pa, auddhatya.*

ninth of the mental abidings[1] preceding calm abiding, let alone calm abiding itself, until scattering and excitement cease. Moreover, because the nature of the sense consciousnesses is to be distracted outward toward objects, if one tried to achieve calm abiding by means of the eye consciousness, the laxity[2] which is a hindrance to calm abiding and which consists of the mind's withdrawing too much inside would not occur because the mind would not be withdrawn inside at all. There would then be the contradiction that laxity, which is widely known as a hindrance to calm abiding, would not be a hindrance to calm abiding, for it would not occur.

Laxity, the mind's withdrawing too much inside, occurs only in connection with a virtuous mind such as that of calm abiding; it does not arise at all with respect to non-virtuous or neutral minds. It is very difficult to distinguish between subtle laxity and meditative stabilization.[3] However, if one asserted that calm abiding is achieved through focusing on an external object, there would be no way at all for laxity to arise. I will explain the way in which calm abiding is achieved in the context of the mental and sense consciousnesses, as well as the way in which faults such as laxity arise, when we talk about the stages of developing calm abiding and the boundaries of its attainment.[4]

HOW TO CHOOSE AN OBJECT OF OBSERVATION

Those who maintain that calm abiding is achieved through the eye consciousness have a reason for their assertion. There are a number of ways of seeking out an object of observation of calm abiding. One way is to investigate among various objects of observation such as a Buddha image to see what works well, or a meditator might read texts to see what objects of observation are recommended or seek the advice of a virtuous spiritual friend, or guide[5]—a lama[6] who can identify a suitable object of observation. It is through mistaking the first method of seeking out an object of observation for the actual training in calm abiding that external objects come to be posited as supports, or bases, of calm abiding.

There are also people who say that whatever occurs to someone to use as an object of observation of calm abiding is fine. They take as their source a

---

1 *sems gnas, cittasthiti.*

2 *bying ba, laya.*

3 *ting nge 'dzin, samādhi.*

4 See pp. 77-82 and 96ff.

5 *dge ba'i bshes gnyen, kalyāṇamitra.*

6 *bla ma, guru.*

line from Atīsha's *Lamp for the Path to Enlightenment* which seems to indicate that any object of observation can be used.[1] Upon investigation of the actual import of this line, however, their interpretation turns out to be incorrect. The reason is that, in cultivating calm abiding, one should take as an object of observation something that causes the mind to be pacified when it is observed. It is not appropriate to use something that will not pacify the mind or cause it to be withdrawn inside. There are many reasons and purposes for each object of observation that can be used as a basis for calm abiding. Thus, it is not true that any object at all will do.

People who take this position say that those desiring to achieve calm abiding should take as an object of observation whatever seems most pleasing or suitable to their minds, whatever appears easily to them. They do not say the object which seems best but that which appears most easily. One might then ask whether it would be best for a person who had become attached to some object earlier in her or his life to meditate on that object. It is definitely pleasant, and the person's mind will take to it very easily. Therefore, according to the above assertion, since this object appears easily to the mind, such a person should be able to achieve calm abiding with it. This is not the case, for the chief purpose of cultivating calm abiding is temporarily to pacify the coarse afflictive emotions[2] included within the Desire Realm.[3] It might be easy to cause the image of a much-hated enemy to appear, but if a meditator took it as an object of observation in generating calm abiding, not only would the afflictive emotion of hatred not be pacified; it would increase.

Nevertheless, there is a reason for such an assertion. The advice to take an object that appears easily is given within the thought that for someone who has no experience with calm abiding, the mode of procedure for attaining it is difficult. If, in addition to this, the object of observation is also difficult, it becomes very hard to achieve calm abiding. Even though this is so, it is not suitable to use an object of observation simply because it appears easily to the mind.

There are two types of persons who cultivate calm abiding, those whose afflictive emotions are definite and those whose afflictive emotions are indefinite. In people of the first type, one of five afflictive emotions—desire,

---

[1] See p. 67.

[2] *nyon mongs, kleśa.*

[3] *'dod khams, kāmadhātu.*

hatred, obscuration, pride,[1] and discursiveness[2]—predominates. There are objects of observation which serve as definite antidotes to each of these afflictive emotions, and such persons would choose their object of observation accordingly. The second type of person has no single predominant afflictive emotion; the afflictive emotions are all equal. It is suitable for this second type of person to take an object from a text or on the advice of a spiritual guide.[3]

There are also two other types of persons, those who can determine a correct object of observation on their own and those who must rely on a spiritual guide. The former have very sharp faculties and are capable of investigating the texts, meditating, and thereby recognizing what is proper for them; most people, however, are of the second type. Persons in whom one of the afflictive emotions is predominant may either consult a text or seek the advice of a teacher in choosing an object of observation that will pacify their dominant afflictive emotion, but usually, persons in whom, for example, desire predominates go to a spiritual teacher, who will examine them in order to ascertain what object would be most suitable for them.

Persons whose afflictive emotions are definite use those objects of observation that will cause their particular predominant afflictive emotions to be pacified. For example, persons in whom desire predominates should take the unpleasant[4] as their object. There are many objects of observation included within the general type of the unpleasant, and these persons should either choose from among what the texts describe or take the advice of a spiritual guide. If, when desirous persons take a certain object to mind, they find that their minds are pacified—withdrawn inside—and that their major afflictive emotion is diminished, they know that they have chosen correctly.

Persons in whom hatred predominates, whether they are capable of choosing their own object of observation or rely on a teacher to choose it, must pacify their hatred before they can achieve the nine mental abidings and calm abiding. To pacify hatred, they meditate on love[5]—its benefits, characteristics, and types. There are many different ways of taking love as one's object of observation, and such persons must choose among them

---

[1] *nga rgyal, māna.*

[2] *rnam rtog, vikalpa.*

[3] *dge ba'i bshes gnyen, kalyāṇamitra.*

[4] *mi sdug pa, aśubha.*

[5] *byams pa, maitri.*

either on their own or with the help of a spiritual guide.

There are also persons dominated by obscuration. A person who wishes to develop calm abiding should minimally have learned about the stages of meditation necessary for its development—the five faults,[1] the eight antidotes, and so forth. Someone who has not done this will not be able to develop calm abiding. In general, obscuration is another word for ignorance,[2] but this is not the meaning here. "Ignorance" usually means the conception of true existence,[3] whose antidote is the wisdom realizing emptiness.[4] Here, however, "obscuration" refers to not having studied and, therefore, not knowing the presentation of phenomena. One must at least be able to identify those things which do not accord with the development of calm abiding. It is necessary either to study or to be taught how the eight antidotes counter the five faults that interfere with calm abiding. Without knowing these, one will not be able to generate even the nine mental abidings that lead to calm abiding.

In general there are two types of ignorance: that which is obscured regarding the cause[5] and effect[6] of actions, and that obscured regarding suchness.[7] A person ignorant about the cause and effect of actions is, for example, an ordinary being[8] who, not knowing the virtues to be adopted and the non-virtues to be discarded, engages in activities such as killing and stealing. Specifically, ignorance regarding the cause and effect of actions consists of not knowing that happiness[9] arises because of having done virtue and that suffering[10] arises because of having done non-virtue. Within not knowing this, one commits many non-virtues. Even if one is not obscured as to actions and their effects, however, one may have ignorance of suchness, the way things are. On the basis of this, one accumulates actions that will cause rebirth in the happy transmigrations[11] in cyclic existence, perhaps thinking, "I will take rebirth as a god."

---

1 *nyes dmigs, ādīnava.*

2 *ma rig pa, avidyā.*

3 *bden 'dzin.*

4 *stong nyid rtogs pa'i shes rab.*

5 *rgyu, hetu.*

6 *'bras bu, phala.*

7 *de kho na nyid, tathatā.*

8 *'jig rtan rang 'ga' ba.*

9 *bde ba, sukha.*

10 *sdug bsngal, duḥkha.*

11 *bde 'gro, sugati.*

When we speak of a person in whom obscuration is predominant, we are referring to the second type of ignorance. The ignorance of suchness can relate to either the superficial or the ultimate nature of phenomena; here we are speaking of someone obscured with regard to the superficial nature of phenomena. This type of ignorance is not a case of being obscured with regard to things such as the attainment of Buddhahood but is simply a matter of not having studied. Such a person would not have learned about topics such as how calm abiding is to be achieved. The antidote to this is to hear about and contemplate the meaning of the scriptures, for this is a person who wants to achieve calm abiding but does not know how.

Persons in whom pride predominates must first weaken, or suppress, their pride before they are able to go through the nine mental abidings and achieve calm abiding. The antidote to pride is meditation on the eighteen constituents.[1] These are the six objects,[2] the six sense powers,[3] and the six sense consciousnesses. All eighteen are included in one's own mental and physical continuum. The meditator is to contemplate four characteristics in relation to these: (1) the fact that many causes are involved in bringing them about, (2) the place in which the causes were amassed, (3) the person who amassed them, (4) the causes through which the eighteen constituents are enhanced. It is so difficult to consider these four in relation to even one small portion of the body that the very act of doing so causes pride to be reduced. Once persons dominated by pride realize that there are many factors in their own minds and bodies whose causes they cannot identify, they also perceive that they cannot identify the causes for other people's minds and bodies either. The recognition that one has a great deal more to learn even about some small part of oneself serves to undermine pride.

Persons in whom discursiveness predominates should meditate on the exhalation and inhalation of the breath.[4] In this case, discursiveness will not be a virtuous mind but a non-virtuous or neutral one. This discursiveness or, more literally, coarse conceptuality is of two types—an innate type and the discursiveness acquired in this lifetime. Discursiveness is included

---

1 *khams, dhātu.* The eighteen constituents are the six objects (forms, sounds, odors, tastes, tangible objects, and other phenomena), the six sense powers (eye, ear, nose, tongue, body, and mental sense powers), and the six consciousnesses (eye, ear, nose, tongue, body, and mental consciousnesses).

2 *yul, viṣaya.*

3 *dbang po, indriya.*

4 *dbugs 'byung rngub, ānāpāna.*

within mental discomfort.[1] How does neutral discursiveness come about? It arises at birth because of one's having felt hatred toward other beings in a former life. The discursiveness that arises in the present life is due to one's having acquired enemies, and hatred for them, earlier in this life. One thereby becomes accustomed to feeling closeness to some people and aversion for others and, because the force of this remains in the mind, coarse conceptuality arises later in life. Meditation on exhalation and inhalation is an antidote to this. It is not an actual antidote, but it will pacify coarse conceptuality, as was explained in the context of setting up the body for meditation and observing the breath going in and out.[2]

The main point to keep in mind in choosing an object of observation for calm abiding is that it should cause one's predominant afflictive emotion to be pacified and the mind to be withdrawn inside.

DISCUSSION

Question: It would seem that meditating on the breath is like meditating on an external object, although it was said that such an object of observation is not conducive to calm abiding. It seems to me to be an external object because it is an object of the body consciousness.

Answer: Watching the breath is not a case of a sense consciousness going out toward an object. If one were using only the body consciousness in observing the breath, this activity would not be able to pacify the other consciousnesses, but it is, in fact, the best way to pacify all coarse minds. When you meditate on exhalation and inhalation, the breath is not your only object of observation. In breathing out, as was mentioned earlier (see p. 28), you imagine that your afflictive emotions go out with the breath and that the white ambrosia[3] which represents all factors that would aid your practice of meditative stabilization comes in as you inhale. These are imagined to be of one entity with your breath as it goes in and out.

The fact that the sense consciousnesses go out to external objects is a sign that they are the coarsest of consciousnesses. When I spoke of how to set up the body for meditation, I said that it was important to set the tongue behind the upper teeth. The reason for doing this is that it will prevent saliva from flowing while you observe the breath. This is necessary because the coarse sense consciousnesses such as the body consciousness

---

[1] *yid mi bde, daurmanasya.*

[2] See p. 26ff.

[3] *bdud rtsi.*

cease during the higher stages of meditative stabilization. This is a correct reasoning proving that calm abiding cannot be achieved in dependence on the sense consciousnesses but, rather, in dependence on the mental consciousness. Further, if it were possible to cultivate and achieve calm abiding through the body consciousness, then calm abiding and the body consciousness would become of one entity, in which case one's meditative stabilization would be a body consciousness. This, in turn, would absurdly mean that the body consciousness itself would perform the activities of meditative stabilization.

Question: Does one visualize the descent of ambrosia and so forth while watching exhalation and inhalation only?

Answer: It is suitable to do this at any time. It is also good to do it when you are actually cultivating calm abiding.

Question: Why is the fault of discursiveness related to hatred rather than desire?

Answer: It indeed arises in connection with desire, but its main source is hatred. Discursiveness, or coarse conceptuality, is mainly identified as a feeling[1]—specifically, the feeling of mental discomfort. This mental suffering arises because of the predominance of anger.[2] Desire and pride usually arise from a feeling of mental pleasure.[3] Doubt[4] and hatred are included within the feeling of mental discomfort, and they give rise to very strong conceptuality.

Conceptuality is, in general, abandoned by the path of seeing[5] because, when one generates the uninterrupted path[6] of the path of seeing in one's mental continuum, one has attained the non-conceptual exalted wisdom.[7] However, this statement has to be seen in context. The non-conceptual exalted wisdom arises through meditation on emptiness, at which time one will certainly have abandoned conceptuality. The conceptuality mentioned here in reference to those who are beginners at calm abiding signifies simply that there are many afflictive emotions in their minds—namely, those factors which hinder calm abiding. In general, conceptuality is very exten-

[1] *tshor ba, vedanā.*

[2] *khong khro, pratigha.*

[3] *yid bde, saumanasya.*

[4] *the tshom, vicikitsā.*

[5] *mthong lam, darśanamārga.*

[6] *bar chad med lam, ānantaryamārga.*

[7] *rnam par mi rtog pa'i ye shes.*

sive; it is said that Buddhahood and the complete elimination of conceptuality are attained simultaneously. It is also said that one has become a Buddha to the extent to which one does not have conceptuality. Thus, some form of conceptuality exists right up to the uninterrupted path that precedes the attainment of Buddhahood.

It is necessary, therefore, to distinguish among the different types of conceptuality. That to be eliminated at the time of assuming the physical posture for meditation and watching the breath is a coarse conceptuality; the type abandoned at the time of achieving calm abiding itself is less coarse. As one goes higher and higher on the path, the conceptuality to be abandoned becomes more and more subtle. Thus, the fact that one has overcome the type of conceptuality that must be abandoned in order to achieve calm abiding does not mean that other, more subtle, types have been overcome. It is important to be careful in distinguishing conceptuality's many varieties.

FOUR TYPES OF OBJECT OF OBSERVATION

What sort of object of observation does one need? How are these identified in our own system? This topic was originally mentioned in the *Sūtra Unraveling the Thought.* It was also explained in Asaṅga's *Grounds of Hearers* and in Kamalashīla's *Stages of Meditation.* There are many explanations of meditation-objects in other texts that follow or comment on these, but all derive from Asaṅga's and Kamalashīla's works.

Four types of object of observation are described:

1 pervasive objects of observation[1]
2 objects of observation for purifying behavior[2]
3 objects of observation for [developing] skill[3]
4 objects of observation for purifying afflictive emotions.[4]

MEANING OF THEIR NAMES

"Pervasive" refers to the fact that this type pervades all objects of observation; this is an etymology (for more discussion see p. 183ff.). Objects of observation for purifying behavior are used by persons in whom one of the afflictive emotions predominates and are named for their ability temporarily to pacify afflictive emotions (for more discussion see the next sec-

[1] *khyab pa'i dmigs pa, vyāpyālaṃbana.*

[2] *spyad pa rnam sbyong gi dmigs pa, caritaviśodanālaṃbana.*

[3] *mkhas pa'i dmigs pa (mkhas par byed pa'i dmigs pa), kauśalyālaṃbana.*

[4] *nyon mongs rnams sbyong gi dmigs pa, kleśaviśodanālaṃbana.*

tion). Objects of observation for developing skill have the feature that, by training in them, one becomes skilled (for more discussion see p. 192ff.). This third category includes objects of observation such as the four noble truths[1] and the twelve-linked dependent-arising;[2] if one studies the texts on these subjects, one becomes skilled in them; "of skill"[3] is an abbreviated expression meaning "to make, or bring about, skill."[4] The fourth type of object of observation is for purifying afflictive emotions (for more discussion see p. 208ff.) What are posited here as afflictive emotions? They are afflictive emotions included within either the Desire Realm or the two upper realms,[5] the Form Realm[6] and the Formless Realm.[7] In dependence on the seven preparations[8] for each of the concentrations and formless absorptions, one separates from the afflictive emotions of desire, and so forth, pertaining to the level below the concentration or the formless absorption [that one is trying to attain].

There is a difference between objects of observation that purify behavior and those that purify afflictive emotions. Objects of observation that purify behavior are for the sake of pacifying a specific afflictive emotion that is predominant, whether it be desire, hatred, obscuration, pride, or discursiveness. The fourth type of object of observation, for purifying afflictive emotions, purifies all afflictive emotions equally. Thus, in dependence on one of the preparations for a concentration or on an actual[9] concentration, a meditator achieves a state of having separated from all afflictive emotions pertaining to the Desire Realm or to a particular concentration or formless absorption.

This is a general division of objects of observation.

Question: When one separates from afflictive emotions through relying on an object of observation of the fourth type, that for purifying afflictive emotions, has one permanently or only temporarily separated from them?

Answer: There are two types of abandonment of the afflictive emotions—

---

1 *'phags pa'i bden pa bzhi, catvāry āryasatyāni.*

2 *rten cing 'brel bar 'byung ba, pratītyasamutpāda.*

3 *mkhas pa'i.*

4 *mkhas par byed pa.*

5 *khams gong ma.*

6 *gzugs khams, rūpadhātu.*

7 *gzugs med khams, ārūpyadhātu.*

8 *nyer bsdogs, samāntaka.*

9 *dngos gzhi, maula.*

temporary and complete. There is much to be said on this topic, but here I will discuss it only briefly.

What is temporary separation from attachment?[1] In dependence on attaining calm abiding and the special insight which allows one to identify Desire Realm afflictive emotions such as desire, hatred, pride, the thought to harm, and so forth, as faulty, one generates a wish to achieve the first concentration.[2] The attainment of a first concentration is simultaneous with the attainment of a state in which one has temporarily eliminated all afflictive emotions pertaining to the Desire Realm. This is called having temporarily separated from attachment.

Complete or permanent abandonment[3] of the Desire Realm afflictive emotions involves a person's first identifying the *root* of these afflictive emotions to be the ignorance that is the conception of true existence. Then, in dependence on calm abiding, meditating on the four noble truths, and generating a supramundane path,[4] one eliminates that very ignorance. In this way, one can completely eliminate the afflictive emotions pertaining to the Desire Realm.

OBJECTS OF OBSERVATION FOR PURIFYING BEHAVIOR

THE UNPLEASANT

We have arrived at the topic of the objects of observation for purifying behavior. The first type is meditation on the unpleasant as an antidote to attachment. There are a number of different meditations on the unpleasant that are antidotes to attachment; the first of these is a meditation on the feeling of suffering.[5] This is one of the three kinds of feeling—those of pleasure, of suffering, or pain, and of neither pleasure nor suffering[6]—that is, neutrality. Among the three kinds of feeling, that of pain is what worldly people mainly do not want. Therefore, the feeling of pain is identified as that which ordinary people do not want and usually make effort to be rid of. The feeling of pleasure is also suffering in the end, but worldly people in general—beginners[7] and ordinary and common beings[8]—con-

---

[1] *chags bral, kāmād virakta.*

[2] *bsam gtan dang po, prathamadhyāna.*

[3] *spangs pa, prahāṇa.*

[4] *'jig rten las 'das pa'i lam, lokottaramārga.*

[5] *sdug bsngal, duḥkha.*

[6] *sdug bsngal ma yin bde ba yang ma yin, aduḥkhāsukha.*

[7] *las dang po pa, ādikarmika.*

[8] *so so'i skye bo, pṛthagjana.*

sider it pleasant and helpful. They make effort only to achieve it, not to get rid of it. Neutral feeling[1] is that which, although capable of changing to happiness or suffering, for the time being gives neither help nor harm. People do not make effort to be rid of it. Because it is temporarily neither pleasant nor painful, people do not think of it as suffering.

What does the world not want, for the most part, and wish to be free of? From among the three types of feeling, it is the feeling of pain. There are many different ways of meditating on the feeling of pain. In the beginning one can meditate on the pain that one experiences in one's own continuum. Later, it is possible to meditate on the suffering of others—those who have been born in the hells, as hungry ghosts, and so forth. Beginners, however, would work with the suffering in their own continuums. Someone who is sick and experiencing suffering can let it serve as an example for the suffering of those born in the bad transmigrations;[2] this suffering is taken as the object of observation and meditated on. However, when we talk about meditation on the unpleasantness of the feeling of pain, we are not talking about the feeling of pain as it is recognized in the world. Rather, this is a case of meditation on the unpleasant as it is set forth in treatises.

The second type of meditation on the unpleasant is contemplation of the foul. Here one observes one's own body and then meditates on putrefaction, rotting, gross dismemberment, and so forth. This is a type of unpleasantness recognized both in the world and in texts.

The third type of meditation on the unpleasant is contemplation of what is unpleasant in relation to something else. Here one meditates on one's own body. Even if we do not now have the type of suffering mentioned above, our bodies are a proprietary effect[3] that has been projected or caused by contaminated[4] actions and afflictive emotions. Such a body is inferior in relation to a Superior's[5] body because, after becoming a Superior, one no longer takes rebirth by the power of contaminated[6] actions and afflictive emotions but by the power of actions. In relation to our own bodies, the bodies of Superiors are very pure; however, in comparison to a

---

1 *btang snyoms, upekṣā.*

2 *ngan 'gro, durgati.*

3 *bdag po'i 'bras bu, adhipatiphala.*

4 *zag bcas, sāsrava.*

5 *'phags pa, ārya.*

6 *zag med, anāsrava.*

Buddha's body a Superior's is unpleasant or inferior. A Buddha's form aggregate—his or her body—only appears to disciples to be form; actually, it has the nature of exalted wisdom.[1] In this way, beginning yogic practitioners can observe their own bodies and meditate on relative unpleasantness.

They also reflect that the body is unpleasant from the viewpoint of its causes, entity, and activities. The causes of one's body are all included within true origins,[2] the second of the four noble truths; specifically, its causes are contaminated actions and afflictive emotions motivated by ignorance. Since such causes have preceded it, the body is also unpleasant from the viewpoint of its own entity because it itself is a true suffering, a case of cyclic existence. It is unpleasant from the viewpoint of its activities because with such a body it is virtually impossible not to meet with birth, aging, sickness, and death. However, Foe Destroyers[3] and high-ground Bodhi-

---

[1] *ye shes, jñāna.*

[2] *kun 'byung bden pa, samudayasatya.*

[3] *dgra bcom pa, arhan.* With respect to the translation of *arhan/ arhant* (*dgra bcom pa*) as "Foe Destroyer," we do this to accord with the usual Tibetan translation of the term and to assist in capturing the flavor of oral and written traditions that frequently refer to this etymology. Arhats have overcome the foe which is the afflictive emotions (*nyon mongs, kleśa*), the chief of which is ignorance, the conception (according to the Consequence School) that persons and phenomena are established by way of their own character.

The Indian and Tibetan translators were also aware of the etymology of *arhant* as "worthy one," as they translated the name of the "founder" of the Jaina system, Arhat, as *mchod 'od* "Worthy of Worship" (see Jam-ÿang-shay-b̄a's *Great Exposition of Tenets,* ka 62a.3). Also, they were aware of Chandrakīrti's gloss of the term as "Worthy One" in his *Clear Words:* "Because of being worthy of worship by the world of gods, humans, and demi-gods, they are called Arhats" (*sadevamānuṣāsurāl lokāt pūnārhatvād arhannityuchyate* [Poussin, 486.5], *lha dang mi dang lha ma yin du bcas pa'i 'jig rten gyis mchod par 'os pas dgra bcom pa zhes brjod la* [409.20, Tibetan Cultural Printing Press edition; also, P5260, vol. 98 75.2.2]). Also, they were aware of Haribhadra's twofold etymology in his *Illumination of the Eight Thousand Stanza Perfection of Wisdom Sūtra.* In the context of the list of epithets qualifying the retinue of Buddha at the beginning of the sūtra (see Unrai Wogihara, ed., *Abhisamayālaṃkārālokā Prajñā-pāramitā-vyākhyā, The Work of Haribhadra* [Tokyo: The Toyo Bunko, 1932-5; reprint ed., Tokyo: Sankibo Buddhist Book Store, 1973], 8.18), Haribhadra says:

> They are called *arhant* [=Worthy One, from root *arh* "to be worthy"] since they are worthy of worship, religious donations, and being assembled together in a group, etc. (W9.8-9: *sarva evātra pūjā-dakṣiṇā-gaṇa-parikarṣādy-ārhatay**arhantaḥ**;* P5189, 67.5.7: *'dir thams cad kyang mchod pa dang // yon dang tshogs su 'dub la sogs par 'os pas na dgra bcom pa'o*).

Also:

sattvas assume bodies through the power of uncontaminated actions, and their bodies, therefore, do not undergo birth, aging, sickness, and death. When one proceeds from the first Bodhisattva ground to the second, the sufferings of sickness, aging, and death are eliminated. Thus, beginning yogic practitioners meditate on relative unpleasantness by observing their own bodies. Reflecting on these reasons, they consider that their own bodies are without essence.

Fourth in this category is meditation on the unpleasant which consists of bad activities. Usually, when people engage in various types of non-virtuous activity such as killing animals, that activity does not appear to them as unpleasant. Yet, although such an action does not seem unpleasant at the time of accumulation of its karmic potency, this practice involves meditating on such actions as unpleasant. One contemplates the effect of a bad activity and observes that as a fruition of such an act one would be reborn in a hell; thus, one would have the body of a hell being, in which one would experience various sufferings. In this way, one considers the unpleasantness of bad actions.

The fifth type of meditation on the unpleasant is on the unpleasantness of the unsteady, also known as the unpleasantness of change. What is the unpleasantness of change? The contaminated aggregates[1] of mind and body which are appropriated through contaminated actions and afflictive emotions disintegrate from one moment to the next. This disintegration can be contemplated in either a coarse or a subtle manner. One can reflect on disintegration in a coarse way by considering that any human being who is born will necessarily die. More subtly, one would consider that the body is disintegrating and approaching closer to death at every moment.

They are called *arhant* [= Foe Destroyer, *arihan*] because they have destroyed (*hata*) the foe (*ari*).

(W10.18: *hatāritvād* ***arhantaḥ***; P5189, 69.3.6. *dgra rnams bcom pas na dgra bcom pa'o*).

(Thanks to Dr. Gareth Sparham for the references to Haribhadra.) Thus, we are not dealing with an ignorant misconception of a term, but a considered preference in the face of alternative etymologies—"Foe Destroyer" requiring a not unusual *i* infix to make *ari-han*, *ari* meaning enemy and *han* meaning to kill, and thus "Foe Destroyer." Unfortunately, one word in English cannot convey both this meaning and "Worthy of Worship"; thus, I have gone with what clearly has become the predominant meaning in Tibet. (For an excellent discussion of the two etymologies of "Arhat" in Buddhism and Jainism, see L.M. Joshi's "Facets of Jaina Religiousness in Comparative Light," L.D. Series 85, [Ahmedabad: L.D. Institute of Indology, May 1981], 53-8).

[1] *phung po, skandha.*

Such disintegration takes place in the time it would take to snap one's fingers. Everyone understands the coarse form of disintegration; even without thinking about momentary disintegration, people recognize that all who are born will die. Subtle momentary impermanence or disintegration does not appear to the minds of ordinary people. To understand subtle momentary impermanence, one must analyze.

I have explained five ways of meditating on the unpleasant in accordance with how they are presented in Asaṅga's *Grounds of Hearers*. A different system of meditating on the unpleasant is given by Vasubandhu in his *Treasury of Manifest Knowledge*. There, he gives three meditations on the unpleasant:

1 the yoga of a beginner at mental contemplation[1]
2 the yoga of someone who is practiced[2]
3 the yoga of one whose mental contemplation is perfected.[3]

The first of these consists of meditating that a piece of skin is removed from the area between one's eyes, exposing the white bone underneath. One is to think that the piece of skin falls off as though causelessly, adventitiously, and one then directs the mind to that white bone. When the meditator is able to set the mind on that, she or he gradually enlarges the area of bone until the entire body is exposed as just bone. After this, the meditator considers that all the lands and oceans of the world are filled with skeletons. Having succeeded in extending the scope of the meditation to include the whole world, one then withdraws the observation gradually until one is again observing just one's own body. At that point, one is seeing just one's own body as a skeleton and remains in contemplation of this as long as possible. This is the meditation which is the yoga of a beginner at mental contemplation.

The second meditation begins as before. The scope is extended to include all the earth and sea and is brought back again, but this time the meditator continues to withdraw the observation so that only the top half of the skull remains as skeleton. One then remains in contemplation of this as long as possible.

The third meditation also begins as before, starting with the white bone at the forehead and extending the scope. The observation is also withdrawn as before, but this time it recedes until only a small area remains

[1] *yid la byed pa las dang po pa'i rnal 'byor, manaskārādikarmika[yoga].*

[2] *yongs su sbyangs pa byas pa'i rnal 'byor, kṛtaparicaya[yoga].*

[3] *yid la byed pa yongs su rdzogs pa'i rnal 'byor, atikrāntamanaskāra[yoga].*

between the eyebrows. The smaller, the better; but if one cannot meditate on a small area, a large one is suitable. It is good, however, to make the area as small as one's mind is capable of observing because, since the mind collects on that area, making that area as small as possible enables the mind to remain steady there. One meditates on this small area as long as one can. This is the subtlest of the ways of meditating on the unpleasant mentioned in Vasubandhu's *Treasury of Manifest Knowledge;* it is called the yoga of one whose mental contemplation is perfected.

DISCUSSION

Question: What does one think about when meditating on putrefaction, rotting, and gross dismemberment in terms of one's own body?

Answer: The point of this meditation is to effect an antidote to desire. Therefore, having taken to mind an object to which one is attached, one imagines it as a skeleton, or as putrefying, or as falling apart. It is difficult to get this to appear to the mind because the object is something very attractive; however, if one makes effort at this, the attachment will later naturally cease. It is difficult for these unpleasant aspects to appear to a beginner's mind in relation to certain objects because of having become accustomed to the pleasant object. Therefore, it is difficult to cultivate a sense of the signs contradicting that object's pleasantness. One should continue to imagine putrefaction, and so forth, forcing the mind into this thought, and eventually it will happen that when the object appears the force of attachment to it will naturally be diminished.

Question: If you are attached to pleasant-tasting food, would you meditate on the food rotting or on your tongue rotting?

Answer: You would meditate on the food itself. It is difficult to meditate on the unpleasantness of taste when one is attached to pleasant taste, because the two are contradictory. However, it is good to take to mind this opposite, contradictory, feature from the beginning, if possible. The meditation explained earlier which involves considering the entire world to be filled with skeletons although it actually is not filled with skeletons will help here too because this also is a case of meditating on something as having a quality which it does not have.

Question: If one meditates on the unpleasantness of an attractive object, will it not happen that hatred will replace the attachment?

Answer: Hatred or aversion will not replace attachment because its motivating cause is different from that which you are cultivating. A yogic practitioner does not cultivate a sense of a certain person as unpleasant within a sense that this person is an enemy but only with the motivation of overcoming attachment. The meditation is not preceded by the motivation, "I am attached to this person, and I will meditate to become angry at him"; rather, one begins the meditation with the purpose of reducing attachment to that person.

Question: If you are very attached to food and then meditate on its repulsive aspects, could not this eventually be brought to the point of having strong aversion for food?

Answer: This comes back to one's motivation for eating. If one eats simply to sustain the body and not because of attachment to taste, one will not have aversion for food. Your thought on this is basically good. You are thinking that if you actually have success with this meditation you will not want to eat because food will seem unpleasant to you. If you do get such an experience and if you have attained the higher stages of yogic practice, it may be that you will be able to put aside food.

Question: It was said that after becoming aware of your own suffering you should meditate on the suffering of hell beings, and so forth. Is this a case of actually making contact with their suffering or of inferring their suffering on the basis of what scriptures say about them?

Answer: This is a case of first having achieved experience in meditating on one's own pain and then using it as an example of the pain that other beings must undergo. This thought is from one's own viewpoint because it involves the realization, "If I am reborn in a hell or as a hungry ghost, I will have such suffering." Persons of greatest capacity—Bodhisattvas—meditate on this by observing suffering in their own continuums and then contemplating the suffering that hell beings, hungry ghosts, and so forth, undergo, reflecting that their suffering is much worse than one's own. Within this thought, Bodhisattvas cultivate a desire to free beings from such suffering.

LOVE

The second group of objects of observation that purify behavior consists of those that act as antidotes to hatred. Hatred mainly involves observing unpleasant persons; one does not speak of hatred in relation to inanimate things. Hatred is a very forceful afflictive emotion, and its antidote is meditation on love. Love itself is the wish that sentient beings have either temporary or final happiness. This should be distinguished from compassion, which is the wish that they be free from suffering.

How does one cultivate love in meditation? There are, in general, three types of objects of observation—attractive, unattractive, and neutral sentient beings. Therefore, you might wonder whether, in the beginning, one should cultivate love observing a pleasant, unpleasant, or neutral person. According to Chandrakīrti, one takes as the initial object of observation a pleasant person—friend, relative, parent, and so forth—and reflects on how nice it would be if he or she had temporary and final happiness. We perceive these people as pleasant because in this life they have been kind and helpful to us. Using this reason as an example, one then observes neutral and unpleasant people in order to cultivate love for them. Some scholars, however, say that one should begin by considering unpleasant persons, but these two systems of quintessential instructions are not contradictory. There is also a third quintessential instruction which says to begin by taking a neutral object of observation to mind.

All three of these are our own system. We accept all of them because there are three types of yogic practitioners who cultivate love. Practitioners of the first type have very sharp faculties and are also said to have a nature of love through having cultivated love in previous lifetimes. If they begin by cultivating love in relation to an unattractive being, their love will become even stronger. People with dull faculties who do not have a nature of love and may even have a nature of hatred would not be cultivating love if they took an unattractive being to mind; they would be cultivating aversion. There are also people who are best able to cultivate love by taking to mind a neutral person. The three types of quintessential instruction are taught to yogic practitioners in dependence on a teacher's analysis of their capacities. The spiritual guide must take the measure of the student's continuum; by looking at the student's mind, the teacher determines what type of object of observation would be best. There are also trainees who determine what object of observation is most suitable by studying the texts and taking the measure of their own minds. In this way, they can decide whether they should first observe attractive, unattractive, or neutral beings in cultivating love. This is one mode of cultivating love. (See also pp. 74-77.)

Another method of cultivating love is to observe sentient beings regardless of whether they are pleasant, unpleasant, or neutral. Here there are three ways to cultivate love, according to the object of observation:

1 love observing mere sentient beings[1]
2 love observing phenomena[2]
3 love observing the unapprehendable.[3]

In the first of these, the meditator cultivates love observing the three types of sentient beings—friend, enemy, and neutral person—without seeing them as qualified by impermanence or the lack of inherent existence;[4] one simply thinks, "May they have happiness!"

The second type involves observing sentient beings within the thought that they are disintegrating moment by moment and that, because of the power of actions and afflictive emotions, they have a nature of impermanence. Within this, one generates love thinking, "May they have happiness!" This is called the love which observes phenomena. Here the yogic practitioner first develops the thought that because of the power of actions and afflictive emotions sentient beings are impermanent and disintegrating moment by moment; conjoining one's mind with this thought, one thinks, "May all these sentient beings have happiness!"

In the third type, love which observes the unapprehendable, the word "unapprehendable" is an abbreviated expression. It means that one observes sentient beings and generates love thinking, "May they have happiness!" within a mind that knows sentient beings do not exist from their own side, or inherently exist, or truly exist.

The first type of love, observing mere sentient beings, is our usual type of love. In the second type, the impermanence of sentient beings appears because, before cultivating love, one reflects how, by the power of actions and afflictive emotions, sentient beings are impermanent and disintegrating moment by moment. Then, without the force of this mind wavering, one begins to develop love. Likewise, the aspect of sentient beings' not existing from their own side appears to the third type of love. One cultivates love—the thought, "May they have happiness!"—toward sentient beings who are without inherent existence and who do not exist from their own side. This is a case of love's being conjoined with a mind that realizes sentient beings to be devoid of inherent existence.

Just as there are three types of love, there are three corresponding types of compassion.

---

[1] *sems can tsam la dmigs pa'i byams pa.*

[2] *chos la dmigs pa'i byams pa.*

[3] *dmigs med la dmigs pa'i byams pa.*

[4] *rang bzhin gyis grub pa, svabhāvasiddhi.*

DISCUSSION

Question: If one reads and thinks about the texts and then chooses an object of observation in dependence on having investigated one's own mental continuum, is it necessary to rely on a spiritual guide?

Answer: You definitely need a spiritual guide in the beginning; otherwise nothing will come. Later on, it is possible to make a decision through reading, and so forth. There are two ways to rely on a spiritual guide. In the first, the spiritual guide teaches the book, explaining what the different objects of observation are, and in this way one comes to know the possible objects of observation. If one then goes off and meditates on the basis of this, the spiritual guide cannot supervise what one does. Therefore, the second way of proceeding, which is to discuss meditation with one's teacher and ask questions as one meditates, is best. Then there is supervision; if there is a fault in your meditation, you will know about it and can eradicate it. One should make a distinction between these two modes of depending on hearing[1] and thinking.[2] There is a difference between, on the one hand, simply reading a text with a teacher and then practicing on the basis of what one has learned and, on the other, first having a teacher teach you the book, then meditating, and then talking with the teacher about your meditation.

Question: Would a disciple have only one teacher or many? Would that teacher necessarily be in the Desire Realm or might she or he be invisible?

Answer: A beginner would have to have a teacher in the Desire Realm because he or she would be unable to see beings in the Form and Formless Realms. It is suitable to depend on many spiritual guides, to ask various teachers for advice on your meditation practice. Still, there are two advantages in staying with one teacher. She or he will know the measure of your continuum and, likewise, you will understand what the teacher is getting at because your sustained dependence on the same teacher will lead to some continuity. This is not a question of whether a teacher is skilled, for you will necessarily need a skilled teacher; this is simply a matter of having a continuous relationship. If you ask questions of a teacher who does not know the measure of your mind, the answer will not be directed specifically to you. Such a teacher will, of course, be able to answer the question because he or she is skilled, but it is not like getting an answer from some-

---

[1] *thos pa, śruta.*

[2] *bsam pa, cintā.*

one with whom you have a long-standing relationship. A teacher with whom you have a long relationship will know what point you have reached in practice and will answer in accordance with what she or he knows about your mind.

There are different types of teachers. The best is one who has attained realization and experience of the meditation. Barring that, a teacher who has heard and thought about many, many texts—not just one or two—and has put together the meaning of all of them is also skilled. The first type of teacher is definitely best.

Studying what is said in books about calm abiding, special insight, the meaning of emptiness, generation of the altruistic mind of enlightenment, and so forth, is different from meditating on a topic and asking questions on the basis of one's meditation. If one does the former, it is better to have a teacher who has gathered and coordinated the meanings of many different texts. With regard to the latter, the Ga̅-gyu-ba̅s have a practice known as "offering the realization" in which the meditator describes to the teacher what he or she experienced in the previous day's meditation—whether there was laxity or excitement, any visions she or he might have had, and so forth.

Question: What is the relationship between meditation on the seven cause-and-effect quintessential instructions for generating the altruistic mind of enlightenment and meditation on love for the sake of developing calm abiding?

Answer: There is no definiteness here. It is possible first to develop calm abiding and then to cultivate the seven cause-and-effect quintessential instructions; it is also possible first to cultivate the seven quintessential instructions and then, when one has generated an altruistic mind of enlightenment—at the time of the Mahāyāna path of accumulation[1]—to develop calm abiding.

When love is used as a means for developing calm abiding, there is no definiteness that the meditator will generate love, compassion, great love,[2] or great compassion[3] in her or his continuum. For example, someone who wishes to develop calm abiding through observing a Buddha's body might be hindered by having hatred in his or her continuum; they may be so accustomed to viewing a certain person as an enemy that when they sit down

[1] *tshogs lam, saṃbhāramārga.*

[2] *byams pa chen po, mahāmaitrī.*

[3] *snying rje chen po, mahākaruṇā.*

to meditate, the enemy appears to mind, interfering with the meditation. In order to overcome this hindrance, the practitioner cultivates love; however, there is no certainty that love will actually be generated in the mental continuum. [It is possible to reduce hatred sufficiently to continue to cultivate calm abiding by observing a Buddha's body, without actually generating love in one's continuum.]

When such persons find that hatred is interfering with the ability to observe the body of a Buddha, they set that practice aside in order to cultivate love. They begin by cultivating even-mindedness, or equanimity,[1] recognizing that they wish their friends to have happiness because they have been good to them in this lifetime and that, except for the fact that the "enemy" was kind to them in a previous life rather than this one, the "enemy" is no different from those regarded as friends. In this way, these practitioners try to cultivate the same type of wish for happiness in relation to the enemy that they already have in relation to friends. This is the type of meditation persons dominated by hatred would need to do in order to develop calm abiding; however, there is no certainty that such practitioners would thereby generate great love at this time.

Question: What about a person whose mind is hateful in general? Even if such a person develops even-mindedness toward one, two, or more persons, there is still hatred for others, so that it seems as though one could never eliminate all the objects of hatred.

Answer: The hatred for different people is all of one type. Therefore, if you overcome hatred for one person, the same antidote should apply to hatred that has other persons as its object. For example, if you cultivate one type of calm abiding, then, at the point of the mental contemplation of thorough isolation,[2] and so forth, it will act as an antidote to all the afflictive emotions of the Desire Realm. This happens because, although there are many different types of Desire Realm afflictive emotions, they are all the same in belonging to the Desire Realm. It is not necessary to cultivate a different antidote for each of the afflictive emotions; the quality of calm abiding applies to them all. Here, similarly, if the love that you cultivate when observing an enemy does not apply to other persons, this is a sign that you have not actually cultivated love.

For example, realization of the impermanence of sound can act as an

---

[1] *btang snyoms, upekṣā.*

[2] *rab tu dben pa'i yid byed, prāvivekyamanaskāra.*

antidote to the conception of permanence[1] in relation to any object, not just sound. One does not need to realize the impermanence of every compounded phenomenon[2] individually. A single realization serves as the antidote for all conceptions of permanence. If this were not so, then it would be necessary to generate a valid cognition[3] with respect to every phenomenon before Buddhahood could be attained because one has the conception of inherent existence with respect to all the countless objects of knowledge.[4] Thus, when you cultivate love, it is necessary to examine very carefully whether or not love is actually being generated.

Question: Would persons of sharp faculties who "have a nature of love" (see p. 51) be meditating on love for the sake of developing calm abiding? My doubt comes because here meditation on love is taught as an antidote for hatred.

Answer: Such persons also have hatred. There is no contradiction. They have a nature of love through having subdued hatred in a past life and, therefore, will be able to achieve calm abiding through cultivating the nine mental abidings in relation to love more quickly than others. The words "hatred" and "nature of love" seem to be contradictory, but it is possible for someone with manifest hatred to have love or compassion in seed form. Persons who have such a seed can develop love very quickly once they begin to cultivate it. All the same, such persons can temporarily have hatred. This is because the boundaries of the afflictive emotions are not definite; sometimes the afflictive emotions are produced, and sometimes they are not.

Question: What are the stages of the third type of love?

Answer: One cannot cultivate love observing phenomena or love observing the unapprehendable without first having cultivated love observing mere sentient beings. This is the order in which the three would be cultivated.

DEPENDENT-ARISING

Now we have arrived at the third group of objects of observation that purify behavior, the meditation on dependent-arising which is the antidote needed by those in whom obscuration predominates.[5] Among those in

---

1 *rtag pa, nitya.*

2 *'dus byas, saṃskṛta.*

3 *tshad ma, pramāṇa.*

4 *shes bya, jñeya.*

5 *gti mug shas cher spyod pa'i gnyen po.*

whom obscuration is predominant are people who have neither heard nor thought about the cultivation of calm abiding yet who desire to cultivate it. For them, the antidote is to study about calm abiding. In order to reduce ignorance about how to develop it, a person must either study and contemplate books or listen to a teacher. Those whose understanding is a little more advanced should use the four reasonings to analyze the meaning of what has been heard and thought about. The four reasonings are:

1 reasoning of the performance of function[1]
2 reasoning of nature[2]
3 reasoning of dependence[3]
4 logical reasoning.[4]

Although these persons may have heard a little of what is said in the texts, at the time of doing analytical meditation they must very clearly understand the reasoning involved and must apply these four reasonings to the meaning of what has been heard and thought about.

The first, the reasoning of the performance of function is, for example, to observe that the activity of the eye consciousness is to see forms. This eliminates obscuration with respect to the three—object, agent, and action.[5]

The second is an analysis of the nature of things. For example, the nature of fire is to burn; that of wind is to be light. How do these reasonings help get rid of obscuration? Using these as examples and extending them makes it possible to know what are and are not the natures of the afflictive emotions to be abandoned and of the various good qualities to be achieved. One can understand what it means for the nature of an afflictive emotion to be established; similarly, one can understand what has the nature of good qualities and recognize that adventitious things do not have the nature of good qualities and can be eliminated.

The third, the analysis of dependence, means, for example, to observe that the person does not exist from her or his own side without depending on the aggregates of body and mind. For instance, the name "pot"[6] is not designated except through dependence on the collection of minute parti-

---

[1] *bya ba byed pa'i rigs pa, kāryakāraṇayukti.*
[2] *chos nyid kyi rigs pa, dharmatāyukti.*
[3] *ltos pa'i rigs pa, apekṣāyukti.*
[4] *'thad sgrub kyi rigs pa, upapattisādhanayukti.*
[5] *bya byed las gsum.*
[6] *bum pa, ghaṭa.*

cles[1] that are a pot's basis of designation.[2] In the same way, a person is designated in dependence on the aggregates; there is no designation of a person that does not depend on mind and body. Of what help is such analysis? It enables one to realize that the person is not something able to stand by itself. This is a very brief explanation.

The fourth, logical reasoning [literally, "the reasoning that establishes correctness"], means, for example, to establish that a pot is impermanent. There are two ways of proving this—by establishing coarse impermanence and by establishing subtle impermanence. This reasoning establishes the correctness of a pot as an impermanent thing. Thus, it is a reasoning that establishes correctness. A yogic practitioner who wishes to develop calm abiding but who is obscured with respect to its presentation must first study this mode of reasoning.[3]

As an alternative, yogic practitioners may think about the twelve-linked dependent-arising. Even practitioners who cannot ascertain subtle dependent-arising can ascertain the coarser form of the order of the twelve-linked dependent-arising, both the forward progression and the reverse one. They can then understand that the other eleven links all derive from ignorance. Thus, even if persons wishing to overcome obscuration cannot observe the subtle dependent-arising, they can in a coarse manner decide that the other eleven links all derive from ignorance; in this way obscuration can be eliminated or suppressed.

DIVISIONS OF THE CONSTITUENTS

The fourth type of object of observation that purifies behavior, an antidote to predominance of pride, involves meditation on the divisions of the constituents. How does this serve as an antidote to pride? Persons dominated by pride not only lack direct knowledge of the mode of being of phenomena but do not even understand well the collection of aggregates in their own continuums. Dividing the various factors into the aggregates of forms, feelings discriminations, compositional factors,[4] and consciousnesses helps to overcome pride. If one looks at the way the body is formed and divides it into smaller and smaller parts, it is impossible to identify everything that is there. Normally, pride is generated through observing one's aggregates of mind and body and thinking, "I." The pride that thinks "I" is based on

---

1 *rdul phra rab, paramāṇu.*

2 *gdags gzhi.*

3 For more on the four reasonings, see *Meditative States,* 155-57.

4 *'du byed, saṃskāra.*

the view that the aggregates are a partless whole.

EXHALATION AND INHALATION OF THE BREATH

The fifth group of objects of observation that purify behavior is comprised of those antidotes needed by persons in whom discursiveness predominates. The antidote to discursiveness is meditation on the exhalation and inhalation of the breath. There are two systems—one explained in Asaṅga's *Grounds of Hearers* and the other, in Vasubandhu's *Treasury of Manifest Knowledge*. I will not explain Asaṅga's system now because the explanation given at the beginning about meditating on the breath can serve as its equivalent; if I explained it, it would take three weeks. Jam-ȳang-shay-b̄a's[1] *Great Exposition of the Concentrations and Formless Absorptions*[2] contains a great deal of material on this system of meditation; once that is translated, you can all read it.

I will explain what is said in Vasubandhu's *Treasury of Manifest Knowledge*, which gives six different ways of meditating on the breath. I have already explained how to set up the body for meditation. Having done this, one withdraws the mind inside and observes the breath. According to one interpretation, these six ways are:

1 meditative stabilization of counting[3]
2 placement[4]
3 investigation[5]
4 change[6]
5 purifying[7]
6 observing the fruit.[8]

[Vasubandhu's own system is described below, p. 61ff.]

The first type involves staying with the breath while counting the

---

[1] *'jam dbyangs bzhad pa*, 1648-1721.

[2] *bsam gzugs chen mo*. The longer title is *Treatise on the Presentations of the Concentrations and Formless Absorptions, Adornment Beautifying the Subduer's Teaching, Ocean of Scripture and Reasoning, Delighting the Fortunate* (*bsam gzugs kyi snyoms 'jug rnams kyi rnam par bzhag pa'i bstan bcos thub bstan mdzes rgyan lung dang rigs pa'i rgya mtsho skal bzang dga' byed*).

[3] *grangs pa'i ting nge 'dzin.*

[4] *'jog pa.*

[5] *nye bar rtog pa.*

[6] *yongs su sgyur ba.*

[7] *yongs su dag pa.*

[8] *'bras bu la dmigs pa.*

breaths from one to ten, without mistaking the count, without letting the mind be distracted to anything, and without letting the mind break its continuum of observation. Someone who can count the breaths from one to ten, keeping the mind on the breath without wandering, is said to have the meditative stabilization of counting.

The second, placement, involves observing wherever in the body wind permeates. There is no certainty that breath, or wind, permeates the body. There are various assertions; some say that breath permeates the entire body, and some say it does not. Whatever the case, one is to observe the breath wherever it goes in the body.

The third, investigation, is a matter of observing not just where wind permeates the body but also where it helps and harms. One analyzes where it causes warmth and where it brings cold.

The fourth, change, involves switching the object of observation. Until now, the object observed has been the breath, but here it changes, so that one observes an object such as the fourth period of the path of preparation,[1] supreme mundane qualities.[2]

The fifth, purifying, involves observing the path of seeing. One is observing higher and higher paths; thus, the objects of observation are becoming more and more subtle.

The sixth, observing the fruit, consists of observation of the paths of meditation and no more learning,[3] and of Foe Destroyers.

Question: How are the fourth, fifth, and sixth types cases of meditating on the exhalation and inhalation of the breath?

Answer: Without first meditating on the breath, one cannot meditate on the subtler objects of observation involved in these last three meditations. Breath is coarse, whereas the paths of preparation, and so forth—which are consciousnesses—are subtle.

According to another interpretation, the fourth meditation, change, is given as the fifth, and the fourth is said to be investigation; this involves observing not only the wind as it permeates the body but all five aggregates of body and mind. The sixth—observing the fruit—is then combined with the fifth—purifying—so that the sixth meditative stabilization is a single meditation in which the paths of seeing, meditation, and no more learning are objects of observation.

---

1 *sbyor lam, prayogamārga.*

2 *'jig rten pa'i chos kyi mchog, laukikāgryadharma.*

3 *mi slob lam, aśaikṣamārga.*

Vasubandhu's own system of meditating on the breath is in six ways:

1 counting[1]
2 following[2]
3 placement[3]
4 investigation[4]
5 change[5]
6 purifying.[6]

In the first list given above (p. 59), "following" was not mentioned, and the sixth was given as "observing the fruit," an item not mentioned here. I will again give a word commentary on this, starting from the beginning.

"Counting" refers to the ability to withdraw the mind inside and count the breaths from one to ten single-pointedly without confusing the order; this count from one to ten comprises one meditative equipoise. "One meditative equipoise" signifies that there is a single continuum of the object of observation, a single continuum of a substantial entity,[7] and a single continuum of mind. There is a constant continuum wherein every instant is a case of meditative equipoise; one does not remain in equipoise for a little while, break it by thinking about something else, and then resume. If the object of observation remains the same but there is no continuum of the substantial entity of consciousness, this does not qualify as a continuum of meditative equipoise. The continuity of the substantial entity of a consciousness of meditative equipoise means that such a consciousness is manifest for the entire time; it is not suitable if it is sometimes manifest and sometimes non-manifest. This is what being included in a single continuum of meditative equipoise means.

The second, following, involves thinking about how the inhaled breath pervades the body. The body has many coarse and subtle channels through which the breath passes. It is easy to recognize its passage through the coarse channels, but for awareness of the subtle channels careful analysis is needed.

After one has practiced observing where the breath does and does not go

---

[1] *grangs pa, gaṇanā.*
[2] *rjes su 'gro ba, anugama.*
[3] *'jog ba, sthāna.*
[4] *nye bar rtog pa, upalakṣaṇā.*
[5] *yongs su sgyur ba, vivartanā.*
[6] *yongs su dag pa, pariśuddhi.*
[7] *rdzas rgyun gcig.*

in the body, it is necessary to examine that which is still unknown—how the breath brings help or harm to the body. Therefore, in the third meditation, placement, the yogic practitioner observes what feelings—pleasurable, painful, or neutral—arise from the breath's movement in the body, and whether there is help or harm.

These three ways of meditating on the breath all involve meditation on the breath itself, which is a tangible object.[1] Breath is wind.[2] Since wind is one of the four elements[3] and is included within the form aggregate, at this point, putting aside the examination of breath as wind, one investigates what is and is not of the nature of the five aggregates in relation to wind. This is the fourth meditation, investigation. One examines whether wind itself is established as having the nature of those aggregates which are not it—whether it is of the nature or entity of that part of the form aggregate which is not wind, or of the feeling aggregate, discrimination, compositional-factor, and consciousness aggregates.

The wind that the yogic practitioner exhales and inhales is included within his or her continuum. The term "body" means the coarse form that can be seen with the eye: a collection of all four elements—earth, water, fire, and wind. This collection is called the body.[4] As long as the body exists, it must depend on consciousness[5] because mind and body have a relationship of support and supported. When this relationship is broken, the person dies; until that time the body depends on consciousness. Since the body depends on consciousness, the earth, water, fire, and wind that make up the body also depend on consciousness, as does the breath we have been talking about. Thus, it can be said that wind depends on the aggregates of consciousness, feeling, and discrimination.

When yogic practitioners have gained facility in these four, they change the object of observation and observe the path of preparation. This is the fifth meditation, change. Previously, the practitioner was observing the breath, which is relatively coarse. We know from experience that form is coarser than consciousness; a path is even more subtle than other types of consciousness.

Then, when these practitioners have gained facility in the fifth medita-

---

1 *reg bya, spraṣṭavya.*

2 *rlung, prāṇa/ vāyu.*

3 *'byung ba, bhūta.*

4 *lus, kāya.*

5 *rnam par shes pa, vijñāna.*

tion, observing the path of preparation, they reflect on the sixth, purifying, which involves observing the paths of seeing, meditation, and no more learning. This is even more subtle than the previous object of observation. Thus, as yogis become practiced in the coarser objects of observation, they move on to more subtle ones.

There are slightly different ways of setting out these six and explaining their meaning; this is probably Vasubandhu's own system. However, there are many interpretations of what Vasubandhu's system is, since there are many different commentaries on the root text of his *Treasury of Manifest Knowledge.*

OTHER OBJECTS OF OBSERVATION

There are other objects of observation, as when one observes a Buddha's auspicious marks[1] or meditates on a divine body, the latter being included within mantra, or tantra. Here one imagines oneself as a divine body; this is a case of bringing about the clear appearance of the body's color and features, from the eyes right down to the soles of the feet. There are also cases of taking hand symbols[2] as the object of observation, or subtle drops[3]—for example, to meditate on such a drop at the center of the heart or at the point between the eyebrows. On Buddha images there is a single hair curled between the eyebrows which is known as a hair-treasury; this is the location of the "point between the eyebrows."

OBJECTS OF OBSERVATION FOR THOSE WHO HAVE NOT AND HAVE ACHIEVED CALM ABIDING

What are posited as objects of observation for those who are newly achieving calm abiding and what are the objects of observation for those who have already attained calm abiding? For the most part, any of the above can be an object of observation for those newly achieving calm abiding. However, there are hardly any people who newly achieve calm abiding by taking emptiness, the twelve-linked dependent-arising, love, the twelve sense-spheres, the eighteen constituents, or analysis of all the five aggregates as an object of observation. These are mostly used as objects of observation by persons who have already attained calm abiding, in order to make further progress. Meditation on the unpleasant or on the body of a Buddha, and so forth, are suitable to be used by those newly achieving

---

1 *mtshan nyid, lakṣaṇa.*

2 *phyag mtshan.*

3 *thig le, bindu.*

calm abiding.

If someone asks whether or not it would be possible to meditate on emptiness when newly achieving calm abiding, the answer is, "Yes. It is possible but extremely difficult." Emptiness is the final mode of phenomena, and analysis of it is very difficult. First, it is necessary to find the object of observation and then, to stabilize on it; here it is difficult even to find the object, much less stabilize on it. One must analyze in order to find it, and for a complete beginner who is analyzing without stability, even the first of the nine mental abidings is impossible. Thus, such meditation is difficult from the viewpoint of the object. It is also difficult from the viewpoint of the subject, the practitioner, because he or she is a person whose conceptions are scattered outside and must be drawn inside. This requires many different techniques such as meditation on the breath. Since it is difficult from the viewpoint of both object and subject, it is indeed very difficult. Therefore, it is said in many sūtras and in Kamalashīla's *Stages of Meditation* that when one achieves calm abiding, one necessarily does so using as an object of observation a phenomenon included within the varieties of conventional phenomena. However, when the cultivation of special insight is set forth, it is done only in the context of meditating on emptiness, not on other topics.

To repeat, it is not that there are no cases whatsoever of persons initially achieving calm abiding using emptiness as their object of observation, but it hardly ever occurs. Once calm abiding has been achieved, that mind of calm abiding can be used as the basis for engaging in analysis to penetrate the mode of being of phenomena. At that point, analysis is rather easy because the meditator has the factor of stability. A person who achieves calm abiding using emptiness as the object of observation and then, still taking emptiness as the object of observation, achieves special insight, has the best type of special insight. Another procedure would be to ascertain emptiness through hearing and thinking and then to achieve calm abiding followed by special insight using emptiness as the object of observation; I think there are no cases of this outside Highest Yoga Tantra.[1]

The fact that certain objects of observation are described as difficult does not mean that they are difficult for everyone; for certain persons a so-called difficult object of observation might be the easiest. How can one tell? Someone with sharp faculties who engages in hearing and thinking can fairly well decide what to do on the basis of the experience that is gen-

[1] *bla med kyi rgyud, anuttarayogatantra.*

erated. It is also possible for a spiritual guide to make an estimate of the practitioner's mental continuum[1] and, based on observation of the practitioner's nature, disposition, and so forth, to decide the type of object of observation most appropriate for a given person.

SEARCHING FOR THE OBJECT OF OBSERVATION

For a beginner, the body of a Buddha is the best of all objects of observation within the sūtra system. Within tantra, there are special meditations for generation of oneself as a deity, but here we are speaking of the sūtra system. The first phase of searching for the object of observation is complete when the entire body of a Buddha appears, even if it is not seen clearly. The whole figure appears at one time in a rough way. Even if what first appears is unclear and without much detail, it is suitable; if only half the image or blackness appears, it is not suitable. If the yogic practitioner works over and over again at visualizing the same complete image, even if it does not appear clearly, eventually confidence will develop in the ability to visualize it at will.

Once the meditator has confidence that the image can be visualized at any time, she or he works on improving the clarity a little. It is necessary to wait until one has achieved a state of confidence before working on clarity because, if one works on clarity before this time, even though there might be some success in making the image clearer, in the end the whole visualization will be lost. When one succeeds in bringing about a steady clarity, it is said that one has sought and found the object of observation.

There are some people for whom a Buddha's body together with the lion-throne, and so forth, will not appear even roughly. It is suitable for such people to visualize only the body. The procedure is then the same as above: first developing confidence with regard to this appearance, no matter how unclear it is, and then working on clarity.

Some people have difficulty visualizing the entire body; it is as though too big. They should take a portion of the body as the object of observation—for example, just the crown protrusion on Buddha's head or the curled hair between Buddha's eyebrows, called the hair-treasury. This is easy because it involves only one specific object.

Sūtra states only that one should seek out a Buddha as object of observation; however, the process of visualizing just a portion of the body is established because in Highest Yoga Tantra it is said that during the stage of

---

[1] *rgyud, saṃtāna.*

generation[1] one should follow such a procedure. Namely, it is said that one can visualize an entire mandala[2] and then attain steadiness with respect to it, after which one would improve the clarity, but if one cannot do this much, it is suitable to meditate on just one's own body. If this is not possible, then it is suitable to take a specific object; for example, if the deity in whose image you are generating yourself has three eyes, it suitable to focus just on the third eye. Then, when this becomes clear, the other parts can be added, as when a person makes an image. This mode of procedure can also be applied to visualization of a Buddha's body in the sūtra system.

If you are able to achieve stability and clarity with respect to a Buddha's body, the lion-throne, and all the figures around the Buddha, you are to maintain them with respect to the entire general image. Then, within maintaining this general appearance, emphasize some particular part of the visualization. Then return to the general, because that is more important.

There are two types of quintessential instruction for finding an object of observation such as the body of a Buddha. One involves a Buddha's body that is newly fabricated by the yogic practitioner and the other, a Buddha's body that is naturally established. With regard to the fabrication of a Buddha's body, we should consider the three-step mantric practice in which the yogic practitioner cleans away defilements, purifies everything into emptiness, and generates him- or herself in a Buddha's body. This practice has two types. In one type of mental generation, everything is purified into emptiness, after which light is emitted; from this light the objects of observation—such as the three objects of refuge—are projected in front of oneself. In the other type, that of taking as an object of observation something that already exists, the meditator emits light and uses it to draw these beings from their natural abode until they are just in front of her- or himself.

Both practices are processes in which the yogic practitioner radiates light. In the first practice, the yogic practitioner generates him- or herself in a divine body and then radiates light that itself creates the objects of refuge. In the second, the light draws Buddhas, and so forth, from their own place of abode. Both of these are mantric, or tantric, and thus are not part of sūtra practice.

In the sūtra system, it is very important to think of the deity as being naturally established, naturally existent and not newly created. This is true whether the yogic practitioner is searching for the object of observation,

---

1 *bskyed rim, utpattikrama.*

2 *dkhyil 'khor, maṇḍala.*

finding it, or continuously meditating on it. When the yogic practitioner enters into meditative stabilization, it is important for him or her to consider the Buddha's body as actually present and to regard it as something which already existed there. Exactly where the meditated object is seen depends on the individual. For some, it is better placed close; for others, it is better a little farther away.

At the end of the session, the yogic practitioner of tantra who has radiated light from which the object of observation arose must without exception again withdraw that object. In the sūtra system, the yogic practitioner contemplates the dissolution of the Buddha's body into an emptiness of inherent existence or, if this is too difficult, into a vacuity. It is also suitable not to cause the Buddha's body to dissolve but to think that the being remains there continuously.

THE LENGTH OF THE SESSION

Once a meditator has found the object of observation, how long should the sessions be? There is no clear exposition of this in relation to the process of achieving calm abiding, but with regard to achieving special insight it is said that the day can be divided into sixteen sessions. This is just a general statement; it depends on the particular person.

It is said that if a yogic practitioner is able to maintain clear observation of the object for a four-hour session, calm abiding can be achieved. Still, it is possible to achieve calm abiding by sustaining a shorter session. The most important factor is for the yogic practitioner to work at gaining confidence that he or she can remain focused on the object of observation as long as wished and to do this every day. It is not possible to achieve calm abiding by practicing some days and not others. As long as one is in a natural state of health without illness, it must be done every day. The length of the session depends mainly on the nature of the meditator.

CHANGING THE OBJECT OF OBSERVATION

In general, it is not suitable to change the object of observation until calm abiding is achieved. As long as the object is appropriate, whether it is chosen by the meditator or given by a teacher, it should not be changed until calm abiding is actually achieved. Atīsha's *Lamp for the Path to Enlightenment* says,[1] "One should set one's virtuous mind on any *one* object of observation."

---

[1] 40c. See Richard Sherbourne, S.J., *A Lamp for the path and Commentary,* 9 and 121. As Leah Zahler points out, this seems to be the stanza that is interpreted to mean that one can set the mind on *any* object of observation that is comfortable.

Is it unsuitable to change the object of observation under any circumstances? No, for once calm abiding has been achieved, the meditator *must* change the object of observation. As Kamalashīla's *Stages of Meditation* says, "When you have entered into mental contemplation, you must change the object of observation." The object of observation is changed in order to increase the mind of calm abiding and cause further progress; even if the object of observation is emptiness, one would at this time change to the eighteen emptinesses. This is done to make the mind more subtle and vast. In order to achieve special insight, it is necessary to have a very powerful mind of calm abiding, but at this point it is new and not very powerful. Therefore, the meditator changes to another object in order to generate more mental power. (See p. 217.)

Is it totally unsuitable to change objects of observation before achieving calm abiding? No; there are exceptions. It is possible to change at the third of the nine mental abidings. For example, a person who finds that thoughts of hatred arise whenever she or he tries to visualize the body of a Buddha took a wrong object of observation to begin with and needs to engage in a technique that will break down hatred. Thus, the object of observation must be changed, and this has to be done during the third mental abiding, not the fourth. I will explain this in more detail when I describe the third mental abiding. (See pp. 74-77.)

4 NINE MENTAL ABIDINGS

Asaṅga's *Grounds of Hearers* sets forth the achievement of calm abiding by way of the nine mental abidings. The fourth chapter of Maitreya's *Differentiation of the Middle and the Extremes,* however, sets forth the mode of achieving calm abiding through overcoming the five faults by way of the eight activities,[1] or antidotes. The context of Maitreya's explanation is the description of a yogic practitioner's meditating on the four noble truths. Such a yogi needs to cultivate the four establishments in mindfulness[2] and the four legs of manifestation.[3] In discussing the four legs of manifestation, Maitreya brings up the topic of the five faults and the eight antidotes.

Maitreya's *Ornament for the Mahāyāna Sūtras* also sets forth the achievement of calm abiding by way of the nine mental abidings. The literal renderings in this text by Maitreya and in Asaṅga's *Grounds of Hearers* are a little different. In Maitreya's *Ornament for the Mahāyāna Sūtras,* the nine are discussed in terms of the progress or improvement of meditative stabilization and the increase of good qualities. In Asaṅga's *Grounds of Hearers,* the nine are discussed from the viewpoint of stopping faults.

I will explain how calm abiding is achieved based on abandonment of the five faults and reliance on the eight antidotes, together with how it is achieved based on the nine mental abidings. My reason is that anyone who cultivates abandonment of the five faults and reliance on the eight antidotes necessarily passes through the nine mental abidings, and, similarly, a person wishing to progress through the nine mental abidings can do so only by abandoning the five faults and relying on the eight antidotes. Therefore, I will lay out what is needed for each of the nine mental abidings in terms of the five faults and the eight antidotes.

---

1 *'du byed pa, abhisaṃskāra.*

2 *dran pa nye bar bzhag pa, smṛtyupasthāna.*

3 *rdzu 'phrul gyi rkang pa, ṛddhipāda.*

SETTING THE MIND

In the first mental abiding, setting the mind,[1] one is able to set the mind a little on the object of observation that has been indicated by a teacher or chosen through one's own study, but one is not able to set the mind there continuously. What appears to the meditator is mostly not the object of observation but many other types of conceptions. It seems that there are more appearances than usual. This is not the case, however; it is not that there is more conceptuality than usual; rather, this is a sign that conceptuality, or discursiveness, is being identified. This was said by Pa-bong-ka[2] from his own experience.

One can pass to the second mental abiding only within the functioning of this continuum of setting the mind.

CONTINUOUS SETTING

The second mental abiding is called continuous setting.[3] At this point one is able to lengthen a little the continuum of observing the object of observation. During this time, distractions and so forth cannot create great interference. In terms of one's own experience, it is as though conceptuality is resting a little.

The most important factor at this time is to identify what is unfavorable to the practice. During the first and second mental abidings, the main obstructions are laziness[4] and forgetfulness,[5] the first two of the five faults. If one has not yet learned the entity and the different types of laziness, it is impossible to rely on the antidotes to them.

The definition of laziness is: a mental factor which, through its own power, causes procrastination with respect to cultivating meditative stabilization.[6] First, it is necessary to think of the entity, or nature, of laziness by way of its defining character. In the oral tradition, it is said that cultivating meditative stabilization is like preparing a meal in that you have to get everything necessary in front of you. It is not good enough just to know it; the understanding has to be made manifest.

There are three types of laziness:

---

1 *sems 'jog pa, cittasthāpana.*

2 *pha bong kha* (1878-1941).

3 *rgyun du 'jog pa, saṃsthāpana.*

4 *le lo, kausīdya.*

5 *gdams ngag brjed pa, avavādasammoṣa.*

6 *ting nge 'dzin sgom par byed pa la rang stobs kyis phyi shol byed pa'i sems byung.*

1 laziness of neutral activities[1]
2 laziness which is an attachment to bad activities[2]
3 laziness of inadequacy[3]

In the first type, the person engages in neutral activities such as sleep through the motivation of putting off meditative stabilization. The second type of laziness usually involves non-virtuous activities; for example, persons cultivating meditation begin to think either about what an enemy will do to them or about what they will do to an enemy. Laziness of inadequacy, or non-affinity, means, for instance, to take cognizance of a Buddha or Bodhisattva's great qualities of mind and to think, "I could not possibly achieve such qualities." The word *sgyid* means "affinity," and *lugs* means "discard"; in other words, because of this type of laziness, one has no sense of affinity with such a high state of mind, as if compatibility or facility with it has been lost. This is the opposite of being able to engage in something fully; it is a case of letting it go altogether. People who have this type of laziness initially want to achieve a Bodhisattva's qualities, and so forth, but when they encounter difficulty in doing so, they give up.

Jam-ȳang-shay-b̄a discusses the word *zhum pa*, or slackness. In general, this term refers to a mental decline. Here it is identified as *yid shi ba'i zhum pa*, meaning "a death of the mind." This decline, or discouragement, is said by Jam-ȳang-shay-b̄a to be equivalent to the laziness of inadequacy. Someone thinks about doing something, and then that thought dies. The word *zhum pa*, or slackness, will be discussed again in relation to laxity. (See p. 80.)

The laziness of inadequacy and the laziness consisting of an attachment to bad activities are indeed bad, but they are quite obvious and easy to identify. The worst laziness is the first, that of neutral activities. Because these activities are not commonly recognized as non-virtuous, the practitioner will tend not to identify them as such. Consequently, he or she does not put much thought into abandoning them. Such activities continually arise when one tries to cultivate meditative stabilization and, thus, are very difficult to abandon. The other types of laziness, although bad, can be identified as non-virtuous as soon as they arise in the continuum. Therefore, when cultivating meditative stabilization the most important type of laziness to abandon is the first. If you fall asleep or want to rest when

---

[1] *snyoms las kyi le lo.*

[2] *bya ba ngan zhen gyi le lo.*

[3] *sgyid lugs pa'i le lo*—literally, "losing affinity."

meditating, or even if you get up and start sewing, these are all instances of the first type of laziness. It is particularly important to identify sleep and a wish to rest, and also talking, as laziness of neutral activities because these are not commonly recognized as non-virtuous. If you began sewing, however, you would be more likely to feel that you should stop that and get back to your meditation.

Question: It seems that sometimes if you are very tired and yet make effort at maintaining the session on the basis of having identified sleep as non-virtuous, the result is that the meditation becomes very bad. Either the object of observation is lost, or uncontrollable fantasies arise.

Answer: There are times when one cannot help going to sleep; at such times the session should be stopped. Then, in the next session, you must start all over at the beginning. If you are having difficulty with sleep[1] or lethargy,[2] you should loosen the mode of apprehension of the object of observation a little.

Each fault has an antidote that can be cultivated. When drowsiness occurs, you can take to mind a brilliant object or think that a hundred thousand suns have simultaneously appeared. This causes the sleepiness to fade away; then you can rejoin meditative stabilization. Similarly, there are specific antidotes for whatever unfavorable conditions might arise.

Of the eight antidotes, four counteract laziness. The first of these is the faith[3] that consists of conviction in the good qualities of meditative stabilization. The second is the generation of an aspiration[4] that is the wish to attain those qualities. The third is exertion,[5] or the effort to attain those qualities. Pliancy is also mentioned as an antidote to laziness, but actually it is a benefit arising from the process of applying the first three antidotes. Still, pliancy itself can be used as an antidote in the sense that one can reflect on the benefit of having pliancy.

Faith is of three types: faith of conviction,[6] faith which is a non-captivated clarity,[7] and aspiration which is a wish to attain.[8] Here the three

---

[1] *gnyid, middha.*

[2] *rmugs pa, styāna.*

[3] *dad pa, śraddhā.*

[4] *'dun pa, chanda.*

[5] *rtsol ba, vyāyāma.*

[6] *yid ches pa'i dad pa.*

[7] *mi 'phrog pa'i dvang pa'i dad pa.*

[8] *'thob 'dod kyi 'dun pa.*

are, respectively, faith of conviction in the effects of meditative stabilization, the aspiration which is a seeking of those qualities, and the exertion involved in trying to achieve those qualities.

The First Three Antidotes to Laziness

1. faith
   - faith of conviction
   - faith which is a non-captivated clarity
   - aspiration which is a wish to attain
2. aspiration
3. exertion

The second type of faith, that which is a non-captivated clarity, means that the meditator will not be captivated by something else.

The third type of faith is defined as: aspiration which is an aspiration for that.[1] What is the difference between the third type of faith—the aspiration which is a wish to attain—and the aspiration which is the second of the four antidotes to laziness? The aspiration included within the types of faith is stronger than the other, which can be understood as a general aspiration; the aspiration which is a wish to attain meditative stabilization is a specific type of aspiration.

Exertion, the third antidote to laziness, means making effort.[2] There are three possibilities[3] between exertion and effort. Exertion is necessary for effort, but effort is not necessary for exertion because effort is defined as an enthusiasm for virtue, whereas it is possible to have exertion in connection with non-virtue.

During the first and second mental abidings it is very important to rely on faith, aspiration, and exertion.

RESETTING

At the third mental abiding, resetting,[4] one is able to set the mind back on the object of observation when the mind has wandered from it. The length of the continuum of meditative stabilization is greater than during the second mental abiding: one can maintain the non-distracted setting of the mind on an object of observation longer than before.

The main faults to be stopped during the first three mental abidings are laziness and forgetfulness. Forgetfulness consists of an afflicted mindful-

---

[1] *de la 'dun pa'i 'dun pa.*

[2] *brtson 'grus, vīrya.*

[3] *mu gsum.*

[4] *slan te 'jog pa, avasthāpana.*

ness.[1] It has the function of causing distraction; it is an unserviceability with regard to cultivating meditative stabilization. The antidote to it is mindfulness.[2] Mindfulness has the feature of an object of observation with which one is familiar; its subjective aspect, or mode of apprehension, is the non-forgetting of the object of observation. In non-forgetting, it is not sufficient merely to be able to recall something that someone asks you about; mindfulness takes place when you are able to remember the object of observation vibrantly.[3] If someone asked you what your object of observation is, you would remember although it had been non-manifest before the question was asked; such is not mindfulness.

During the first three mental abidings, or placings of the mind on the object of observation, the greatest faults are laziness and forgetfulness. Thus, as we have said, it is very important to rely on the antidotes to these during this time. If, during these three mental abidings, you are so beset by laziness or forgetfulness that even though you rely on the antidotes—faith, aspiration, exertion, and mindfulness—you do not succeed in overcoming the faults, you must analyze the situation. There are many such cases in which meditators cannot conquer the difficulties and cannot go on. A very sharp person can do her or his own analysis at this time. Otherwise, as in the Ga-gyu-ba tradition, you offer your realization[4] to your teacher—that is, you tell her or him about your meditation. Your teacher will then tell you what to do. The practice of offering one's realization to a spiritual guide comes at this point in the nine mental abidings. Thus, if you arrive at the third mental abiding and, because of a predominant afflictive emotion such as hatred, are unable to progress to the fourth mental abiding, you ask for advice.

In cultivating meditative stabilization, one must draw the mind inside. At that time, whatever is strongest in the mind will become manifest. For example, a person much accustomed to hatred is unable to advance because hatred becomes manifest when she or he cultivates calm abiding. When this person is not cultivating meditative stabilization, however, hatred does not become manifest because the mind is distracted.

Most people have a particular afflictive emotion, and some also have unusual diseases which impede progress at this time; thus, it is necessary to

---

[1] *dran pa nyon mongs can.*

[2] *dran pa, smṛti.*

[3] *thu re.*

[4] *rtogs pa phul ba.*

reduce these. To do so, it is necessary to set aside the previous cultivation of calm abiding and engage in the cultivation of love, for instance, by way of analytical imputed special insight. There is no stabilizing meditation[1] here, just analytical meditation[2] to reduce the force or vibrancy of the hatred. One must rely on the antidotes to hatred from the viewpoint of many reasonings. No stabilizing meditation is permitted at this juncture because it would only cause the afflictive emotion to return. Thus, the meditator must analyze: "What is my reason for being angry at this person? What did this person do that was wrong?" Then one should reflect further: "If my mother did to me what this person has done, would it be suitable for me to be angry at her?" It should be suitable, for in that case one's mother would have done the same thing that the person at whom one is angry with has done but it is not suitable to be angry at one's mother. This implies that one's anger is not suitable.

In cultivating love, it is not appropriate for most people to begin by taking an enemy as the object of love. One should first observe one's own mother and cultivate a wish that she have happiness and the causes of happiness. Next, one should cultivate a wish that a friend have happiness and its causes. Following this, take to mind a neutral person and wish the same for him or her. It is not possible to begin by meditating on the generality of "all sentient beings" because one does not have love with respect to even one sentient being. Therefore, it is necessary to begin with a particular person such as one's mother and then to think of a friend; then extend this wish for happiness to a neutral person, and, when you are able to have such a wish for the neutral person, examine whether or not you can generate this wish with respect to an enemy. If it seems that you have made some progress, then in the next session, instead of beginning over again by thinking of your mother, go directly to taking a friend as the object of observation. When progress is very good, it is possible to concentrate specifically on the wish that an enemy have happiness and its causes.

If, having gone through the process, you are still unable to generate love for an enemy, it must be that you have not really cultivated love for your mother or for a friend. What you thought was love for them was not. Since you do not have love for anyone, it is necessary to analyze whether there is such a thing as the love for all sentient beings about which one hears people talk. Is there such a thing as a Buddha who has brought to

---

1 *'jog sgom.*

2 *dpyad sgom.*

completion the cultivation of love and compassion as set forth in sūtras and tantras? If there is not, then the four noble truths do not exist, the paths do not exist, and cause and effect of actions do not exist. Then reflect, "If there is such a thing as bringing to fulfillment the cultivation of love and compassion as a Buddha, why is it that I myself do not have these qualities?"

That is one technique. Another method is to analyze the three factors involved in hatred—the person who hates, the action of hating, and the person hated—and to meditate on these as not existing inherently or from their own side, in the sense that when they are sought analytically they cannot be found. For example, in analyzing the object of hatred one can analyze whether the hated person's afflictive emotions are the enemy or try to discover what among his or her five aggregates could be considered the enemy. In time, if one is able to contemplate in this way, one will come to feel that the hatred is a bit senseless.

When the hatred has been reduced, the meditator again takes a friend as an object of observation and cultivates the love which is the wish that this friend have happiness and its causes. As before, the process is repeated with regard to a neutral person and an enemy. Hatred will then naturally diminish, and when it does, when the meditator has confidence that hatred cannot harm her or his mental process, he or she again begins to cultivate the nine mental abidings.

If one is acquainted with the systems of the texts, one can also reflect on the causes of the hated person's activities. They were done through the force of contaminated actions and afflictive emotions. It is also appropriate to think about the equality of love and hatred in the sense that if love were inherently existent, hatred would be also, and if hatred were inherently existent, love would be. If love is not inherently existent then hatred is not, and the other way around also. In this sense they are equal. The nature of this process of thought is such that when, after reflecting in this way, the meditator again withdraws the mind, hatred will have decreased.

After investigation through analytical meditation, the mind becomes neutral. Even when the vibrancy of hatred has been reduced, however, it is still not suitable to cultivate the nine mental abidings. First, one must rest for a while—just leave things alone for the time being. This was stated by Bhāvaviveka in his *Heart of the Middle* and his own commentary on it, *Blaze of Reasoning.*

Hatred is discussed here only as an example. As was explained earlier, meditation on the unpleasant can be used as a means of reducing desire, and so forth. (See also p. 44ff.) When the process of reducing the vibrancy of hatred or another predominant afflictive emotion is completed, the meditator again begins to cultivate the nine mental abidings using the body of a Buddha, and so forth, as the object of observation. The practice now continues as before.

CLOSE SETTING

The fourth mental abiding is called close setting.[1] Through the strong force of mindfulness, the mind now remains on its object of observation. From the fourth mental abiding on, the object of observation is not lost. However, within not losing the object of observation, one is bothered by strong laxity and excitement.

Until now we have discussed only laziness and forgetfulness. Someone might wonder whether or not laxity and excitement also occur during the first three mental abidings, since they are being mentioned only now. They certainly do occur, but until the fourth mental abiding laziness and forgetfulness are grosser and stronger and thus must be countered first. It is possible to err on the basis of how these topics are presented in the great texts, as opposed to experiential order. Teachers' talk about laxity and excitement might lead one to think that they do not occur before the fourth mental abiding, but, as we have said, this is not the case.

Question: If you identify laxity or excitement during the first three mental abidings, is it suitable to apply the antidotes to them?

Answer: Yes. It is suitable to resort to the antidotes to laxity and excitement; however, laziness and forgetfulness are grosser and worse at this time. Your development in terms of the nine mental abidings depends on the manifestation of unfavorable factors. If you do not have laziness or forgetfulness, you will immediately be in the third mental abiding. It is not always necessary to progress from the first to the second to the third. Some people begin with the second and some, with the third.

During the fourth mental abiding, as was mentioned earlier (p. 77), the mind is thoroughly set inside through the power of strong mindfulness. However, within non-forgetfulness of the object of observation it is still possible for laxity and excitement to be generated. There is no longer much danger from laziness and forgetfulness because one has developed such strong mindfulness that, even if laziness and forgetfulness arise, one

---

[1] *nye bar 'jog pa, upasthāpana.*

can immediately get rid of them, but there is great danger of laxity because the mind is strongly withdrawn inside. Laxity arises only during the cultivation of meditative stabilization because one of its causes is the withdrawal of the mind inside.

Question: If you begin to get dull while listening to a lecture, is that not laxity?

Answer: No, it is lethargy. Lethargy is included within the factor of obscuration. Laxity is non-defiled and neutral or virtuous; lethargy is necessarily afflicted,[1] and thus laxity and lethargy are mutually exclusive.[2] We can settle qualms about this after the nature of laxity has been set forth.

It is necessary to identify the causes producing laxity. It can be produced in three ways: (1) by diminution of the intensity of meditative stabilization; (2) through sleepiness or lethargy; (3) by the mind's being overly withdrawn inside.

When laxity is produced in the first way, the intensity of meditative stabilization diminishes; its heightened quality decreases. The generation of laxity in the second way, through sleepiness or lethargy, is like the casting of a shadow. The mind becomes cloudy, as if something that was illumined had become dark. Sleepiness and lethargy are not causes in the sense of preceding laxity but in the sense that, instead of going to sleep, the mind has become lax.

When laxity is produced in the third way, it is caused by the mind's being overly withdrawn inside. This is because the excessive withdrawal of the mind causes the intensity of clarity to diminish—that is, the heightened quality of the meditative stabilization decreases. However, the mind need not be overly withdrawn inside for laxity to arise. For example, if, while you are in meditative stabilization on the body of a Buddha, love and compassion arise, these are not actual instances of love and compassion but are cases of laxity. One would think that love and compassion would be included among virtuous phenomena, but here they are deceivers and a type of subtle laxity. As an antidote, one meditates on the difficulty of finding a human life with leisure[3] and fortune,[4] and the importance of having gained them. Or one might meditate on the major and minor marks of a Buddha in order to heighten the mind.

1 *nyon mongs can, kliṣṭa.*

2 *'gal ba, virodha.*

3 *dal ba, kṣaṇa.*

4 *'byor ba, saṃpad.*

If, by relying on introspection,[1] the meditator suspects that laxity is about to arise through the force of sleep or lethargy, it is definitely necessary to meditate on a bright object. A well-educated person could meditate on the nature of the mind as clear light.[2] Most people will be helped by meditation on a bright object, but someone who has engaged in a good deal of analysis and obtained some understanding of what it means that the defilements are adventitious and the mind's nature is clear light will find the second antidote even more helpful than the first. When laxity arises in the third way, through withdrawing the mind too much inside, it is necessary to revivify or heighten the mind. One does this by causing the meaning of sūtras, and so forth, to appear to the mind.

The antidotes to the first and third types of laxity are set forth in Bhāvaviveka's *Blaze of Reasoning*, his commentary to his *Heart of the Middle*. The antidote to the second is set forth in the *Sūtra Unraveling the Thought* and Asaṅga's *Grounds of Hearers*, as well as in all presentations of the stages of the path.[3]

Laxity occurs only when one is fairly advanced in cultivating meditative stabilization. Thus, it is said to be necessary to identify the nature and mode of production of the three types of laxity before cultivating meditative stabilization.

The entity, or nature, of laxity is explained as an internal distraction which is a mental factor that destroys the intensity of clarity in [a mind of] meditative stabilization.[4] This is the definition of laxity. There are two forms of laxity, neutral and virtuous. Four terms are relevant here:

1 factor of stability[5]
2 factor of subjective clarity[6]
3 factor of clarity[7]—both subject and object have to be clear
4 intensity[8]

In the second factor above, one has stability and subjective clarity but not intensity. Subtle laxity is virtuous—for example, when a little stability has

---

[1] *shes bzhin, saṃprajanya.*

[2] *'od gsal, prabhāsvara.*

[3] *lam rim.*

[4] *ting nge 'dzin gyi gsal ngar gzhom par byed pa'i sems byung nang gi g.yeng ba.*

[5] *gnas cha.*

[6] *dvang cha.*

[7] *gsal cha.*

[8] *ngar.*

been lost but there is still an intensity to the clarity. Thus, there are three possibilities. One might have only subjective clarity but not objective clarity and not intensity; one might have both subjective and objective clarity but not intensity; and as a third possibility one might have intensity and subjective and objective clarity but be a little lacking in the factor of stability. It is more important to be able to identify these forms of laxity than to identify meditative stabilization.

In coarse laxity, one has subjective clarity but there is some fault with the factor of stability; nevertheless, there is subjective clarity.

Subtle laxity is of two types, coarse subtle and subtle subtle. In the coarse form of subtle laxity, one has the first three factors—stability, subjective clarity, and both subjective and objective clarity—but lacks the fourth, intensity. In the subtle form of subtle laxity, one has all four qualities, but there is a slight fault with the factor of stability.

In an example used to illustrate this practice, it is said that two guards, representing mindfulness and introspection, are protecting the jewels of meditative stabilization from the robbers, laxity and excitement. The factors of mindfulness and introspection survey the mind to see whether laxity or excitement is arising. From the time of the fourth mental abiding, mindfulness has come into its own and does not deteriorate. This is because the power[1] of mindfulness is fulfilled in the fourth mental abiding. Thus, one continually maintains mindfulness of how the factors of stability, subjective clarity, objective and subjective clarity, and intensity are faring.

How does laxity differ from slackness?[2] Many texts, such as the *Sūtra Unraveling the Thought*, Asaṅga's *Grounds of Hearers*, and Bhāvaviveka's *Heart of the Middle* and *Blaze of Reasoning*, discuss slackness instead of laxity. Even though the word "laxity" may be mentioned, "slackness" appears even more frequently. These two are not entirely the same; however, the slackness to which these texts refer is laxity. In the context of their explanation, slackness can be only neutral or virtuous—there is no afflicted slackness. Thus, since what they are calling slackness actually signifies laxity, it can occur only during meditative stabilization.

In general, however, there are three different types of slackness: (1) observing a virtuous object, (2) observing a neutral object, and (3) observing a non-virtuous object. The mental decline or disheartenment mentioned

---

[1] *stobs, bala.*

[2] *zhum pa.*

earlier occurs when, for example, after observing the meditative stabilizations of Buddhas and generating a wish to attain them, a slackness or disheartening sets in. This is an instance of slackness that has a virtuous object. It is also called the laziness of inadequacy, or the laziness of putting oneself down, feeling "I could not possibility do this." If a person wants to murder someone and then becomes disheartened, this is a case of slackness having a non-virtuous object, which would not occur during the cultivation of meditative stabilization. This disheartenment with respect to murder is non-virtuous because if the person could do it, she or he would. Although the person is discouraged about his or her ability to accomplish the murder, the would-be murderer is not renouncing it, for that would be a virtue. A case of neutral slackness would be, for example, if a person had been walking a long way to a certain destination, become tired, and met another person who said that the distance yet to be covered was even greater than that covered already. The traveler's disheartenment would be neither virtuous nor non-virtuous, but neutral.

The three cases just mentioned are instances of slackness that are not instances of laxity. Thus, the two are not equivalent. However, whatever is a case of laxity is a case of slackness. Laxity necessarily has a factor of non-clarity with respect to the object of observation, but in the three types of slackness, or disheartenment, discussed just above, the object of observation can still remain vivid; indeed, it is because the object is so clear that the person becomes disheartened. Thus, Jam-ȳang-shay-b̄a makes a distinction between slackness and laxity, although other monastic colleges consider them to be equivalent. Some people say that the original Sanskrit for these two is a single word; however, there are three possibilities between them: whatever is laxity is necessarily slackness, but whatever is slackness is not necessarily laxity.

The greatest error comes from confusing laxity and lethargy. What is the difference between them? Lethargy is included within the factor of obscuration. For this reason, laxity and lethargy are necessarily mutually exclusive. Laxity occurs only when the mind is withdrawn inside in the process of developing meditative stabilization, whereas lethargy can be produced either when the mind is withdrawn inside or when the mind is scattered outside. Lethargy accompanies all root and secondary afflictive emotions.[1] Even when one experiences excitement, lethargy—a factor of heaviness of mind and body—is present at the root of its generation; it is due to the

---

[1] *rtsa nyon, mulakleśa; nye nyon, upakleśa.*

factor of lethargy that, even if you become excited and the mind is heightened, afterward you sink back down. The fact that you come back down indicates that lethargy is at the root of the excitement. Therefore, through the mind's scattering outside, more obscuration can be produced.

Thus, the first quality of lethargy is that it is included within obscuration. The second is that it accompanies all root and secondary afflictive emotions. Third, it indirectly interrupts the cultivation of meditative stabilization, for, through its force, laxity and excitement are produced. Its fourth quality is that it causes darkness of mind and heaviness of body. The first three features are set forth in Asaṅga's *Summary of Manifest Knowledge*. The fourth can be divided into two parts, darkness of mind and heaviness of body. These two are set forth in Vasubandhu's *Treasury of Manifest Knowledge;* they comprise the function of lethargy.

Usually the teaching on laxity is given at the time of explaining the fourth mental abiding, but this is not because laxity does not occur before this time. It is just that laxity is dealt with experientially at a time when, for the most part, meditative stabilization is coming continuously, and this occurs at the fourth mental abiding. (See p. 77.)

DISCIPLINING

At the fifth mental abiding, disciplining,[1] yogic practitioners, through their own power, know the good qualities of meditative stabilization. At this point, they generate the power of introspection; although they had introspection earlier, this is when the *power* of introspection is generated. During this period, too, there is great danger of laxity because previously, in the fourth mental abiding, the mind was strongly withdrawn. Thus, it is necessary to revivify or heighten the mind. There are probably no instances of coarse laxity's occurring during the fifth mental abiding, but subtle laxity does. Meditators, who now know through their own experience the qualities of meditative stabilization and have generated the power of introspection, pass on to the sixth mental abiding in that same session.

PACIFYING

During the sixth mental abiding, pacifying,[2] meditative stabilization is improved through knowledge of the faults of distraction, laxity, excitement, and so forth. The power of introspection is fulfilled; through one's own power, one is able to inspect for laxity and excitement. However, through

---

[1] *dul bar byed pa, damana.*

[2] *zhi bar byed pa, śamana.*

excessive heightening of the mind, there is danger of subtle excitement. Therefore, at this point, it is appropriate to explain the entity and divisions of excitement.

The entity, or definition, of excitement is: (5) a mental factor, included within the class of desire, which—(1) observing its object, an attractive contaminated thing—(2) has the subjective aspect of not being pacified, (3) is a scattering of the mind to the outside, and (4) interrupts the cultivation of meditative stabilization.[1] The main points of the definition are numbered and discussed in the order in which they appear in the Tibetan.

1 The object of excitement is necessarily an attractive, contaminated object. It is attractive or pleasant in the sense that the excited consciousness views it as such; there is no definiteness that the object is pleasant for everyone.
2 The objective aspect of the excitement is that it is not pacified. This means that while the mind views such an object, it cannot be recalled inside.
3 Excitement is a scattering of the mind outside. Afflictive emotions are of two types—one when the mind is too withdrawn inside and the other when it is scattered outside. Excitement signifies desire within the context of scattering outside; this scattering occurs because of desire.
4 Excitement interferes with the cultivation of meditative stabilization. It causes an unserviceability of mind due to the contradiction between withdrawing the mind inside in meditative stabilization and the mind's being scattered outside.
5 Excitement is included within the class of desire.

To be able to identify the presence of excitement, one must know not only this fivefold description of its entity, or nature, but also its causes. Asaṅga's *Grounds of Hearers* and the *Sūtra Unraveling the Thought* say that an excited consciousness is one that takes to mind the signs of excitement. The word "sign"[2] has various meanings: aspect,[3] cause,[4] and nature.[5] There is a

---

[1] *rang yul zag bcas kyi dngos po yid du 'ong ba la dmigs nas* (1) *rnam pa ma zhi par byed pa* (2) *sems phyir 'phro ba* (3) *ting nge 'dzin sgom pa la bar du gcod pa* (4) *'dod chags kyi char d'ogs pa'i sems byung* (5). For a discussion of the divisions of excitement, see *Meditative States,* 61-62.

[2] *mtshan ma, nimitta.*

[3] *rnam pa, ākāra.*

[4] *rgyu, hetu.*

[5] *rang bzhin, svābhāva.*

term, *mtshan mar 'dzin pa,* which is usually translated "apprehension of signs" and means, to apprehend the nature incorrectly. Thus, it could be translated "perverse conception of the nature"—that is, the holding of what is actually the opposite of the nature of things to be the nature of things. In this way, the term "apprehension of signs" sometimes refers to the conception of true existence.[1] Understood in another way, however, it is the definition of "discrimination." In the latter case, it means, to apprehend the nature of things correctly. Discrimination is of two types: (1) apprehension of signs—that is, inherent existence—and (2) apprehension of what actually is there;[2] the conception of true existence is a case of the first type, apprehension of the opposite of what is there.

Asaṅga's *Grounds of Hearers* and the *Sūtra Unraveling the Thought* refer to "taking to mind the signs of excitement."[3] "Signs of excitement" here refers to causes of excitement.

Haughtiness[4] is a cause of excitement. Haughtiness consists of a heightening or pumping up of the mind within an attachment to one's own qualities. When this is generated, excitement automatically comes along with it. Thus, it is necessary to identify the causes generating haughtiness. Nāgārjuna's *Friendly Letter*[5] identifies these causes of haughtiness:

1 Lineage. One's class or social status being taken as a basis for generating haughtiness.
2 Body, or form. If one has a body that others admire, one might generate haughtiness.
3 Hearing, or learning. There are three types that are causes of haughtiness: (a) having heard, or learned, a great deal;[6] (b) holding learning;[7] (c) having accumulated learning.[8] (a) This type of hearing related to haughtiness is of greatest danger to a person who wishes to cultivate hearing, thinking, and meditating. For example, someone who is in meditative stabilization may begin to stray from it through thinking

[1] *bden 'dzin.*

[2] *bkra bar 'dzin pa.*

[3] *rgod pa'i mtshan pa yid la byed pa.*

[4] *rgyags pa, mada.*

[5] *bshes pa'i spring yig, suhṛlekha;* P5682, vol. 129. This is stanza 12; see *Nāgārjuna's Letter,* trans. Geshe Lobsang Tharchin and Artemus B. Engle (Dharamsala: Library of Tibetan Works and Archives, 1979), 46.

[6] *mang du thos pa.*

[7] *thos pa 'dzin pa.*

[8] *thos pa bsags pa.*

about the many things that he or she has heard; that person may then reflect on them in such a way that they turned into a basis of desire: she or he may think, "I have heard a great deal, I am very learned," or may become distracted into running through topics studied. (b) The second type of hearing that is a cause of haughtiness is a person's feeling that he or she not only has heard a great deal but also is capable of engaging in a great deal of thought. (c) Asaṅga's text does not comment on the third type of haughtiness related to hearing—that of having accumulated learning. There is no doubt about what the first two mean, but there are two different interpretations on what the third signifies. "Having accumulated learning" might mean that one has heard or studied many different texts on a given topic. My own opinion, however, is that "having accumulated learning" refers to having haughtiness in connection with states arisen from meditation,[1] because the first type of haughtiness regarding learning had to do with hearing and the second, with thinking; thus, it seems reasonable that the third be associated with meditation. For example, some scholars in Tibet engaged in a great deal of study and then went into retreat out of haughtiness, so that people would know that they had entered a phase of no activities and were in deep meditation. Among people who wish to cultivate meditative stabilization, there is not too much danger of their thinking that their lineage or body is great, but they must be learned and thus could be attached to their own learning—to the fact that they have heard a great deal.

4 Youth.[2] Haughtiness regarding youthfulness refers to pride in one's own beauty.

5 Power, or authority.[3] There are people who, when they have control over an area, develop haughtiness by observing their own authority.

Still, it is the third type of haughtiness—that related to learning—that is most likely to arise in educated people.

We have discussed methods for revivifying or heightening the mind. (See p. 78ff.) One of the three antidotes mentioned is to meditate on a bright object; another is to meditate on the nature of the mind as clear light. Still another is to do reflective meditation on the meaning of scriptures. The third involves the danger that, even if one originally set out to reflect on the meaning of scriptures for the sake of overcoming laxity, in

---

1 *sgom byung, bhāvanāmayī.*

2 *lang 'tsho.*

3 *dbang thang che ba.*

time this reflection may turn into haughtiness. Therefore, in his *Grounds of Hearers*, Asaṅga emphatically sets forth the types of haughtiness related to learning; nevertheless, no commentary on them is given in Tibet.

These three types of haughtiness related to learning are most significant. A person wishing to cultivate meditative stabilization must be learned, that is to say, must engage in a great deal of hearing. Thus, this fault will arise. When Asaṅga and the *Sūtra Unraveling the Thought* speak of "taking to mind the signs [i.e., causes] of excitement," they are referring to the types of haughtiness just mentioned, which are causes of excitement. It is Bhāvaviveka's *Blaze of Reasoning* that explicitly states haughtiness as a cause of excitement.

During the sixth of the nine mental abidings, the power of introspection is fulfilled—that is, one improves meditative stabilization through recognizing by one's own power the faults of distraction, laxity, excitement, and so forth.

When cultivating meditative stabilization, one must inspect from time to time whether or not laxity or excitement has arisen. Does one temporarily give up meditative stabilization when inspecting in this way? No. Inspection must be done within not giving up meditative stabilization. The inspection lasts neither for a very long nor for a very short time. Once the yogic practitioner has confidence that the mind will stay on the object of observation, it is possible to have an inspection that functions simultaneously with observation of the object.

One needs to engage in inspection before losing the intensity of meditative stabilization. There are two reasons for doing so: (1) Such inspection causes the meditative stabilization to continue; one can then lengthen the continuum of meditative stabilization and thereby advance to a higher state. If one can remain in meditative stabilization for four or five hours, then by engaging in inspection toward the end of that period, one will be able to remain in meditative stabilization still longer. (2) If laxity or excitement has arisen or is about to arise, inspection allows one to realize that this is the case. If one has a vibrancy[1] of meditative stabilization with respect to remaining on the object of observation, it is possible to tell when laxity or excitement is about to arise. As an additional minor purpose, introspection enables mindfulness to hold on to the object of observation.

During the first two mental abidings, it takes most of one's force to cause the mind to stay on the object of observation; from the third and

---

[1] *thu re.*

fourth mental abidings on up, one is able to engage in the techniques of introspection. A person who has developed vibrancy in meditative stabilization can immediately recognize that laxity or excitement is about to arise. What does one do then? One merely loosens the mode of apprehension of the object of observation a little and then engages in a technique for removing the laxity or excitement in accordance with how these methods are explained in the texts. Once the laxity or excitement has been removed, it is said that one again tightens observation of the object of observation. Kamalashīla's *Stages of Meditation* says, "Having removed laxity, tighten the mind on the object of observation." The Tibetan conjunction *la* [in the phrase "having removed laxity"] indicates that persons trained in meditative stabilization can recognize when laxity or excitement will arise, at which time they loosen the mode of apprehension of the object of observation a little, engage in a technique to overcome laxity or excitement, *and*[1] then again tighten down on the object of observation. This summarizes how one engages in techniques for removing laxity and excitement while cultivating the nine mental abidings.

Kamalashīla's statement above applies, not to a beginner, but to a person who has attained some dexterity with respect to meditative stabilization, for a beginner who loosens the mode of apprehension of the object of observation a little will lose the object of observation entirely.

Question: How do you set it up so that you will engage in introspection while the meditation is going well? There seems to be a great tendency only to do this when the meditation is not going well and you have strayed from the object.

Answer: Introspection has two functions. One, near the beginning of the process, is concerned with inspecting whether or not the mind is abiding on the object of observation; this causes the mind to remain on the object of observation. Later, introspection is more concerned with whether or not laxity or excitement has arisen; at this time, its function is to cause application of the appropriate antidote. These two modes of introspection occur within a single continuum; it is not necessary to posit two consciousnesses with respect to them.

It is necessary to inspect while you are abiding on the object of observation; this is like one mind's looking at another mind. Before dexterity has been attained, this type of inspection must be done continually through-

[1] *la.*

out the session. How does one do this? The main mind[1] observing the object of observation is manifest; the inspecting mind is somewhat nonmanifest. It is as though looking from one side, like someone spying. Once dexterity has been attained, it is no longer necessary to inspect all the time.

Question: What is the etymology of the sixth mental abiding? Why is it called "pacifying"?

Answer: It stops the discordant factors and, through its own power, induces increase of meditative stabilization.

THOROUGH PACIFYING

The seventh mental abiding is called thorough pacifying.[2] At this point, the power of effort is generated. There is no longer much danger—as there was during the fifth and sixth mental abidings—that laxity or excitement will arise. If they do arise, however, one is able to suppress them.

What is the effort the power of which is generated in the seventh mental abiding? This effort has six qualities:

1 intense application[3]
2 continuous application[4]
3 causally concordant application[5]
4 effort arising from application[6]
5 undisturbed effort[7]
6 effort which is insatiable[8]

These are not qualities of effort in general but must be present in the power of effort discussed here.

The first of these, intense application, is a sense of intentness with regard to the qualities of meditative stabilization—that is, when one thinks about these qualities, the mind is intent on them.

The second, continuous application, means that one continuously applies oneself to the task of cultivating meditative stabilization; one does not just do it sometimes.

---

[1] *gtso sems.*

[2] *nye bar zhi bar byed pa, vyupaśamana.*

[3] *gus sbyor.*

[4] *rtag sbyor.*

[5] *rgyu mthun pa'i sbyor ba.*

[6] *sbyor ba las byung ba'i brtson grus.*

[7] *mi 'thugs pa'i brtson grus.*

[8] *chog ma shes pa'i brtson grus.*

Causally concordant application, the third, means that it is necessary to have a single continuum of effort. Thus, when one begins the task, one continues to progress on the basis of the effort as a causal concordance; it all flows from the same stream of effort.

The fourth quality, the effort arising from application, is to be distinguished from the effort resulting from having made effort in past lifetimes. What is needed here is an effort generated from application in this lifetime.

Undisturbed effort, the fifth quality, is not disturbed by hardships such as heat.

The last quality, the effort which is insatiable, is motivated by one's not being satisfied with what has been accomplished up to now.

In order to have the *power* of effort, one must have these six types of effort.

Question: Is it the case that laziness can exist in the seventh of the nine mental abidings but would probably not exist in the eighth?

Answer: In my opinion, when the power of effort is attained, laziness will not arise. At that time, one has already fulfilled the powers of mindfulness and introspection. The power of effort is fulfilled at the level of the eighth mental abiding; I do not think you could have laziness in the seventh. There is no clear explanation of the boundary. One has completed the powers of mindfulness and introspection; if one were to generate laziness, this would mean that one could not notice it with mindfulness.

MAKING ONE-POINTED

In the eighth mental abiding, making one-pointed,[1] one is able, through merely relying on mindfulness and introspection at the beginning of the session, to remain with the object of observation. Because the strength of laxity and excitement has deteriorated, it is not necessary to rely on mindfulness and introspection while one is actually cultivating meditative stabilization. At this point, the power of effort is fulfilled, and by maintaining the continuum of this meditative stabilization one passes into the ninth mental abiding.

SETTING IN EQUIPOISE

In the ninth mental abiding, setting in equipoise,[2] one is able, through merely directing the mind toward the object of observation, to stay in

---

[1] *rtse gcig tu byed pa, ekotīkaraṇa.*

[2] *mnyam par 'jog pa, samādhāna.*

meditative stabilization spontaneously. It is automatic; the meditation has its own flow. At this point one has achieved the power of familiarity;[1] one is free from laxity and excitement, is able to set the mind continuously in meditative stabilization, and has subjective and objective clarity. Which of the eight antidotes applies at this time? Desisting from application[2] is equivalent with the ninth mental abiding. It is through the functioning of such desisting that one is spontaneously able to maintain the continuum of meditative stabilization in the ninth mental abiding.

The term *btang snyoms* is often translated as "equanimity" or "neutrality." Here it is being translated as "desisting." There are three types of *btang snyoms:*

1 neutral feeling[3]
2 immeasurable equanimity[4]
3 desisting from application.[5]

The factor of desisting from application of the antidote is itself a mental factor but is not included among the fifty-one mental factors. There are scholars who assert the existence of mental factors other than the fifty-one. The factor of desisting serves as an antidote to unnecessary application of other antidotes.

THE FOUR MENTAL ENGAGEMENTS

I have shown how the nine mental abidings are achieved by way of the six powers.[6] Now I will explain how they are achieved by way of the four mental engagements.[7]

The first two mental abidings are achieved by way of forcible engagement.[8] The third through seventh are included within the mental engagement of interrupted engagement.[9] The eighth is included within uninterrupted engagement[10] and the ninth, within spontaneous, or one-pointed,

---

[1] *yongs su 'dris pa, paricaya.*

[2] *btang snyoms, upekṣā.*

[3] *tshor ba btang snyoms.*

[4] *btang snyoms tshad med.*

[5] *'du byed btang snyoms.*

[6] For further discussion of the six powers, see Lati Rinbochay's oral presentation in *Meditative States,* 53, 54, 57, 69, 71, 72.

[7] *yid la byed pa, manaskāra.*

[8] *sgrim ste 'jug pa, balavāhana.*

[9] *bar du chad cing 'jug pa, sacchidravāhana.*

[10] *chad pa med par 'jug pa, nischidravāhana.*

engagement.[1]

The first two mental abidings are included within forcible engagement because the meditator must tighten the mind and force it to stay on the object of observation. At this point, one engages in techniques designed not to *keep* the mind on its object of observation but to *put* it there. From the third through seventh mental abidings, one engages in techniques to cause the mind to remain on its object of observation. During these mental abidings, the mind is sometimes able to stay on its object of observation and sometimes not; thus, they are characterized by interrupted engagement.

During the eighth mental abiding the mind stays on its object of observation without being interrupted by laxity and excitement. It is thus characterized by uninterrupted engagement.

The ninth mental abiding is included within spontaneous, or one-pointed, engagement. This is because the ninth mental abiding does not depend on the exertion that observes whether laxity or excitement has arisen: the mind is one-pointedly engaged with the object of observation and is able to operate according to the meditator's own intention. For all these reasons, the ninth mental abiding is included within spontaneous, or one-pointed, engagement. This, in brief, is how the nine mental abidings are included within the four mental engagements.

FIVE FAULTS AND EIGHT ANTIDOTES IN RELATION TO THE NINE MENTAL ABIDINGS

Let us relate the five faults and the eight antidotes as set forth in Maitreya's *Differentiation of the Middle and the Extremes* to the nine mental abidings set forth in the *Sūtra Unraveling the Thought*, Asaṅga's *Grounds of Hearers*, and Maitreya's *Ornament for the Mahāyāna Sūtras*. As was mentioned above (p. 69), whoever cultivates the nine mental abidings overcomes the five faults through the eight antidotes, and whoever overcomes the five faults through the eight antidotes must cultivate the nine mental abidings.

Among the eight antidotes, faith, aspiration, and exertion are important in the beginning; mindfulness and introspection are important in the middle, and desisting from application of the antidotes is important at the end. The application of the antidotes is important from the first through the eighth mental abidings. What remains? Pliancy, which is important for all nine mental abidings. It is called a branch which is a benefit.[2] Pliancy is

---

[1] *lhun grub tu 'jug pa, anābhogavāhana.*

[2] *phan yon gyi yan lag, *anuśaṃsāṅga.*

posited as an antidote to laziness; it is the fourth of the four antidotes to laziness but it is important in the beginning, middle, and end.

Pliancy is called a branch which is a benefit because it is a benefit, or effect, of having cultivated the nine mental abidings. The pliancy of the first concentration would be the final aim of a person cultivating a mundane path of meditation.[1] The purpose of cultivating the nine mental abidings is to attain calm abiding, which is conjoined with the pliancies. Thus, because they are the aim, the pliancies are important throughout all nine mental abidings.

Faith, aspiration, and exertion are techniques for striving toward meditative stabilization. Mindfulness and introspection are techniques for aiming the mind at meditative stabilization. The application of the antidotes is an incentive to meditative stabilization; it urges one on. Desisting from application is a technique for stopping the application of antidotes when, because the mind is spontaneously set in meditative stabilization, they are no longer necessary.

Whose system is it to put together the five faults, eight antidotes, and nine mental abidings with regard to the cultivation of calm abiding? This is a system of the Ḡa-dam-b̄a[2] School, which stems from Atīsha. There are two Ḡa-dam-b̄a lineages—the preceptual[3] and the textual.[4] The preceptual lineage consists of those who mainly engage in practice by way of a transmission of preceptual instructions.[5] The textual lineage consists of those who engage in practice from the viewpoint of maintaining a continuum of explanation of the great texts. The system explained above is that of the textual Ḡa-dam-b̄as.

Unless I identify the tradition from which I speak, it might be thought that I was making up something new. Therefore, I have identified this explanation as from the textual Ḡa-dam-b̄a tradition. The definitions, divisions, causes, and so on, that were set forth in relation to excitement, and so on, came from many different sources, such as Vasubandhu's *Treasury of Manifest Knowledge* and Asaṅga's *Summary of Manifest Knowledge.* It is suitable to bring these together because they all speak to the same topic. It sometimes happens that different topics have the same name, in which

---

[1] *sgom lam, bhāvanāmārga.*

[2] *dka' gdams pa.*

[3] *gdams ngag pa.*

[4] *gzhung pa pa.*

[5] *gdams ngag, avavāda.*

case it is not suitable to fuse the two explanations, but that is not the case here.

The sections eliminating qualms were all taken from the literature of Jam-ȳang-shay-b̄a. There is not much in Indian texts that settles qualms in this way. In Tibet, many texts set forth the definitions, or entities, of these topics, but only Jam-ȳang-shay-b̄a's *Great Exposition of the Concentrations and Formless Absorptions* does so by putting together many different texts, examining them, and then eliminating a great variety of qualms. I have also added occasional phrases from quintessential instructions. It would be suitable for someone to cultivate the nine mental abidings on the basis of this explanation and by extending their understanding through examining the great texts.

DISCUSSION

Question: What causes someone to rise from meditative stabilization? It sounds as though, since the mind and the object of observation are united, one would need to be roused by someone else.

Answer: This is not necessary. Meditative stabilization is not like going to sleep. Even if it were, when we go to sleep at night, we can sometimes set it up so that we awaken early. Among the many causes required for meditative stabilization, there is one that sets up how long the meditator will remain in it. This causes it to cease when the determined amount of time has passed. When one rises from calm abiding, the mind of calm abiding becomes somewhat non-manifest, but its ability to function does not deteriorate, for, as soon as one again withdraws the mind inside, it immediately recurs. If the functioning had deteriorated, however, the mind would have separated from meditative stabilization, and it could happen that, when the mind was again withdrawn inside, something other than calm abiding would arise. Thus, one is able to rise from meditative stabilization because one decides beforehand how long one will remain in it.

Question: If you develop calm abiding and then do not meditate for ten years, will calm abiding immediately arise again when you sit down again in meditation?

Answer: There is no certainty. It could happen that even after a day you would no longer have calm abiding. It could also be that after a hundred years it would still remain. This depends on various functions in the mind.

Question: What type of mental function determines this?

Answer: If someone cultivates and achieves calm abiding and then decides that there are many more important things to be done and meditative stabilization is a waste of time, this decision would cause calm abiding to deteriorate. Not only would calm abiding deteriorate but so would one's virtuous roots[1] in general because one would have come under the influence of a wrong idea. This wrong conception is one of the causes severing virtuous roots. For a person who had achieved calm abiding and continued to value it highly, it would still arise ten or twenty years later.

Question: What has been explained so far does not seem unique to Buddhism. If non-Buddhists were to cultivate these mental abidings, would they go about it in the way described here?

Answer: The object of observation would be different, and the special methods would be different—taking refuge,[2] generating the altruistic mind of enlightenment, reflecting on the importance of having leisure and fortune, and so forth. The [non-Buddhist] Forders[3] cultivate calm abiding for the sake of achieving causal meditative absorptions[4] so that they can be reborn in high states within cyclic existence. They seek either to remain in a long life or to take rebirth as a god of long life or in the Form or Formless Realm. This does not require refuge, the thought definitely to leave cyclic existence, or the altruistic mind of enlightenment.

Question: Is reflective meditation[5] included within either analytical or stabilizing meditation, or is it a third category?

Answer: Reflective meditation—so called because the meditator causes certain meanings to appear and reflects on them—can be a form of either analytical or stabilizing meditation. For example, we refer to reflective meditation on the stages of the path. We distinguish between verbal and factual reflective meditation, the latter being the type that deals with the actual meaning. With regard to the stages of the path leading to highest enlightenment, one first goes through the words or names of these and then makes an imitation, as if the actual fact were appearing to the mind, and in time it appears.

In verbal reflective meditation, a series of sound generalities appears to

1 *dge ba'i rtsa ba, kuśalamūla.*

2 *skyabs, śaraṇa.*

3 *mu steg pa, tīrthika.* "Forders" is a term for non-Buddhist religious practitioners in India; they are so called because of propounding a ford, or means to reach, to liberation.

4 *rgyu snyoms 'jug, *kāraṇasamāpatti.*

5 *shar sgom.*

the mind. In factual meditation, one reflects not only on the words but on the meaning, ranging from the beginning of the path—reliance on a spiritual guide—right up through the stages of union of pure mind and pure body. In this type of reflective meditation, the subjects seem to diminish in number; the words become more and more condensed while still retaining all the meaning. Thus, reflective meditation helps one not to forget whatever topic is contemplated.

Question: Is it possible to attain calm abiding in this country? There are so many other activities to perform!

Answer: I do not think there is any difference between this country and my own. It is difficult to withdraw from all activities and just cultivate calm abiding, however helpful this might be for practice. Thus, it is important to reduce activities, to get rid of those that are not important.

We do many things mostly because we are used to doing them, without analyzing which are sensible and which are not. Among the great many activities we perform, a large number are pointless. We can conclude for ourselves that it would be all right not to do those that serve very little purpose. Important activities could be somewhat reduced; for example, instead of spending two hours on them, spend only one. It is not said in texts that beginners should cultivate calm abiding all day long, nor would it be possible for them to do so. Whether you are in Europe, America, or wherever, it is possible to find the time; the important factor is to have the quintessential instructions so that you can cultivate calm abiding.

In comparison with my own country, there are indeed more activities here—industry, and so forth—but I doubt that there is anyone who has no time to cultivate calm abiding. No one has to work all the time. We are just not analyzing our activities to see what actually needs to be done and what does not; we just go on doing what we have always done. There must be time if one puts aside activities of little meaning. This requires analysis, and if analysis is done, I think we would find that we have time.

5 ACHIEVING CALM ABIDING

In the meditative stabilization of the ninth mental abiding, one is free of laxity and excitement and is able to engage the object of observation one-pointedly. Not only this, but one is also able continuously to engage the object of observation spontaneously and has the factors of stability and clarity. However, the attainment of such meditative stabilization is *not* the attainment of calm abiding.

PLIANCY

What is the measure of having attained calm abiding? As was mentioned, the ninth mental abiding has spontaneity[1] and the features, or factors, of stability and clarity. The texts speak of the latter two, but it is better to think in terms of three factors—spontaneity, stability, and clarity. A meditative stabilization that has these three features is a meditative stabilization of the ninth mental abiding. Nevertheless, someone who has attained this has not attained calm abiding because, before attaining calm abiding, one must attain the stages of pliancy;[2] the consciousness of calm abiding must be conjoined with special pliancy. As to why the ninth mental abiding is not calm abiding, the *Sūtra Unraveling the Thought* says that it is a mind *concordant with* calm abiding, not a mind *of* calm abiding. Asaṅga's *Actuality of the Grounds*[3] gives another reason:

> Such a meditative stabilization is not actual calm abiding because one has not achieved special pliancy or supreme joy and bliss and because [the ninth mental abiding] has not been achieved by means of special pliancy and supreme joy and bliss.

Because the instrumental case ("by means of") was used, one can understand that special pliancy and supreme joy and bliss must precede calm abiding. The explanation of pliancy is very important; listen to it well.

---

[1] *lhun gyis grub pa, anābhoga.*

[2] *shin tu sbyangs pa, praśrabdhi.*

[3] *sa'i dngos gzhi, bhūmivastu;* P5536-5538. Also known as *Grounds of Yogic Practice* (*yogacaryābhūmi, rnal 'byor spyod pa'i sa*).

There is a certain omen of pliancy.[1] Following this, pliancy itself is generated. Then there are the stages by which those pliancies cease; this is very important and is often not explained in the texts. After this, calm abiding is attained. There are four types of pliancy: mental pliancy, physical pliancy, the bliss of physical pliancy (bliss[2]), and the bliss of mental pliancy (joy[3]). The passage from Asaṅga's *Actuality of the Grounds* also mentions a state of supreme joy and bliss.

First the omen is generated, then mental pliancy, then physical pliancy, then the bliss of physical pliancy, and finally, the bliss of mental pliancy. These are the stages by which pliancy is generated.

MENTAL PLIANCY

In order to understand what we mean when we say that mental pliancy is generated, it is necessary to know what the entity, or nature, of mental pliancy is. When yogic practitioners cultivate meditative stabilization, they remove bad states that are unserviceabilities with regard to engaging in meditative stabilization. The definition of mental pliancy is: (7) An other (*or* special) compositional factor which is a mental factor that (1) removes the functioning of assumptions of bad mental states, (2) is in the class of very pure phenomena, (3) takes to mind a true [object] (*or*, is a pure taking to mind), (4-5) joyfully and happily engages its object of observation unimpededly, and (6) is a factor of lightness.[4]

1 The source for the statement that pliancy removes the functioning of assumptions of bad mental states[5] is Asaṅga's *Summary of Manifest Knowledge.*

2 All phenomena are included within 108 categories that fall into two divisions, thoroughly afflicted phenomena and thoroughly pure phenomena.[6] The removal of assumptions of bad mental states is included within the class of very pure phenomena. It is virtuous, although some

---

[1] *shin sbyangs skye ba'i snga bltas.*

[2] *bde ba, sukha.*

[3] *dga' ba, prīti.*

[4] *sems kyi gnas ngan len gyi byed las sel bar byed cing* (1) *rnam byang gi phyogs su gyur pa* (2) *yang dag pa(r) yid la byed pa* (3) *dmigs pa la dga' mgur thogs med du 'jug pa* (4-5) *yang ba'i char gyur pa'i* (6) *sems byung 'du byed gzhan* (7). The main points of the definition are numbered and discussed in the order in which they appear in the Tibetan.

[5] *sems kyi gnas ngan len.*

[6] For a listing with brief identifcations of these see Jeffrey Hopkins, *Meditation on Emptiness* (London: Wisdom Publications, 1983), 201-212.

virtues are objects of abandonment.[1] Nevertheless, even the virtues to be abandoned are included within the class of pure phenomena because they are virtuous. For example, all the virtues in the continuum of a person who has attained the ninth mental abiding or calm abiding are contaminated and, thus, are to be given up, but they are included within the class of pure phenomena. This is what the second section of the definition indicates.

3 Pliancy is a taking to mind of something true, or a pure taking to mind. The difference lies in whether or not the reading is *yang dag pa* or *yang dag par*, since the *ra* ending makes the phrase an adverbial accusative.

4 and 5 The mind happily[2] and unimpededly[3] engages its object of observation. The word *mgur ba* signifies a special kind of joy.

6 Pliancy is a mental factor which is a factor of lightness. There are times when a yogic practitioner is not enthusiastic but has a heaviness of mind with respect to engaging in meditative stabilization. In pliancy, however, such heaviness is totally absent; the mind is light.

7 Mental pliancy is a special compositional factor, not an ordinary one, because it has arisen by the power of meditative stabilization; it is other[4] than the ordinary because, unlike ordinary virtues, pliancy arises through one's having cultivated meditative stabilization. Mental pliancy is called a compositional mental factor because it is engaged in exertion.[5]

All these factors must be complete for something to be a mental pliancy. These seven are not explained in any one text but are drawn from many different sources. (1) That a mental pliancy removes the functioning of bad mental states is from Asaṅga's *Summary of Manifest Knowledge.* (2) That it is included in the class of very pure phenomena is from Asaṅga's *Grounds of Hearers.* (3) That it is a taking to mind of something true, or a pure taking to mind, is from Sthiramati. (4 and 5) That it is a mind happily and unimpededly engaging in the object of observation is from Bhāvaviveka's *Blaze of Reasoning.* (6) That it is a mental factor which is a factor of lightness is from Sthiramati. (7) That it is a special compositional factor is also from Sthiramati. It is suitable to draw all these points together in forming the definition of mental pliancy because they all explain

[1] *spangs bya, prahatavya.*

[2] *dga' mgur.*

[3] *thogs med du.*

[4] *gzhan.*

[5] *rtsol ba, vyāyāma.*

the same mental pliancy. Scholars sometimes draw points from a variety of texts in order to fill in a definition. Thus, this is the meaning of mental pliancy.

What is the function of the assumptions of bad mental states[1] that mental pliancy removes? When a yogic practitioner makes effort at cultivating meditative stabilization, there are factors that interrupt unimpeded setting [of the mind] on the object of observation, as well as those that interrupt the abandonment of afflictive emotions. These assumptions of bad mental states are, therefore, included in the class of afflicted phenomena. They are factors involving a sense of heaviness. Although they are mental factors, they need not be included among the fifty-one mental factors.

Many factors accompany any main mind, and whatever object is observed by any one of them is observed by all the others. For example, the mental factor of wisdom[2] that accompanies a main mind engages *by its own power* in differentiating phenomena. Thus, the main mind itself also differentiates phenomena but does not do so by its own power; it does so by way of the force of the mental factor of wisdom. When blissful feeling accompanies the main mind, it is not only the factor of feeling that experiences bliss; the main mind does also, but its experience of bliss is not by its own power. A main mind and its accompanying mental factors have the five similar associations.[3] This means that whatever the one experiences, the other does also; whatever the one observes, the other also observes, and so forth. The difference is that a certain mental factor observes or feels by its own power and the others do so by way of the power of that mental factor. That the factor of feeling experiences bliss occurs through its own power; that the main mind which accompanies that mental factor of feeling experiences bliss is due to the fact that it is accompanied by that factor of feeling.

Since the assumptions of bad mental states are consciousnesses themselves, mental pliancy is also a consciousness. Assumptions of bad physical states and physical pliancy are forms. When one attains calm abiding, these assumptions of bad mental and physical states are not abandoned from the root but are only temporarily stopped. It is not possible actually to abandon these except through the Mahāyāna path. Nevertheless, although calm abiding does not remove them from the root, their manifest

---

1 *gnas ngan len.*

2 *shes rab, prajñā.*

3 *mtshung ldan, saṃprayukta.*

function of interrupting meditative stabilization is removed; they are not removed from the root until Buddhahood. They are more difficult to abandon than the afflictive emotions. It is said that in the continuum of a Foe Destroyer there are assumptions of bad mental and physical states. For example, Foe Destroyers when just walking along will sometimes suddenly jump as if they are playing. This is due to distraction and is considered an assumption of a bad physical state.

Bodhisattvas have assumptions of bad physical and mental states that contradict vows taken. For instance, while eating, they might become distracted and, as though automatically, do something foolish. The assumptions of bad mental and physical states that prevent meditative stabilization are stopped when mental pliancy is attained. These unfavorable states are abandoned over the ten grounds of the Mahāyāna; they are the opposite of mental pliancy.

PHYSICAL PLIANCY

The definition of physical pliancy is: a special, light tangible object that removes physical tiredness, and other unfavorable physical functionings illustrated by this, when a wind moves in the body through the force of meditative stabilization while engaging in cultivating meditative stabilization, and that is in the class of very pure phenomena.[1]

The reason physical pliancy is a special tangible object is that it is not an ordinary form but a form generated by meditative stabilization; it is a special touch generated by meditative stabilization. The opposite of a physical pliancy is an assumption of a bad physical state.[2] This is a factor of heaviness that brings about bodily fatigue when the winds circulate in the body while one is engaged in cultivating meditative stabilization; it is included within the class of thoroughly afflicted phenomena. The main bad physical state is that which causes a lack of enthusiasm for, or lack of wanting to engage in, meditative stabilization. Because this is the main function, it is the one mentioned by Asaṅga's *Grounds of Hearers* in connection with assumptions of bad physical states.

A physical pliancy is a tangible object. A mental pliancy is a mental factor. However, Indian commentaries present two different systems of interpretation. According to one, both physical and mental pliancy are consid-

---

[1] *ting nge 'dzin sgom pa la 'jug pa na ting nge 'dzin gyi mthus lus la rlung rgyu ba na lus ngal ba dang 'dis mtshon pa'i byed las gzhan sel bar byed pa rnam par byang pa'i phyogs su gyur pa'i yang ba'i reg bya khyad par ba.*

[2] *lus kyi gnas ngan len.*

ered to be mental factors, the former being associated with sense consciousnesses and the latter, with mental consciousnesses. However, Sthiramati specifically interprets physical pliancy as a tangible object, and most Tibetan commentaries follow him in this.

The general meaning of an assumption of a bad state is: a factor which cannot bear the mind's being aimed at its object of observation. The general meaning of a pliancy is: a factor of being able to take to mind, or a factor of facility with aiming the mind at, an object of observation. That which causes the yogic practitioner to dislike aiming the mind at an object of observation is called an assumption of a bad state.

BLISS OF PHYSICAL PLIANCY AND BLISS OF MENTAL PLIANCY

The bliss of physical pliancy occurs when the mental factors of feeling that accompany sense consciousnesses are blissful. The blisses of mental pliancy are the mental factors of blissful feelings associated with mental consciousnesses. In general, feelings accompany the five types of sense consciousnesses.

Can all five sense consciousnesses be accompanied by the blisses of physical pliancy? There are two interpretations. Vasubandhu's *Treasury of Manifest Knowledge*, said to be the system of the Vaibhāṣhikas, asserts that all five sense consciousnesses can be accompanied by blissful feelings that are blisses of physical pliancy. This is because the bliss of physical pliancy pervades all of them. According to the upper schools of tenets[1] [Chittamātra and Mādhyamika], a bliss of physical pliancy is solely a blissful feeling that accompanies the body consciousness. There is no very clear source for this position, but by using reasoning one can understand that, while one is in meditative stabilization, there would not be a bliss of physical pliancy that accompanied, say, an eye consciousness. Among the five sense consciousnesses, the body consciousness is chief. From the viewpoint of perception of forms, the eye consciousness is chief, but from the viewpoint of experience, the body consciousness is chief. Similarly, from among the five sense powers, the physical sense power[2] is chief.

The physical sense power pervades the entire body, from the soles of the feet to the crown of the head. No matter where the body is touched, even if it is in a place in which some other sense power and consciousness, such as the eye, abides, that touch is felt because the body sense power is present there also. If someone is hurt and thereby loses an eye, the damage occurs

[1] *grub mtha', siddhānta.*

[2] *lus kyi dbang po, kāyendriya.*

just to the area of the eye consciousness without affecting the rest of the body. However, if the body consciousness is stopped, all the other sense consciousnesses also stop and the person dies. This is the basis of the statement in Āryadeva's *Four Hundred* that obscuration (ignorance) accompanies all afflictive emotions like the body sense power:[1]

> Just as the body sense power [pervades] the body,
> Obscuration abides in all.
> Therefore, through destroying obscuration
> All afflictive emotions will also be destroyed.

The body sense power pervades the entire body; if it stops, then all the other senses stop. Similarly, if ignorance ceases, all other afflictive emotions cease from the root. Thus, the body sense power and the body consciousness are chief, and whatever is a bliss of physical pliancy is necessarily a blissful feeling accompanying a body consciousness. This is the system of the upper schools of tenets. Thus, we have settled that according to the upper systems all cases of blisses of physical pliancy are cases of blisses that accompany the body consciousness.

Feelings are divided into three: pleasant, or blissful, painful, and neutral. This division is more common in the treatises. The bliss of physical pliancy is a case of the first type of feeling.

Feelings can also be divided into five types:

mental bliss[2]
bliss[3]
mental discomfort[4]
pain[5]
neutral feeling.

This fivefold division occurs in the second chapter of Vasubandhu's *Treasury of Manifest Knowledge*. Here the blisses of mental and physical pliancy are cases of the first and second types of feeling, respectively. The bliss of mental pliancy is a blissful feeling that accompanies the mental consciousness; therefore, in the threefold division of feelings it is the first type, bliss, and in the fivefold division it is specified as mental bliss. The two blisses,

[1] *bstan bcos bzhi brgya pa zhes bya ba'i tshig le'ur byas pa, catuḥśatakaśāstrakārikā;* P5246, vol. 95. This is VI.10.

[2] *yid bde, saumanasya; = bliss of mental pliancy.*

[3] *bde ba, sukha; = bliss of physical pliancy.*

[4] *yid mi bde, daurmanasya.*

[5] *sdug bsngal, duḥkha.*

of physical and mental pliancy, are contaminated blissful feelings because any blissful feeling before calm abiding is necessarily contaminated.

Through what force are these blisses generated? Are they caused in the same way in which ordinary pleasures are caused—say, by heat or cold? No. They are induced by the force of the generation of mental and physical pliancy. This makes them special.

The entities of mental and physical pliancy and the blisses of these two pliancies have been briefly explained, as well as the opposites of mental and physical pliancy—the assumptions of bad mental and physical states. First, merely their names were set forth; then their entities, or nature; and then the order of their generation, which we are about to discuss.

ORDER IN WHICH THE PLIANCIES ARE GENERATED

The order of generation is:

1 omen of pliancy
2 (coarse special) mental pliancy
3 (coarse special) physical pliancy
4 bliss of physical pliancy
5 bliss of mental pliancy
6 stages of cessation of the blisses of physical and mental pliancy
7 generation of calm abiding.

Persons who have attained the meditative stabilization of the ninth mind of the Desire Realm[1]—that is, the ninth mental abiding—know from their own experience that they will be attaining calm abiding. As these meditators condition themselves again and again to this meditative stabilization, an omen arises that is a forerunner of the coarse special pliancy. There comes to be a sense that the brain is very heavy. In the Tibetan commentaries, which use the genitive case here, it is said that there comes to be the sense of a heavy brain. However, Asaṅga's *Grounds of Hearers* has a *ra* ending; thus, it reads, "There is a sense of a heavier brain." When physical pliancy is generated, one's body feels like cotton—very, very light. As an omen of the generation of such pliancy, one has a sense of a heavy brain. I think that the use of the adverbial *ra* ending is much better, for, once calm abiding has been attained, one's brain seems to be heavier than one's body. The *ra* ending allows one to understand that the brain appears to be heavier than the body. However, the Tibetan commentaries quote this using the genitive—"an appearance of a heavy brain." In any case, this sense of

[1] *'dod sems dgu pa'i ting nge 'dzin.*

the brain's being heavy is an omen of the generation of physical pliancy.

Immediately afterward, one generates the coarse special mental pliancy which removes the assumption of bad mental states that make for an unserviceability of mind. It is at this point that the mental pliancy having the seven features is generated. (See p. 97.)

In dependence on the force of this mental pliancy, a special type of wind moves about, pervading the entire body. Asaṅga's *Grounds of Hearers* states this as *rlung rgyu ba'i rgyus na*, whereas the Tibetan commentaries read *rlung rgyu ba'i dus na*, "at the time of the movement of this wind," which is easy to understand. The first reading, however, is better; it means, "when the movement of the wind pervades all the channels throughout the body." This has more the sense of "pervade" than the Tibetan texts; it signifies that this wind pervades all the consciousnesses and channels. In any case, when this special wind pervades the entire body, the wind and the body become as though undifferentiable. An observer could still see the yogic practitioner's body, but from the point of view of the meditator's own experience, it is as though only wind remained. The time of this pervasive wind marks the generation of physical pliancy. When this wind moves in the body, all factors of bodily heaviness are removed, so that it does not even seem as though one thing—wind—is moving inside the other—the body; rather, it is as though they are completely mixed. This is called the coarse special physical pliancy. Similarly, the mental pliancy generated [just before the coarse special physical pliancy] is a coarse special mental pliancy.

Immediately after the generation of the coarse special physical pliancy, the yogic practitioner has an experience of great physical bliss. This is the blissful feeling of physical pliancy.

Because of the connection between mind and body—the latter being the support[1] and the former, the supported[2]—once there is a bliss of physical pliancy, a sense of great mental bliss is experienced. For most beginners, mental pleasure comes from physical pleasure or bliss. For people abiding in higher realization, physical pleasure or bliss comes from mental bliss. It is a general principle for ordinary people that mental pleasure is produced from physical pleasure, and this is also true of the bliss of mental pliancy's being generated from the bliss of physical pliancy.

In this way, the mental and physical pliancies and the blisses of these

---

1 *rten, āśraya.*

2 *brten pa.*

pliancies are produced. Do they remain? No. When they cease, the first to fade is the coarse special physical pliancy. Asaṅga's *Grounds of Hearers* says that its initial force gradually stops. This means that the intense feeling becomes more subtle. This coarse factor of physical pliancy was initially generated; it was the first occurrence of a state that one had never known before, and it had a strong charge to it. This coarse charge becomes more subtle, gradually diminishing until it becomes like a shadow of the body; that is, it exists together with the body. When this occurs, it is called a shadow-like physical pliancy.

The coarse sense of great joy that accompanies the initial generation of the bliss of mental pliancy ceases immediately after the cessation of the physical charge. After that, the meditator again makes special earnest effort at setting the mind on the object of observation in the meditative stabilization of the ninth mental abiding.

Earlier, one was able to set the mind on the object of observation but had not gotten rid of the obstacles—the assumptions of bad physical and mental states. Now these are overcome, and, therefore, one has a stability and peacefulness due to the fact that these states have been pacified. Having again made the mind stable with respect to the object of observation and having pacified the assumptions of bad physical and mental states, one attains actual calm abiding.

Simultaneously with calm abiding, one attains a mind of an upper realm—a mind included within the levels of an upper realm [in this case, the Form Realm]. One also attains a special physical and mental pliancy included within the levels of an upper realm. This is also the time of attaining the mental contemplation of a mere beginner,[1] as well as the time of attaining a preparation[2] for the first concentration. These are all simultaneous. This is a continuation of the earlier meditative stabilization of the ninth mental abiding.

If even the great joy of the bliss of mental pliancy must cease, then clearly calm abiding is attained by a mental consciousness, not a body consciousness. The stages of cessation of the [coarse special] physical pliancy and the bliss of mental pliancy are signs that this is the case. If calm abiding were achieved by a sense consciousness, then it would not be necessary first to stop these coarse winds.

Jam-ȳang-shay-b̄a's *Great Exposition of the Concentrations and Formless*

---

1 *las dang po pa tsam gyi yid byed.*

2 *nyer bsdogs, sāmantaka.*

Absorptions and Ḏzong-ka-ḇa's great, middling, and small *Expositions of the Stages of the Path to Enlightenment* say that when one achieves a non-fluctuating meditative stabilization conjoined with special pliancy, one achieves calm abiding. This means that when the mind is again made stable with regard to the object of observation, the continuation of the earlier shadow-like pliancy—which had ceased in the meantime—turns into the pliancy included within the levels of an upper realm.

There is a great difference between being *conjoined with* a special pliancy and being *achieved by* a special pliancy. The meaning of calm abiding's being *conjoined with* special pliancy is that they are thoroughly mixed, the shadow-like pliancy at this time having turned into a pliancy included in an upper realm. When we speak of something's being *achieved by* special pliancy, there are two types of pliancy involved—coarse and subtle special pliancy. The coarse mental and physical pliancies are the initially generated mental and physical pliancy (see p. 103). Subtle special pliancy is the shadow-like special pliancy. This is the special direct cause of a calm abiding. Therefore, when we speak of calm abiding which is achieved by a special pliancy, we are referring to the shadow-like special pliancy that is calm abiding's uncommon direct cause. This is why Asaṅga's *Grounds of Hearers* uses the instrumental: "due to special pliancy." This is mentioned in the context of the special pliancy which precedes special insight and is its uncommon direct cause. On the other hand, when Asaṅga speaks about a calm abiding that is *conjoined with* special pliancy, he is referring to a special pliancy included in the levels of an upper realm; this is what the shadow-like pliancy has become. The pliancy referred to in the statement, "Calm abiding is conjoined with special pliancy," and that indicated in "the calm abiding which is achieved by special pliancy" are very different; in fact, they are mutually exclusive.

ELIMINATION OF QUALMS WITH RESPECT TO PLIANCY

The first topic was the measure of having achieved calm abiding, wherein just the name was given. The second topic, the individual natures and definitions of the various pliancies, was followed by an indication of the sources for each of the parts of the definitions. After this came an indication of the stages of the generation and cessation of those pliancies and, next, an indication of the mode of achieving calm abiding in dependence on those stages of generation and cessation of the pliancies, as well as an indication of the qualities that are attained simultaneously with calm abiding, such as a mind of an upper realm. We are yet to discuss the elimination of qualms.

MEANING OF THE NAMES GIVEN TO THE PLIANCIES EXPLICITLY SET FORTH IN ASAṄGA'S *GROUNDS OF HEARERS*

These are:

1 the pliancy difficult to analyze,[1] or subtle pliancy[2]

2 the pliancy easy to analyze,[3] or coarse pliancy.[4]

These verbal conventions openly appear in Asaṅga's *Grounds of Hearers*. I will explain these clearly and at length because this is not done in most Tibetan commentaries.

The pliancy difficult to analyze, or subtle pliancy, is generated first; the pliancy easy to analyze, or coarse pliancy, is generated second. The pliancy easy to analyze is equivalent to coarse pliancy—that is, the mental and physical pliancies whose generation was explained earlier. They occur after the omen has arisen—that is, after one experiences a heaviness of the brain. As was mentioned (p. 103), one experiences such a heaviness when one again enters into meditative stabilization after achieving the ninth mental abiding. Asaṅga's *Grounds of Hearers* states that the pliancy generated immediately after the omen is easy to analyze. It is easy to understand that one has it; hence the name.

Before the generation of coarse pliancy, one must generate what is known as subtle pliancy, or the pliancy difficult to analyze. Most Tibetan commentaries identify the subtle pliancy as what arises before coarse pliancy is generated. Thus, the numbers (1) and (2) above refer to the order of generation. "Subtle pliancy" refers to a non-manifest, or non-obvious, generation of mental and physical pliancy in yogic practitioners who have the ninth mental abiding, at the time when they again enter into meditative stabilization. They are not able to identify the presence of that pliancy, but it is present.

It is said that the meditative stabilization of one who has the ninth mental abiding and is again entering into meditative stabilization both assists that pliancy and is assisted by that pliancy. As much as the factor of meditative stabilization increases, so much does the factor of pliancy increase, and vice versa. At some point, in the manner of a substantial cause,[5]

---

[1] *brtags par dka' ba'i shin sbyangs.*

[2] *phra ba'i shin sbyangs.*

[3] *brtags par sla ba'i shin sbyangs.*

[4] *rags pa'i shin sbyangs.*

[5] *nyer len, upādāna;* the text says *len pa'i tshul gyis,* but this means *nyer len pa'i tshul gyis.*

the subtle pliancy induces the pliancy easy to analyze—that is, the coarse pliancy. With the meditative stabilization and subtle pliancy mutually increasing each other, the omen of pliancy appears when the subtle pliancy reaches the point of acting as a substantial cause of the coarse pliancy. Thus, the cooperative condition is the meditative stabilization of the ninth mind of the Desire Realm. The substantial cause of the coarse pliancy is the pliancy difficult to analyze, or the subtle pliancy. Thus, in the manner of acting as a substantial cause, the subtle pliancy induces the coarse one, with the meditative stabilization of the ninth mind of the Desire Realm acting as the cooperative condition.

As one continues to cultivate meditative stabilization, the ninth mental abiding of the Desire Realm acts as the substantial cause of calm abiding, and the shadow-like pliancy acts as the cooperative condition for producing calm abiding.

If the pliancy difficult to analyze, or the subtle pliancy, acts as the substantial cause of the coarse pliancy, when is this subtle pliancy first generated? Some say it is simultaneous with the initial generation of the meditative stabilization of the ninth mind of the Desire Realm. However, it seems that, according to a literal reading of Asaṅga's *Grounds of Hearers*, the two—the subtle pliancy and the meditative stabilization of the ninth mind of the Desire Realm—are not simultaneous, for Asaṅga's *Grounds of Hearers* says:

> Subtle [pliancy] is [generated] when (6) [the yogic practitioner] makes effort [at meditative stabilization] (5) at just the beginning of abiding in that stretch of time in which one has (4) removed the three [faults]—(1) exertion, (2) covetousness for the world, and (3) mental discomfort.[1]

The first word, *brtun pa*, means "exertion." (2) The phrase *'jig rten la brnabs sems*, "covetousness for the world," refers to attachment to body, resources, and so forth. (3) "Mental discomfort"[2] refers to a strong functioning of conceptuality. (4) *bsal* means "to remove"; the three just mentioned are removed when one attains the meditative stabilization of the ninth mind of the Desire Realm. Thus, this meditative stabilization is said

---

[1] *brtun pa* (1) *dang 'jig rten la brnabs sems* (2) *dang yid mi bde ba* (3) *rnam par bsal ba'i* (4) *bar la gnas pa de'i dang po kho nar* (5) *brtson pa de'i tshe...ni* (6) *phra ba yin no.* The key terms of the passage are numbered and discussed in the order in which they appear in the Tibetan.

[2] *yid mi bde ba, daurmanasya.*

to be triply qualified because of its three features of removing exertion, covetousness, and mental discomfort. The point at which these are removed is simultaneous with the attainment of the meditative stabilization of the ninth mind of the Desire Realm. (5) In the phrase *bar la gnas pa de'i dang po kho nar, bar la gnas pa* means "while abiding"; it indicates a stretch of time. The term *kho na* means "just." Thus, the phrase means, "at just the beginning[1] of abiding in a stretch of time" in which one has removed these three. This phrase identifies the point at which yogic practitioners first generate subtle pliancy, and it indicates that subtle pliancy is generated at that time "when yogis make effort [at meditative stabilization] at just the beginning of abiding in that stretch of time when they have removed the three [faults]." If subtle pliancy were attained simultaneously with the attainment of the meditative stabilization of the ninth mind of the Desire Realm, Asaṅga would have said *rnam par bsal ba'i tshe na*—"at the time of having removed [exertion]..."—instead of *bar la*, indicating a stretch of time. Thus, it is explicitly said in Asaṅga's *Grounds of Hearers* that when yogic practitioners who have the ninth mental abiding *again* enter into meditative stabilization, subtle pliancy is generated

It is necessary to identify the boundaries at which states are generated. The subtle physical pliancy, although not obvious, is generated by meditative stabilization and is a meditative-stabilization form. What is usually referred to as pliancy is the coarse pliancy that is generated after the omen of pliancy arises.

Usually, what is subtle comes after what is coarse, just as the more difficult to realize follows the easier to realize. For instance, the subtle and difficult paths are attained after the easy ones; doctrines difficult to realize are those that are non-manifest, non-obvious, and realized later. In this context, however, the meanings of "coarse" and "subtle" are different. It is difficult for yogic practitioners themselves to know or establish this subtle pliancy; if they do not know about it, how do we know that such a thing exists? By their own experience, yogic practitioners know that they have achieved the meditative stabilization of the ninth mind of the Desire Realm. Beyond that, the generation of the omen of pliancy is obvious, as is the generation of the mental and physical pliancies. In dependence on the obviousness of the meditative stabilization of the ninth mind of the Desire Realm and of the mental and physical pliancies, yogic practitioners understand that the subtle pliancies—mental and physical—act as the coopera-

[1] *dang po.*

tive condition and substantial cause of the coarse pliancy. Thus, they understand that the existence of the establishment of the beginning of the continuum of the coarse pliancy depends on these other pliancies.

Asaṅga's *Grounds of Hearers* says that when the coarse pliancy becomes more and more subtle it comes to be called the shadow-like pliancy; this is a subtle pliancy, but it should not be confused with the subtle pliancy that precedes the coarse one and is said to be subtle because it is not obvious. This latter is called subtle only because it is not manifest to the yogic practitioner; it is like something just newly growing. In the former case, the shadow-like pliancy is subtle in the sense that familiarity with the coarse pliancy is brought to fulfillment, whereby the coarser parts of it drop off and one is left with just its essence. These coarser parts drop away as one cultivates meditative stabilization and pliancy in union; finally, just the essence—the shadow-like pliancy—remains. Unless you distinguish between the two verbal designations of subtle pliancy, you will think they refer to the same thing and that the explanation is redundant. Because the Indian texts are very deep and profound, the meaning needs to be clarified even though it is right there in those texts.

OMEN OF PLIANCY

The omen of pliancy[1] consists of the sense that the brain is heavy in comparison to the body. Everyone agrees that this is because physical pliancy can be generated everywhere in the body except in the brain. However, the texts do not give any *reason* why physical pliancy cannot be generated in the brain. I think that it is related to tantra.

When a person is conceived, the mixture of the father's semen and the mother's blood splits into portions, with one segment going up to the top of the head and the other descending to the solar plexus. I doubt that the brain is so bad that pliancy cannot be generated there; rather, I believe that the entity of one type of subtlest mind is with that portion of the blood-and-semen mixture which is at the top of the head and the entity of another type of subtlest mind is with the portion of blood-and-semen mixture at the solar plexus. Through the paths and meditative stabilizations set forth in the sūtra systems, it is not possible to affect the subtle minds that abide in the center of the blood-and-semen mixture in the brain. The larger portion of the blood-and-semen mixture is probably in the brain, and the smaller, at the solar plexus. Most probably, it is only in dependence on Highest Yoga Tantra that pliancy can be generated where the

[1] *shin sbyangs skye ba'i snga bltas.*

mind abides in the red and white constituents in the brain. This is my own thought; the actual reason why pliancy is not generated in the brain should be examined.

Both male and female have the white constituent primarily at the top of the head and the red constituent primarily at the solar plexus. The white constituent at the top of the head is in the shape of an upside-down Sanskrit syllable *haṃ*, and the red constituent at the solar plexus is like a line that is wider at the top and narrower at the bottom. At the heart, there is the shape of a covered jewel case; the top is white, and the bottom, red.[1] At the time of death, when the white moves down, there is a radiant white appearance, and when the red moves up, there is a radiant red appearance. To achieve mental and physical pliancy in those places, one must rely on Highest Yoga Tantra; it cannot be done through paths common to Buddhists and non-Buddhists, and beyond that, it cannot be done through the Perfection Vehicle[2] or the three lower tantra sets. Most of the red and white constituents is at the top of the head; the other areas—solar plexus and heart—have less. There is no difference between male and female with regard to these. The place where the red and white constituents join at conception is where the heart starts. Texts say that the mind is at the heart, but people in the world [i.e., the West] say that they think in their heads. This is not entirely wrong because an essence of the red and white constituents exists in the brain.

Question: When the portions of the red and white constituents split apart, does the mind that abides within them split up also?

Answer: We do not say that the mind divides. The mind pervades the whole body. The place where its functioning is strongest is at the heart and at the top of the head. We speak of the "spirit" as residing in various places in the body, and of these, the main one is where the mind abides—the heart or the top of the head. At conception, the two portions grow from the center; similarly, at death, the two come back together. When the "jewel case" opens, death occurs. At that time, the relationship of the body as the support and the consciousness as the supported is severed. When does the mind abide *only* inside the case? This happens at death, and, in terms of cultivation of the path, it occurs in people who are on high levels

---

[1] For more on the consciousnesses that manifest during the process of dying, see Lati Rinbochay and Jeffrey Hopkins, *Death, Intermediate State and Rebirth* (Ithaca, NY: Snow Lion, 1980).

[2] *phar phyin gyi theg pa, pāramitāyāna.*

of the stage of completion of Highest Yoga Tantra. Thus, it is only when one arrives at a high level of the stage of completion that one is capable of stopping the mind in all other places so that it operates only at the heart, and then one is able to use that mind to cultivate the path—to realize emptiness, and so forth. There are only two occasions on which the mind stops in, or withdraws from, all places and dwells only inside the heart: at a high level of the stage of completion and when one abides in the subtle mind of death.

Question: Is there any fault in an ordinary person's being handled while abiding in the subtle mind of death?

Answer: No. Although the person has not yet died, anyone in that state is definite to die. The subtle state that is being manifested is due to the power of karma, not to cultivation of the path. It is harmful to touch such a person only when she or he is in meditative stabilization.

Question: Is there any harm if a person is handled at the point at which the outer breath ceases?

Answer: I doubt that it matters for an ordinary person.

Question: How does the white constituent account for the lack of pliancy in the brain?

Answer: The predominantly white constituent in the form of an upside-down *haṃ* is situated in the brain, and in order for physical pliancy to be generated with the mind that dwells inside it, practice of Highest Yoga Tantra is necessary. The method of generating calm abiding discussed here does not involve any practice of Highest Yoga Tantra; thus, it is not capable of affecting the area where this constituent abides.

STAGES OF GENERATION AND CESSATION OF THE PLIANCIES AS PRESENTED IN ASAṄGA'S *GROUNDS OF HEARERS*

The topics about which we have eliminated qualms are (1) analysis of the meaning of the terms "the pliancy difficult to analyze" and "subtle pliancy," on the one hand, and "the pliancy easy to analyze" and "coarse pliancy," on the other, and (2) the omen of generating pliancy. These eliminations of qualms have all been done with respect to the literal or explicit meaning of Asaṅga's *Grounds of Hearers.*

Now we begin elimination of qualms with respect to the stages of the generation and cessation of pliancy as presented in Asaṅga's *Grounds of Hearers.* We said that mental pliancy is generated first, then physical pliancy, then the bliss of physical pliancy, and finally, the bliss of mental pliancy. The stages of cessation are (1) cessation of coarse physical pliancy and (2) cessation of the coarseness of the bliss of mental pliancy. That was how we delineated it (see p. 103). Asaṅga's text itself explicitly indicates that mental and physical pliancy are generated; it does not explicitly indicate that the bliss of physical pliancy is generated. However, the text explicitly states that just after the generation of physical pliancy, the bliss of mental pliancy is generated.

Stages of Generation and Cessation of Pliancies
According to Asaṅga's *Grounds of Hearers* & Tibetan Commentaries

Stages of Generation		*Stages of Cessation*
mental pliancy		
physical pliancy	———	coarse physical pliancy
(bliss of physical pliancy)	———	(bliss of physical pliancy)
bliss of mental pliancy	———	[coarseness of] bliss of mental pliancy

Most Tibetan commentaries other than D̄zong-ka-b̄a's *Great* and *Medium Exposition(s) of the Stages of the Path to Enlightenment* insert an explanation of the generation of the bliss of physical pliancy, although it is not mentioned in Asaṅga's *Grounds of Hearers;* they explain that when physical pliancy ceases, the bliss of physical pliancy, which is caused by it, must also cease. The source for these commentaries is held to be D̄zong-ka-b̄a's *Great* and *Medium Exposition(s) of the Stages of the Path to Enlightenment,* even though these texts themselves do not explicitly mention the generation of the bliss of physical pliancy. There is no other source for this explanation. What words from D̄zong-ka-b̄a's texts are taken as the source for this?

The words are *lus la bde nyams 'char,* "A sense of bliss[1] dawns in the body." Later texts take this as a source for the statement that a blissful *feeling* is generated in the body. However, there is no definiteness that if a *sense* of bliss dawns in the body, a bliss has actually been generated. It is possible that even if an actual bliss has not been generated, a yogic practitioner has a sense of bliss. In fact, texts sometimes say that the words "a *sense* of bliss is generated" serve as an indication that actual bliss has not been generated. For instance, let us consider the precursor of the feeling of bliss that is initially generated at the time of the mental contemplation of

---

1 *bde nyams* = *bde ba'i nyams* = sense of bliss.

joy-withdrawal.[1] According to the upper, or Mahāyāna, system of Manifest Knowledge:

> At the time of the mental contemplation of joy-withdrawal, the feeling of bliss that accompanies a preparation is initially generated.[2]

At the time of attaining the path of preparation, one attains a mental contemplation called arisen from belief, which precedes the mental contemplation of joy-withdrawal; at that time, one has a *sense* of bliss but does not have bliss:

> At the time of the mental contemplation of belief, a sense of bliss dawns. From the viewpoint of progress on the path, attainment of the mental contemplation of belief and the path of preparation are simultaneous.[3]

Thus, when the text says that a sense of bliss is generated at the time of the mental contemplation arisen from belief, it is saying that an actual feeling of bliss is not generated. Therefore, the later interpreters who take D̄zong-ka-b̄a's statement as indicating that an actual bliss is generated in the body can be supported only through reasoning; there is no scriptural citation which says this, for, if there were such a scriptural proof, it would have to be from Asaṅga's *Grounds of Hearers.* This is not because all scriptural proofs have to come from Asaṅga's text but because there is no text superior to the *Grounds of Hearers* with regard to discussing the pliancies and other topics of calm abiding. There are many texts which explain how calm abiding is generated, but only Asaṅga's text presents in such great detail the generation of the pliancies, the measure of having generated various states, and so forth. Therefore, Asaṅga himself says in his *Compendium of Ascertainments*[4] that one should look in his *Grounds of Hearers* in connection with these topics. This is because the topics are explained in detail there.

One cannot say that the later Tibetan commentaries are mistaken, for not just one but nearly all state that an actual bliss is generated in the body. As was mentioned, they depend on D̄zong-ka-b̄a's *Great* and *Me-*

---

1 *dga' ba sdud pa, ratisaṃgrāhaka.*

2 *dga' sdud yid byed kyi skabs su nyer bsdogs 'khor gyi tshor ba bde ba dang por skye.*

3 *mos pa yid byed kyi skabs su bde ba'i nyams 'char/ lam bgrod pa'i dbang du byes na mos pa yid byed dang sbyor lam thob pa dus mnyam red.*

4 *gtan la dbab pa bsdu ba, nirṇayasaṃgraha.*

dium Exposition(s) of the Stages of the Path, which state that a sense of bliss dawns in the body. Since nothing is explicitly said about this in Asaṅga's *Grounds of Hearers* and since Asaṅga's *Grounds of Hearers* is the only source on which one could rely, it is necessary to establish this point through reasoning. The text one would depend on here should set forth the generation of physical pliancy, describing the wind that pervades the entire body, and so forth. That wind serves as an observed-object condition[1]—that is, as a cause generating the physical feeling of bliss.

For example, in the systems that set forth external objects, colors[2] and shapes[3] are in a cause-and-effect relationship with the eye consciousness. (In the systems that do not assert external objects, it is said that the two—colors and shapes, on the one hand, and the consciousness which observes them, on the other—are generated simultaneously.) In the systems of those who assert external objects, it is said that through the power of meditative stabilization, the wind pervading the body arises and serves as a cause of the body consciousness that experiences bliss. There is nothing in Asaṅga's *Grounds of Hearers* that can be taken as proof of this, except that it says that such a wind pervades the body. If you look at these texts, you will understand the points I am making.

So far, we have eliminated qualms with respect to the stages of generating the pliancies, and so forth. This was done through discussion of the explanation in Dzong-ka-ba's *Great* and *Medium Exposition(s) of the Stages of the Path* and the explanations of later Tibetan interpretations of this. I will now set forth qualms with respect to the stages of cessation of the pliancies.

Asaṅga's *Grounds of Hearers* sets forth the stages of generation of the pliancies as mental pliancy, physical pliancy, and the bliss of mental pliancy. Immediately after this, he sets forth the cessation of physical pliancy, and then the cessation of the coarseness of the bliss of mental pliancy. He does not mention the bliss of physical pliancy in the stages of either generation or cessation. He speaks of the cessation of physical pliancy between the two pliancies, and he speaks of the cessation of the bliss of mental pliancy between the two blisses of pliancy.

It is important to know what is explicitly indicated in Asaṅga's *Grounds of Hearers*, what words are used in Dzong-ka-ba's *Great* and *Medium Ex-*

---

[1] *dmigs rkyen, ālambanapratyaya.*

[2] *kha dog, varṇa.*

[3] *dbyibs, saṃstāna.*

position(s) of the Stages of the Path to Enlightenment, and how later commentaries interpret the thought of these. Asaṅga's text makes two statements using the words "after that."[1] In the first case the referent, or antecedent, of "that" is "the generation of the bliss of mental pliancy"; "after that" means "after the generation of the bliss of mental pliancy." Just at the point of the generation of calm abiding, Asaṅga's text again says, "after that": "After that, the beginner yogi possesses a mental contemplation"[2]—that is, calm abiding.

This indicates that coarse physical pliancy has ceased, as has the coarseness of the bliss of mental pliancy. When the yogi again makes the object of observation very steady, calm abiding is attained. It may wrongly seem that the "after that" in this passage of Asaṅga's text has to mean "after the cessation of the coarse physical pliancy and the coarse bliss of mental pliancy, when the yogi again makes meditative stabilization very firm." However, what it actually means is that *at the same time* that the yogi again sets [the mind] very steadily on the object of observation, calm abiding is attained. This occurs *just after* attainment of the shadow-like pliancy; when the yogi then settles very steadily on the object of observation, calm abiding is simultaneously achieved. The antecedent of "that" here is, therefore, the statement, "The yogi comes to possess the shadow-like pliancy." It is after this that the beginner yogi comes to possess a mental contemplation[3]—that is, calm abiding. The shadow-like pliancy is an uncommon direct cooperative condition producing calm abiding. Because of the way the text unfolds, it is possible to misunderstand it as indicating that the yogi achieves calm abiding *after* setting the mind steadily on the object of observation once he or she has gained the shadow-like pliancy. The actual meaning is that just at that time when, after attainment of the shadow-like pliancy, the yogi's meditative stabilization becomes very firm, calm abiding is achieved.

This completes the third elimination of qualms. I think that even though we have not written out all of Asaṅga's *Grounds of Hearers* on these topics, we probably have not missed even a syllable regarding the measure of achieving calm abiding. I have explained calm abiding's entity and filled this out with material from other texts. We have also eliminated qualms with respect to the stages of generation and cessation of the pliancies.

---

1 *de'i 'og tu.*

2 *de'i 'og tu rnal 'byor pa las dang po pa yid la byed pa dang bcas pa yin de.*

3 *yid la byed pa, manaskāra.*

QUALMS CONCERNING THE SIGNS OF CALM ABIDING

It is usually said that a yogic practitioner who has attained calm abiding can fly, and so forth. Some scholars say that someone who attains calm abiding can pass unimpededly through a wall, and there are many accounts of such occurrences. Indeed, there must be such attainments with the achievement of calm abiding. What is such a person's body like?

The yogic practitioner's body, to begin with, is an obstructive body produced from past contaminated actions and afflictive emotions. Through the power of having cultivated meditative stabilization, the practitioner has made a form that is equal to the space of, and occupies the same area as, her or his obstructive body. Not only does the shadow-like pliancy pervade the entire body; it becomes of an undifferentiable entity with that body. Whatever potencies physical pliancy has arise for the body.

The form generated by meditative stabilization is also called a mental body,[1] or an unimpeded mental body.[2] It is "the form of one who has attained mastery."[3] It is not a body that has external matter as its basis of formation; rather, it is a form generated by internal meditative stabilization. Thus, there is no reason for it to be obstructed or impeded. Moreover, once it is generated by meditative stabilization, it must be like a consciousness. It pervades and is equal with the body, its entity being undifferentiable from the body's own. For example, when iron burns, the fire and the iron become entirely undifferentiable; wherever the iron is touched, the potency of fire is there. It must be for this reason that such a yogic practitioner is able to pass through walls without obstruction.

It might be thought that the yogic practitioner's brain would remain on the other side of the wall as, indeed, pliancy is not generated in the brain, but because it is a form generated by meditative stabilization there must not be any such fault.

It is said, for instance, that through cultivating an actual first concentration and then engaging in the meditative stabilization of the inhalation and exhalation of the breath, Hīnayāna sages are able to live for eons. If there were no such special form generated by meditative stabilization, then, since that person's body is composed only of matter produced through contaminated actions and afflictive emotions, in time that body would be overcome by some cause. However, even though the body arose

---

[1] *yid lus.*

[2] *yid lus thogs pa med pa.*

[3] *dbang 'byor ba'i gzugs.*

through contaminated actions and afflictive emotions, because the yogic practitioner has created such a form by meditative stabilization—that form being one with the body—the contaminated actions and afflictive emotions cannot, for the time being, affect it. By the power of this form, such a sage can live for an eon.

In meditative stabilization, it is through the power of the shadow-like pliancy that the body becomes unimpeded. There is another cause of becoming unimpeded: meditation on emptiness. It is said that a person who realizes emptiness—even one who does not have a union of calm abiding and special insight[1]—also has an unimpeded body. A person who realizes emptiness before achieving calm abiding realizes it by an inferential consciousness[2] and, thus, has a mind arisen from thinking,[3] not arisen from meditation.[4] For instance, we mentioned a person who seeks meditation based on the view. (See p. 15.) The unimpeded body of a person who has realized emptiness but has not attained calm abiding comes about not through the shadow-like pliancy but through an internal familiarization with this utter vacuity. Such a person has not achieved an exalted knower of all aspects—an omniscient consciousness—but has brought to completion familiarization with the utter vacuity. Such a person has a sense that if there were something that could impede, it would have to be truly existent. The very fulfillment of familiarity with searching for objects through analysis and then not finding them *is* the realization of emptiness. Since the seeking for and not finding objects has been brought to completion, whatever appears to the practitioner appears to be empty. Therefore, the reasons why the body of a person who has realized emptiness is unimpeded and why the body of a person who has achieved calm abiding is unimpeded are different.

DISCUSSION

Question: Can it be said that the continuum of a body produced by contaminated actions ceases when one attains calm abiding and that it is replaced by a continuum of a body produced by meditation?

Answer: The body produced by contaminated actions and afflictive emotions has not ceased, and the person has not assumed a new body. How-

---

[1] *zhi lhag zung 'brel.*

[2] *rjes dpag, anumāna.*

[3] *bsam byung, cintāmayī.*

[4] *sgom byung, bhāvanāmayī.*

ever, even though the former body remains, certain of its functions cease temporarily through the power of the practitioner's having cultivated meditative stabilization; these are its function of being impeded—which is due to past contaminated actions and afflictive emotions—and its functions of pain, and so forth, which are all functions of the body's being a true suffering.

In a similar case, a person who attains the first Bodhisattva ground[1] is included in the same physical basis as that same person who was formerly on the path of preparation and whose body is impelled by contaminated actions and afflictive emotions. Even though the first-ground[2] Bodhisattva still has a body impelled by contaminated actions and afflictive emotions, these functionings completely stop.

Question: Dzong-ka-ba's *Great Exposition of the Stages of the Path* says that it is a mistake to consider impedance to be the object of negation[3] of emptiness. How can this be?

Answer: Impedance, or obstructiveness, is coarser than inherent existence, which is the subtle meaning of the object of negation. It is inherent existence, not impedance, that is being refuted. However, if the person does not first understand an absence of impedance, it is doubtful that she or he could understand the absence of inherent existence.

Question: Dzong-ka-ba's *Medium Exposition of the Stages of the Path* says that the four mental engagements are also involved in the cultivation of special insight. If that is so, then would not the first of the four mental engagements, called forcible engagement,[4] be involved? But, why would it be needed at the time of cultivating special insight when calm abiding has already been achieved?

Answer: These four mental engagements are different from the four at the time of developing calm abiding. They have the same names, but the sense is different. We will discuss this topic later.

Question: Then why are the nine mental abidings not present again, with a different sense?

Answer: If you want to designate them as being present at that time, it is suitable to do so. However, that terminology is not used, whereas the ter-

---

1 *sa dang po, prathamabhūmi.*

2 *sa dang po, prathama-bhūmi.*

3 *dgag bya, pratiṣedhya.*

4 *sgrim ste 'jug pa, balavāhana.*

minology of the four mental engagements is.

Question: The fourth of the four mental engagements is spontaneous engagement.[1] Is that present with calm abiding?

Answer: That verbal convention is not used. Thus, all four precede calm abiding. The designation "spontaneous engagement" is used with reference to the meditator's initial engagement of the object of observation without any exertion, and so forth. When calm abiding is achieved, not only does one have such lack of exertion; one also has pliancy. [Hence, there is no need to use the designation "spontaneous engagement."]

As was mentioned earlier (p. 117), the body of a person who has attained physical pliancy is like a mental body.[2] Thus, the term "the form of one who has attained mastery"[3] can refer either to the state of meditative stabilization or to the person who has it.

When one directly realizes emptiness, a mental body is achieved. The body of a Foe Destroyer in a non-abiding nirvāṇa is also a mental body. The body of a Bodhisattva on one of the pure grounds—eighth through tenth—is a mental body. However, the Form Bodies of a Buddha do not receive the designation "mental body," for this term is used only to refer to states preceding the attainment of Buddhahood.

"Mental body" does not mean a body which is of one entity with the mind; it means a body which, like the mind, is unimpeded. The body of a being in the intermediate state,[4] therefore, is also called a mental body. All these various mental bodies are different; they are not the same. They are, however, similar in that at their own time they are unimpeded.

There are also bodies which are imperceptible by others. Their imperceptibility depends on the degree of realization possessed by a person with meditative stabilization.

Question: Is it the case that our mind and body are of one entity but then become different entities at the time of death?

Answer: A person's mind and body are in a relationship of being one entity of support and supported. At death these become separate. Nihilists say that mind and body are of one entity because the mind has a nature of the four elements. Thus, they maintain that without depending on a similar

---

1 *lhun grub tu 'jug pa, anābhogavāhana.*

2 *yid lus.*

3 *dbang 'byor ba'i gzugs.*

4 *bar do, antarābhāva.*

type of consciousness that precedes it, a consciousness can be produced in dependence on the elements. The Buddhist meaning of mind and body being of one entity includes that consciousness must depend on a former moment of similar type—that is, a former consciousness.

Question: If mind and body are of one entity, are they like the iron and fire which *become* of one entity, since before birth and after death they are separate?

Answer: They are not of one entity like iron and fire; their relationship is just that of the support—body—and that which is supported—consciousness.

Question: If the body of someone who has achieved calm abiding, for instance, is really unimpeded, it would seem that one's clothes would fall off. If not, is it the case that one can control the degree of unimpededness one has? Also, if there is nothing obstructive, it would seem that the body no longer has any mass, in which case it would also seem that gravity would no longer affect the body and one would float away.

Answer: Your clothes are not left behind when you pass through a wall. There is also no need to take them off, since passing through a wall occurs through the power of meditative stabilization. If you want to be perceived as impeding—for example, if you wish to shake hands with someone—you can do so. However, I do not think that a person who has achieved calm abiding can be unimpeded whenever he or she wishes. It is necessary for such a person to enter into meditative stabilization and, while in that state, would be able to pass through walls, and so forth. It is not something one could do at all times, for such a person still has coarse exertion. Outside of actualized meditative equipoise, this person would not be unimpeded.

Question: In order for a beginner to establish that there are former and later rebirths, it is necessary to establish that the substantial causes of mind and body are necessarily different. However, since mind and body are of one entity and we experience them as of one entity, it would seem to be very difficult for a beginner to understand their substantial causes as different.

Answer: Pot and *thing* are of one entity. The continuum of *thing* always remains; if a pot breaks, the continuum of *thing* is not ended. *Thing* and *pot* are different in that the pervasion of the former is greater than the pervasion of the latter. Nevertheless, these two are said to be of one entity. While a pot exists, it is said that it is of one entity with *thing*, but after it disintegrates, it is not. The continuum[1] of the substantial entity of the mind continues, but bodies are changed. It is from the viewpoint of this temporary state that mind and body are said to be of one entity.

Question: Is it possible to identify mind and body as different in terms of one's own experience?

Answer: When you say "mind," you are referring to the aggregate of consciousness. We also speak of the aggregate of form. A person is something that is imputed or designated to the five aggregates.

We are born into realms that have form and into the Formless Realm. In the latter, there is no form among the bases of designation of the person. From this point of view, it can be established that at some time there is a separation of mind and body. When one is born in the Formless Realm, one has already been separated from the former body. Hence, there is a time when mind and body are separate. This is a coarse example of the fact that separation of mind and body occurs.

---

1 *rgyun, saṃtāna.*

6 SIGNS OF CALM ABIDING

I have explained the preparation for calm abiding—the nine mental abidings—and the actual achievement of calm abiding, as well as the "end"—that is, the type of capacity possessed by someone who has calm abiding. A yogic practitioner, having attained calm abiding, has special abilities such as the capacity to fly and a special type of body. These can be applied to the previous discussion of the elimination of qualms. (See pp. 117-118.) Now we will also discuss the signs of having achieved calm abiding, but we do not need to hold that the discussions of the "end" and of these signs are mutually exclusive.

INCREASE OF MEDITATIVE STABILIZATION DUE TO PLIANCY

A sign of having achieved calm abiding is the increase of meditative stabilization, which is due to the fact that pliancy and meditative stabilization assist each other. At this point, one has attained mental pliancy and brought its capacity to fulfillment. One has also attained physical pliancy and brought its capacity to fulfillment. Thus, these pliancies are capable of serving as special aids to meditative stabilization.

VANISHING OF ALL COARSE APPEARANCES

A second sign of calm abiding is that, when the yogic practitioner sets the mind in meditative equipoise, all coarse appearances vanish. Most texts refer to this but do not specify clearly just which coarse appearances have vanished. Because the texts do not have any clear statement on what sorts of appearance cease when calm abiding is attained, we must infer these on the basis of the entity and signs of calm abiding.

In general, there are several types. Coarse appearances to the sense consciousnesses cease. Another type of cessation of coarse appearance consists of the stopping of manifest coarse afflictive emotions.[1] Beyond this, there is a cessation of the manifest operative consciousnesses.[2] These are called operative consciousnesses because they operate on the six types of object;

[1] *nyon mongs rags pa mngon gyur ba.*

[2] *'jug shes.*

the reference here is to cessation of the coarser forms of these. There is also a stoppage of the subtle operative consciousnesses.

Thus far we have mentioned stoppage of sense consciousnesses, manifest coarse afflictive emotions, coarse operative consciousnesses,[1] and subtle operative consciousnesses.[2] There are also very subtle operative consciousnesses.[3] The next-to-last type is subtle from within the division of operative consciousnesses into very subtle and subtle; however, there is no stoppage of the very subtle.

STOPPAGE OF THE SENSE CONSCIOUSNESSES

When one sets the mind in a meditative equipoise of calm abiding, the sense consciousnesses necessarily stop. A sign of this is that when one is in a deep meditative equipoise of calm abiding, a great deal of saliva flows. Because consciousness is not holding on to that spot, without any choice on the part of the practitioner, a great deal of saliva flows naturally. Since, in meditative equipoise, one withdraws all sense consciousnesses, it is as though the sense consciousnesses cannot hold on to the body, or as though one has forgotten about the body, inasmuch as one is incapable of being mindful of it.

STOPPAGE OF THE MANIFEST COARSE AFFLICTIVE EMOTIONS

Furthermore, while in meditative equipoise, one is able to stop the manifest coarse afflictive emotions. There are two reasons for this. The first is that afflictive emotions are operative consciousnesses, and a mind of calm abiding is also an operative consciousness. It is a fact that two consciousnesses which are different substantial entities *and* of the same type—such as two mental consciousnesses or two eye consciousnesses—cannot operate in one person's continuum at the same time. Thus, two mental consciousnesses which are different substantial entities cannot operate simultaneously. Hence, there are three parts to the reason why the manifest coarse afflictive emotions cannot operate during meditative equipoise: (a) coarse afflictive emotions are mental consciousnesses; (b) they are of similar type with that of meditative stabilization; and (c) they are different substantial entities from meditative stabilization. Two such consciousnesses cannot operate in one individual continuum at the same time; there is no sentient being in whom two of these can operate simultaneously. This is the first

1 *'jug shes rags pa.*

2 *'jug shes phra mo.*

3 *'jug shes shin tu phra mo.*

reason why manifest coarse afflictive emotions cannot be present in person who has a mind of calm abiding. However, this is not an especially wonderful reason.

Whether by means of a path that is common to Buddhists and non-Buddhists or in conjunction with the thought definitely to leave cyclic existence, and so forth, a person cultivates calm abiding within viewing the afflictive emotions pertaining to the Desire Realm[1] as faulty and for the purpose of stopping them. Even if it is merely the Desire Realm that is seen as faulty, the meditator will be able to suppress afflictive emotions of similar type pertaining to the upper realms—the Form and Formless Realms. This ability comes from the fact that she or he is viewing that type of afflictive emotion pertaining to the Desire Realm as faulty and, therefore, wishes to be rid of it; for the functioning of afflictive emotions pertaining to the Desire, Form, and Formless Realms is similar. Thus, even though only Desire Realm afflictive emotions are explicitly viewed as faulty, whereas those of the Form and Formless Realms are not, the meditation extends to other afflictive emotions of similar type pertaining to the Form and Formless Realms, and the meditator is able to correct them as well. This is the main reason why a person who has achieved calm abiding does not have any manifest coarse afflictive emotions. Moreover, for such a person the coarse Desire Realm afflictive emotions also do not become manifest in states subsequent to meditative equipoise, when the functioning of the meditative stabilization has ceased.

A mind of calm abiding can suppress afflictive emotions but cannot abandon any. Asaṅga's *Grounds of Hearers* says that for a person who has attained calm abiding, a covetous or harmful mind for the most part does not occur: such manifest coarse afflictive emotions pertaining to the Desire Realm[2] tend not to occur for such people. This does not mean that they have been abandoned, however, or that they will not arise in the future.

What is the difference between calm abiding and a mundane type of special insight? With mundane special insight, one is able to stop the afflictive emotions even more forcefully. It is necessary to distinguish between suppression and separation from attachment—that is, the freedom from attachment which is generated by mundane paths of special insight. Having suppressed afflictive emotions through calm abiding, one is still ready to generate them very quickly when the appropriate circumstances

---

1 *'dod pa'i nyon mongs.*

2 *'dod pa'i nyon mongs rags pa.*

arise. One has not yet abandoned them from the root, as one does with the achievement of a supramundane path.

Through cultivation of the fourth, fifth, and seventh of the seven preparations for a concentration, it is possible to achieve a separation from attachment; this is achieved through a mundane path. Like suppression of the afflictive emotions through calm abiding, such separation is to be distinguished from the abandonment from the root that is achieved through a supramundane path; even when one attains such separation from attachment, one is still ready to generate the afflictive emotions. Nevertheless, there is a great difference between suppression of an afflictive emotion through calm abiding and separation from attachment by way of a mundane path. In the latter case, one attains a situation in which, temporarily, the afflictive emotions cannot be generated. A mundane path has an uninterrupted path and a path of release[1]—a true cessation of afflictive emotions, temporarily. In the case of suppression, however, the afflictive emotions are not generated when one is in meditative equipoise, but when one rises from that state and becomes distracted, the afflictive emotions are ready to be generated.

There are texts which say that one cannot suppress afflictive emotions through calm abiding. This is said to prevent error; someone who newly attains calm abiding has the feature of having attained meditative stabilization, and the mind is conjoined with physical and mental pliancy; one has a mind of an upper realm, not the type of disturbed or unpeaceful mind of the Desire Realm. Therefore, it is possible to err in identifying the state attained. When some people achieve calm abiding, they think they have attained the stage of completion in Highest Yoga Tantra. The sense consciousnesses have stopped; the manifest afflictive emotions have temporarily ceased, and there is a special sense of physical and mental bliss.[2] Descriptions of the stage of completion say that the winds enter, dissolve, and remain in the central channel and also set forth features that have some similarity with the state of calm abiding; thus, some mistakenly think that the stage of completion has been attained. Others, because their mental continuums have become peaceful, think they have separated from attachment. The texts which say that calm abiding cannot suppress afflictive emotions indicate that the meditator not only has not attained the completion stage of Highest Yoga Tantra but has not attained even a

---

1 *rnam grol lam, vimuktimārga.*

2 *bde ba, sukha.*

Mahāyāna path; not only that, but one has not attained a path of any type. Not only has one not abandoned even a single afflictive emotion; one has not even separated from attachment to a single afflictive emotion.

To abandon an afflictive emotion from the root, it is necessary to attain a supramundane path. To separate completely from attachment to Desire Realm afflictive emotions, it is necessary to attain an actual first concentration. To attain that, it is necessary to have the seven preparations, the first of which is the mental contemplation of a mere beginner—calm abiding. Thus, the point being made is that by achieving calm abiding one has not abandoned any afflictive emotions. Texts sometimes give coarse explanations—saying that one has abandoned distraction, excitement, and so forth—that are not detailed.

The term "manifest coarse afflictive emotion of the Desire Realm"" appears frequently in the Tibetan commentaries. In Asaṅga's *Grounds of Hearers*, however, two phrases appear at this point: "the thorough entanglements do not occur strongly and the obstructions do not course forcefully."[1]

"Obstructions" here does not refer to obstructions in general but to the elements among Desire Realm afflictive emotions that prevent meditative stabilization. The main of these are "covetous attitude, harmful intent, and desire included within the level of the Desire Realm,"[2] or associated with the Desire Realm. Thus, the thorough entanglements that Asaṅga states do not occur strongly are probably the same as what we call "coarse" afflictive emotions. Even if one of the entanglements is about to arise, the yogic practitioner is able to suppress it immediately by relying on its antidote.

The word *shas cher* (see note 1) has two meanings: "mostly" and "strongly." Here I think it should be understood as "strongly" because it modifies the word "course." This means that the manifest obstructions do not course or, if they do, are easily suppressed. Nevertheless, terms such as "manifest coarse afflictive emotions of the Desire Realm" do not appear explicitly in Asaṅga's *Grounds of Hearers*, although there are words that mean the same thing.

We must make fine distinctions with respect to the words "do not arise" or "are abandoned" in the great texts. For instance, when speaking about the attainment of pliancy, Asaṅga's *Grounds of Hearers* refers to the "abandonment" of assumptions of bad states. The context here lets us know that

---

1 *kun nas dkris pa drag po mi 'byung zhing sgrib pa rnams shas cher kun tu mi rgyu zhing.*

2 *'dod pa'i sas bsdus kyi brnabs sems gnod sems chags pa.*

"abandonment" does not mean that these assumptions of bad states are abandoned from the root but that, when their manifest form is about to be produced, one can suppress it temporarily through relying on the antidote.

When are assumptions of bad mental and physical states abandoned from the root? This does not occur when one attains calm abiding, or even when one attains Foe Destroyerhood. There are many texts, such as Ḏzong-ka-ḇa's *Illumination of the Thought of (Chandrakīrti's) "Supplement to (Nāgārjuna's) 'Treatise on the Middle,'"*[1] which say that Foe Destroyers have in their continuums the assumption of bad physical and mental states. According to the Prāsaṅgika system, a person whose lineage is definite in the Mahāyāna would begin abandoning these on the eighth Bodhisattva ground. It is then be even more difficult, according to the Prāsaṅgikas, to abandon from the root the assumptions of bad mental and physical states than to abandon the obstructions to liberation.[2]

Similarly, the texts speak of an abandonment, on the path of preparation, of those afflictive emotions which are to be abandoned by a path of seeing, these being divided into the four levels of the path of preparation—namely heat,[3] peak,[4] forbearance,[5] and supreme mundane qualities. However, these are not actually abandoned at that time. What such statements mean is that over the series of the four levels of the path of preparation the coarsest of these afflictive emotions are first suppressed on the level of heat and the more subtle are suppressed or diminished over the other levels of the path of preparation. Not one type of afflictive emotion is actually abandoned before the attainment of a supramundane path.

The texts also say that when one attains a concentration there is an abandonment of the afflictive emotions pertaining to the lower level. For example, it is said that when one attains the first concentration one abandons or separates from attachment to the nine cycles of afflictive emotions pertaining to the Desire Realm. The verbal convention, or term, "abandonment" is used in order to indicate the temporary suppression of the manifest form of these afflictive emotions. The temporary separation from attachment is merely *called* abandonment; it is not an actual abandonment. The Indian texts speak only of abandonment; therefore, Ḏzong-ka-

---

[1] *dbu ma la 'jug pa'i rgya cher bshad pa dgongs pa rab gsal;* P6143, vol. 154.

[2] *nyon mongs pa'i sgrib pa, kleśāvaraṇa.*

[3] *drod, uṣmagata.*

[4] *rtse mo, mūrdhan.*

[5] *bzod pa, kṣānti.*

b̄a's *Golden Rosary of Eloquence,*[1] having given an extensive explanation that the references to abandonment are not to actual abandonments because, in order to abandon the seeds of these afflictive emotions, one must become a Foe Destroyer, says that, except for the use of the verbal convention "abandonment" for a temporary diminution or suppression, these are not actual abandonments and that, "beyond that, one also needs to make a fine distinction with respect to abandonments by a member of the spiritual community[2] who proceeds in the manner of leapover."[3] The leapover practitioners are those who have previously separated from attachment; for example, a Once Returner[4] who has previously separated from attachment[5]—that is, who has separated from six of the nine cycles of afflictive emotions pertaining to the Desire Realm. This type of fine distinction—that such a person, who had previously separated from attachment, has only temporarily suppressed or diminished the manifest form of the first six of the nine cycles of afflictive emotions pertaining to the Desire Realm—should be made with respect to the various usages of the term "abandonment."

STOPPAGE OF THE COARSE OPERATIVE CONSCIOUSNESSES

Next, let us consider the stoppage of the coarse operative consciousnesses. It is impossible for this to be accomplished through calm abiding. Such cessation occurs only through the attainment of the supramundane paths, and it occurs at the time of an exalted wisdom of meditative equipoise. At this time all coarse operative consciousnesses stop. Thus, even if there is an operative consciousness at that time, it is only a subtle one. For example, in the continuum of a person on the uninterrupted path of a Mahāyāna path of seeing, there is a conventional altruistic mind generation,[6] but this is a subtle consciousness. At that time, the minds of compassion, the thought definitely to leave cyclic existence,[7] and so forth, exist, but in a

[1] *legs bshad gser gyi phreng ba;* P6150, vol. 154. The longer title is *Extensive Explanation of (Maitreya's) "Ornament for Clear Realization, Treatise of Quintessential Instructions on the Perfection of Wisdom," As Well As Its Commentaries* (*shes rab kyi pha rol tu phyin pa'i man ngag gi bstan bcos mngon par rtogs pa'i rgyan 'grel pa dang bcas pa'i rgya cher bshad pa*).

[2] *dge 'dun, saṃgha.*

[3] *de'i steng nas thod rgal ba'i dge 'dun gyi spangs pa la yang zhib cha zhig 'don par bya'o.*

[4] *phyir 'ong, sākṛdāgāmin.*

[5] *chags bral sngon song gi phyir 'ong.*

[6] *byang chub sems bskyed, bodhicittotpāda.*

[7] *nges 'byung, niḥsaraṇa.*

subtle way. The exalted wisdom of meditative equipoise itself is an operative consciousness and is coarse, but it is the only one that is manifest.

Question: With respect to the stoppage of the coarse operative consciousnesses, if, during that time, the exalted wisdom of meditative equipoise—which is said to be coarse—occurs, then everything except meditative equipoise has stopped. In calm abiding, there is a stoppage of the sense consciousnesses, which are coarse, and the only operative consciousness that remains is the mind of calm abiding. Since the mind of calm abiding itself is coarse, why cannot the attainment of calm abiding be referred to as a stopping of coarse operative consciousnesses?

Answer: It depends what you consider "coarse" to mean. If you take it as meaning "manifest," then you can say that, at the time of the stoppage of the coarse manifest consciousnesses, a coarse manifest consciousness remains—namely, the wisdom of meditative equipoise. However, if you consider "coarse" in a negative sense, the wisdom of meditative equipoise would not be coarse, but subtle. Thus, there is a difference between the stoppage of sense consciousnesses and of coarse operative consciousnesses. However, when I said that, at the time of meditative equipoise of a person on the uninterrupted path of the Mahāyāna path of seeing, there is a coarse consciousness present, I meant that there is a manifest consciousness.

STOPPAGE OF THE SUBTLE OPERATIVE CONSCIOUSNESSES

With regard to the stoppage of subtle operative consciousnesses, the altruistic mind generation, and so forth, in the continuum of a person on an uninterrupted path of a Mahāyāna path of seeing are subtle operative consciousnesses. In some cases, these subtle ones stop and only very subtle ones remain. This occurs only in Highest Yoga Tantra. Here "very subtle" refers to the four subtle minds, among which, again, there are levels of subtlety. When we speak of the sense consciousnesses' stopping, we are referring only to certain members within the class of operative consciousnesses.

At the time of the meditative equipoise of the uninterrupted path of a Mahāyāna path of seeing—the time of directly realizing emptiness—there is a conventional mind generation existing in a subtle way. However, many texts say that the conventional mind of enlightenment does not exist at that time. They say that it exists only in the manner of non-degeneration—meaning that it itself is not present. Others say that at the time of the meditative equipoise of an uninterrupted path of a Mahāyāna path of seeing, there is an altruistic mind generation but it exists in a subtle way. There are also people who say that the assertion that "whatever is a consciousness in the continuum of a person having a learner's meditative equipoise is necessarily an exalted wisdom of meditative equipoise" is a good assertion and that it accords with tantra.

It appears that their thought is this. No matter what is said in the sūtra system on whether or not an altruistic mind generation exists during the exalted wisdom of meditative equipoise on emptiness, or whether it is subtle or not, in tantra there is great meaning in asserting that it does not occur during meditative equipoise, for at that time all that exists is the mind of clear light, which itself is the exalted wisdom of meditative equipoise. All other manifest and non-manifest minds have ceased. There are no minds such as the altruistic mind generation, and so forth, in the continuum of a person who has just attained the first of the ten Bodhisattva grounds according to the tantra system. There is no mind other than this mind of clear light. This is why some people say that in the continuum of a person still on the path of training no altruistic mind generation exists at the time of meditative equipoise on emptiness. They point to the tantric explanation as the reason why this has a great deal of meaning.

However, when I think about it, it does not seem to be very sensible to say that a statement is meaningful just because it accords with Highest Yoga Tantra, for it is by the power of having attained the stage of completion through depending on the stage of generation in Highest Yoga Tantra that one is capable of stopping all other consciousnesses. According to the sūtra system, far from stopping other consciousnesses, one is not capable even of abandoning any of the innate afflictive emotions at the time of achieving the first ground. There is a tremendous difference with regard to coarseness and subtlety between the exalted wisdom of meditative equipoise as explained in sūtra and as explained in Highest Yoga Tantra.

The exalted wisdom of meditative equipoise of the first Bodhisattva ground as generated in the sūtra system is something that is stopped before the generation of the exalted wisdom of meditative equipoise on the first Bodhisattva ground in the system of Highest Yoga Tantra. Thus, I think, the fact that in Highest Yoga Tantra all other consciousnesses can be stopped at the time of the exalted wisdom of meditative equipoise is due to the great difference of subtlety and power between this exalted wisdom and that of the sūtra system. Therefore, it is not reasonable to say that the assertion, "During the exalted wisdom of meditative equipoise in the sūtra system all other consciousnesses have stopped," is good because it accords with Highest Yoga Tantra.

To give an example from the viewpoint of the abandonment of afflictive emotions: A person definite in the Mahāyāna lineage who enters the path for the sake of abandoning artificial and innate afflictive emotions must abandon them over the first seven of the ten Bodhisattva grounds. They are abandoned gradually, by degrees, over these grounds. The afflictive emotions are divided into coarse, middling, and subtle according to the Prāsaṅgika assertions on the sūtra system. However, in Highest Yoga Tantra, a person abandons all afflictive emotions right at the first Bodhisattva ground. There is no need to divide them into artificial and innate afflictive emotions, coarse, subtle, and so forth; they are all abandoned simultaneously. This is due to the difference in the subtlety and power of the consciousnesses.

There are some who say that the uninterrupted path of the Mahāyāna path of seeing is a manifest coarse operative consciousness, whereas others say it is a manifest subtle operative consciousness, but these propounders have different things in mind when they say "coarse" or "subtle."

TURNING SLEEP INTO MEDITATIVE STABILIZATION

A sign of having achieved calm abiding is that sleep turns into meditative stabilization. How does one have this capacity? There is no way to go to sleep except for the mind to be withdrawn inside. A person who has attained calm abiding is so familiar with meditative stabilization that when he or she withdraws the mind inside, sleep becomes of the entity of meditative stabilization. Does this mean that sleep has become calm abiding? No.

There are, in general, three types of sleep: virtuous, non-virtuous, and neutral. These types are determined by the motivation a person has before going to sleep; if a person goes to sleep with a non-virtuous motivation and the sleep is conjoined with the force of that motivation, then the sleep itself will be non-virtuous. Similarly, if one goes to sleep within a state conjoined with a neutral or virtuous motivation, the sleep itself becomes neutral or virtuous. From within these three, a person who has attained calm abiding has achieved a virtuous motivation—namely a state arisen from meditation which is such that it affects any type of behavior. Thus, whenever this person withdraws the mind, it becomes an entity of meditative stabilization. There are, in general, the three ways already mentioned by which sleep becomes virtuous, non-virtuous, or neutral, and for a person who has calm abiding, this is even stronger. Such a person has the capacity to awaken sleep into meditative stabilization.[1]

Why is it that sleep is not calm abiding? What would be the fault if it were? Sleep can serve as an entity of meditative stabilization, but it cannot be a calm abiding because calm abiding is a state arisen from meditation which must be a continuation of the substantial entity of a state arisen from hearing, from thinking, and from meditation. Sleep, however, is not such a state. One does not meditatively cultivate sleep. The sleep of a person who has calm abiding is a meditative stabilization but not a calm abiding. It is of the same entity as the mental factor of stabilization[2] that accompanies it and thus is an entity of meditative stabilization, but that is just the stabilization factor that accompanies a virtuous mind and is not a state arisen from meditation.

In general, when the texts speak of the attainment of meditative stabilization, they are indeed referring to the attainment of calm abiding. However, we also speak of a meditative stabilization of any of the nine mental abidings. All nine are meditative stabilizations, and the cultivation of these is called a cultivation of meditative stabilization. It is necessary to look at the context of the statement in order to discover what the word "medita-

---

[1] Gedün Lodrö gives another example of the mind automatically becoming an entity of meditative stabilization. It is so involved that it is a digression from the main topic:

> It is said that in the Form and Formless Realms there are no states arisen from thinking but only states arisen from hearing (*thos byung, śrutamayī*) or arisen from meditation. In the Form Realm there are states arisen from hearing and meditation, but not states arisen form thinking. In the Formless Realm, there are only states arisen from meditation. Why is this? If a Form Realm being hears something that she or he wishes to think about, just that intention to think about it will cause the mind to turn into an entity of meditative stabilization. It is said that "without thought, it turns into meditative stabilization." This occurs because the continuum is moistened with calm abiding. How, then, does one posit the mental contemplation of individual knowledge of the character, the second of the preparatory mental contemplations, for a person in an upper realm? In the Form Realm it is a state arisen from hearing. In the Formless Realm there are no states arisen from hearing, and, since it is also not possible to accomplish individual knowledge of the character from within a state arisen from meditation, it is said that it occurs through one's having been born in the Formless Realm in this or a previous lifetime. This is stated in D̄zong-ka-b̄a's *Notes on the Concentrations and Formless Absorptions* (*bsam gzugs zin bris*).

[2] *ting nge 'dzin, samādhi.* See Jeffrey Hopkins, *Meditation on Emptiness,* 246 and 247; also, Lati Rinbochay and Elizabeth Napper, *Mind in Tibetan Buddhism,* 144.

tive stabilization" means. For instance, if one asks whether a person who has attained the nine mental abidings has attained meditative stabilization or not, this refers to the attainment of calm abiding.

Similarly, the word *yid la byed pa*[1]—a mental engagement, mental contemplation, or taking to mind—is a mental factor, but when Asaṅga's *Grounds of Hearers* mentions the attainment of a mental contemplation, this also refers to calm abiding. There is a passage that states, "A yogi at that point has a mental contemplation," meaning that she or he has calm abiding. In this context, the term "mental contemplation" is to be understood only as calm abiding. This word has another meaning when we speak of the seven mental contemplations and the preparations for the concentrations. Thus, one must look at the context to determine which of the different meanings of a term is being indicated.

Question: Does sleep's turning into the entity of meditative stabilization mean that the yogic practitioner can at that time see his or her object of observation?

Answer: It is possible for a yogic practitioner meditating on, for example, the body of a Buddha, to see the body of a Buddha in that sleep state of meditative stabilization. There is no definiteness. Usually, at the time of sleep, we see what we are most used to. For example, if you are thinking very strongly about a passage in a book, you tend to dream about it.

Question: An ordinary person might think of something virtuous while falling asleep—a visualization or mantra, for example—but later in the night might have a distinctly non-virtuous dream. How would this be classified?

Answer: That virtuous attitude preceding sleep sets up a period of sleep that is virtuous, but it is only a period. Later, something non-virtuous arises. The sleeper does not have this under control and cannot determine what comes after the initial period of sleep.

SENSE OF HAVING ADVENTITIOUSLY ACQUIRED A BODY

The next sign of calm abiding is that, when one rises, it is as though one had adventitiously acquired a body. "Body" here refers to our gross body, but there is no clear explanation for this in any Indian or Tibetan commentary. There are, however, many explanations of the powers of meditative stabilization; these can be used as means of illustrating this capacity. For instance, when a person with calm abiding withdraws the mind and goes to sleep, that sleep turns into an entity of meditative stabilization. All

[1] *manaskāra.*

that is manifest to this person is sleep; only the sleep consciousness is manifest. When one awakens, the sense consciousnesses become manifest, at which time the places where the sense consciousnesses reside also become manifest. The person then has a sense of acquiring a new body and feels that it is not just the body that he or she had formerly. This happens because, when the mind becomes of the entity of meditative stabilization in sleep, it is as though the body has ceased or has become of the entity of consciousness. Similarly, when a person who has attained the shadow-like pliancy sets up a situation of walking through walls, and so forth, and then returns, the reappearance of the gross body is like the attainment of a new body. While that person is moving about unimpededly, the body is unimpeded, just as the mind is. To that person's sense of appearance, no gross body appears. Similarly, when sleep becomes manifest, all appearances are only unimpeded. When the sense consciousnesses become manifest, their bases also become manifest, and the person has an uncomfortable sense of acquiring a new gross body. This sense of adventitiously acquiring a body and sleep's turning into an entity of meditative stabilization thus have the same reason as their basis.

DAWNING OF MANY PURE APPEARANCES

It is said that many pure appearances dawn when calm abiding has been attained. It is not necessarily the case, however, that when pure appearances occur they do so by the power of meditative stabilization. Thus, it is necessary to analyze the various types of pure appearance.

In general, there are three different types.

1 Sometimes, through the force of winds' entering into channels in which they usually do not course, appearances arise that do not occur otherwise. There are various good and bad appearances. Some people have hallucinations or go crazy, and there are many cases of pure appearances' dawning for such people.

2 There is a dawning to the mind of meditative visions.[1] Earlier (p. 113), we spoke of *bde nyams 'char*, the dawning of a sense of bliss; there, *nyams* was translated "sense," but here it is more like a spiritual vision. This might consist of the natural appearance of a Buddha field,[2] for example, to a person who has attained calm abiding; such an appearance would be due to the force of that person's familiarity with meditative stabilization. It would occur not only during the session but outside it also, without

[1] *bsgoms pa'i nyams yid la 'char ba.*

[2] *sangs rgyas kyi zhing, buddhakṣetra.*

the person's even seeking to think about a Buddha field; however, if the person wanted to think about a Buddha field, it might not appear very well. Such appearances are spontaneous. They are innate and like our usual appearances, but are such that they would start to disappear upon analysis, whereas, without too much attention, they are very clear. Such appearances occur without a person's specific intention, in the course of usual activities.

3 The third type of pure appearance is of a sense consciousness actually perceiving pure appearances. For example, people speak of seeing the face of a deity; this means that they see the deity, not just the face. It might be said that a certain person has seen the face of the goddess Sarasvatī. This is a case of her or his directly seeing the deity with the eye consciousness.

The type of pure appearance that is being referred to here regarding a person who has attained calm abiding is the second, the dawning to the mind of meditative visions.

DISCUSSION

Question: Which of the three types of visions would include the person who has not attained calm abiding and who has a vision of a Buddha?

Answer: If the person has been meditating on a Buddha's body, this can be a case of the second type—that is, of meditative vision dawning to the mind.

Question: What about a person who has not been cultivating meditative stabilization at all?

Answer: This would be a case of someone who, in a former lifetime, meditated on the body of a Buddha. There are two kinds of virtue: virtues which arise from training in this life[1] and virtues due to the force of one's having become conditioned to them in a past lifetime.[2]

Question: Would it be possible for a person who practiced deity yoga and had not first attained calm abiding to achieve the appearance of a deity?

Answer: This would be the second type, that of a meditative vision dawning to the mind because of its cultivation in meditation.

Question: Then why is this type of vision a sign of calm abiding?

Answer: There is a difference in the strength of the meditative vision when

[1] *sbyor byung gi dge ba.*

[2] *skyes stobs kyi dge ba.*

it dawns to the mind through the achievement of calm abiding. It is very important to make these distinctions. There could indeed be cases of meditative visions dawning to the mind before calm abiding.

Question: It seems that these three types of vision are hierarchical. The second type, which appears to the mind, cannot be subjected to analysis, but in the third type the deity is seen directly; this seems to indicate that it could be analyzed. Is that correct?

Answer: Yes, the third is probably stronger than the other two. The first type, the pure appearances which arise through the winds' coursing in channels which they usually do not enter, occurs only in states unrelated to meditation. Although, on the stage of completion of Highest Yoga Tantra, one purposely causes winds to enter channels in which they usually do not go, visions occurring at that time would be cases of meditative visions dawning to the mind—the second type. Thus, the first occurs only in the ordinary context.

The three ways in which pure appearances can arise are set forth in reference to a beginner who has newly attained calm abiding. Such a beginner can be someone who is about to attain calm abiding, someone who has attained it, and so forth. However, pure appearances that arise for a person on the stage of completion of Highest Yoga Tantra occur in dependence on the power of meditation, which causes the winds to enter and dissolve into the central channel.

With regard to the immaculate vacuity that appears to a subtle mind of death, there are two types: (1) an immaculate vacuity that appears through the force of karma and (2) another that appears through the power of meditation. The first of these is not an actual emptiness but a general type of vacuity that appears ordinarily at death. The immaculate vacuity that appears through the force of meditation is the actual emptiness; it arises through the force of the winds' having entered, dissolved into, and remained in the central channel by the power of meditation. Thus, this state occurs through the force of meditation and not just through the winds' entering into and coursing in unusual channels.

Question: In what sense and in what manner does meditative equipoise degenerate at the time subsequent to meditative equipoise?

Answer: With respect to the meditative equipoise of, for example, a person who has attained calm abiding, it is definite that its functioning will not have degenerated when that person is in a state subsequent to meditative equipoise. Nevertheless, this state is a conventional mind. The person who has such a state is one who has risen from meditative equipoise. "Rising from meditative equipoise" does not mean that the person has to stand up, and so forth; it means that the meditator has left that particular meditative equipoise and has a conventional mindfulness. The person is now mindful of something else.

Whatever is an actual meditative equipoise is a meditative equipoise on emptiness. This is the Prāsaṅgika assertion. In a state subsequent to meditative equipoise, whatever appears seems to be empty. During meditative equipoise, the "all-emptiness" appears; this means that the meditator is concentrating one-pointedly on just emptiness. In a state subsequent to meditative equipoise, conventional things appear. Nevertheless, they do not appear in their ordinary way but from within a non-diminishment of that emptiness. Thus, when one sees a conventional phenomenon from within a state subsequent to meditative equipoise, one indeed sees a conventional phenomenon. A person who has not realized emptiness also sees conventional phenomena. The difference between them is that the first person, through the essential of having become familiar with emptiness of everything at the time of meditative equipoise, automatically ascertains during the state subsequent to meditative equipoise that whatever phenomena appear are empty. This is like what happens when one is initially taught the connection between a name and an object. For example, if you make the connection with respect to an oak tree and think, "This is a tree," then later, when you see a willow, you automatically think, "This is a tree," without someone else's having to make the connection for you. This occurs through the power of your having made the original connection, "tree," regarding the oak tree. Similarly, when one rises from meditative equipoise, no matter what kind of conventional phenomenon is seen, a mind that thinks, "This is empty," is automatically generated. This is what should be understood by the term "subsequent to meditative equipoise." It is induced through the power of meditative equipoise. This is the actual state subsequent to meditative equipoise.

A state similar to this occurs for a person who has newly attained calm abiding; although it is not a real state subsequent to meditative equipoise, it is designated by that name. At the time of a state subsequent to meditative equipoise, there is no deterioration of the meditative equipoise that preceded it. This is because the force of the meditative equipoise has remained without diminishment. When one passes beyond the state subsequent to meditative equipoise and engages in some other activity, the state subsequent to meditative equipoise no longer remains. This is the case for most ordinary people; however, it is possible to engage in activities without losing that state. If the meditative equipoise is very strong, then moving about and doing various things will not harm its force. The strength of the state subsequent to meditative equipoise depends mainly on the strength of the meditative equipoise. Therefore, when one engages in an ordinary activity, it is entirely possible that the functioning of the meditative equipoise will degenerate.

There are many different types of Desire Realm afflictive emotions and many differences in their strength. However, if we consider an ordinary being who has newly attained calm abiding, such a person has not abandoned harmful intent,[1] which is a mind of the Desire Realm; because this person's familiarity with harmful intent is still greater than his or her familiarity with meditative equipoise, that attitude of harmful intent will be generated outside of meditative equipoise. Thus, far from abandoning harmful intent, such a person has not even separated from attachment to it, and therefore, when, after the state subsequent to meditative equipoise, she or he meets with conditions for its generation, it will be generated. If, when harmful intent is about to become manifest, one is capable of relying on its antidote, then not much fault will come from it, but if, as it is about to be produced, one is unable to rely on its antidote, it will become manifest, and at that point it is said the functioning of calm abiding has deteriorated.

What is the functioning of calm abiding that deteriorates? Calm abiding has one-pointed engagement in the object of observation, clarity of the object, spontaneous engagement in the object of observation, and the serviceability of mental and physical pliancy. When the mind of harmful intent becomes manifest, these functionings shrivel. In the beginning they are very vibrant, but they wilt like a plant in the hot sun. If one is still incapable of relying on the antidote, then the afflictive emotion will flourish, and calm abiding will become weaker and weaker until it finally disappears. At this point its continuum is severed. When the afflictive emotion first becomes manifest, one still has a chance to prevent such deterioration by relying on the appropriate antidote. Calm abiding will not be as vital as it was, but it can be refurbished. No matter what type of afflictive emotion one has, even if it is of a peaceful type, its functioning will continue to in-

---

[1] *gnod sems, vyāpāda.*

crease unless, at that point, one relies on an antidote. Its increase eventually causes the continuum of calm abiding to be severed.

Some texts use the term "state subsequent to meditative equipoise" very broadly to refer only to some state that occurs after meditative equipoise. The actual state subsequent to meditative equipoise, however, must be one that is induced by meditative equipoise itself. Thus, at the time of a state subsequent to meditative equipoise, the functioning of meditative equipoise has not deteriorated.

We usually refer to the space-like meditative equipoise[1] and the illusion-like state subsequent to meditative equipoise.[2] The space-like meditative equipoise is so named because, during it, whatever appears is necessarily just this immaculate vacuity. At the time of the state subsequent to meditative equipoise, things appear as like illusions and as capable of performing functions, even though they are empty of true existence. During the state subsequent to meditative equipoise, one is able to induce ascertainment with respect to this fact.

Generation of an afflictive emotion is one way in which the functioning of calm abiding can deteriorate. It can also deteriorate through the process of death and rebirth. If someone who has attained calm abiding is an ordinary person who has not attained the independence through which birth and death occur under one's own power, then, at the time of death, attachment and grasping for the next lifetime necessarily become manifest. Since attachment and grasping—which are included within the Desire Realm—must be generated, one powerlessly comes under their influence. This, in turn, necessitates that the *functioning* of attachment and grasping become manifest. At that time, calm abiding will degenerate. Therefore, since the calm abiding attained in this lifetime through cultivating the path is subject to deterioration through the process of death and rebirth, it is said that we must attain power over death and birth. These must come under the meditator's control.

How is it that calm abiding or another path will not deteriorate for someone who has attained control over death and birth? When such a person is about to die, when the signs of death appear, the practitioner effectively *stops* attachment and grasping and instead manifests path states. Because the continuum of those paths is not cut, one is able to take rebirth without the substantial continuum of those states being severed. Even if

---

1 *mnyam bzhag nam mkha' lta bu.*

2 *rjes thob sgyu ma lta bu.*

one cannot maintain the state consciously, one can carry a healthy seed for the generation of that particular path. Then, in a future lifetime, when one meets with conditions suitable for the generation of that state, it is ready to be produced.

This entire discussion is still within the framework of taking rebirth in cyclic existence. Birth and death are under one's control, but one is still being reborn in cyclic existence by the power of karma; this process can take place without manifest attachment and grasping, but even if the usual coarse attachment and grasping are not present, some type of attachment and grasping is there. However, this is not of a faulty type and cannot bring harm to oneself.

Question: If you do not have control over death and rebirth, and the path does deteriorate, what does it take to generate that path again in the next life?

Answer: There is no definiteness that the path will become manifest again in the next lifetime. One does not know where the next rebirth will be. Until one attains the forbearance level of the path of preparation, it is still possible to be reborn in a hell. Thus, there are people who have attained the path of accumulation and then been reborn in a hell. However, if we take as an example someone who has attained a path, does not have control over birth and death, and is reborn as a human, the necessary concordant circumstances for achieving the path again would arise through wishes made in the previous lifetime. To accomplish this, it will be necessary to engage in hearing, thinking, and meditating and to develop the power of wishes for the path.

Many external and internal conditions must come together. One internal condition is the attainment of a path in the past. Unlike a person who had never attained calm abiding, someone who had attained it in a previous lifetime would have the seed for generating it, which would make its cultivation easier. However, one must also have hearing, thinking, and so forth.

It is not necessary to be a Superior to have death in one's control. One probably does not even need to have attained a path. For example, someone who cultivates love, compassion, or the altruistic mind of enlightenment[1] can eventually manifest this cultivated attitude no matter what type of afflictive emotion is about to be generated. Such a person's meditation would even become stronger in the midst of severe pain due to sickness.

---

[1] *byang chub kyi sems, bodhicitta.*

Although an ordinary meditator would give up the meditation at that time, the more developed meditator attains a confidence such that the attachment and grasping which manifest at the time of death do not overcome her or him. When the signs of death are about to appear, the meditator manifests the mind to which he or she has become accustomed through long cultivation, and even though attachment and grasping become manifest in some form, the mind is not carried away by this attachment and grasping as an ordinary person's mind would be.

If the meditator is capable of manifesting the cultivated mind at that time, then the subtle mind of death will be conjoined with it. The type of rebirth depends on what affects the subtle mind of death. Thus, if one has manifest afflictive emotions before death, the subtle mind of death will be conjoined with those afflictive emotions. If one can stop the gross manifestation of attachment and grasping and is capable of manifesting a mind of love or compassion or the altruistic mind of enlightenment, then when one becomes unconscious in the subtle mind of death, that subtle mind is affected by one of those minds.

Question: Does this mean that one of those minds is manifest at that time?

Answer: No. Rather, it is as though its shadow, or its scent, is there. In the process of death the coarse consciousnesses cease, and gradually the more subtle ones also cease. They stop within the manifest mind of, for example, compassion, whereby the functioning of compassion remains. This is what is left. If attachment and grasping become uncontrollably manifest, then the mind stops within that, and it is the functioning of attachment and grasping that remains. Thus, one needs the confidence, built on experience, that one could manifest a mind of, for example, compassion at the time of death. There are people who die very gently or slowly, and this makes it easier to manifest a mind of meditation such as compassion or love. Some people die with great pain from disease; unless such a person has great familiarity with meditation, the mind will become attached to the pain, and one will die within that attachment. If, when you have such a painful feeling, you have an attachment to your body such that you do not want that pain, attachment to the body increases. Within the non-deterioration of the functioning of that attachment, the various minds cease and the subtle mind of death becomes manifest. For this reason, we usually make wishes that severe pain may not occur at the time of death. When you have strong pain, then whatever your practice is, it usually falls apart—it gets lost.

Question: What occurs as a result of the functioning of love, and so forth, affecting the subtle mind of death?

Answer: One will still be reborn by the power of karma but will be able to carry over to the next lifetime whatever one has meditated. This is all within the context of being reborn in cyclic existence. It is not necessary to have a Superior path or even a path of a common being[1] to have such control over death. There are also cases of being reborn in a pure land[2] through the power of wishes, but this is not what we are talking about. We are referring only to an ordinary person who is taking rebirth as, for instance, a human.

Question: What is a pure land?

Answer: For instance, according to the texts there is a place called the Joyous,[3] which is one of the six areas of Desire Realm gods. There is in the Joyous a pure land called the Pleasant Doctrine-Bearing Joyous Place.[4] The protector Maitreya lives there. The Joyous itself is contained within cyclic existence because it is one of the six areas of gods of the Desire Realm; it is not a pure land. However, the Pleasant Doctrine-Bearing Joyous Place is a pure land. It is in the Joyous but away from it, just as monasteries are within cities but at a distance from them. The Pleasant Doctrine-Bearing Joyous Place is not contained within cyclic existence.

Another pure land is the Blissful Place,[5] Amitābha's pure land. Texts explain these pure lands as having a definite location. However, I doubt that people who are to be reborn there all go to one place, like going to New York. I think that someone is reborn there as a result of having thought about it greatly and that the place itself is an appearance factor[6] of that person's mind; for rebirth in a pure land is due to one's own practice and meditation. The type of resources that one uses in such a land, and so forth, are achieved by the power of one's own meditation. I do not think it could be the case that everyone meditating on, for example, Amitābha, could be going to a single place; rather, the appearance factor of their own minds would produce such a place.

There is great purpose in being born in a pure land. One is never after-

---

[1] These are the paths of accumulation and preparation.

[2] *dag zhing, kṣetraśuddhi.*

[3] *dga' ldan, tuṣita.*

[4] *dga' ldan yid dga' chos 'dzin.*

[5] *bde ba can, sukhāvatī.*

[6] *snang ngo.*

ward reborn in a bad transmigration because, having been born in a pure land, one listens to doctrine[1] and practices it, so that one is only reborn from one pure land to another. Even though the land is produced from the appearance factor of the mind, one listens to doctrine coming from the outside. These two are not mutually exclusive. As Shāntideva says, there are hells; there is suffering; and these are established within one's own mind. I think it must be the same with pure lands. It is difficult to explain because it depends on the structure of the mind and on karma, which are two very difficult topics.

Question: If the subtle mind of death is conjoined with compassion, is it definite that one will be reborn in a happy transmigration? My doubt comes because it is possible to generate compassion in a hell.

Answer: There are very many karmas in the continuum of a given person. Each person has hundreds of thousands of karmas that would cause rebirth in a hell, hundreds of thousands that would cause rebirth as a human. Rebirth in a hell by the power of karma cannot occur under the influence of compassion. Persons who have death under their control can usually bring it about that they will not be born in a bad transmigration. Such persons would have countless karmas for being reborn as a human and could bring it about that they are reborn as a human.

There are several factors that determine which of a person's countless karmas impels the next rebirth. One way in which rebirth takes place is that the earlier actions fructify first. Another is according to which is strongest. Rebirth due to the strength of actions has precedence over rebirth due to temporal proximity of actions. Thus, if all the strengths of the actions are equal, one's birth will be produced by whichever action is earliest. There are exceptions, however. For example, a person who has accumulated a strong action for rebirth in a hell can stop that through meditation. Meditation on the mind of compassion stops the generation of the gross minds of attachment and grasping that would cause rebirth in a hell. Such meditation is virtuous and nourishes a karma that accords with it. The person would take rebirth by its power of that. It is probably entailed that if the subtle mind of death is conjoined with a mind of compassion, and so forth, there will not be rebirth in a bad transmigration.

---

[1] *chos, dharma.*

7 RISING FROM MEDITATIVE EQUIPOISE

Our discussion of the deterioration or non-deterioration of the functioning of calm abiding (see pp. 137-141) was subsidiary to the topic of the signs of calm abiding. Now I will explain the mode of rising from meditative equipoise. It should be thought about this way: A person is set in the meditative equipoise of calm abiding; rising from that is like awakening from sleep. This "rising" does not mean that the body rises; rather, it is the end of a period of being in meditative equipoise on, for example, emptiness. During this meditative equipoise, nothing appears except emptiness, and it comes to an end after a predetermined amount of time. Thus, rising from meditative equipoise does not mean that one rises and engages in conventional activities.

Right after one rises from meditative equipoise, one's mind—no matter what object it is considering—remains conjoined with the force of calm abiding. There are persons who rise from a meditative equipoise of calm abiding that observes one of the varieties of conventional phenomena; others rise from the meditative equipoise of a calm abiding observing the mode, emptiness. Still others initially cultivate and achieve a calm abiding observing one of the varieties but have as their final intention meditation on emptiness; even though such persons have not realized emptiness, they have some understanding of it. Our discussion of rising from meditative equipoise mostly has to do with this third type of person.

When such a person rises from meditative equipoise and conventional phenomena appear to the mental consciousness or the sense consciousnesses, they appear as produced from causes and conditions. One contemplates that these have been produced through the aggregation of many causes and conditions and that for this reason they are appearing to oneself. This is a contemplation of dependent-arising; therefore, it is a contemplation of freedom from the extreme of annihilation.[1] One then con-

[1] *chad mtha', ucchedānta.*

templates the fact that, although these phenomena appear in various ways to various sentient beings through the power of causes and conditions, they do not have even a particle of inherent existence. One reflects that all phenomena abide in the middle way, free from the extremes of permanence[1] and annihilation. Within that contemplation, one rests a little.

Although phenomena do not inherently exist, persons who lack the eye of wisdom which sees the absence of inherent existence conceive the opposite—inherent existence—and thereby travel in cyclic existence. One rests a little, contemplating the way in which beings travel in cyclic existence. One then contemplates the fact that people who are stuck in cyclic existence and wish to get out of it sometimes seek this escape for their own sake and thereby fall into the attitude of Hearers and Solitary Realizers. Bodhisattvas, who possess in their continuums paths that stop both the extreme of cyclic existence[2] and the extreme of solitary peace,[3] contemplate and abide in the Bodhisattva deeds—the six perfections,[4] and so forth. They reflect on the fact that the Buddhas of the ten directions became familiar with these Bodhisattva deeds at the time of the paths of learning and, having brought them to completion, are now engaged in activities for the sake of setting sentient beings in the non-abiding nirvāṇa.[5] The meditator rests a little in that contemplation.

The yogic practitioner then thinks, "I also will strive at the remaining paths of calm abiding and special insight in order to attain the highest object of attainment—Buddhahood—for the sake of others' welfare." The meditator has this motivation and rests a little in that thought.

All this is within the state subsequent to meditative equipoise, and this is how you should consider this state to be. This is the real state subsequent to meditative equipoise.

Question: It seems that this is an analytical meditation?

Answer: It could be posited as an analytical meditation.

These are all the modes of thinking or contemplation during the state subsequent to meditative equipoise. First, the yogic practitioner is set in a meditative equipoise of calm abiding for perhaps an hour. Or, if the length of the session is an hour, a half-hour would be spent in meditative equi-

---

[1] *rtag mtha', śaśvatānta.*

[2] *srid pa'i mtha', bhavānta.*

[3] *zhi mtha', *śāntānta.*

[4] *pha rol tu phyin pa, pāramitā.*

[5] *mi gnas pa'i mya ngan las 'das pa, apratiṣṭhanirvāṇa.*

poise and a half-hour in the state subsequent to meditative equipoise. This is an example.

When the contemplation is finished, the person gently frees himself or herself from the meditative posture. One does not just jump up and run about immediately. It is said that the practitioner then bows down to the Buddhas of the ten directions. The period of freeing oneself from the cross-legged posture is the rising from the state subsequent to meditative equipoise, but some refer to the state subsequent to meditative equipoise much more loosely as involving everything that happens after meditative equipoise.

I have been explaining the rising from meditative equipoise of the third type of person, someone who deeply wants to attain a union of calm abiding and special insight realizing emptiness, who has not yet realized emptiness, but who has an understanding of it. There are other presentations of rising from meditative equipoise based on the various system of tenets. There is no definiteness of its being only the way I have explained.

PART TWO:
EXPANSION

8 TEXTBOOKS AND DEBATE

Question: You have referred a great deal to Asaṅga's work. Is this how the topic would be taught in Tibet? Would the students already have read the *Grounds of Hearers*, or is it merely studied by way of a teacher's drawing out quotations from it?

Answer: I would lecture on these topics within citing Asaṅga's work as a source. Each of the monastic colleges has its own textbooks;[1] however, all the textbooks derive from Indian texts. It is in terms of the Indian commentaries that debate is carried out between the colleges. Within one's own college, however, it is not necessary to debate on that basis; it is possible to debate on the basis of one's own textbook. However, even though, when we go to the great debates set up by the Tibetan government, our minds might reflect on our own textbooks, we cannot debate from them. It is necessary to cite the generally accepted Indian texts. Thus, the Indian texts are taken by everyone as the basis. Everyone has the words, but when they get together to debate, they do not agree at all on the meaning of the Indian texts.

As I mentioned earlier in connection with calm abiding and special insight (p. 114), there is nothing on these topics that surpasses Asaṅga's *Grounds of Hearers*. One must consult that text. Our Go-mang[2] College has a bit of an advantage with regard to the Indian texts because many of these are cited in the Go-mang literature—more so than in the writings of other monastic colleges. The Go-mang texts are filled with quotations from Indian commentaries. Although both challenger and defender must know the various Indian citations involved, whether the challenger is familiar with them or not does not make much difference; for the defender, however, such familiarity makes a great deal of difference; he profits greatly. Something that does not appear in an Indian commentary is not acceptable.

---

[1] *yig cha.*

[2] *sgo mang.*

Question: Does that mean one could not quote Ḏzong-ka-ḇa?

Answer: When people of the different orders debate, it is not possible to quote Ḏzong-ka-ḇa. Within the Ge-luk-ḇa[1] order, one can cite Ḏzong-ka-ḇa.

If, inappropriately citing a passage, someone gives the reason, "Because such-and-such was said," you would answer, "The reason is not established,"[2] for if you said, "There is no entailment,"[3] it would mean that you yourself had a different interpretation. To answer here that the reason is not established really does not mean that the person quoted did not make the statement attributed to him but that one does not accept that statement as authoritative. You would think that the answer here would be, "There is no entailment," but it is not.

If, in a debate, a defender says something that contradicts his own textbook, the challenger can point out that he is contradicting his own textbook. There are times when such can be said. If it is an important issue, the challenger can point out what the defender's own textbook says and ask, "Is it that you do not know what your own textbook says or that you disagree with it?" This sometimes happens.

Question: Can you disagree with your own textbook?

Answer: There are many cases of internal contradictions within our own textbooks. Thus, there are many instances of not agreeing with one's own textbook. The better ge-s̄hays know what positions there are on topics such as whether or not there are actual minds which are non-manifest. If I, being from Go-mang, said that there was no such thing, everyone would be amazed. The people from Go-mang would also be amazed. If I said, "Yes, I know that text says that, but I do not accept it," then, too, everyone would be amazed because I would have given up my textbook. On smaller points, however, there are cases of people who do not know their text's assertion.

Question: Does everyone agree on what the original authentic text is?

Answer: Often different Indian sources are cited. Both challenger and defender must know the Indian citations involved and be able to interpret them.

Question: But would it be the case that you would accept everything stated

[1] *dge lugs pa.*

[2] *rtags ma grub.*

[3] *ma khyab.*

by any Indian writer?

Answer: No. For example, with regard to the topics of the Perfections,[1] we mainly follow Haribhadra and Vimuktisena. These are the main Indian commentators for that topic. Also, Dharmamitra's *Clear Words*[2] is sometimes used, but not very much. Its assertions are sometimes stated and refuted.

Question: To what class of commentary do monastic textbooks belong?

Answer: There are two main types of monastic literature, or textbook:[3] those that set forth the general meaning[4] and those that engage in final analyses.[5] The general-meaning type sets forth definitions, divisions, and so forth. The section of final decisions is mainly concerned with eliminating qualms. Thus it is not definite that everything would be discussed; only important points of difference would be.

---

[1] *pha rol tu phyin pa, phar phyin; pāramitā.*

[2] *shes rab kyi pha rol tu phyin pa'i man ngag gi bstan bcos mngon par rtogs pa'i rgyan gyi tshig le'ur byas pa'i 'grel bshad tshig rab tu gsal ba shes bya ba, abhisamayālaṃkāraprajñāpāramitopadeśaṭīkāprasphuṭapadā;* P5193.

[3] *yig cha.*

[4] *spyi don.*

[5] *mtha' dpyad.*

9 HĪNAYĀNA AND MAHĀYĀNA

Since the two terms "Hīnayāna" and "Mahāyāna" have two distinct meanings, I will clarify their usage. The word "Hīnayāna" can refer to the Hīnayāna tenet systems—Vaibhāṣhika and Sautrāntika—or to a person who is a Hīnayānist, someone whose main motivation is merely to get out of cyclic existence oneself. Similarly the word "Mahāyāna" can refer to the Mahāyāna tenet systems—Chittamātra and Mādhyamika—or to a person who is a Mahāyānist, someone whose main motivation is to establish all sentient beings in Buddhahood.

There is further danger of confusion because the Hīnayāna systems themselves explain ways of achieving calm abiding and special insight by Hīnayānists *and* Mahāyānists. Similarly, the Mahāyāna systems explain how both Hīnayānists *and* Mahāyānists achieve calm abiding and special insight.

	Hīnayāna		***Mahāyāna***
System	Vaibhāṣika Sautrāntika	System	Chittamātra Mādhyamika
Person	Hīnayānist	Person	Mahāyānist

This is a basis of error nowadays, both for those who have not studied and for those who have studied somewhat but without becoming acquainted with the breadth of Buddhist texts. Even in Tibet, because of such error some people made the following mistaken equations: Hīnayāna with Hearers;[1] Chittamātra with Solitary Realizers;[2] Mahāyāna with proponents

[1] *nyan thos, śrāvaka.*

[2] *rang sangs rgyas, pratyekabuddha.*

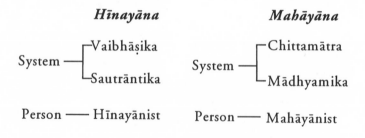

of Mahāyāna tenet systems. The source for these erroneous equations is that there are texts which, in presenting the Hīnayāna, primarily discuss Hearers; which, in presenting Solitary Realizers, primarily discuss such Chittamātra topics as the lack of a difference of entity between subjects and objects; and which, in presenting the Mahāyāna, primarily discuss the direct realization of emptiness, a topic mainly but not exclusively associated with the Mahāyāna.

Why are the Vaibhāṣhika and Sautrāntika schools called Hīnayāna and the Chittamātra and Mādhyamika, Mahāyāna? After Buddha became enlightened, he set forth, in general, three turnings of the wheel of doctrine. The sūtras spoken during the first stage of his teaching are included within the Hīnayāna and those of the middle and final stages, within the Mahāyāna. Thus, the Vaibhāṣhika and Sautrāntika systems are Hīnayāna because they derive their presentations of the bases, paths, and fruits from the sūtras taught during the first stage. They are also known as the two schools of Hearers because, when one practices the paths as presented in the Hīnayāna sūtras, one achieves the fruits of Hearers and Solitary Realizers. Hearers are slightly lower than Solitary Realizers, but the scriptural sources for both are the Hīnayāna sūtras. Except in the system of Yogāchāra-Svātantrika-Mādhyamika, Hearers and Solitary Realizers do not differ in their type of realization; they differ in their mode of amassing the collections of merit.[1] Similarly, a Mahāyānist—a Mahāyāna person—is one who practices the path as it is set forth in Mahāyāna sūtras.

It is possible for one person to be both a Mahāyānist [in terms of motivation] and a proponent of Hīnayāna tenets. For example, there was a Bodhisattva known as Proponent of One Consciousness, and he is said to be a Vaibhāṣhika.

Question: Would a Bodhisattva who propounds Hīnayāna tenets be one who has an altruistic aspiration to achieve enlightenment for the sake of all sentient beings but does not have the Mahāyāna view of emptiness?

Answer: Yes. One becomes a Bodhisattva, or Mahāyānist, through cultivating the altruistic aspiration to the enlightenment of a Buddha for the sake of all beings. It is only due to this that one is called a Mahāyānist. If Bodhisattvas were posited by way of view, it would be impossible for a single person to be both a Bodhisattva and a Vaibhāṣhika.

There are, however, roughly three types of Bodhisattvas—dull Bodhisattvas, Bodhisattvas who initially proceeded on the Hīnayāna path, and

[1] *bsod nams, puṇya.*

very sharp Bodhisattvas. A very sharp Bodhisattva could not also be a follower of Hīnayāna tenets because, before generating an aspiration to attain the enlightenment of a Buddha for the sake of all beings, she or he has two valid cognitions. To explain this, let us consider what, in ordinary language, the nature or entity of this aspiring to enlightenment is. It is the attitude, "I will attain highest enlightenment for the sake of all other sentient beings." There are many ways of training in this mind of enlightenment. One method, which stems from Shāntideva, is called the exchange of self and other; another, from Chandrakīrti, is known as the seven cause-and-effect quintessential instructions. "Altruistic mind of enlightenment"[1] is the name designated to an attitude in which one seeks Buddhahood oneself in order that others may attain Buddhahood.

A person who is definite in the Mahāyāna lineage[2] is one who enters the Mahāyāna path from the beginning without previously generating any of the Hīnayāna paths. Very sharp Bodhisattvas engage in two types of analysis before actually generating the altruistic aspiration. First, they consider whether or not it is possible for all sentient beings to attain Buddhahood; this must be investigated with reasoning. They must also analyze whether, even if such might be possible, it could actually happen. By using reasoning, very sharp Bodhisattvas come to understand that all persons *can* attain Buddhahood and that they are definite to do so. These are the two valid cognitions that necessarily precede the actual intention of very sharp Bodhisattvas to achieve Buddhahood for the sake of others.

On what types of reasons do these valid cognitions depend? They depend on two facts: (1) that the nature of the mind is clear light and (2) that all defilements of the mind are adventitious, or temporary. Sentient beings abide in a state of being obscured by defilements. A very sharp Bodhisattva engages in a great deal of analysis to discover whether or not it is possible to separate the mind from its defilements. If the possibility of separation from these obstructive defilements did not exist for all sentient beings, the wish to attain Buddhahood so that others might attain it would be a fruitless meditation.

In dependence on reasonings set forth in texts of valid cognition[3] and Mādhyamika, the practitioner realizes that the nature of the mind is clear light and that its defilements are temporary. Realizing that defilements do

---

[1] *byang chub kyi sems, bodhicitta.*

[2] *theg chen gyi rigs nges.*

[3] *tshad ma, pramāṇa.*

not abide in the nature of the mind, he or she realizes that even though the mind is defiled by the conception of true existence, that conception is merely adventitious, for at that time the meditator realizes that the conception of true existence does not accord with the actual nature of things. Seeing that defilements do not abide in the nature of the mind is itself the realization of truthlessness, or emptiness. To put it another way, seeing that what is conceived by the conception of true existence is not established or substantiated in accordance with its mode of apprehension is itself the realization of selflessness.[1] When the Bodhisattva realizes that it is possible, at some time, to separate from the conception of self, or of true existence, she or he recognizes that the conception of self does not inhere in the nature of the mind. The sign that this is so is the fact that, in time, the conception of a self of persons, or of true existence, can be separated from the mind. If the conception of self inhered in the nature of the mind, getting rid of that conception would mean getting rid of the mind. They could not become separate. For example, there is no way to separate fire and heat, or air and lightness.

The realization that what is conceived by the conception of true existence, or the conception of self, does not exist in accordance with the way it is conceived is a realization of selflessness, or truthlessness. That very non-existence in accordance with the way it is conceived is the emptiness of the mind. It is this emptiness which the very sharp Bodhisattva who is definite in the Mahāyāna lineage must realize before generating the altruistic mind of enlightenment. It would not be sufficient to realize the emptiness of a pot or a pillar at this time. This is why the texts explain that a very sharp Bodhisattva must realize emptiness before generating the mind of enlightenment.

A person who follows a Hīnayāna tenet system, such as Vaibhāṣhika, and yet is a Bodhisattva must be either a dull Bodhisattva or a person who initially proceeded on the Hīnayāna path. In our own oral transmission the latter is usually posited as an example of someone who, though a Bodhisattva, is a follower of a Hīnayāna system. Such a person first trains in Hīnayāna tenets and, while still maintaining that system's view, meets with a Mahāyāna spiritual guide or a text from which he or she receives instructions on generating the altruistic aspiration to enlightenment, and thereby generates it. This has been a brief explanation of how there can be Bodhisattvas who maintain Hīnayāna tenets.

---

[1] *bdag med pa, nairātmya.*

Question: What would you consider a Bodhisattva who himself or herself followed Mahāyāna tenets but who taught tenets of the Hīnayāna to those disciples for whom this was most helpful?

Answer: Such a Bodhisattva does this only for the sake of taking care of others. For example, it has to be said that the final thought of Shākyamuni Buddha himself is that of the Prāsaṅgika Mādhyamika system; yet, in order to take care of various types of disciples, Buddha set forth the paths of the three types of persons—Hearers, Solitary Realizers, and Bodhisattvas—as well as the four schools of tenets.

Bodhisattva Superiors still training in the path are persons who have directly realized emptiness and who frequently engage in direct cognition of it. They have no need to meditate on impermanence or on coarse selflessness because they have already directly realized the subtle selflessness, and when there is a subtle realization, the coarser misconceptions are abandoned along the way. Nevertheless, even though such Bodhisattvas would not take impermanence or coarse selflessness as their main object of meditation, it is said that they mainly meditate on impermanence, coarse selflessness, the four truths, and so forth. They do this not for their own sakes—their own path is only to meditate on emptiness—but in order to be able to care for and teach Hearers and Solitary Realizers.

Bodhisattva Superiors must generate two types of paths of seeing: (1) the means of passage which is the wisdom directly realizing emptiness and (2) that which is passed beyond—the wisdoms realizing coarser topics such as impermanence. The reason is that, when a Bodhisattva becomes a Buddha, she or he must teach all three types of sentient beings and, to be able to teach them, must generate their type of realization in his or her own continuum. The necessity for this is set forth in the second chapter of Dharmakīrti's *Commentary on (Dignāga's) "Compilation of [Teachings on] Valid Cognition."* He sets forth these topics loosely without formally applying them to the path.

Question: When on the five paths do sharp Bodhisattvas have their two valid cognitions?

Answer: Realization comes before the first path—the path of accumulation; one becomes a Bodhisattva at the beginning of that path. One initially achieves this path upon generation of the altruistic mind of enlightenment, and these two valid cognitions precede the generation of that mind. They occur at the time of the unusual attitude,[1] the high resolve.

When the altruistic aspiration is generated through the seven cause-and-effect quintessential instructions,[2] the first six occur when the person has not attained any of the five Mahāyāna paths. With the generation of the seventh—the altruistic aspiration itself—the meditator achieves the Mahāyāna path of accumulation. A person who enters the Hīnayāna before taking up the Mahāyāna can generate the first five of the seven quintessential instructions while still on the Hīnayāna path. The sixth, the generation of the unusual attitude, is contradictory with the Hīnayānist attitude, which must be forsaken before the unusual attitude can be generated. Those definite in the Mahāyāna lineage, who do not enter a Hīnayāna path, do this type of investigation and analysis at the point of the sixth of the seven quintessential instructions.

Your question touches on a difficult point. Those who engage in these analyses and achieve these two cognitions are included within the sphere of Mahāyāna practitioners. This is because one who has generated the sixth quintessential instructions is a person whose Mahāyāna lineage has been awakened.[3] Even Hearers and Solitary Realizers can have mere great compassion, but in generating the sixth quintessential instruction one has the great compassion in which one takes upon oneself the burden of freeing all sentient beings. This sixth step, called the unusual attitude, is of two types: unusual compassion and unusual love. This compassion is called unusual, or special, because it exceeds great compassion. Similarly, this type of love is unusual, or special, because it exceeds even the great love that Hearers and Solitary Realizers can possess.

Love is the wish that all sentient beings have happiness and the causes of happiness. Compassion is the wish that they be free from suffering and its causes. A person definite in the Mahāyāna lineage first has a sense of how nice it would be if sentient beings were free from suffering and its causes and were joined with happiness and its causes. Then, at the point of generating the unusual attitude the meditator feels, "Indeed, sentient beings must come to possess happiness and must come to be free from suffering, and *I myself* must take on the burden of making them so." The meditator then analyzes whether or not he or she, and all sentient beings, have the

[1] *lhag bsam, adhyasaya.*

[2] Recognition of all sentient beings as one's mothers, becoming mindful of their kindness, promising to repay their kindness, love, compassion, the unusual altruistic attitude, and generation of the aspiration to Buddhahood for the sake of all beings.

[3] *theg chen gyi rigs sad pa'i gang zag.*

possibility of becoming free from all defilements. This is where the two cognitions come.

Thus, a person definite in the Mahāyāna lineage who is at the point of the sixth of the seven quintessential instructions has no path at all. She or he has not attained any Mahāyāna path. Nevertheless, such a person is someone definite in the Mahāyāna lineage, and her or his Mahāyāna lineage has been awakened.

The generation of the altruistic mind of enlightenment is very important. The intention to gain highest enlightenment for the sake of others is included within the factor of method, but when one searches for its root, or that from which it derives, one finds that it derives from the view of emptiness.[1]

---

[1] To summarize: Those who have an altruistic intention to become enlightened are Mahāyānists, but they do not have to be followers of a Mahāyāna system of tenets—Chittamātra or Mādhyamika. Similarly, followers of a Mahāyāna system of tenets do not have to be Mahāyānists in the sense of having developed this altruistic motivation; they could be Hīnayānist in terms of motivation, seeking for the time being merely to leave cyclic existence. In the context of the two ways of presenting calm abiding and special insight, the terms "Hīnayāna" and "Mahāyāna" refer to tenet systems and not to categories of persons as determined by motivation. For more on this topic, see Jeffrey Hopkins' supplement in H.H. the Dalai Lama, Tsong-ka-pa, and Jeffrey Hopkins, *Tantra in Tibet* (London: George Allen and Unwin, 1977; reprint Ithaca: Snow Lion, 1987), 173-179.

10 ORDER AND BENEFITS OF CULTIVATING CALM ABIDING AND SPECIAL INSIGHT

ORDER OF CULTIVATION

We have discussed the objects of observation of calm abiding, how to search for and find the object of observation, and the suitability or unsuitability of changing it. The next topic is the cultivation of calm abiding and special insight while observing an object of observation.

Calm abiding must be achieved before special insight. This being so, why do some texts seem to say that special insight comes first? In terms of the order of practice, calm abiding comes first, and in terms of their generation in the mental continuum calm abiding is also first. Some topics, however, can be presented in more than one order. For example, when the four noble truths are explained, true sufferings are discussed first, then true origins. This is because a yogic practitioner must see the faults of suffering and then search for its causes; the practitioner must then find out whether there are true cessations[1] of suffering, whereupon he or she will practice the path leading to those cessations. Sūtra, however, contains explanations of the four truths in which true origins are explained first and the actual sufferings second, in accordance with the sequence of cause and effect, since ignorance precedes suffering and leads to suffering as its impelled effect. However, there is no such variety of explanation in relation to calm abiding and special insight because, whether one considers them from the viewpoint of practice or in terms of actually generating them in one's continuum, calm abiding comes first and then special insight. Thus, it is necessary to achieve calm abiding before special insight.

Consequently, when Asaṅga's *Summary of Manifest Knowledge* says, "Some have achieved special insight but not calm abiding; some have

---

1 *'gog pa'i bden pa, nirodhasatya.*

achieved calm abiding but not special insight," the statement, "Some have achieved special insight but not calm abiding," does not refer to actual special insight. Similarly, the statement, "Some have achieved calm abiding but not special insight," also does not refer to actual special insight. According to another statement, "There are some who achieve calm abiding based on special insight." This can be interpreted in two ways, with regard to actual and imputed calm abiding and special insight. The referent here is a person who has one of the five predominant afflictive emotions and, therefore, is not able to achieve calm abiding simply through meditating on the body of a Buddha by proceeding through the nine mental abidings up to calm abiding but must break down some hatred, for instance, before being able achieve calm abiding. Such a person wishes to achieve calm abiding using the body of a Buddha as the object of observation but is prevented from doing so by a predominance of hatred. To break down hatred, this practitioner must achieve experience on the level of analytical meditation with regard to hatred. Once this is achieved, it is possible to pass through the nine mental abidings leading to calm abiding. Without engaging in such analytical meditation, this person might achieve even the ninth mental abiding but would not be able to attain calm abiding. This is because, before achieving calm abiding, many types of mental and physical pliancy[1] must be attained; many winds must be purified, and this cannot be done by a person dominated by hatred. No matter how much progress is made, she or he would get no farther than the ninth mental abiding.

The above is a case of achieving an imputed calm abiding based on an imputed special insight. In this example, "imputed calm abiding" refers to the ninth mental abiding, and "imputed special insight," to the experience of analytical meditation used to break down hatred. Following this, the person will indeed achieve actual calm abiding. The analytical meditation engaged in before the ninth mental abiding is included within the class of special insight but is not actual special insight. Achievement of the ninth mental abiding based on such analytical meditation is included in the class of calm abiding but is not actual calm abiding. Indeed, the final achievement in this series will be actual calm abiding, but the ninth mental abiding is achieved on the basis of an imputed special insight.

I shall now speak about achievement of an actual calm abiding in dependence on an actual special insight. For example, let us consider a per-

---

[1] *shin sbyangs, praśrabdhi.*

son who has already attained the meditative stabilization which is a union of calm abiding and special insight and then achieves an actual first concentration in dependence on the seven mental contemplations. This achievement of the first concentration is a time of achieving an actual calm abiding in dependence on an actual special insight. However, this is not a case of *newly* achieving calm abiding. The meditator has already achieved calm abiding, and at this time his or her goal is the attainment of the first concentration.

Thus, when Asaṅga's *Summary of Manifest Knowledge* states that there are cases in which calm abiding is achieved in dependence on special insight, it refers either to the achievement of an imputed calm abiding in dependence on an imputed special insight or to the attainment of an actual calm abiding in dependence on an actual special insight—this latter not being a *new* achievement of calm abiding. The point is that one must initially achieve calm abiding before achieving special insight and that, when Asaṅga's statements are explained as above, they do not contradict this.

Is it necessary to achieve a calm abiding observing emptiness before one can achieve a special insight observing emptiness? Yes. Not only is it definite that one must, in general, achieve calm abiding before achieving special insight, one must also have a calm abiding observing emptiness before one can have a special insight observing emptiness. This, however, does not mean that it is necessary, before this special insight, to have a calm abiding in which all nine mental abidings have observed emptiness. Since, indeed, it is impossible to achieve calm abiding without the nine mental abidings, one might wonder how the special insight observing emptiness could be achieved without the meditator's passing through the nine mental abidings observing emptiness. What happens is this: first the meditator achieves a calm abiding that observes one of the varieties of phenomena, not emptiness. Having done this, he or she works at the first of the seven mental contemplations, which is called "thorough knowledge of the character."[1] This is an analytical meditation on emptiness; in dependence on such analysis, special insight is achieved. The meditator thus uses the mind of calm abiding as a mental basis[2] for engaging in analysis on emptiness. At the end of a period of analytical meditation, she or he again sets the mind in stabilizing meditation. At that time, the practitioner has a mind of calm abiding that observes emptiness without having gone through the

---

1 *mtshan nyid rab tu rig pa.*

2 *sems rten.*

nine mental abidings with emptiness as the object of observation.

Because this person has already achieved calm abiding, the many physical and mental pliancies that accompany calm abiding have already been generated. Thus, when the meditator again sets the mind in meditative stabilization after completing analytical meditation through the mental contemplation called thorough knowledge of the character, the pliancies easily reappear. They now occur automatically, by their own force.

There are two ways of achieving calm abiding observing emptiness. In the first, an initial attainment of calm abiding gained through observing emptiness, one relies on scriptures that set forth the modes of correct and fallacious reasonings and engages in hearing, thinking, and meditating, thereby coming to understand what emptiness is and passing through the nine mental abidings observing it. In the second, a person who has achieved calm abiding observing one of the varieties uses this special mind as a mental basis and, with the force of that meditative stabilization, analyzes with respect to emptiness by using minds of hearing and thinking. Because of this special type of mind, he or she does not have to depend on the processes of reasoning in the way in which they are usually laid out—using proof statements,[1] and so forth. Most cases of a realization of emptiness are of this second type.

Thus it is definite that before achieving special insight, one must have calm abiding, and, similarly, before one can have special insight observing emptiness, one must have calm abiding observing emptiness. This is true in all forms of sūtra and the three lower tantra sets. In Highest Yoga Tantra, however, there are cases of achieving calm abiding and special insight simultaneously. Jam-ȳang-shay-b̄a's *Great Exposition of the Concentrations and Formless Absorptions* and other texts state that in Highest Yoga Tantra there are cases of achieving calm abiding and special insight simultaneously through the force of the blessed empowerment of various special objects of observation and the force of special meditative stabilizations. Jam-ȳang-shay-b̄a's text on the concentrations and formless absorptions does not give a clear explanation of how this takes place because he explains it in detail elsewhere in relation to Highest Yoga Tantra, but we can explain it here in a rough way.

At the beginning of the stage of completion[2] in Highest Yoga Tantra, a yogic practitioner definitely must have the ability to take as an object of

---

[1] *sgrub ngag.*

[2] *rdzogs rim, niṣpannakrama.*

observation that which is a composite of an ascertainment factor[1]—an absence of inherent existence—and an appearance factor[2]—a divine body. These are not two different consciousnesses but a single consciousness that is described as having two factors, ascertainment and appearance. For this type of yoga to be generated, all coarse conceptions[3] must be stopped, and this necessitates the stopping of all winds that serve as the mounts of such conceptions. Before the stage of completion, during the stage of generation, the yogic practitioner stops these winds of coarse conceptions.

When the yogic practitioner has achieved either the eighth or ninth mental abiding preceding calm abiding, she or he meditates on emptiness—on the lack of inherent existence of object, agent, and action.[4] Then, from within a meditative equipoise on emptiness, the practitioner emanates and withdraws a mandala. This emanation and withdrawal is done with the seal[5] of emptiness—that is, it is done while sustaining the force of the practitioner's realization of emptiness. Through just this practice, the eighty coarse conceptual thoughts are naturally stopped. Not only do the many types of coarse conceptions described in sūtra cease through this practice of emanating and withdrawing the mandala; even the altruistic mind of enlightenment ceases at that time.

As for the attainment of calm abiding and special insight, the main obstacles to it are two types of wind, one that interferes with analysis and another that interferes with stabilization. This practice purifies both of these winds simultaneously. Since these two winds are the chief obstacles to the attainment of calm abiding and special insight and since this yogic practitioner abiding in the eighth or ninth mental abiding preceding calm abiding engages in the emanation and withdrawal of the mandala, thereby purifying these winds, there is no reason why he or she should not attain special insight. Thus, in Highest Yoga Tantra, there is no need to engage in the additional preparatory practices explained in sūtra, nor is it necessary to achieve calm abiding specifically in order to calm and purify the winds.

The purpose in practicing the emanation and withdrawal of a mandala is to achieve the stage of completion and not mainly to purify the winds.

---

[1] *nges ngo.*

[2] *snang ngo.*

[3] *rnam rtog, vikalpa.*

[4] *bya byed las gsum.*

[5] *phyag rgya, mudrā.*

Nevertheless, the winds are automatically purified by this practice. Thus, for this practitioner, the attainment of calm abiding and special insight is also simultaneous with the attainment of the stage of completion. In all probability, this attainment is also simultaneous with that of the mantric path of preparation, but this point is not clearly stated in the texts; in the sūtra system, the attainment of a union of calm abiding and special insight observing emptiness is simultaneous with the attainment of the path of preparation.

BENEFITS OF CULTIVATION

I will briefly mention the benefits of cultivating calm abiding and special insight. The *Sūtra Unraveling the Thought* states that all good qualities of the three vehicles—Hearer, Solitary Realizer, and Bodhisattva—are fruits of calm abiding and special insight. This is said from the viewpoint of the types of meditation: there is no practice of meditation that is not included within analytical or stabilizing meditation.

If persons who have attained calm abiding keep their minds in calm abiding, not only does the force of their meditative stabilization remain but their other good qualities increase and do not degenerate. Similarly, persons who have achieved special insight have clear perception not only with respect to the object of observation on which they have been meditating but also with respect to any other object to which they turn their minds. Persons who cultivate calm abiding but not special insight will gain the factor of stability but not that of an intense clarity; they will not be able to manifest any antidote to the afflictive emotions. One must achieve an intensity of clarity in order for anything to serve as an antidote to ignorance, and to achieve that clarity one must cultivate special insight.

The first of the actual antidotes of any vehicle is an uninterrupted path. The uncommon direct cause of an uninterrupted path is a meditative stabilization which is a union of calm abiding and special insight. Therefore, it is definite that one must cultivate special insight. If someone cultivated special insight without calm abiding—if we pretend that there is such a possibility—then even if that person achieved intense clarity, she or he would not have the factor of stability and would come under the influence of excitement, thereby eliminating the possibility of developing calm abiding.

These are, in brief, the benefits and purposes of cultivating calm abiding and special insight. I have mentioned them in accordance with the Tibetan tradition of explaining these topics. In India this topic was not set forth separately but was included in the explanation of how to achieve calm abiding and special insight.

DISCUSSION

Question: Since practitioners of Highest Yoga Tantra automatically purify the winds that are obstacles to calm abiding and special insight through practice aimed at attaining the stage of completion, do they not need to use the nine mental abidings in order to achieve calm abiding? It was stated that practitioners engaging in emanation and withdrawal abide in the eighth or ninth mental abiding; did they have to pass through the previous mental abidings to reach that point?

Answer: Yes. Persons practicing Highest Yoga Tantra pass through the first eight or nine mental abidings just as in the sūtra system. However, the power of mind is completely different. The order of the mental abidings is the same, but the mode of generating the object of observation is different.

In general a person who is a special trainee of tantra is sharper than one of sūtra; within the four tantra sets, a special trainee of Highest Yoga Tantra is very sharp, but there are differences even within this group of very sharp trainees. The sharpest among them will practice the emanation and withdrawal of the mandala at the eighth mental abiding rather than the ninth. Highest Yoga Tantra does not have a separate description of how to achieve calm abiding and special insight because, through the practices of Highest Yoga Tantra, the obstacles to achieving calm abiding and special insight are removed along the way.

Question: A person cultivating calm abiding through observing emptiness does so by observing a generic image of emptiness. What does this image consist of? What is it like?

Answer: It is difficult to talk about such a generic image, or meaning generality. When people like ourselves hear the word "emptiness," only a sound generality[1] appears to the mind, not a meaning generality. For a person who has done a great deal of hearing about emptiness and has engaged in thinking based on what has been heard, something that accords with emptiness appears to the mind. That which appears to such a person is the meaning generality, or generic image, of emptiness. When one first hears or thinks about emptiness, only a coarse type of thought arises and probably all that appears to the mind is a sound generality. When one gets

[1] *sgra spyi, śabdasāmānya.* In brief, this is a rough image of an object that appears to the mind merely from hearing the name or the description of it.

a little closer to the meaning of emptiness—through thinking about what has been heard, and so forth—one comes closer to the appearance of a generic image of emptiness. A person to whom a meaning generality of emptiness has appeared is necessarily one who has formed an understanding of emptiness. For example, when a meaning generality of a pot appears, an image concordant with a pot appears to the mind. For a meaning generality of emptiness to appear, a person must have engaged in a good deal of thought based on correct reasoning about emptiness, even if he or she has not gone so far as to realize emptiness with valid cognition.[1]

Question: When a person who has achieved calm abiding does analysis on emptiness in dependence on the mental contemplation of individual knowledge of the character and again achieves calm abiding, is that latter calm abiding achieved during the mental contemplation of individual knowledge of the character?

Answer: No, it is not. The calm abiding observing emptiness is not included among the seven mental contemplations. More specifically, it is not individual knowledge of the character because that mental contemplation is a mind of hearing or thinking—of analysis. The calm abiding observing emptiness cannot be any of the higher mental contemplations either, nor is it an actual first concentration.[2]

There is a great difference between achieving calm abiding when one sets the mind in stabilizing meditation after analyzing [with respect to emptiness] by means of the first mental contemplation—that is, after individual knowledge of the character—and the topic of Asaṅga's reference to attaining actual calm abiding based on actual special insight. This latter "actual calm abiding" is a first concentration.

The initial achievement of the first concentration is the first achievement of an object—the joy[3] and bliss[4] of the first concentration—for which one hopes and wishes. That is why Asaṅga mentions that an actual calm abiding is achieved in dependence on an actual special insight.

Question: Does one go through the nine mental abidings in order to achieve imputed calm abiding based on imputed special insight? If so,

---

1 *tshad ma, pramāṇa.*

2 Some Tibetan scholars hold that individual knowledge of the character is not limited to hearing and thinking but does include states arisen from meditation such as calm abiding.

3 *dga' ba, prīti.*

4 *bde ba, sukha.*

what is the difference between this and achieving actual calm abiding based on actual special insight?

Answer: Earlier, we eliminated qualms concerning whether calm abiding or special insight is achieved first. (See pp. 159-164.) It was explained that there are two ways of interpreting Asaṅga's statement in the *Summary of Manifest Knowledge* that calm abiding can be achieved in dependence on special insight. One interpretation is that this refers to attainment of an imputed calm abiding in dependence on an imputed special insight, and the other considers these to be actual.[1] I identified the latter interpretation as referring to a situation in which a meditator achieves calm abiding, then the special insight which is a union of calm abiding and special insight, and after that, works at cultivating a meditative stabilization which is a union of calm abiding and special insight for the sake of attaining the first concentration. The stage of working toward that goal is called special insight, and actual attainment of the first concentration is again calm abiding.

When persons cultivating a mundane path attain the first concentration of a mundane path, the final object sought has been attained. Their hope and wish are fulfilled. Such persons' initial attainment of calm abiding is simultaneous with the attainment of a mind included within the level of an upper realm—here, the Form Realm. Their attainment of the first concentration is by no means a new attainment of calm abiding, but it is a new attainment of a special calm abiding endowed with joy and bliss.

There was also a question in connection with the first of the seven mental contemplations, individual, or thorough, knowledge of the character. This is an entirely different subject and should not be confused with the above discussion. In general, in order to attain special insight one must first attain calm abiding. Also, in order to attain a special insight observing emptiness it is necessary first to attain a calm abiding with respect to emptiness. However, there is the difference that, to attain a calm abiding observing emptiness, it is not necessary to achieve a calm abiding that is pre-

---

[1] "Achieving an imputed calm abiding based on an imputed special insight" refers to the achievement of the ninth mental abiding by means of the type of analytical meditation that is begun at the third mental abiding for the purpose of eliminating a predominant afflictive emotion such as hatred. The imputed calm abiding is the ninth mental abiding, and the imputed special insight is simply the analysis used to overcome hatred, for instance. In the other interpretation as actual rather than imputed, calm abiding observing emptiness is achieved based on the analytical meditation of the first of the seven mental contemplations—individual knowledge of the character.

ceded by the nine mental abidings observing emptiness. The meditator begins this process by attaining calm abiding through observing one of the varieties of conventional phenomena, not emptiness. Then, within the non-deterioration of the calm abiding observing the varieties, she or he engages in the analysis called thorough knowledge of the character. The meditator does this because of not yet having realized emptiness and needing to realize it. At the end of this analysis, the meditator sets the mind in meditative stabilization; at this time, he or she has a calm abiding observing emptiness.

Thus, these are two very different topics. The former has to do with an actual first concentration, whereas the latter refers to an achievement of calm abiding observing emptiness that follows the mental contemplation of thorough knowledge of the character. The achievement of calm abiding observing emptiness as just explained is a case of seeking out the view of emptiness within a meditative state because one has already attained calm abiding. This is different from seeking out calm abiding from within the view. It cannot be included within the mental contemplation of thorough knowledge of the character because it is a state arisen from meditation. Nor is it a case of special insight; thus, it cannot be a case of the second mental contemplation, known as arisen from belief.[1]

Jam-ȳang-shay-b̄a has given a very good explanation of this—namely, that a person who has already achieved calm abiding does not need to progress through the nine mental abidings observing emptiness in order to achieve the calm abiding that takes emptiness as its object of observation. This calm abiding is achieved automatically through the investigation and analysis that takes place during the mental contemplation of thorough knowledge of the character. He does not explicitly state the reasons for this, but we can easily understand them, for, before achieving calm abiding, one must achieve physical and mental pliancy. In order to do that, one must stop all unfavorable physical and mental states which prevent this pliancy. The person engaging in analysis has already achieved calm abiding observing the varieties and, therefore, has already eliminated the situations unfavorable to mind and body. Since the meditator is merely changing the object of observation, it is not necessary to eliminate states or conditions that prevent calm abiding. These are the reasons why it is unnecessary to progress through the nine mental abidings at this time. In addition, it is also unnecessary again to achieve physical and mental pliancy.

---

[1] *mos pa las byung ba, adhimokṣika.*

11 PHYSICAL BASIS

I will now discuss the physical basis[1]—that is, beings who can and cannot achieve calm abiding. Two types of activity are involved: newly cultivating calm abiding and maintaining possession of the calm abiding that has already been achieved. Beings in the hells[2] can do neither of these, nor can hungry ghosts.[3] Demigods[4] are also unable either newly to develop calm abiding or to maintain possession of it. Among humans,[5] those on the northern continent,[6] known as Unpleasant Sound,[7] can neither newly develop calm abiding nor maintain possession of it. Animals[8] cannot do these either. Among gods,[9] some can and some cannot; we will leave them aside for the time being. These are the six types of physical bases that one can have; with five of these, one is unable to engage in either of the two activities relating to calm abiding, and humans on one of the four continents where humans live cannot do these either.

The reason hell beings can neither newly cultivate nor maintain possession of calm abiding is that they are troubled by both physical and mental suffering to such a degree that they have no chance to think of calm abiding. In considering who is able to achieve calm abiding, one must take note of both the physical basis and the type of mind. Hell beings not only have physical suffering but are particularly tormented by mental suffering; their physical suffering is great, but their mental suffering is even greater. Therefore, they have no opportunity to focus the mind on an object of ob-

---

1 *lus rten.*

2 *dmyal ba, naraka.*

3 *yi dvags, preta.*

4 *lha ma yin, asura.*

5 *mi, manuṣya.*

6 *gling, dvīpa.*

7 *sgra mi nyan, kuru.* In this ancient cosmology there is a huge mountain at the center with four continents surrounding it; India, or our world, is the southern continent.

8 *dud 'gro, tiryañc.*

9 *lha, deva.*

servation.

Similarly, hungry ghosts can neither newly attain calm abiding nor maintain possession of it because they are troubled by the sufferings of hunger and thirst. Besides this great suffering, they are tremendously afflicted with jealousy of those who have food and drink. Therefore, they are unable to practice calm abiding; they have both physical and mental suffering in strong force.

Animals are unable to engage in either of the activities involved in calm abiding because, although they do not have as great physical and mental suffering as hungry ghosts, they are so stupid that they have no basis for focusing on objects or for the operation of discriminative wisdom. The faculties of hell beings and hungry ghosts are sharper than those of animals.

Demigods are unable either newly to generate or to maintain possession of calm abiding because their rebirths as demigods are impelled by an action conjoined with a mind of jealousy regarding the wealth and resources of the gods. While they accumulated the karma that caused their rebirth as demigods, they were overcome by jealousy and hatred of the gods and, as a fruition of this, are now continually troubled by the mental suffering of jealousy.

Among the four continents where humans live, there is neither new generation nor maintaining possession of calm abiding on the continent of Unpleasant Sound. This is because, even though the beings there do not have the suffering of physical or mental pain, they do not have any strong force of thought to engage in either virtue or non-virtue. The commentaries on Vasubandhu's *Treasury of Manifest Knowledge* state that such persons are without capacity because they do not have sufficient force of thought to carry anything through.

On the other three continents inhabited by humans, there exist new generation and maintaining possession of calm abiding. Gods are also able to engage in these activities, although among both gods and humans there are exceptions, beings who cannot newly achieve or maintain calm abiding. The main human exceptions are those who are insane, those whose elements are physically disturbed, and beings emanated by another being. Beings of this last type are incapable of deciding to generate calm abiding because they depend on the mind of the emanator. Another exception among humans is someone overpowered by poison; this also probably means someone who is crazy. The difference between the two types of insane or crazy persons is that the first is naturally crazy, whereas the one overpowered by poison is someone whose mind has been affected by certain substances. These are the main cases of the mind's not abiding in a normal state. These people not only cannot generate calm abiding or an actual absorption[1] of a concentration, they also cannot generate a vow of individual liberation,[2] a Bodhisattva vow, or a tantric vow.

Other humans who cannot cultivate calm abiding are those who lack normative maleness[3] or who are neuter[4] or are androgynous;[5] this last means that they change from one gender to another without the intervention of an operation. Neuter beings, like those in the northern continent, are unable to carry anything through to a conclusion. They do not have sufficiently strong force of thought. Androgynous humans, those who have both male and female signs, have the afflictive emotions of both male and female and thus have too many afflictive emotions to be able to generate calm abiding.

It is said that hungry ghosts and demigods have too great a fruitional obstruction to work at calm abiding. This means that the actions, or karmas, that caused such persons to be reborn as hungry ghosts or demigods were such that their mere fruition prevents them from engaging in virtuous activity. Hell beings, of course, have a fruitional obstruction inasmuch as they have been born as hell beings and are undergoing tremendous suffering. The fruition of the action that impels birth as a hungry ghost or demigod causes that very type of mind to be continually manifest, and hungry ghosts and demigods continue to engage in this type of activity even within the awareness that such a non-virtuous mind is manifest.

A difference between hell beings and animals is that even though animals have a fruitional obstruction—the maturation or fruition of the karma that caused them to be born that way—they do not know that this suffering is due to a given action whereas hell beings do.

These are the main types of beings who can neither newly develop calm abiding nor maintain possession of it. A secondary group of those unable

---

1 *dngos gzhi'i snyoms 'jug, maulasamāpatti.*

2 *so sor thar pa, pratimokṣa.*

3 *ma ning, paṇḍaka.* For a very clear and thorough discussion of the term *paṇḍaka,* see Leonard Zwilling, "Homosexuality as Seen in Indian Buddhist Texts," in *Buddhism, Sexuality, and Gender,* edited by José Ignacio Cabezón (Albany: State University of New York Press, 1992), 203-214.

4 *za ma, ṣaṇḍha.*

5 *mtshan gnyis pa, ubhayavyanjaña.*

to engage in these activities are humans or gods at a time of sleeping, fainting, the meditative absorption of cessation,[1] or the meditative equipoise of non-discrimination.[2] For example, there are gods dwelling in areas of non-discrimination. They cannot newly generate that meditative equipoise which would be necessary for taking rebirth in the next lifetime in a higher realm of cyclic existence.

INVESTIGATION OF QUALMS

Now let us consider some objections to what I have just said.

Objection: You say that hell beings cannot newly develop calm abiding. Yet, the *Kāraṇḍavyūha Sūtra*[3] says that there are cases of hell beings who newly saw the truth. "Newly seeing the truth" means that one is achieving the path of seeing, and in order to achieve that path it is necessary to achieve the path of preparation, the sign of which is the attainment of the meditative stabilization which is a union of calm abiding and special insight. Thus, before that path one must have achieved a full-fledged calm abiding.

Answer: Some textbooks of the monastic universities in Tibet give the answer that in the case of "newly seeing the truth" the word "truth" does not refer to the path of seeing but to the generation of the altruistic mind of enlightenment. Indeed, many sūtras say that there are cases of hell beings, hungry ghosts, and nāgas[4] who newly generate the mind of enlightenment during that lifetime and become Bodhisattvas.

Another answer: "Seeing the truth" really does mean achieving the path of seeing, and the moment such a person attains the path of seeing, she or he ceases to be a hungry ghost or a hell being.

Objection: How could one be able to newly generate the altruistic mind of enlightenment and yet be unable to generate calm abiding?

Answer: In order to generate calm abiding, one must be able—from the viewpoint of both the physical basis and the type of mind—to analyze objects of observation, subjective aspects,[5] and so forth. Although texts sometimes say that one can have special insight before achieving calm

---

1 *'gog pa'i snyoms 'jug, nirodhasamāpatti.*

2 *'du shes me pa, asaṃjñā.*

3 *'phags pa za ma rtog bkod pa zhes bya ba theg pa chen po'i mdo, āryakāraṇḍavyūhanāma-mahāyānasūtra;* P784, vol. 30.

4 *klu.*

5 *rnam pa, ākāra.*

abiding, this does not refer to actual special insight but only to the analytical faculty of searching out an object. One must have not only an interest in the object but also a strong factor of wisdom[1] with respect to it. This latter is the wisdom analyzing the object. With regard to the altruistic mind of enlightenment, it is sufficient to have great faithful interest and aspiration. Although one does not engage in a great deal of analysis during the cultivation of calm abiding, being told about an object by someone else is not sufficient to cause that object to appear to your own mind; you yourself must investigate it carefully. For the generation of an altruistic mind of enlightenment, however, it is enough to be told that there is such a thing as Buddhahood, and if you come to believe this and can thereby generate great effort, the altruistic mind of enlightenment can be attained. As Asaṅga says, a stage of something called special insight precedes the process of developing calm abiding. This is not really special insight, but it involves the minds of hearing and thinking that research an object.

A spiritual guide can identify what the object should be, but that is not sufficient. One must engage in hearing, thinking, reading texts, and so forth, in order to figure out what the object is. Having researched the object, one is said to find, or gain, the object, and then it is taken as the continual basis. One settles on just that object with stabilizing meditation, no longer engaging in analytical meditation. After calm abiding is achieved, one works at achieving actual special insight.

In the case of the altruistic mind of enlightenment, it is sufficient to gain belief in the existence of Buddhahood which is the perfection of one's own and others' welfare and on the basis of that to engage in great effort for the sake of generating the mind of enlightenment. Of course, it is all the better if one also engages in analysis. When non-artificial, spontaneous experience arises regarding the wish to attain highest enlightenment for the sake of all sentient beings, the altruistic mind has been generated. "Non-artificial experience" means that the strength of one's altruistic aspiration to enlightenment is as strong during any of the four types of behavior—walking about, sitting down, lying down, and eating—as it is during an actual strong session of meditation; the experience is equally strong both in and out of meditation.

DISCUSSION

Question: I had the impression that hungry ghosts could see only other

---

[1] *shes rab, prajñā.*

hungry ghosts, but the fact that they are said to have jealousy for those with food and drink seems to indicate that they can see other types of beings.

Answer: Hungry ghosts have the sharpest faculties of beings who cannot generate calm abiding; thus, they not only see others' resources but, because of their own karma, also know about what others have.

Question: It was said that one cannot develop calm abiding from within the meditative absorption of cessation or that of non-discrimination. Might one have attained calm abiding before achieving either of those states?

Answer: Whether one is talking about achieving a meditative absorption as a human or about a god who is born into that area, there indeed is no need to newly generate calm abiding. What I meant, however, was that such persons cannot begin to cultivate the new meditative stabilizations that are needed in order to be reborn into a higher state.

Question: Would people who take marijuana, and so forth, be included among those who are crazy because of a poison?

Answer: Yes. There are grasses such as the *da-du-ra*,[1] but there are also drugs that can be manufactured [according to the Tibetan system]. These would prevent cultivation of calm abiding. They cause temporary interference; when their force is dispelled, the interference is no longer there.

Question: What is the difference in afflictive emotions possessed by male and female?

Answer: In general, we refer to the three poisons, the six root afflictive emotions,[2] and the twenty secondary afflictive emotions.[3] Both males and females have all these. The male and female afflictive emotions that I was referring to are the desire each has for the other. Males have an attraction to females, and females, to males. A person who had both types of desire would have a great deal. There are cases of such people.

Nowadays a fetus is photographed in order to discover whether it is male or female. In the past there were no such devices, but people could tell the child's gender by its position in the womb. If it was to be born as a

---

[1] *da du ra.* In Tibetan this is *thang phrom*, which is also spelled *thang khrom*. The latter is identified as *dhūstūra* (thorn-apple) in Sarat Chandra Das's *Tibetan-English Dictionary*, 568. Thanks to Professor Guy Newland for the note.

[2] *rtsa nyon, mūlakleśa.*

[3] *nye ba'i nyon mongs, upakleśa.*

male, its position in the womb would be that of having desire for the mother; if as a female, it would be in a position of desire for the father—that is, facing outward. A mother knows which way the child faces and thus can tell its sex. This difference in position is due to the mode of entry to the womb.

There are two types of knowledge of this type of topic, that based on clairvoyance[1] and that based on reasoning.[2] Most of these matters can be determined through reasoning. Error seldom occurs because of the reasoning process, but it sometimes occurs in clairvoyance. For example, Asaṅga and his brother, Vasubandhu, were once invited to a family's home to predict what type of calf was about to be born to one of their cows. Asaṅga, relying on the clairvoyance for which he was famous, answered that a calf with a white tail would be born. Vasubandhu, who gave an answer based on reasoning, said that the calf would have either a white tail or a white mark on its forehead. Soon afterward, the calf was born with a white spot in its forehead. When a calf is in the womb, its tail is curled around so that the tip touches the center of its forehead. Asaṅga directly perceived the white spot there. Vasubandhu, who was very skilled in the knowledge of phenomena, knew how calves were positioned in the womb and thus realized that the white spot Asaṅga referred to could be either on the tip of the tail or on the forehead. Thus, reasoned knowledge is very important. We consider the coming to decisions based on textual sources to be of great significance.

Question: With regard to eunuchs, neuter, and androgynous humans who cannot attain calm abiding, if someone has already attained calm abiding and then through accident or illness falls into one of these categories, would that person lose her or his attainment or would he or she be able to hold on to it by using what has already been understood?

Answer: There is no definiteness that the person's calm abiding will deteriorate. However, if the accident is very strong, it will deteriorate.

Question: We know that the gods of no discrimination cannot cultivate calm abiding. Other than these, which gods can and cannot cultivate calm abiding?

Answer: There are very few gods of the Desire Realm who can cultivate calm abiding. The six types of Desire Realm gods can be included in the

---

1 *mngon shes, abhijñā.*

2 *rigs pa, yukti.*

two, those who depend on the earth and those who do not. I think that the gods who depend on the earth can cultivate calm abiding and that the others, who are in the sky, cannot, for one cannot do this without seeing the faults of the Desire Realm.

Question: What type of meditation did the gods of no discrimination cultivate in order to be reborn as such?

Answer: Such persons are concerned with overcoming coarse states of mind and, on the basis of that, achieve a meditative absorption.[1] They mistake the factor which is pacification of coarse minds for liberation; thus, they view the meditative absorption of non-discrimination as being a path to liberation and see birth in that level as liberation. That is the main cause for birth as a god of no discrimination.[2] Such persons must also achieve an absorption which is a concentration.

Question: How does the meditative absorption of non-discrimination differ from the formless absorption of nothingness?[3]

Answer: There is a great difference. In the level of Nothingness, there is no appearance of form,[4] and one does not have the mistaken discrimination that the meditative absorption of non-discrimination is a path to liberation and that birth at that level is liberation.

---

[1] *snyoms 'jug, samāpati.*

[2] *'du shes med pa'i sems can, asaṃjñisattva.*

[3] *ci yang med, ākiṃcanya.*

[4] *gzugs, rūpa.*

12 MENTAL BASES

The great texts have two ways of setting forth the mental basis[1] of calm abiding. One is simply to present it, and the other is first to explain two other meanings of basis that would be inappropriate in the context of the mental basis of calm abiding and then to give the appropriate meaning. I will use the latter method.

In general, bases, or supports, can be divided into two types, those prior to that which they support[2] and those simultaneous with it.[3] Prior bases [literally, "bases involved in an earlier-and-later sequence"] can be explained in relation to the sense consciousnesses and the mental consciousness. I will take one type of sense consciousness as an example. An eye consciousness has three bases which are its causes. In relation to an eye consciousness that apprehends form, these three are (1) the uncommon proprietary condition[4]—the eye sense power;[5] (2) the immediately preceding condition[6]—the immediately preceding moment of consciousness that ceases just before the first moment of an eye consciousness; (3) the observed-object condition[7]—the form which is the object of that eye consciousness. The support, or basis, of calm abiding is not like any of these three types of prior basis.

What are the prior supports of a mental consciousness? In terms of a mental consciousness that knows a pot, the pot itself is the observed-object condition. The mind that induces the conceptual consciousness is its immediately preceding condition. A conceptual consciousness that knows a pot arises in dependence on a prior basis, whether this be the term "pot" or a memory of a pot.

---

1 *sems rten.*

2 *snga phyi ba'i rten.*

3 *dus mnyam pa'i rten.*

4 *thun mong ma yin pa'i bdag rkyen, asadhāraṇādhipatipratyaya.*

5 *mig gi dbang po, cakṣurindriya.*

6 *de ma thag rkyen, samānantarapratyaya.*

7 *dmigs rkyen, ālaṃbanapratyaya.*

In both of the examples above, the basis, or support, is involved in a temporal sequence; it precedes that which arises in dependence on it, and the two have a cause-and-effect relationship. The basis of calm abiding, however, is not like either of these.

A basis can also be simultaneous within being a different entity from the supported,[1] like a table and a book. If I place this book on the table, the table acts as a basis of the book. They are simultaneous, but they are different entities. The basis of calm abiding is also not like this. Both this and the prior bases mentioned above are brought up for the sake of clarifying what the basis of calm abiding is not; it is not like the prior or the simultaneous bases, both of which involve support and supported being two separate entities. These types of basis are objects to be negated in the course of finding out what the mental basis of calm abiding is.

What is the mental basis of calm abiding? It is of the same entity as calm abiding itself. When one cultivates the nine mental abidings that precede calm abiding, these nine are all minds included within the Desire Realm. When, however, after achieving these nine, one attains calm abiding, one has attained a mind that is included within an upper realm. The upper realms are the Form Realm and the Formless Realm.

This mind is of the same entity as calm abiding. The mind included within an upper realm is itself calm abiding, and calm abiding is a mind included within an upper realm.

To give another example, if one takes as one's mental support a meditative equipoise which is an actual concentration and on the basis of this cultivates the path of preparation, at first the actual concentration and the path of preparation are different. However, when, within the mind of an actual concentration, one attains the path of preparation, then the concentration and the path of preparation are of one entity. The mind of the actual concentration becomes of the entity of the mind of the path of preparation. At this point, the two cannot be separated; the one is the other. It is important that this should appear to your minds well.

There is also an example given in the texts. When a piece of iron is placed in fire, the iron becomes red hot; at that point, it is impossible to distinguish or separate the iron from the fire. However, when the iron has just been placed in the fire and is just becoming red, the two can be separated. The texts do not spell out how this example applies to the exemplified, but it is easy to understand. The fire is like the meditative equipoise

[1] *brten pa.*

which is an actual concentration, and the iron is like the path of preparation. If one takes an actual first concentration as one's basis and cultivates the path of preparation, when the path of preparation is attained the mental basis becomes the path of preparation just as the iron takes on the nature of fire.

We are beings of the Desire Realm, and thus our minds are also included within Desire Realm minds. If we cultivate great compassion, our own minds are the basis for great compassion. By contemplating countless sentient beings and meditating to develop great compassion, one eventually achieves great compassion. At that point, the mental basis—one's own mind—has become of the entity of great compassion. There is no distinguishing the two at that time. Meditating on great compassion does not mean taking compassion as an object and looking at it; it means taking sentient beings as one's object and developing compassion for them such that the mind comes to be of the nature of great compassion.

The texts frequently speak of different mental bases: the basis for calm abiding, the basis for meditative absorption, the basis for achieving a path. The way of understanding all of these is the same. You may wonder whether, when one cultivates a certain path, the mind becomes of the entity of that path. It is important to understand this question because that is, in fact, what occurs when one cultivates calm abiding. The mental basis becomes of the nature of calm abiding. Therefore, we can ask whether it is the case that when one cultivates any of the paths, such as the path of seeing and the path of meditation, or the altruistic aspiration to enlightenment, the mental basis and the thing meditated on come to be one in entity. If the mind does not become of the entity of a path, and so forth, then how is that path produced? For example, when we speak of a Bodhisattva Superior meditating on emptiness, we do not mean that the Bodhisattva Superior's mind becomes of the entity of emptiness; emptiness here is indicated as the apprehended object.[1] However, when we speak of meditating on compassion and love, we mean that the mind becomes of the entity of these; meditating on love means taking sentient beings as the object and then developing experience with regard to them, thereby generating the mind into the entity of love.

When someone on the Mahāyāna path of accumulation cultivates the meditative stabilization of a first-ground Bodhisattva, she or he neither takes this path as the object nor generates his or her mind into the entity

[1] *bzung yul, grāhyaviṣaya.*

of that path. Rather, he or she cultivates a subjective aspect which is an aspect of that meditative stabilization. The Bodhisattva on the path of accumulation comes to understand well the entity, subjective aspect, object of observation, and so forth, of the concentrations of a first-ground Bodhisattva—for instance, the going-as-a-hero meditative stabilization[1]—and becomes very familiar with what that state is like and makes an aspiration to be able to generate it in her or his own mind. This process is known as generating a similitude of that concentration. There is no other way for such a person to meditate on a state that has not yet been achieved. It cannot be taken as an object of observation, nor can the mind of a Bodhisattva on the path of accumulation be generated into the entity of a first-ground Bodhisattva's concentration, for the ability to do so has not yet been developed. Thus, what is cultivated is a similitude of that meditative stabilization.

Similarly, you might ask how common beings—those on the Mahāyāna paths of accumulation or preparation, for example—meditate on the three exalted knowers,[2] these being the exalted knower of all aspects,[3] the knower of paths,[4] and the knower of bases.[5] They cannot do it by way of taking the three exalted knowers as their apprehended object until they actually attain these knowers at the time of becoming Superiors, nor can they generate their minds into the entity of these exalted knowers. They cultivate the three exalted knowers by meditating on that which has a similar type of realization. For example, the exalted knower of bases is of the same type of realization as direct realization of the selflessness of persons.[6] Thus, persons on the path of accumulation can take as their object a mind that exists in their own mental continuums—namely, their own [conceptual] realization of the selflessness of persons. Through meditating on this, they achieve the first moment of a continuum which later turns into the fruit of an actual exalted knower of bases. Similarly, by meditating with their own [conceptual] realization of emptiness as an object, they set in motion a continuum that will later become an exalted knower of paths and an exalted knower of all aspects. This last is a direct perception of the

---

[1] *dpa' bar 'gro ba zhes bya ba'i ting nge 'dzin, śūraṃgamo nāma samādhi.*

[2] *mkhyen pa, jñāta.*

[3] *rnam pa thams cad mkhyen pa nyid, sarvākārajñatā.*

[4] *lam shes, mārgajñatā.*

[5] *gzhi shes, vastujñatā.*

[6] *gang zag gi bdag med, pudgalanairātmya.*

aspects of all phenomena and occurs only at Buddhahood.

In the continuum of a Buddha are inconceivable secret qualities. Only other Buddhas can understand them; even Bodhisattva Superiors cannot perceive them directly. How, then, can one meditate on these inconceivable hidden qualities? One can cultivate these through aspirational prayer.[1] Within an understanding of the characteristics and types of these special qualities, one makes an aspiration to achieve them quickly.

We can speak of four types of beings. The highest are Superiors, those who have attained at least the path of seeing. Next are common beings who have attained the paths of accumulation or preparation. Third are ordinary beings who know something about the paths but have not achieved any. Finally, there are commonplace ordinary beings who do not even know anything about the paths.

How would ordinary beings meditate on the eight categories[2]—the three exalted knowers, the four trainings,[3] and the fruit,[4] the Wisdom Truth Body[5] of a Buddha? Such persons can meditate on these by examining their definitions, characteristics, boundaries, and the means of attaining them. Even though one has not attained special insight, one can analyze these eight by means of a similitude of special insight. In this way one is able to meditate on the eight categories.

DISCUSSION

Question: In descriptions of the direct cognition of emptiness, it is said that emptiness and the mind cognizing it are like water poured into water. How is this different from the mind's becoming of the entity of emptiness?

Answer: When one speaks of the Mahāyāna path of seeing as being like water poured into water, it is not meant that the subject is generated into the entity of the object. Rather, it indicates that once the uninterrupted path is attained, all conventional appearances disappear for this mind. Only emptiness appears, and thus it is said that the mind and emptiness are of one taste. Before this time, the mind's object is only a mental image[6] of emptiness. This image exists between subject and object and, therefore, subject and object seem to be different. When the uninterrupted path of

[1] *smon lam, praṇidhāna.*

[2] *dngos po brgyad, aṣṭau padārthāḥ.*

[3] *sbyor ba, prayoga.*

[4] *'bras bu, phala.*

[5] *ye shes chos sku, jñānadharmakāya.*

[6] Or, meaning-generality (*don spyi, arthasāmānya*).

the path of seeing is attained, only actual emptiness appears; thus, there is no longer a distinction between subject and object.

Question: Why is it that compassion and the three exalted knowers, cannot be taken as objects of observation in meditation?

Answer: Once something is the object of the mode of apprehension, it is necessarily "over there" in front of you and, therefore, different from your own mind. For example, to set compassion up as an object of reflection and then to consider its qualities, and so forth, is a case of investigating compassion. It is not meditation of compassion [that is, meditative cultivation of compassion], for this involves generating one's own mind as compassion.

Question: It was said that all conventional appearances disappear when one attains the uninterrupted path of the path of seeing. After this, however, at the time of the wisdom subsequent to meditative equipoise,[1] do conventional appearances again appear?

Answer: All conventional phenomena will again appear after you rise from meditation. However, there is a great difference in the way they appear to people like ourselves and to people who have actually cognized emptiness. The phenomena that appear are the same, but the way they appear is different. A person who has directly realized emptiness has a subsequent realization of phenomena as illusory. There are two types of emptiness being spoken of here. One is the emptiness of the space-like meditative equipoise; the other is the emptiness of the subsequent realization, which is like an illusion. The second is not an actual emptiness but is given that name.

During meditative equipoise directly realizing emptiness, only the non-affirming negative[2] which is a mere vacuity appears. When one rises after having attained the uninterrupted path and path of release of the path of seeing:, one has what is known as a subsequent realization.[3] At that time, whatever appears is perceived as being like an illusion. This is because the subsequent realization is conjoined with the previous realization of emptiness, and thus all phenomena are seen as qualified by emptiness.

1 *rjes thob ye shes, pṛṣṭhalabdhajñāna.*

2 *med dgag, prasajyapratiṣedha.*

3 *rjes thob, pṛṣṭhalabdha.*

13 MORE TYPES OF OBJECTS OF OBSERVATION

PERVASIVE OBJECTS OF OBSERVATION

The first of the general categories, pervasive objects of observation, has four subdivisions:

1 non-analytical image[1]
2 analytical image[2]
3 observing the limits of phenomena[3]
4 thorough achievement of the purpose.[4]

Regarding the order of these, there is a system explaining the second, the analytical image, first, and the non-analytical image second. The order above, however, is given in Kamalashīla's *Stages of Meditation.*

The names of the first two, non-analytical and analytical image, are posited from the viewpoint of the subject. The names of the last two, observing the limits of phenomena and thorough achievement of the purpose, are posited from the viewpoint of the object.

NON-ANALYTICAL AND ANALYTICAL IMAGE

By conceptual[5] and non-conceptual,[6] we generally mean, for instance, the non-conceptuality of the non-conceptual exalted wisdom of meditative equipoise. Although the [Tibetan and Sanskrit] words are the same in both cases, the meaning is not. Non-conceptuality, or non-analysis, is so called

---

1 *rnam par mi rtog pa'i gzugs brnyan, nirvikalpakapratibimba.*

2 *rnam par rtog pa dang bcas pa'i gzugs brnyan, savikalpakapratibimba.*

3 *dngos po'i mtha' la dmigs pa, vastvantālaṃbana.*

4 *dgos pa yongs su grub pa, kṛtyānuṣṭāna.*

5 *rnam par rtog pa, savikalpaka.* The word *rtog pa,* which is most often translated as "conceptual," is being translated as "analytical" in the names of the two images to convey the specific meaning intended in this context.

6 *rnam par mi rtog pa, nirvikalpaka.*

[in this context] because it does not analyze the mode[1] of phenomena—their nature[2] or emptiness—but, rather, is a type of calm abiding that takes as its object of observation the varieties[3]—that is, conventional phenomena—without analyzing their nature. Thus, it is important to be very clear that "non-analytical" [in the term "non-analytical image"] specifically refers to the fact that one is not analyzing or investigating the mode [of being] of phenomena, their emptiness. This explanation accords with Kamalashīla's *Stages of Meditation*, although other explanations exist.

This first of the pervasive objects of observation is also described as observation of the sign[4] of a reflection,[5] or image. The meaning in this context is the same. The object itself is said to be an image because the varieties of objects are not observed nakedly but are perceived by means of an image. Dharmakīrti's *Commentary on (Dignāga's) "Compilation of [Teachings on] Valid Cognition"* specifically refers to this type of object as a generic image, but the higher systems do not use this term here. According to Dharmakīrti's text, the image involved with a conceptual consciousness is a generic image which that consciousness takes as its object. This generic image is said to be related to the actual object to which it corresponds.

When one begins to cultivate calm abiding, one has no direct perception of the object but is working with conceptuality in that an image of the actual thing is taken as the object of observation. This consciousness does not perceive objects nakedly; it operates by way of an image. In the *Sūtra Unraveling the Thought* and in Asaṅga's *Grounds of Hearers*, there is an explanation of this image as being a likeness of that object.

The second of the four types of pervasive object of observation is an analytical image. According to Kamalashīla's *Stages of Meditation*, this is a case of special insight. It receives the name "analytical image" because it involves special insight taking to mind (or analyzing) the nature of phenomena. Since the nature of phenomena is being analyzed, this is said to be an analytical image.

Both of these objects of observation are discussed from the viewpoint of the subject, the viewing consciousness. The first, a non-analytical image, is posited according to how calm abiding observes phenomena; the second is

---

1 *ji lta ba.*

2 *rang bzhin, svābhāva.*

3 *ji snyed pa.*

4 *mtshan ma, nimitta.*

5 *gzugs brnyan, pratibimba.*

posited according to how special insight observes its object. Calm abiding is non-analytical in the sense that it does not analyze the mode, or final nature, of phenomena. Since special insight analyzes the mode, the second type is analytical.

Question: The first type has to do with how calm abiding observes phenomena?

Answer: Yes. Its objects of observation are always the varieties, not the mode. It does not matter which of the varieties (that is, which conventional phenomenon) is its object—you could be meditating on the unpleasant, on love, and so forth.

Question: Does "calm abiding" here mean full-fledged calm abiding?

Answer: Yes. Remember that all four here are called pervasive objects of observation. This category includes all objects of observation—all the varieties. Which varieties of objects should be meditated upon—the unpleasant, and so forth—is ascertained in accordance with the meditator's needs.

Question: Would the body of a Buddha be an example of the first type of pervasive object of observation and would the sevenfold reasoning [establishing the selflessness of persons[1]] necessarily be indicated by the second type?

Answer: The body of a Buddha would be included among objects of the first type. Since the reference here is to a general type of calm abiding, meditation on the body of a Buddha, on love, on the unpleasant, and so forth, are all suitable to be included. There is no definiteness as to what the actual object of observation might be. Similarly, the second type of pervasive object of observation refers to special insight in general. Since the sevenfold reasoning relates to a specific type of special insight, there is no definiteness that it would be indicated as the second type of pervasive object of observation.

According to the order of the four pervasive objects of observation given in Asaṅga's *Grounds of Hearers* and the *Sūtra Unraveling the Thought,* the second type—analytical, image—is put first. The meaning there is also a little different from what has been explained so far. Nevertheless, there is no contradiction. According to these texts, the name "non-analytical" is given because, for the most part, calm abiding involves stabilizing meditation, not analytical meditation. Asaṅga's text and the *Sūtra Unraveling the*

---

[1] See Hopkins, *Meditation on Emptiness,* 48-51, 176-92, 687-97.

Thought do not classify the first two types of pervasive object of observation by making a division of phenomena into the mode and the varieties, or into ultimate and conventional truths.[1] Rather, they say that because calm abiding is mainly a case of stabilizing meditation, it is non-analytical, and because special insight is mainly a case of analytical meditation, it is analytical. These two ways of interpreting the categories are not contradictory. They are based on different reasons, for there are different things to be understood in relation to Kamalashīla's and Asaṅga's presentations.

The reason Kamalashīla's presentation makes the first type—the non-analytical image—a case of taking one of the varieties of conventional phenomena as the object of observation and the second—the analytical image—a case of taking to mind the mode of phenomena is that ordinary beings who are beginners at meditation must achieve calm abiding first and then special insight. There is almost no case of a beginner taking the mode [of being] of phenomena as the object of observation in developing calm abiding, although it could happen. A person who has attained calm abiding can then take the mode of phenomena as an object of observation and, in dependence on that, generate special insight. This is why Kamalashīla's *Stages of Meditation* distinguishes between non-analytical and analytical in this way.

Asaṅga's *Grounds of Hearers* and the *Sūtra Unraveling the Thought* set forth the first two pervasive objects of observation on the basis of a division into analytical and stabilizing meditation without making a division into the mode and the varieties. Whether one is observing the mode or the varieties, as a beginner one first mainly practices stabilizing meditation and then, once calm abiding has been achieved, cultivates analytical meditation and thereby achieves special insight.

Question: Would the seven cause-and-effect quintessential instructions[2] for generating the altruistic mind of enlightenment be included within the category of the non-analytical image?

Answer: Yes. However, if you are mainly doing this meditation by way of analytical meditation, using reasons, and so forth, then, since this is not primarily a stabilizing meditation, it would be included within the category of analytical images. It is important to bear in mind that, according to Kamalashīla, "analytical image" refers only to observation of the mode or nature of phenomena. In Asaṅga's system, the analyzed image can be

[1] *don dam bden pa, paramārthasatya; kun rdzob bden pa, saṃvṛtisatya.*

[2] *rgyu 'bras man ngag bdun.*

any object—either the mode or the varieties of conventional phenomena—as long as it is an object of observation of analytical as opposed to stabilizing meditation. Thus, in Asaṅga's system, since the seven cause-and-effect quintessential instructions are mainly involved with analytical meditation, they would be included among analytical images.

Thus, it is important to be aware of what meaning is being given to the terms "analytical image" and "non-analytical image"—to know whose system is being applied. Sometimes, as with Kamalashīla, non-analytical refers only to taking the mode, emptiness, to mind; in Asaṅga's system, it refers to any object that is observed in analytical or investigative meditation.

OBSERVING THE LIMITS OF PHENOMENA

The third type of pervasive object of observation is called observing the limits of phenomena. This can be posited from the viewpoint of either the object or the subject. What would the limits of phenomena signify from the viewpoint of the object? The impermanence of sound[1] is not a limit of phenomena. The limit of phenomena is their not existing from their own side, which is the mode of subsistence[2] of all phenomena whatsoever. According to Prāsaṅgika tenets, this is the limit of phenomena.

If the limit of phenomena is posited from the viewpoint of the subject, one is said to be observing the limit of phenomena only when emptiness is nakedly observed. Until that time, even if emptiness is one's object of observation, the limit of phenomena is not seen. Thus, if observing the limits of phenomena is understood as an object, it means observation of the final or ultimate mode of being[3] of some phenomenon. If taken from the viewpoint of the subject, it means nakedly observing that nature. For this reason, the *path* of observing the limits of phenomena is simultaneous with attainment of the first Bodhisattva ground. This is the point at which there is no generic image intervening between the consciousness and its object of observation, emptiness, and thus the nature of phenomena is observed nakedly.

What are the boundaries of observing the limits of phenomena according to Kamalashīla's *Stages of Meditation?* A very important term relevant to this is *khong du chud pa*—to internalize or realize. Kamalashīla uses this term, as do the Indian texts in general. "Internalizing enlightenment"

---

[1] *sgra mi rtag pa.*

[2] *gnas lugs.*

[3] *yin lugs.*

means either the attainment of enlightenment or the attainment of direct realization.[1] Thus, it has two meanings: to attain and to realize directly. Therefore, from the viewpoint of the object, it is necessary to internalize the path of observing the limits of phenomena. It is because such internalization involves direct perception of emptiness that Kamalashīla asserts the path of observing the limits of phenomena to be simultaneous with attaining the first Bodhisattva ground.

DISCUSSION

Question: Is the third pervasive object of observation, observing the limits of phenomena, being equated with attainment of the path of seeing?

Answer: For one who is definite in the Mahāyāna lineage, attainment of this path is equated with attainment of the first Bodhisattva ground and, therefore, with the path of seeing. There is an explanation of how these four pervasive objects of observation are used in the context of achieving the five Mahāyāna paths in dependence on calm abiding and special insight. That type of explanation belongs to the style of teaching known as instruction from experience.[2] What I have been explaining on the basis of various texts is known in Tibet as textual instruction.[3] This is a matter of explaining how things are set forth in the texts without relating them to the way in which one progresses along the stages of the path. Instruction from experience is done in the context of the teacher's own meditative experience; the yogi gives instruction on the basis of what appears to his or her mind through their own practice and experience of calm abiding or special insight. There is also a third type of instruction known as practical instruction,[4] in which the teacher does not just state a presentation as it is given in the texts but sets it out so that it can be practiced. This type of instruction is done especially for the sake of the practice of the paths. Another type of instruction is known as bare or naked instruction.[5] Here the words of a text are explained in terms of what they actually refer to, not merely in terms of their literal meaning.

Question: Would the third of the pervasive objects of observation, observing the limits of phenomena, necessarily be related to a supramundane

[1] *mngon sum du rtogs pa thob pa.*

[2] *myong khrid.*

[3] *gzhung bshad.*

[4] *nyams khrid.*

[5] *dmar khrid.*

path? Would the first two pervasive objects of observation as presented by Kamalashīla also necessarily be supramundane?

Answer: Not necessarily. The non-analytical image can be related to the path of accumulation. The second—the analytical image—can be put with the path of preparation. Neither of these two paths—which are, respectively, the first and second of the five Mahāyāna paths—is [necessarily] supramundane. The third pervasive object of observation is related to the paths of seeing and meditation, the third and fourth Mahāyāna paths. The fourth type of pervasive object of observation, thorough achievement of purpose, can be put with the fifth Mahāyāna path, that of no more learning—the path of a Buddha.

Question: Does this mean that the first two types of pervasive object of observation can also be observed on a mundane path[1] of meditation?

Answer: Yes.

Question: Why are these called pervasive objects of observation?

Answer: Because all objects are included among them (see p. 42). For example, the first type includes all varieties of conventional phenomena—meditation on love, on the unpleasant, on the sevenfold reasoning, and so forth. The last three types of pervasive object of observation involve emptiness; emptiness is also classified as an object of observation for purifying afflictive emotions. In general, therefore, all objects of observation are included among what we call pervasive objects of observation.

Question: Is there no contradiction in calling the latter two, which are objects of observation of a supramundane path, objects of observation for the development of calm abiding? There appears to be a contradiction because calm abiding has already been attained by the time one reaches a supramundane path.

Answer: This would be the case if you considered them in terms of their order and their relation to the five paths, but they need not be considered like that. This is not a laying out of a mode of progress by one individual; it is not the case that the same person attains the first, then the second, and so forth, and attains calm abiding only after completing the fourth. Rather, these are four types of objects of observation that four different people might take up at a time when they have not yet achieved calm abiding or special insight. For example, persons who have already attained

---

[1] *'jig rten pa'i lam, laukikamārga.*

the first Bodhisattva ground will have the third object of observation, observing the limits of phenomena, in their continuums. Persons who have attained the path of preparation will have an analytical image in their continuums. Such persons do not need to go back and work with a non-analytical image because they have already attained calm abiding. The application of these four objects of observation to the Mahāyāna paths should not be confused with the way in which they are set out as a classification of objects of observation by which calm abiding can be achieved.

For example, when one attains the path of observing the limits of phenomena, one also attains the first Bodhisattva ground. A person on the first Bodhisattva ground has already achieved calm abiding; however, it is suitable for [a beginner] to take the observation of the limits of phenomena as an object of observation for generating calm abiding at a time when calm abiding has not yet been attained. It can be used as an object of observation for cultivating calm abiding.

Question: I do not understand how emptiness can be an object of observation in the development of calm abiding, since it is a slightly hidden phenomenon[1] and an object of analytical meditation.

Answer: There is no definiteness concerning whether emptiness is an object of analytical meditation. People who generate calm abiding using emptiness as their object of observation are extremely rare; most achieve calm abiding through taking one of the varieties of conventional phenomena as an object of observation and will turn to emptiness and use analysis after calm abiding has been achieved. However, it is possible for those with sharp faculties and those with high realization to cultivate calm abiding by taking emptiness as their object of observation initially.

Most people who try to use emptiness as an object of observation in developing calm abiding encounter two difficulties, one in relation to the object and one in relation to the subject. From the viewpoint of the object, because emptiness is profound and difficult to understand, most people lose the factor of stability[2] of mind when they think about or contemplate it, and if they do not think about it, what they are doing cannot be called meditation. From the viewpoint of the subject, it is difficult for a person who is initially training in calm abiding to calm down and stop discursiveness. Therefore, most texts set forth the development of calm abiding through using one of the varieties of conventional phenomena as the ob-

[1] *cung zad lkog gyur.*

[2] *gnas cha.*

ject of observation. Once calm abiding is achieved, emptiness is taken as the object of observation in cultivating special insight.[1]

Most people start with some [easier] conventional object of observation when they first develop calm abiding and then change to another when they are working on special insight. There are, however, people who achieve calm abiding with emptiness as their object of observation and then, staying with that same object of observation, achieve special insight. Such persons are called "those whose special insight is best among all."

THOROUGH ACHIEVEMENT OF THE PURPOSE

The fourth pervasive object of observation, thorough achievement of the purpose, is actually a Buddha's Nature Body.[2] Therefore, those who actually possess this in their continuums are Buddhas. "The *path* of thoroughly achieving the purpose" refers to something which exists only in the continuum of a Buddha Superior.[3] All the same, it is possible to take a Buddha's Nature Body as an object of observation in order to cultivate and achieve calm abiding. As an object of observation, thorough achievement of the purpose can be used in the development of both calm abiding and special insight.

The fourth of the pervasive objects of observation, thorough achievement of the purpose, is not a temporary purpose but the ultimate one; the final purpose of generating the paths and the grounds is to attain Buddhahood. The object observed when the purpose has been achieved is a Buddha's Nature Body; the one who is achieving this purpose is a first- through tenth-ground Bodhisattva, and one who has actually achieved the purpose is a Buddha.

Someone whose continuum is different from a given Buddha's can observe that Buddha's Nature Body. In dependence on observing it, such a person can attain calm abiding, special insight, and the first Bodhisattva ground. Therefore, it is necessary to distinguish when "thorough achievement of the purpose" refers to something that one has in her or his own continuum and when it refers to observing what exists in another's continuum. There are people who attain the first Bodhisattva ground and Buddhahood through observing the Nature Body of a Buddha's continuum. A person who has generated the path observing the limits of phenomena in his or her own continuum is a first-ground Bodhisattva; such a

---

[1] See Hopkins, *Meditation on Emptiness,* 70-71.

[2] *ngo bo nyid sku, svabhāvikakāya.*

[3] *sangs rgyas 'phags pa.*

person can take a Nature Body as an object of observation and thereby achieve Buddhahood. One should think carefully about the distinction between an object of observation in one's own or in another's continuum and about the fact that there are objects of observation included in the varieties of conventional phenomena as well as in the mode of phenomena, their emptiness.

DISCUSSION

Question: Is it possible for someone who has not achieved the first Bodhisattva ground to take the Nature Body as an object of observation?

Answer: Yes, it is possible. Even someone who has not entered any path can take it as an object of observation. One can also take observing the limits of phenomena as an object of observation before entering the path, but it is not said that one has generated the path of observing the limits of phenomena until one achieves the path of seeing and, simultaneously, the first Bodhisattva ground. Similarly, one can begin to achieve thorough achievement of the purpose even before entering the path, but a person who has thoroughly achieved the purpose is a Buddha.

Question: What is the difference between the middle two pervasive objects of observation—the analytical image and observing the limits of phenomena. It would seem that both are observing the mode of phenomena; is there a difference in what is appearing to the mind?

Answer: The object of observation is emptiness in both cases, but there is a difference in how it appears to the mind. In talking about a path observing the limits of phenomena we are referring to the clear appearance[1] of emptiness. This means there is direct perception in which there is no generic image between subject and object.

When observing an analytical image, one has overcome the coarse type of generic image, but a subtle type remains. At this point, one is on the path of preparation and has achieved a union of calm abiding and special insight; a subtle appearance of duality is still present. This is, however, a realization arisen from meditation, a high state of mind.

OBJECTS OF OBSERVATION FOR DEVELOPING SKILL

AGGREGATES

Objects of observation for [developing] skill[2] are objects with respect to

---

[1] *gsal snang.*

[2] *mkhas pa'i dmigs pa, kauśalyālambana.*

which a yogic practitioner becomes skilled. A yogic practitioner who desires to become skilled with respect to the nature of compounded phenomena must know the entity,[1] divisions,[2] definition,[3] enumeration,[4] and mode of production[5] of the aggregates. For example, to know the mode of production of the form aggregate, which is an instance of coarse form, is to know it arises from or is compounded from an aggregation of minute particles and to know that when it disintegrates there is a dissolution of those particles.

It is particularly difficult to understand the mode of production of feelings. How are the feelings of pleasure, pain, and neutrality produced? Someone skilled in the feeling aggregate would know what causes bring about each of these and would also understand how each of the three disintegrates.

Someone skilled in knowledge of the aggregate of discriminations understands that, in general, discrimination accompanies every main mind. We say that persons without discrimination do not know anything, that they are as though crazy. To have discrimination means that one can think. This does not mean merely to see something or to have thought but refers to discrimination in the sense of motivation. For example, someone who speaks harshly may have a purpose in doing so, or the words may have simply rushed out without prior consideration. Harsh words spoken without prior thought are said to be without motivation and without discrimination. If the harsh words were said intentionally and unmistakenly, the speaker is said to have motivation or discrimination; she or he has spoken exactly in accordance with their own thought. Thus, discrimination comes about because of the presence of intention and lack of error.

The fourth aggregate, compositional factors, is a making of effort at activity. The generation of an altruistic mind of enlightenment can serve as an example. There are two types of altruistic mind of enlightenment—an aspirational one, which is just the thought, "I would like to attain Buddhahood," and a practical one, which is not merely a thought or wish but involves actually making effort at the practices leading to the attainment of Buddhahood. Shāntideva's *Engaging in the Bodhisattva Deeds* gives

[1] *ngo bo, vastu.*

[2] *dbye ba.*

[3] *mtshan nyid, lakṣaṇa.*

[4] *grangs nges.*

[5] *skyed tshul.*

the following example: a person who wishes to go somewhere is like someone who has the aspirational mind of enlightenment, and a person actually traveling toward that place is like someone who has the practical mind of enlightenment. The latter does not merely *want* to attain Buddhahood but is actually making effort toward it by practicing the six perfections—giving, ethics, patience, effort, concentration, and wisdom. Similarly, "discrimination" refers to thought, whereas the aggregate of compositional factors involves actually making effort.

The aggregate of consciousness is the basis of everything. With regard to the form aggregate, for example, the activities of the body depend on consciousness. The activity of experiencing pleasant, unpleasant, and neutral feelings also has consciousness as its basis. Discrimination is the mental factor of taking up a motivation and, therefore, has a consciousness as its main mind. Finally, with respect to the compositional factors, if there were no consciousness there would be no basis of making effort. The assertion of many schools of tenets that the person[1] is the continuum of consciousness derives from just this fact that the aggregate of consciousness is the basis of the others.

How is the continuum of consciousness asserted to be the person? This is the person in relation to whom there is a going from a past life to the present one and from there to a future life. It is in relation to the person that deeds are accumulated, and so forth.

CONSTITUENTS

What would a yogic practitioner who wished to become skilled in the nature of causes do? Every compounded phenomenon has both a substantial cause[2] and a cooperative condition.[3] The yogic practitioner analyzes the mode of arising of constituents.[4] For example, he or she would examine the substantial cause and cooperative condition of a particular form constituent. The word "constituent"[5] has many different meanings. It can

---

[1] *gang zag, pudgala.*

[2] *nyer len, upādāna.*

[3] *lhan cig byed rkyen, sahakāripratyaya.*

[4] The eighteen constituents are the six sense powers (eye, ear, nose, tongue, body, and mental sense powers), the six objects (forms, sounds, odors, tastes, tangible objects, and other phenomena), and the six consciousnesses (eye, ear, nose, tongue, body, and mental consciousnesses).

[5] *khams, dhātu.*

mean cause, mode of being,[1] nature,[2] or a potency[3] for the arising of something. When the meaning behind any of these terms is sought, however, one finds a casual activity.

Even in relation to the final nature of phenomena, emptiness—which is permanent—it is very suitable to reflect on causes. Chandrakīrti's *Supplement to (Nāgārjuna's) "Treatise on the Middle"* says that in the end all arise from emptiness. This means that all causes and effects operate within the context of emptiness; it also signifies that for those with high realization emptiness itself appears as cause and effect. This does not mean that emptiness is a functioning thing,[4] or is impermanent, or is a cause from which things arise. To those whose understanding is well formed, emptiness appears as cause and effect because they understand that all phenomena are empty in the same way and that cause and effect operate with the context of emptiness.[5] They understand that if all phenomena were not of one taste with emptiness, cause and effect could not operate. Thus, saying that all arise in the end from emptiness does not mean that causes and effects arise from emptiness. In this way, "constituent" comes to mean cause, final nature, nature, or potency. Thus, not only the eighteen constituents but any compounded product whatsoever can be analyzed endlessly.

TWELVE SENSE-SPHERES

A person wishing to become skilled in conditions must be skilled in the presentation of the twelve sense-spheres.[6] For example, the mental sense-sphere, which is one of the internal sense-spheres, arises from three conditions: an object-of-observation condition, an immediately preceding condition, and an uncommon proprietary condition. Each of the twelve sense-spheres can be taken as a continuum requiring these three conditions. A person who is skilled in how one of the twelve sense-spheres arises from the three conditions is said to be skilled in conditions.

TWELVE-LINKED DEPENDENT-ARISING

One who wishes to become skilled in the twelve-linked dependent-arising

---

1 *yin lugs.*

2 *rang bzhin, svābhāva.*

3 *nus pa.*

4 *dngos po, bhāva.*

5 *stong pa'i ngang.*

6 *skye mched, āyatana.* The twelve sense-spheres are the six objects (forms, sounds, odors, tastes, tangible objects, and other phenomena) and the six sense powers (eye, ear, nose, tongue, body, and mental sense powers).

must meditate on either the forward or reverse progression of the twelve. There are many different ways of explaining how one person cycles in cyclic existence by way of the twelve-linked dependent-arising.[1]

The Twelve-Linked Dependent-Arising[2]

1 ignorance[3]
2 compositional action[4]
3 consciousness[5]
  a. cause consciousness
  b. effect consciousness
4 name and form[6]
5 sense-spheres[7]
6 contact[8]
7 feeling[9]
8 attachment[10]
9 grasping[11]
10 existence[12]
11 birth[13]
12 aging and death[14]

How are the twelve presented in terms of the lives of a single person? First, the natures, entities, and divisions of the twelve links individually must be explained. This is the basis for understanding how one person travels in cyclic existence by way of these twelve. Does a person achieve the twelve simultaneously or serially? We need not discuss the many different ways in

---

[1] See Hopkins, *Meditation on Emptiness*, 275 and Appendix 2, 707, for a discussion of these interpretations.

[2] Simplified from Hopkins, *Meditation on Emptiness*, 276.

[3] *ma rig pa, avidyā.*

[4] *'du byed kyi las, saṃskārakarma.*

[5] *rnam shes, vijñāna.*

[6] *ming gzugs, nāmarūpa.*

[7] *skye mched, āyatana.*

[8] *reg pa, sparśa.*

[9] *tshor ba, vedanā.*

[10] *sred pa, tṛṣṇā.*

[11] *len pa, upadana.*

[12] *srid pa, bhava.*

[13] *skye ba, jāti.*

[14] *rga shi, jarāmaraṇa.*

which the twelve are presented in Vasubandhu's *Treasury of Manifest Knowledge* but will take the upper systems' presentation as our basis.

Let us say that a person accumulates in her or his present life an action that will cause rebirth as a god in the future. Once an action has been committed, there are said to be twelve links of dependent-arising which are of one completion[1] with it. Thus, the twelve links related to a particular virtuous action are a different group from the twelve related to a particular non-virtuous one. The rebirth someone takes as a god is the projected effect[2] of a virtuous action. How many of the twelve links connected with that action arise in this lifetime and how many in a future lifetime? How many would have arisen in a past life?

As soon as an action has been completed, the second link, compositional action, is established. This action was preceded by the motivation of beginningless ignorance. The action arises immediately after the ignorance; there is no interruption between them. The action itself is the mental factor of intention.[3] As the intention is approaching its cessation, it comes to abide in the entity of a potency.[4] Once the intention has become a potency, consciousness—the third link of dependent-arising—is established, for, as the compositional action deposits a potency on the consciousness, it becomes of the nature of consciousness.

The accumulation of an action and the compositional action occur in the same instant. There are two different systems concerning the arising of the remaining nine links of dependent-arising. It can happen that a person who accumulates an action that would cause future rebirth as a god is in the very next life reborn as a god. It can also happen that one or many lives intervene between the lifetime during which the action is performed and that in which the person is reborn as a god.

When a person who will immediately be reborn as a god is about to die, the eighth, ninth, and tenth links—attachment, grasping, and existence—arise. Grasping is appropriation of the next rebirth. Existence is a potency or latency. We have said that when an action is about to cease, it deposits a potency on the third link, consciousness. "Existence," the tenth link, is the name given to that potency when it has been nurtured by the eighth and ninth links, attachment and grasping. When the potency is first produced,

---

1 *tshar gcig pa.*

2 *'phangs 'bras.*

3 *sems pa, cetanā.*

4 *nus pa.*

it does not have the ability to produce a new life, but once it has been nurtured by attachment and grasping it is able to function as an entity capable of taking up a new life. Thus, these are the five links which occur in the same life in which the action was committed: ignorance, compositional action, consciousness, attachment, and grasping.

The third link, consciousness, is really two consciousnesses, the cause consciousness and the effect consciousness. Because only the first of these is a projecting cause, there are said to be five and one-half projectors[1]—the first, second, and half the third, as well as the eighth, ninth, and tenth of the twelve links of dependent-arising.

The remaining six and one-half links are all projected effects.[2] Before rebirth as a god, the person is in the intermediate state, or *bar-do*. The projected effects arise after the intermediate state at the time of birth[3] as a god; five and one-half of them are simultaneous with that rebirth. The twelfth link, aging and death, is established in the second moment after taking rebirth.[4] There is no certainty whether that second moment will be a case of aging or death since there are, for example, humans who are born and then die in the very next moment. This never happens with gods. [Thus, for them, the second moment after taking rebirth is always a time of aging.]

How many of the twelve arise when a human is to be reborn as a human without having another type of rebirth between those two? In this life there are five and one-half links; in the next life there are said to be seven and one-half; the halves are not counted, however, because there is only one consciousness. The division of the third link, consciousness, is made only from the viewpoint of that consciousness' being a cause or an effect. In this case, the twelve links of dependent-arising are complete in two lifetimes.[5]

MEANING OF DEPENDENT-ARISING

In the Tibetan word *rten cing 'brel ba*, "dependent-arising," the two words to be commented on are *rten* (literally, "base," "support," that which is depended on) and *'brel* (literally, "connection" or "relation"). These two

[1] *'phen byed phyed lnga*—literally, "the five projectors of which one is [only] a half."

[2] *'phangs 'bras phyed bdun*—literally, "the seven projected effects, of which one is [only] a half."

[3] *skye srid.*

[4] *skye ba, jāti.*

[5] For other presentations, see Hopkins, *Meditation on Emptiness*, 275-83, 707-711.

words are very important. Sūtras, and so forth, use the long form of this term, *rten cing 'brel bar 'byung ba*, which means "dependently and relatedly arisen." The shortened Tibetan phrase *rten 'brel* uses only the words "dependently, relatedly."[1]

Briefly, "dependent" means that in these twelve links the arising of a link depends on the preceding one. For example, if there is no ignorance, action will not arise; in this way, action is dependent on ignorance.

If ignorance does not precede action as a cause, the action will not arise. Thus, we can establish that there is a relationship between ignorance and action within the context of their being different entities. That is why they are said to be "related."

The two words "dependent relationship" are put together in order to eliminate the misconception that the twelve links are unrelated and independent. In Sanskrit "dependent-arising" is *pratītyasamutpāda*. Many Tibetan texts comment on three aspects of this term: the arising dependently, the dependent relationship, and the establishment of dependence. In general, these three are equivalent, but they have different potencies[2] or connotations, just as the words "impermanent" and "compounded" are equivalent but have different potencies.

Because the first of these three expressions, "dependent-arising," is the most inclusive, the Mādhyamikas take this as the king of reasonings that analyze the ultimate. This is the most extensive of such reasonings.

THE TWELVE LINKS INDIVIDUALLY

The above has been an explanation of the meaning of dependent-arising in general. Now I will explain each of the twelve links individually. It is necessary to know the nature of these to ascertain their order and to know which are afflicted[3] and which are not.

The first link, ignorance, is the motivation. Ignorance is a factor of obscuration, of which there are two modes: (1) with respect to actions and their effects and (2) with respect to suchness but not actions and their effects. To be obscured with respect to actions and their effects means not to understand what kinds of fruition—happiness, suffering, and so forth—will result from a particular action that has been committed. For example, a person engaged in killing may not understand that it is a non-virtuous activity; or, even if the person sees it as non-virtuous and a cause of future

[1] For more on this topic, see Hopkins, *Meditation on Emptiness*, 163-167, 662-676.

[2] *nus pa.*

[3] *nyon mongs can, kliṣṭa.*

suffering, she or he engages in killing anyway because of not fully believing that suffering will result. This latter is also actually a case of not knowing that killing is a non-virtue because, even though the person has heard that it is non-virtuous and a cause of suffering, he or she has not realized it with valid cognition and does not believe it. From this point of view, the person's motivation in killing is ignorance. Because this motivation is not merely present but also manifest, the person either directly engages in killing or has someone else do it for him or her.

When the life-faculty[1] of the victim ceases, the murderer accumulates the second of the twelve links, action. There are two aspects to this action, that of intention and the physical deed of killing. The latter is accumulated in the killer's continuum when the victim's life-faculty ceases. This is true regardless of whether the perpetrator does the killing her- or himself or orders another person to do it.

Question: Then ignorance is the motivation for non-virtuous actions?

Answer: Yes, and the same principle can be applied to virtuous actions. An action is virtuous, non-virtuous, or neutral in dependence on its motivation. With regard to virtuous action, if one is going to meditate, for example, one first has the motivation, "I am going to meditate." When, because of this motivation, one engages in meditation, one accumulates a virtuous activity.

Question: How is it that a person who sends another to commit murder will generate the third link of dependent-arising—the cause consciousness—when that murder is effected?

Answer: The first two of the three types of physical non-virtue, killing and stealing, can be delegated to someone else. One can send someone to kill another person, and in the very next moment after the victim's life-faculty is cut off, a complete path of action is accumulated in one's own continuum. This is the time of acquiring the second link, action. After sending off the actual murderer, the person who gave the order may engage in a virtuous activity while the murder is being committed. Even so, when the victim's life-force ends, the path of action for the one who initiated the murder becomes complete. How can this occur? No new consciousness arises in the person who is back home engaging in a virtuous activity. What, then, is the nature of the action that is actualized? Is it of the entity

---

[1] *srog gi dbang po, jivitendriya.*

of consciousness, matter,[1] or non-associated compositional factors?[2] The four schools of tenets have different answers to this question.

According to the Chittamātrins and the Yogāchāra-Svātantrikas, this action becomes of the nature of a potency and is deposited in the consciousness. According to most other proponents of tenets, it becomes a non-revelatory form;[3] a bodily action can be either a revelatory form[4] or a non-revelatory form, which is not a potency but an entity of an action that will later turn into the entity of the tenth link of dependent-arising, known as existence. Thus, even though the person who gave the order is engaging in a virtuous activity, the fruition of his or her non-virtuous activity in initiating the murder will not be wasted. She or he will have to undergo the effect of that action. The same is true of a virtuous action initiated by one person and carried out by another, such as when someone makes a charitable donation through an agent.

Ignorance in general is a little different from the ignorance which is the first of the twelve links of dependent-arising, for the latter is either non-virtuous or neutral. The ignorance that motivates an action impelling rebirth in a bad transmigration cannot be neutral but must be non-virtuous and must be a case of obscuration with respect to actions and their effects. Such obscuration is necessarily non-virtuous. The ignorance that serves as the motivator for taking rebirth in the upper realms [that is, the Form and Formless Realms] or in happy transmigrations [in the Desire Realm] cannot be virtuous; rather, it is neutral because it is not a case of being obscured with respect to the fact that pleasure is produced in dependence on a virtuous action and that pain is produced in dependence on a non-virtuous one. Someone who has such a neutral ignorance not only is unobscured with respect to these facts but also has belief in them. Such a person engages in actions within a belief in the relationship of actions and their effects; therefore, he or she engages in an action in order to take rebirth in a happy transmigration. Although such a person has a mistaken conception of the self,[5] because she or he engages in an action believing in the cause and effect of actions and out of fear of a bad rebirth, the ignorance that motivates the action is neutral.

---

[1] *bem po, kanthā.*

[2] *ldan min 'du byed, viprayuktasaṃskāra.*

[3] *rnam par rig byed ma yin pa'i gzugs, avijñaptirūpa.*

[4] *rnam par rig byed kyi gzugs, vijñaptirūpa.*

[5] *bdag, ātman.*

This motivation has two parts. Not wanting to be reborn in a bad transmigration has a factor of ignorance—the misconception of the nature of the I.[1] This is an ignorance which is an obscuration with respect to suchness. The other factor of motivation is that which draws the person into doing a virtuous action out of concern for avoiding rebirth in a bad transmigration. This part of the motivation is virtuous.

The second of the twelve links of dependent-arising is compositional action. Although action, or karma, in general can be virtuous, non-virtuous, or neutral, the compositional action that is the second link of dependent-arising must be either virtuous or non-virtuous because it brings about rebirth. This is because it functions as the cause of either a happy or bad transmigration, and these rebirths must have, respectively, a virtuous or non-virtuous action as their cause. This distinction is very important because the actions included in the twelve are actualizers of a rebirth.

According to the upper systems, but not Vasubandhu's *Treasury*, there are three exceptions to this: the action which brings about Foe Destroyerhood, an act of confession[2] which destroys a previously accumulated projecting action, and an action projecting rebirth in a pure land.[3] Except for these three, all actions will definitely cause rebirth. This is the assertion of the higher tenet systems; it is not asserted by Vasubandhu, for he states in the *Treasury* that *any* action will have a rebirth as its projected effect.

An action that impels rebirth in one of the upper realms—Form Realm or Formless Realm—is an unfluctuating[4] action, and one that impels a happy transmigration [in the Desire Realm] is called a meritorious[5] action. Both of these must be virtuous. For someone to be impelled into a bad transmigration there must be a non-virtuous, or non-meritorious,[6] action. In chart form:

---

1 *nga, ahaṃ.*

2 *bshags pa, deśanā.*

3 *dag zhing, kṣetraśuddhi.*

4 *mi g.yo ba, āniñjya.*

5 *bsod nams, puṇya.*

6 *bsod nams ma yin pa, apuṇya.*

Types of Rebirth

Rebirth	*Impeller*	*Type*
Formless Realm	unfluctuating action	virtuous
Form Realm	unfluctuating action	virtuous
Happy transmigrations in Desire Realm	meritorious action	virtuous
Bad transmigrations	non-virtuous actions	non-virtuous

Because of ignorance, an action is accumulated, and in the next moment there is consciousness, the third of the twelve links of dependent-arising. This means that as an action approaches cessation it deposits a potency on the consciousness. Actualization of the third link—consciousness—and cessation of the second—action—are simultaneous. At this time, the action has become of the entity of a potency that remains with the consciousness. Since the second link—action—cannot remain permanently, what can remain, and how, until its effect ripens in another rebirth, possibly far in the future? This question is much debated, and all four schools of tenets have different answers. (See p. 201.)

The third link, consciousness, has two factors, the consciousness at the time of the cause and the consciousness at the time of the effect. The first refers to the consciousness that exists at the time of the action, until the new consciousness impelled by that potency is appropriated—that is, until the rebirth which is an effect of that action takes place.

The fourth link is name and form which is more precisely called "name and/or form." The last four of the five aggregates—feeling, discrimination, compositional factors, and consciousnesses—are called the name basis.[1] "Form," then, refers to the form aggregate. This link is to be understood as "either name or form" because, if an action impels a rebirth into the Formless Realm, there are only the four name-basis aggregates; the form aggregate is absent. Thus, the person is designated just in dependence on the four name aggregates.

The fifth link, sense-spheres, refers to the twelve sense-spheres, which are actualized simultaneously with assuming a new rebirth.

The sixth, contact, refers to the ability of the body consciousness to make contact with tangible objects.

The seventh, feeling, means the ability to know which of the three feelings—pleasure, pain, or neutrality—is arising.

The eighth, attachment, refers to the desire for taking rebirth. This

[1] *ming gzhi.*

could mean wanting to be reborn as a god or some type of attachment related to the rebirth one will take. For example, if at the time of death one feels, "I want to be warmer," or, "I want to be colder," this is not the usual attachment but an uncommon form of it that has bearing on the type of rebirth one will take.

The ninth link, grasping, is also a case of attachment but is distinguished by the fact that, whereas the attachment previously discussed is a mere aspiration, this link refers to the actual taking up of the next life.

The tenth, existence, is really similar to action but, as was already mentioned, the action has ceased and become of the nature of consciousness; until the occurrence of the birth of which that action is the cause, the latency or potency of that action remains as a neutral phenomenon. "Existence" is the name given to the latency when it has been nurtured by attachment and grasping and thereby becomes able to produce the effect of taking up the new life.

The eleventh link, birth, refers to the actual taking of rebirth through the power of that action.

The twelfth is either aging or death. In the first moment, rebirth is taken; in the second, aging is actualized. This link is called "aging and/or death" because there are cases of taking rebirth and dying in the very next moment, without aging.

This is a rough explanation of the names of the twelve links of dependent-arising. Are the twelve actualized in this order? No, this is not the order of their actualization but the order in which they are taught.

ORDER OF ACTUALIZATION

Let us take an example. If someone newly accumulates an impelling action, motivated by ignorance, that would bring about rebirth as a human, which of the twelve links are included in the present life? Ignorance is actualized, and in the next moment, action is actualized. When that action is approaching cessation, consciousness is actualized. At this point, two and one-half links have been actualized, and the action has become of one entity with consciousness. In order for this action which is to impel a human rebirth actually to cause rebirth as a human, three other links—the eighth, ninth, and tenth—must be actualized when the person is about to die. The attachment involved here is a taking pleasure in rebirth; in the very next moment, without any further exertion, this attachment becomes grasping—an actual exertion of effort toward taking rebirth. Once the potency has been nurtured by this attachment and grasping, it becomes strong, much as a seed nurtured by water becomes able to grow. This strengthened state is what is meant by existence; it would be a great mistake to think that the tenth link, existence, signified something new, for this potency has existed since the time of the third link, consciousness. Now, nurtured by the eighth and ninth links, it has the power to ripen into an effect.

After the person dies, the eleventh link, birth, is actualized when he or she takes rebirth. The fourth, fifth, sixth, and seventh links—either name or form, sense-spheres, contact, and feeling—are also simultaneously actualized at birth. In the next moment the twelfth link, either aging or death, is actualized.

The consciousness at the time of the effect is also actualized simultaneously with the fourth, fifth, sixth, and seventh links at the time of birth. This consciousness is known as a cause consciousness before rebirth and as an effect consciousness after rebirth. The former is a case of abiding as a latency; because it ripens and attains the power to bring about its effect at the time of the tenth link, existence, it is then no longer a cause but an effect consciousness.

It is important not to mistake the word "existence"[1] that refers to the tenth link with the more common meaning of that word—namely, cyclic existence. "Cyclic existence"[2] is a name that applies to all true sufferings[3] and true origins[4] of suffering. The "existence" which is the tenth link of dependent-arising refers specifically to a latency that has become qualified by the ability to bring about its effect.

This explanation has been from the viewpoint of the twelve links' being complete in two lifetimes. The first lifetime was the time of accumulating the action. The first, second, half of the third, and the eighth, ninth, and tenth links are all established in relation to the support that does the action. The others are all established in the subsequent lifetime.

The twelve can also be completed in three lifetimes. As before, an action motivated by ignorance is done, actualizing the cause consciousness. This is not different from the above. If the lifetime immediately following is not impelled by that particular action, it is possible for an eon[5] or more to intervene before the rebirth impelled by that action occurs. There is no cer-

---

1 *srid pa, bhava.*

2 *'khor ba, saṃsāra.*

3 *sdug bsngal bden pa, duḥkhasatya.*

4 *kun 'byung bden pa, samudayasatya.*

5 *bskal pa, kalpa.*

tainty of the amount of time here. Let us say that five lives intervene between the commission of an action and the taking of the rebirth impelled by it. If the sixth life is to be taken up through that action, then at the end of the fifth life, as the person is about to die, the eighth, ninth, and tenth links of the dependent-arising related to that particular action will become manifest. The taking of rebirth in the sixth life will be the eleventh link, birth; the way the others are actualized is as before. The five intervening rebirths are the results of actions other than the one which gives rise to the sixth rebirth; they constitute different series of dependent-arisings. It might happen that a hundred thousand years intervene between a certain action and the rebirth that results from it. People have amassed countless actions. No matter how long the process takes, the twelve links are completed over three lifetimes; at the very least they will be completed within two lifetimes.

Question: Can they ever be completed in one lifetime?

Answer: No, because one will take birth through the power of that action, and taking rebirth involves a new life.

This ordering of the twelve links of dependent-arising is how they are presented in the texts and in sūtra. As I have explained, their order of actualization is that the first three—ignorance, action, and the cause —arise; then attachment, grasping, and existence; and finally, there is the simultaneous arising of birth, effect consciousness, name and/or form, sense-spheres, contact, and feeling, which are immediately followed by aging and/or death.

When the twelve links are complete in three lifetimes, ignorance, action, and the cause consciousness are known as the two and one-half projectors.[1] The eighth, ninth, and tenth links are called the three actualizing causes.[2] The rest are known as the six and one-half projected effects.[3]

This has been a general explanation. There is no case in which, when the three actualizing causes—attachment, grasping, and existence—arise, another life intervenes between them and the rebirth that they actualize. Generally speaking, it is impossible not to take rebirth once these three have become manifest. However, according to Asaṅga's *Summary of Manifest Knowledge*, there can be exceptions. It is possible for the eighth,

1 *'phen byed phyed gsum*—literally, "the three projectors of which one is [only] a half."

2 *'grub byed rgyu gsum.*

3 *'phangs 'bras phyed bdun*—literally, "the seven projected effects of which one is [only] a half."

ninth, tenth links to be actualized and for the person to die and enter the intermediate state without then having to take rebirth.

In general, the second and tenth links—action and existence—are different, but if one commits a very strong virtuous or non-virtuous action it immediately becomes of the nature of the tenth link.

I have explained a little about how the twelve links of dependent-arising are actualized because this is one of the topics in which one may become skilled. Buddha first set forth the *Sūtra on Dependent-Arising*[1] in the country of Magadha using a certain rice seedling as an example and speaking about how it grows. Nāgārjuna wrote a commentary on this, as did Vasubandhu. Many of these teachings were also set forth in the *Sūtra of Teaching to Nanda on Entry to the Womb*.[2]

APPROPRIATE AND INAPPROPRIATE

The next object of observation in which one can become skilled is that of actions and their effects. This means understanding that virtue is a cause giving rise to happiness and that non-virtue is a cause giving rise to suffering. It also involves an understanding of what constitutes a complete action. There are actions which are accumulated but not committed; there are also actions which are committed but not accumulated. For example, if one has the motivation to do an action but does not act on it, the action is accumulated but not committed. An action done accidentally or in a dream is committed but not accumulated. In this case, there is no motivation for the action; it comes about unintentionally. Actions that are both accumulated and committed are complete activities.

A complete action is one in which the preparation, carrying out, and conclusion of the activity are complete. In the case of a virtuous action, the motivation consists of a wish to do it; the action itself consists of carrying out that wish, and the conclusion or culmination is to feel happy afterward that one has done a given virtuous activity.

This is the fifth of the five objects of observation that make one skilled. It is sometimes called "the appropriate and the inappropriate,"[3] the appropriate being virtues and the inappropriate, non-virtues.

Question: Since the objects of observation that make one skilled involve so

---

1 *Rice Seedling Sūtra; sā lu'i ljang pa'i mdo, śālistambasūtra;* P876, vol. 34.

2 *tshe dang ldan pa dga' bo mngal du 'jug pa bstan pa, āyuṣmannandagarbhāvakrāntinirdeśa;* P760.13, vol. 23.

3 *gnas dang gnas ma yin pa, sthānāsthāna.*

much analysis, how can they be used to develop calm abiding?

Answer: These objects of observation are used by someone who has already achieved calm abiding in order to extend and strengthen it. It is indeed possible initially to achieve calm abiding with these objects of observation but, as with emptiness, it would be very difficult for a beginner to do so.

OBJECTS OF OBSERVATION FOR PURIFYING AFFLICTIVE EMOTIONS

The fourth category of objects of observation is of two types. One object is to view a lower level (such as the Desire Realm) as gross[1] and an upper level (such as the First Concentration) as peaceful.[2] At this time, the practitioner has achieved calm abiding and, in dependence on the analysis that takes place during the mental contemplation of individual knowledge of the character,[3] achieves a mundane path.

Once calm abiding has been achieved, there are two paths that one can take, mundane and supramundane. I will later explain these extensively. (See pp. 215-235.)

---

[1] *rags pa, audārika.*

[2] *zhi ba, śānta.*

[3] *mtshan nyid so sor rig pa'i yid byed, lakṣaṇapratisaṃvedīmanaskāra.*

14 PATH OF SEEING AND RELATED QUESTIONS

Question: What types of bases are used for attaining the path of seeing?

Answer: There are Hīnayānists who use the not-unable[1] preparation as a mental basis for the path of seeing—specifically, Stream Enterers who proceed in a simultaneous[2] manner. Such persons will not attain the first concentration; they have nothing better than the not-unable. However, those on the Mahāyāna path of preparation attain all four concentrations; thus, of course, those persons would use a better type of mind as the basis—specifically, the fourth concentration. There is nothing better than using the fourth concentration as a basis for the path of seeing.

In dependence on the not-unable preparation, one can abandon all the afflictive emotions, and this preparation can serve as the basis for either contaminated or uncontaminated consciousnesses. The term "not-unable preparation" is used for all the preparations for the first concentration. All of them can be considered not-unable preparations, but the three actual uncontaminated ones are the mental contemplations of individual knowledge of the character, thorough isolation, and final training.

In the Mahāyāna it is necessary to overcome not only the afflictive emotions but also the obstructions to omniscience. Although there is no clear statement to this effect, I believe that in order to overcome the artificial obstructions to omniscience it would not be sufficient to have just a preparation; an actual concentration would be necessary. A person on the Mahāyāna path of seeing is a beginning Superior and must get rid of the artificial obstructions to omniscience. If, however, you said that it does not necessarily follow that for a Mahāyāna Superior to abandon obstructions to omniscience the basis would necessarily have to be an actual concentration, that would be correct. A preparation, and even a mind of the Desire Realm, can act as a mental basis. This is not contradictory because these

---

[1] *mi lcog med, anāgamya.*

[2] *gcig car, sakṛt.*

latter cases occur when someone has achieved a high Bodhisattva ground. Thus, there are the three possible types of mental basis—a preparation, an actual concentration, or even a mind of the Desire Realm. Dzong-ka-ba's *Great Exposition of the Stages of the Path* refers to the fact that a Desire Realm mind can act as a mental basis. He then asks, "Does this also illustrate the case with regard to the path of seeing? No."

The fourth concentration referred to here is also called a final concentration.[1] If a mind of the Desire Realm is added to the eight meditative absorptions and if the meditator passes through these in the forward and reverse process in meditative equipoise, then at the end she or he sets the mind in the fourth concentration. This is the final concentration. The meditator begins with a mind of the Desire Realm, proceeds up to the eighth absorption, then back down to the mind of the Desire Realm, and then up again to the fourth concentration. *That* fourth concentration receives the name "final concentration."

Another way of positing this concentration is that one goes from a mind of the Desire Realm, up through the eight absorptions, and on to the meditative absorption of cessation; then back down through all of them to the Desire Realm mind, and then back up to the fourth concentration. Mostly, however, it is the first method that is done.

In the systems of the higher schools of tenets, all four concentrations receive the name "final concentration." In other words, one would begin with the Desire Realm mind, progress up to an absorption of the peak of cyclic existence or on to the meditative absorption of cessation, go back down to the mind of the Desire Realm, and then up to any of the four concentrations, any of which could be called a final concentration. However, in the system of Vasubandhu's *Treasury of Manifest Knowledge* only the fourth concentration is so designated. Even in the Mahāyāna tenet systems, the fourth is still the best of the final concentrations, although all four are final in the sense that they are at the end of this process of progressing up and down the levels.

Question: Why is the fourth concentration best?

Answer: In the first concentration, one has separated from attachment with respect to painful feelings. In the second concentration, there is not much fluctuation of investigation[2] or analysis.[3] However, in the first two con-

---

[1] *rab mtha'i bsam gtan.*

[2] *rtog pa, vitarka.*

[3] *dpyod pa, vicāra.*

centrations, one assumes bliss. In the third concentration, even though one voluntarily assumes bliss, it is not assumed in so strong a manner as in the first two. In the fourth concentration, one has separated from attachment not only with respect to suffering but also with respect to pleasure. If one voluntarily assumed bliss, it would harm one's meditative stabilization. These reasons also probably explain why it was previously necessary to diminish strong bliss and joy.

The word *chags bral*, which we are translating "separated from attachment" is explained thus: *chags pa*, like *sred pa*, means attachment. In this case, one voluntarily assumes bliss in the first three concentrations, but in the fourth one leaves bliss; one has separated from attachment to it.

Question: How can you speak of separation from attachment with respect to the feeling of suffering? No one is attached to suffering.

Answer: One separates from attachment with respect to suffering in the sense of becoming free from the afflictive emotions that produce it.

Question: Why is a concentration a better mental basis than a formless absorption?

Answer: In the formless absorptions, there is a predominance of calm abiding. One is as though dissolved into the factor of calm abiding. The meaning of calm abiding's being too predominant is probably that the mind is not very clear.

Question: Are concentrations themselves unions of calm abiding and special insight? For example, the fourth concentration.

Answer: You could not say, "The subject, the fourth concentration, is a meditative stabilization which is a union of calm abiding and special insight." That would be too general. However, the fourth concentration can be said to accompany a union of calm abiding and special insight. If you stated that the fourth concentration is a meditative stabilization, that would be unsuitable. The fourth concentration is many things—main mind, mental factors, and so forth. You could speak of the factor of meditative stabilization that accompanies the fourth concentration, or of the wisdom that accompanies the fourth concentration, and so forth.

Question: Does special insight turn into some other consciousness on the path, or is the mind of special insight realizing emptiness over the ten Bodhisattva grounds, also a case of special insight?

Answer: Yes; the term "special insight" extends right through to Buddhahood. "Meditative stabilization which is a union of calm abiding and special insight" is not a case of a term's being imputed to a specific state; rather, its own states as it advances are given different names—the path of preparation, the path of seeing, and so forth. Thus, there is a great difference between the terms imputed to certain entities and those imputed to certain states. If you speak of the special insight directly realizing emptiness, it is not a reference to a certain level of the path because that entity exists at many places along the path. However, if you speak of an uninterrupted path which is a special insight directly realizing emptiness, the consciousness of a specific state is designated. The five paths are posited from the viewpoint of wisdom. Hīnayāna and Mahāyāna paths, however, are not posited by way of wisdom but by way of method.

How is it that the five paths are posited by way of wisdom? The wisdom realizing emptiness can be posited as the general entity that exists over all five paths. From the viewpoint of how much familiarity one has with it, the states are designated as the paths of accumulation, preparation, and so forth.

I would like to clarify my previous statement that on the Mahāyāna path of preparation it is necessary to attain all four concentrations, since there is a difference between attaining the four concentrations *at the time of* the path of preparation and their attainment *by a person on* the path of preparation. It is definite that the four concentrations will be attained by the time of the path of preparation, but not necessarily by someone on the path of preparation. One could easily make the mistake, on the basis of the words, that since the four concentrations are achieved at the time of the path of preparation they are necessarily achieved by someone on the path of preparation.

How is it that there could be a person on the path of preparation who has not attained the four concentrations? Take the example of a person who is definite in the Mahāyāna lineage and has attained a calm abiding observing emptiness beforehand. In terms of that person's progressing on the supramundane path, that person is someone who, when he or she attains the path of preparation, will necessarily simultaneously attain a meditative stabilization which is a union of calm abiding and special insight observing emptiness. On the path of accumulation, that person would attain the mental contemplation of individual knowledge of the character and, before that, calm abiding. From that point, the person will pass on to the path of preparation, at which time there is simultaneous attainment of the Mahāyāna path of preparation, the mental contemplation arisen from belief, and a union of calm abiding and special insight. This means that the person at this point is at the third preparation. The rest of the preparations are yet to be achieved; therefore, the person has not yet achieved any actual concentration. This explains how there can be a person on the Mahāyāna path of preparation who has not attained the concentrations.

Why is it said that one must attain the four concentrations at the time of the path of preparation? This is because the first of the achievings through engagement[1] are attained at the path of preparation. There is no clear statement on this, but it can be virtually settled by reasoning. Achieving through engagement, or entry into the concentrations and formless absorptions, is attained from the path of preparation. The path of preparation is extremely long, and before the path of seeing it is necessary to attain the achieving of entry into the concentrations and formless absorptions. Even though there is no clear statement on why the four concentrations must be attained on the path of preparation, I think it is because of the achieving of entry into the concentrations and absorptions.

1 *'jug sgrub, prasthānapratipatti.*

PART THREE:
SPECIAL INSIGHT

15 MODES OF PROCEDURE

MUNDANE AND SUPRAMUNDANE PATHS

There are only two modes of procedure for progressing through the remaining paths in dependence on calm abiding. One progresses in dependence on either a mundane path or a supramundane path. How do these differ?

To understand these two modes of procedure, it is necessary to understand the presentation of the three realms and the nine levels[1] (see chart).

The Three Realms and the Nine Levels

(Read from bottom to top.)[2]

formless realm	peak of cyclic existence	ninth level
	nothingness	eighth level
	infinite consciousness	seventh level
	infinite space	sixth level
form realm	fourth concentration	fifth level
	third concentration	fourth level
	second concentration	third level
	first concentration	second level
desire realm		first level

The three realms are the Desire Realm, the Form Realm, and the Formless

[1] *khams gsum sa dgu.*

[2] For more detail see the chart in Geshe Lhundup Sopa and Jeffrey Hopkins, *Cutting Through Appearances: The Practice and Theory of Tibetan Buddhism* (Ithaca: Snow Lion, 1990), 213.

Realm. The nine levels are the Desire Realm, the First Concentration,[1] the Second Concentration,[2] the Third Concentration,[3] the Fourth Concentration,[4] Limitless Space,[5] Limitless Consciousness,[6] Nothingness,[7] and the Peak of Cyclic Existence.[8] Someone who wishes to separate temporarily from attachment to afflictive emotions pertaining to the Nothingness level—that is, the eighth level—and below, can do so by depending on a mundane path. Someone who wishes to get rid of the afflictive emotions pertaining to the Peak of Cyclic Existence must definitely depend on a supramundane path. Asaṅga's *Grounds of Hearers* says that there is no third category of path other than the mundane and the supramundane. However, whether one progresses through the remaining paths in dependence on a mundane or a supramundane path, it is necessary to depend on preparatory training[9]—even though it is said that there is no third path.

FOUR ATTRIBUTES OF PREPARATORY TRAINING

If a person who has achieved calm abiding wishes to proceed over some of the remaining paths—for example, if she or he wishes to progress over the rest of the supramundane paths—that person must consider what preparatory trainings are necessary. Similarly, a person who wishes to progress over the remaining paths in dependence on a mundane path must work on the preparatory trainings for a mundane path. What are the preparatory trainings? The practitioner must cultivate again and again the calm abiding and physical [and mental] pliancy that have already been attained. It is necessary, according to Asaṅga's *Grounds of Hearers,* to "pass days and nights"—that is, a great deal of time—in this endeavor. The practitioner's meditation must come to have the four attributes of preparatory training.[10]

---

[1] *bsam gtan dang po, prathamadhyāna.*

[2] *bsam gtan gnyis pa, dvitīyadhyāna.*

[3] *bsam gtan gsum pa, tritīyadhyāna.*

[4] *bsam gtan bzhi pa, caturthadhyāna.*

[5] *nam mkha' mtha' yas, ākāśānantya.*

[6] *rnam shes mtha' yas, vijñānānantya.*

[7] *ci yang med, akiṃcanya.*

[8] *srid rtse, bhavāgra.*

[9] *sngon 'gro'i sbyor ba.*

[10] *sngon 'gro'i sbyor ba'i khyad par bzhi.*

The Four Attributes of Preparatory Training

1 first attribute
  a advancing the entity
  b increase
  c breadth
2 second attribute
  a tightness
  b steadiness
  c hardness
3 third attribute: aspiration toward a true object of observation and engagement in it
4 fourth attribute: skill in the causes of calm abiding and special insight (For detail, see chart, p. 219.)

The first attribute has three aspects: advancing the entity,[1] increase,[2] and breadth.[3] The first of these is that the entity of the calm abiding and physical [and mental] pliancy advances. The relevant passage of Asaṅga's *Grounds of Hearers* is quoted in D̄zong-ka-b̄a's *Great Exposition of the Stages of the Path to Highest Enlightenment* but is not explained there. Therefore, we must arrive at an explanation through reasoned analysis. "Advancing the entity of calm abiding and physical [and mental] pliancy" refers to making their continuum steady, such that it will not be interrupted. The second aspect, increase, means that the entity not only continues but becomes strong. Thus, "advance" refers to the continuation of the substantial continuum of calm abiding and physical [and mental] pliancy, whereas "increase" is designated from the viewpoint of that entity's becoming stronger. The third aspect, breadth, is extremely important and was mentioned earlier at the time of discussing the object of observation of calm abiding. Here "breadth" refers to developing the capacity for engaging in many objects of observation. Most beginners must observe only one object of observation before achieving calm abiding. It is said that if, instead of observing one object, a meditator changes objects and observes many, it will be impossible to achieve calm abiding. After achieving it, however, one definitely must engage in techniques for broadening one's objects of observation. Thus, the statement that one should make the object of observation broader refers to the time after achievement of calm

---

[1] *ngo bo 'phel ba.*

[2] *rgyas pa.*

[3] *yangs pa.*

abiding. There are many different interpretations of Atīsha's statement that, in achieving calm abiding, "one should set one's virtuous mind on any *one* object of observation," but in any case, a meditator [usually] stays with just a single object until calm abiding is achieved. Some say that this particular passage means that one may choose any object of observation; [this position is refuted on p. 35].

The three aspects of the second attribute are tightness,[1] steadiness,[2] and hardness.[3] "Tightness" refers to the object of observation and the subject, the mind of calm abiding, being stuck together such that they cannot be separated. For example, when we tie things together well, they cannot be separated. "Steadiness" refers to the fact that the mind at this point cannot easily come to have an unfavorable state. "Hardness" is not to be understood as a coarse or gross quality; rather, it indicates that this is not a meditation whose capacities have not been fulfilled but one that is developed.

The third attribute is the aspiring toward a true or correct object of observation and engagement in it.[4] The word for "aspiration" here, *mos pa,* has many meanings. It may mean "aspiration" or "wish," as it does here. It may also mean "belief." Sometimes it refers to pretense, as when you think you are something you are not, or that something is what it is not. For example, the word *mos pa* is used in the instruction to think that an area is filled with water; the area is not filled with water, but there is a meditation in which one imagines that it is. In this case, the word has nothing to do with belief, or faith. Therefore, it cannot be said one-pointedly that the word *mos pa* has only a single meaning; the meaning depends on the context.

What is a correct object of observation? There are some people who, although they achieve calm abiding and have the breadth of being able to engage in many objects of observation, are unable to engage in a certain special object of observation because it is too subtle. The word "correct" does not mean that such an object must necessarily be emptiness. It could be a phenomenon other than the profound emptiness, such as an exalted knower of all aspects.[5] To have the third attribute is to have the aspiration

---

[1] *dam pa.*

[2] *brtan pa.*

[3] *sra ba.*

[4] *yang dag pa'i dmigs pa la mos pa dang de la 'jug par 'gyur ba.*

[5] It seems, then, simply to indicate an exalted object of observation.

to observe a special object of observation and, furthermore, to be able to engage in observing such an object.

The fourth attribute is skill in the causes of calm abiding and special insight.[1]

Skill in Causes of Calm Abiding and Special Insight

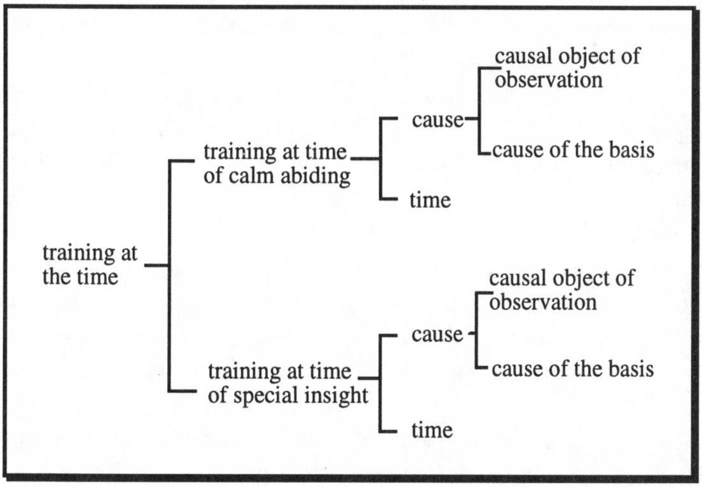

"Training at the time"[2] refers to the ability to do whatever is necessary for a particular practice at that time. This applies to both calm abiding and special insight. As it applies to the topic of calm abiding, there are two subtopics: the cause[3] of calm abiding and the time[4] of calm abiding. The cause of calm abiding is also divided into two: the causal object of observation[5] and the cause of the basis.[6] Training at the time of special insight[7] has a similar set of subdivisions, which are not discussed here.

With regard to training at the time of calm abiding,[8] what is the causal object of observation? It is the main object of observation itself. In dependence on the object of observation, the mind becomes pacified. Thus,

[1] *zhi gnas dang lhag mthong gi mtshan ma la mkhas pa.*

[2] *dus kyi sbyor ba.*

[3] *mtshan ma.*

[4] *dus.*

[5] *dmigs pa'i mtshan ma.*

[6] *gzhi'i mtshan ma.*

[7] *lhag mthong gi dus kyi sbyor ba.*

[8] *zhi gnas kyi dus kyi sbyor ba.*

pacification of the mind is a fruit, or effect, of the object of observation, and for this reason the object of observation is called a cause of calm abiding. Here the word *mtshan ma* does not in the least mean "mark" or "sign"; its only meaning here is "cause." Thus, the object of observation is an imputed but not an actual cause of the pacification of the mind. Therefore, it should be understood as a causal object of observation. The object of observation is a cause in the sense that in dependence on it the mind becomes pacified.

In order to purify or advance calm abiding, one engages in training in special insight. Therefore, in the term "cause of the basis,"[1] "basis" refers to the purification of calm abiding, or the advance of calm abiding. The cause of this is engagement in training in special insight. When does one have the purification of calm abiding? It is attained when one achieves the meditative stabilization which is a union of calm abiding and special insight. Therefore, in order to achieve the purification of calm abiding, one engages in the training in special insight which will act as the cause of the purification of calm abiding—or, in other words, the cause of the basis. One cultivates special insight in order to purify calm abiding. If, when one cultivates special insight, the calm abiding is ruined, it is necessary to begin training from the beginning. If, however, when one cultivates special insight for the sake of calm abiding, the calm abiding not only does not deteriorate but advances because of this practice, then one is well along in preparation for the higher paths.

The topic of training at the time of calm abiding is divided into two parts: cause, which has just been discussed, and time. (See chart, p. 219.) Here "time" refers to the ability to engage immediately in the object of observation either when excitement arises or when one has a sense that it is about to arise.

These four preparatory attributes are all preparatory trainings for going on to the remaining paths, in dependence on either a mundane or a supramundane path. Although Asaṅga's *Grounds of Hearers* does not designate them as preparatory trainings, it sets them forth at this point as attributes which must be developed. The point is that, if one is going to attain special insight, one's mind must have these four attributes. Therefore, before going on to all the steps in cultivating special insight, one would continue to cultivate meditation so that it would come to have these four qualities. In general, all that is being said is that one must have a developed

---

[1] *gzhi'i mtshan ma.*

entity of calm abiding which can then be used for cultivating special insight.

Calm abiding must be developed to such a degree that it cannot be ruined by analysis.[1] Not only that; it must be able to advance as the analysis advances. It might seem that this is very close to having actual special insight; however, it is suitable to say that having the four attributes means that one's calm abiding is developed merely until it will not be disturbed by analysis, whereas having special insight means that one has both wisdom and meditative stabilization in equal force. The first stage shown in the chart (p. 219) refers to the factor of wisdom in meditative stabilization while cultivating calm abiding; and the second stage, to the factor of wisdom in meditative stabilization while cultivating special insight. The third stage occurs when one has special insight. At this time, one's mind is accompanied by factors, equal in strength, of meditative stabilization and wisdom. This is why it is said that the attainments of special insight and of a union of calm abiding and special insight are simultaneous. Whenever actual special insight is attained, one attains a union of calm abiding and special insight.

In terms of the mode of practice needed to bring about the fourth attribute, the practitioner who has good stabilizing meditation seeks to increase its clarity. When this practice begins to affect the stabilizing meditation [by interfering with it], one sets the mind more in stabilizing meditation. In this way, the mind is increased.

It is necessary here to understand the difference between two points. If excitement is being generated or is about to be generated, one engages in stabilizing meditation to prevent it. If one feels that laxity is being generated or is about to be generated, one engages in analytical meditation as an antidote to that.

Moreover, at the time of working on stabilizing meditation, with a corner of the mind one remains wary or cautious about becoming lax. It may be asked how one mind can be set in meditative equipoise while another mind is looking as though from a corner of the mind. I do not think this is very difficult, since this is a case of the mind's being set in meditative equipoise while a corner of the mind watches it. For example, if you are walking along a path with someone and are engaged in intense or important conversation, you are involved in two activities. Mostly you are concerned with what the other person is saying, but a small remaining portion

---

[1] *dpyod pa, vicāra.*

of your mind is engaged in keeping you on the path. We have all experienced this.

There are probably no qualms with respect to the first three attributes of preparatory training. You may have qualms about the fourth, however. In discussing it, I specifically referred to becoming skilled in the causes of calm abiding. Asaṅga's *Grounds of Hearers* clearly sets forth *how* one becomes skilled in calm abiding and special insight, although this is not explained clearly in the Tibetan commentaries.

The first topic regarding this is the training at the time of calm abiding. This has two parts, the cause and the time of calm abiding. The cause of calm abiding is broken down into the causal object of observation and the cause of the basis. Since it is in dependence on the object of observation of a calm abiding that the mind becomes peaceful, the object is itself called a cause. With respect to the cause of the basis, this was explained as cultivation of special insight for the sake of purifying calm abiding. One might indeed have qualms about this.

There are several different types of meditation:

1 meditating for the sake of attaining that which one has not yet attained[1]
2 meditating for the sake of the non-deterioration of that which has been attained[2]
3 meditating for the sake of increasing that which has already been attained.[3]

"Cultivating special insight for the sake of purifying calm abiding" refers to the first type.

If we illustrate the above with people who are cultivating the path, there are two types: those who have and who have not entered the path. This is because hearing, thinking, and meditating are preparations for the path; having first relied upon these three, one generates a path. In the case of cultivating special insight for the sake of purifying calm abiding, one is engaging in meditation for the sake of attaining what has not yet been attained. The actual attainment of special insight occurs with attainment of the third of the seven preparations, which is called the mental contemplation.[4] Here, at the time following the first preparation [calm abiding], and before attainment of the third, one has not yet attained special insight.

[1] *ma thob pa 'thob pa'i phyir du sgom pa.*

[2] *thob pa mi nyams pa'i phyir sgom pa.*

[3] *thob pa gong 'phel du 'gro ba'i phyir sgom pa.*

[4] *mos pa las byung ba'i yid byed, adhimokṣikamanaskāra.*

Between the first and the third preparation is the mental contemplation of thorough knowledge of the character. Calm abiding has been attained, and in order to attain special insight one engages in the mental contemplation of thorough knowledge of the character, which itself is mainly analytical meditation.

Question: It seems that, on the one hand, in order to attain special insight, you are required to do things which would require that you already have special insight. On the other hand, it seems that in order to purify calm abiding you are required to do certain things that seem to indicate that you do not already have calm abiding—for example, the necessity of being aware that excitement is about to arise.

Answer: First, it should be made clear that the fourth attribute of preparatory training mentioned above (p. 217) is not the mental contemplation of thorough knowledge of the character, for that is mainly analytical meditation. At this point, one must find out whether or not one can do that analytical meditation. I am now talking about the period between the attainment of the first preparation, calm abiding, which is a mental contemplation, and actually beginning to work at the second. This is the preparatory training for *beginning to work at* the second preparation, the mental contemplation of thorough knowledge of the character.

With regard to the qualms about excitement arising, this is entirely different from what was done while cultivating calm abiding. The strength of it is very different. Before, one was seeking to enhance meditative stabilization, or one-pointedness of mind, whereas here one is enhancing pliancy and meditative stabilization.

Question: Since at this point one is not cultivating the mental contemplation of thorough knowledge of the character, why is this called a cultivation of special insight for the sake of purifying calm abiding?

Answer: Because what one is mainly aiming at is special insight. Special insight is sought for the sake of attaining a union of calm abiding and special insight. The measure of having thoroughly purified special insight is the attainment of a union of calm abiding and special insight. The measure of having thoroughly purified calm abiding is also the attainment of that union.

Question: What would the fault be if one did not engage in this training—if one immediately attempted to cultivate the mental contemplation of thorough knowledge of the character?

Answer: This mental contemplation is mainly analytical meditation and is specifically aimed at attaining special insight. If one began the analytical meditation of the mental contemplation known as thorough knowledge of the character without this training, the one-pointedness of one's meditative stabilization would deteriorate.

Question: What is the object of observation in the preparatory training of cultivating special insight for the sake of purifying calm abiding?

Answer: It could be the same as the object of observation formerly used in cultivating calm abiding, but if one's meditative stabilization has become developed, it is possible to use a special object. If the yogic practitioner does not have high realization, he or she would stay with the former object, but someone with high realization uses the ability gained through the attainment of calm abiding—the ability to engage in many objects of observation—and directs the mind to higher objects. There is no definiteness here; it depends on the level of realization.

Question: If the object of observation at this time is still the body of a Buddha, then in what sense is one cultivating special insight?

Answer: One could engage in analytical meditation on the major and minor marks of a Buddha, how they are achieved, and so forth.

Question: Then one does engage in analytical meditation at the time of cultivating special insight for the sake of purifying calm abiding?

Answer: Yes, because one is trying to find out whether or not one can cultivate special insight. How is this done? The context is the same as before. First one achieves the factor of clarity[1] and then, the factor of stability. While working on the factor of clarity, one has to be wary of the possible arising of excitement. If one finds that excitement is indeed beginning to arise, one works on the factor of stability. The work on stability is done within being wary of the possible arising of laxity. If laxity begins to develop, one works on clarity.

In this way, one analyzes to see whether or not it is suitable to pass on to the cultivation of the mental contemplation of thorough knowledge of the character. This mental contemplation is mainly a mixture of hearing and thinking and is also mainly analytical meditation. Thus, if meditative stabilization is not very firm, it will be ruined by engaging in this mental contemplation.

---

[1] *gsal cha.*

16 PROGRESSING ON THE MUNDANE PATH

PERSONS ON THE MUNDANE PATH

Persons who have generated in their mental continuums the four features of meditative stabilization through engaging in the preparatory trainings progress by way of either the mundane path or the supramundane path. I will explain here how one proceeds on the mundane path.

With regard to progressing on the mundane path, there are two topics: the person who is progressing and the path of progress. With regard to persons, Asaṅga's *Grounds of Hearers* sets forth four types of person who can progress by way of a mundane path:

1 all Outsiders [non-Buddhists][1]
2 Buddhists of dull faculties[2]
3 Buddhists of sharp faculties whose virtuous roots are not thoroughly ripened[3]
4 Bodhisattvas who are one lifetime away from achieving Buddhahood.[4]

OUTSIDERS

Asaṅga's *Grounds of Hearers* says, "all Outsiders," but this does not mean that whoever is an Outsider is necessarily one who can progress by a mundane path. The word "all" is used because any Outsider who has achieved calm abiding and wishes to progress higher must do so by way of a mundane path. The reason for this is that if one is going to progress in this lifetime by way of a supramundane path, one must at the least achieve a supramundane uncontaminated path. Even if one is only going to begin the process in this lifetime, it is necessary to achieve a path which has as its aspect realization of the truths. Because non-Buddhists do not accept the

---

[1] *phyi rol pa thams cad.*

[2] *dbang rdul gyi nang pa.*

[3] *dbang rnon gyi dge rtsa yongs su ma smin pa.*

[4] *skye ba gcig gis thogs pa'i byang chub sems dpa'.*

four noble truths and their sixteen attributes, non-Buddhists do not have such path.

What do non-Buddhists have? They have attainment of calm abiding and of the first five of the six clairvoyances. It is impossible to attain the first five clairvoyances without having attained an actual absorption of a concentration; the first five clairvoyances and the four immeasurables[1] must be attained in dependence on an actual concentration. Without depending on an actual concentration, no person—whether Buddhist, non-Buddhist, Bodhisattva, or whatever—can attain any of the first five clairvoyances or any of the four immeasurables. Asaṅga's *Summary of Manifest Knowledge* says that whether one is Buddhist or non-Buddhist, whether a Hearer, Bodhisattva, or whatever, the immeasurables are achieved in dependence on the four concentrations, and the same is true of the five clairvoyances. Thus, non-Buddhists can have attainment of an actual concentration.

Among non-Buddhists, the Nihilists[2] are of two types: Dialecticians[3] and Meditators.[4] There are Nihilist Meditators who achieve an actual concentration. In dependence on that, they achieve a clairvoyance that is mainly the memory of former lifetimes. This is done mainly in dependence on the meditative stabilization of the inhalation and exhalation of the breath. The clairvoyant consciousness itself acts as the subject which examines the inhalation and exhalation. That clairvoyance is a direct perception;[5] therefore, it sees things clearly. It observes former inhalations and exhalations because, being a clairvoyant consciousness, it is able to move back through the inhalations and exhalations. This is not something that thought is able to accomplish. It seems easier to move back within this lifetime because it is manifest; it is easy to remember back to the point of conception, the joining of the two lifetimes in the womb. There are clairvoyant consciousnesses of greater and lesser power and of higher and lower realization. For those of higher realization it is possible to pass back to the intermediate state that preceded this lifetime. There are some who are able to remember one, two, or three lifetimes. This depends on the strength of the clairvoyant consciousness. Nihilist Meditators then come to the one-

---

1 *tshad med, apramāṇa.*

2 *rgyang 'phen pa, āyata.*

3 *rtog ge pa.*

4 *snyoms 'jug pa.*

5 *mngon sum, pratyakṣa.*

pointed decision that nothing exists before the one, two, or three lifetimes that they are able to perceive clairvoyantly. This is how the system of Nihilists having clairvoyance becomes established. They identify their own direct perception, the clairvoyant consciousness, as an omniscient consciousness and thereby decide from the depths of their minds that nothing existed before what they can see.

This is, indeed, not an ordinary consciousness; it is included within the level of an upper realm. With a union of calm abiding and mundane special insight preceding it, an actual concentration acts as the mental basis of this clairvoyant consciousness. In dependence on this clairvoyant consciousness, Nihilist Meditators are able to understand many things that ordinary persons cannot. They feel that the clairvoyant consciousness is so trustworthy that whatever it does not see does not exist. When they do not see lifetimes beyond the first few past lifetimes, then, from the depths of their minds, they come to the conclusion that such lifetimes do not exist. With that decision, a Nihilist Meditator's clairvoyant consciousness and calm abiding deteriorate. It is said that the person's virtuous roots simultaneously deteriorate. In general, there are some people who, when their actual concentration deteriorates, fall only to the level of having a union of calm abiding and mundane special insight. Here, however, not only the actual concentration but also the union of calm abiding and mundane special insight, as well as mundane special insight, deteriorate.

Beyond this, there are many other non-Buddhist sages who have achieved clairvoyances. Those who attain an actual concentration are able to remain in meditative equipoise even for an eon through the meditative stabilization observing the inhalation and exhalation of the breath. There are those who, by their clairvoyant consciousnesses, are able to bring to mind the formation of the world system[1] and to extend their perception to the disintegration of the world system. Others are capable of seeing places ranging from the areas of the concentrations down to the levels of the hells. It is more difficult to view one's own continuum than external objects.

An Outsider who has attained calm abiding and wishes to progress further on the path can do so only by means of a mundane path.

BUDDHISTS OF DULL FACULTIES

The second category consists of Buddhists having dull faculties. These are persons who have attained calm abiding but are unable to achieve a special

---

1 *'jig rten gyi khams, lokadhātu.*

insight observing any of the four noble truths. Such persons are bothered by the afflictive emotions of the levels of Nothingness and below from among the nine levels (see chart, p. 215). Although anyone troubled by any type of afflictive emotion of cyclic existence has two choices, the supramundane or the mundane path, this second type of person has no ability to practice the supramundane path, which would involve achievement of a union of calm abiding and special insight observing a coarse or subtle selflessness and is unable to develop special insight observing any of the four noble truths.

BUDDHISTS OF SHARP FACULTIES WHOSE VIRTUOUS ROOTS ARE NOT THOROUGHLY RIPENED

The third type is a person whose virtuous roots are not thoroughly ripened. Asaṅga's *Grounds of Hearers* makes this statement without specifying its meaning; however, Ḏzong-ka-ḇa's *Exposition of the Stages of the Path* identifies persons of this type as those who, although they have understood[1] emptiness, have not ripened the virtuous roots needed for directly realizing emptiness. Thus, this third type is different from the second because persons of the third type have sharp faculties and, whether they have entered a path or not, have realized emptiness; nevertheless, the virtuous roots needed for direct realization of emptiness in this lifetime have not ripened. Such persons, being troubled by afflictive emotions pertaining to the Desire Realm, wish to separate from attachment to Desire Realm afflictive emotions and must accomplish this goal by means of a mundane path. There is no other choice because, in order to separate from attachment to afflictive emotions by way of a supramundane path, one has to cognize emptiness directly and persons of this third type are incapable of doing so at that time.

Let us discuss the meaning of the word *khong du chud pa*, translated here as "understand." In the Tibetan commentaries, it has the same meaning as "realize."[2] In Indian commentaries, however, the term has two meanings. For instance, if the term *khong du chud pa* is used in relation to enlightenment, it means "to attain"[3] enlightenment; similarly, when Kamalashīla uses this term in his *Stages of Meditation*, he is referring to attaining the first Bodhisattva ground. If *khong du chud pa* is used in relation to such-

1 *khong du chud pa.*

2 *rtogs pa.*

3 *thob.*

ness, it means "to directly realize"[1] suchness, or, "to make [suchness] manifest."[2] Thus, in Indian commentaries the term *khong du chud pa* means either "to attain" or "to make manifest"; if it is traced back, it probably means "to make manifest," for we refer to a person who has attained enlightenment as one who has manifested or actualized enlightenment. There are also many references, in both Indian and Tibetan commentaries, to manifesting or actualizing suchness. To actualize enlightenment is to attain it; to make suchness manifest is to realize it directly.

For example, on the path of training there are cases of having first a prime cognition,[3] then a subsequent cognition,[4] and then again a prime cognition. The second attainment of a prime cognition would occur when one directly realized emptiness. The mode of realization is so different from what came before that this perception is called a prime cognition. The term "actualize suchness" refers to such an occasion of directly realizing emptiness. Thus, in Indian commentaries, the term *khong du chud pa* is used for *mngon du gyur pa* (to make manifest). The term "actualization of exalted wisdom"[5] appears frequently in the discipline[6] texts. Here, "exalted wisdom" refers only to the exalted wisdom which directly realizes the truth. The term *stong pa nyid mngon du 'gyur pa*—"to make emptiness manifest"—means "to realize emptiness directly." Thus, it seems that in the Tibetan commentaries *khong du chud pa* means "to realize." I offer this to you as something to be examined later.

BODHISATTVAS ONE LIFETIME AWAY FROM ACHIEVING BUDDHAHOOD

Persons of the fourth type are Bodhisattvas who are one lifetime away from achieving the full enlightenment of a Buddha. This means that there will be one lifetime between their present life and the attainment of Buddhahood. According to Vasubandhu's *Treasury of Manifest Knowledge*, whoever is a Bodhisattva one lifetime away from achieving Buddhahood is necessarily a person on the path of accumulation; a person who is to achieve enlightenment in this lifetime is called a final-lifetime Bodhisat-

---

1 *mngon sum du rtogs pa.*

2 *mngon du gyur pa.*

3 *tshad ma, pramāṇa.* This first prime cognition would occur when first realizing emptiness inferentially.

4 *bcad shes.*

5 *ye shes mngon du 'gyur pa.*

6 *'dul ba, vinaya.*

tva.[1] In the Mahāyāna systems of tenets a Bodhisattva who is one lifetime away from Buddhahood probably is necessarily on one of the three pure grounds—the eighth, ninth, or tenth. Thus, there is a great difference between the Mahāyāna sūtra tenet systems and the system of the *Treasury*. The three lower tantra sets[2] agree with the Mahāyāna sūtra system on this point.

According to Highest Yoga Tantra, a Bodhisattva who is one lifetime away from Buddhahood is on the path of accumulation. This means a Bodhisattva of the Highest Yoga Tantric system.

Question: What about a tenth-ground Bodhisattva who is yet to enter Highest Yoga Tantra?

Answer: Such a Bodhisattva is already necessarily in her or his last lifetime. Someone who has entered Highest Yoga Tantra from the very beginning and achieves the path of preparation by way of Highest Yoga Tantra is necessarily a person who will achieve the illusory body[3] in that very lifetime. This means that such a person is beyond death; thus, Buddhahood will be achieved right within that lifetime. Therefore, anyone who achieves the path of preparation by way of the path of Highest Yoga Tantra will necessarily achieve an illusory body on that very life-basis. One who has achieved the illusory body will necessarily connect to Buddhahood.

Entry into Highest Yoga Tantra occurs either on the paths of accumulation or preparation or on the tenth ground. In the latter case, one would follow the sūtra system until achieving the initial uninterrupted path of the tenth ground and would then enter Highest Yoga Tantra.

Within the Mahāyāna sūtra tenet systems, is it definite on which of the three pure grounds the Bodhisattva who is one lifetime away from Buddhahood will be? I feel it must be the tenth ground. The tenth ground should not be thought of as something that goes quickly. Rather, it has some duration; it can take several lifetimes. There is no very clear source in texts stating that a Bodhisattva one lifetime away from Buddhahood is necessarily on the tenth ground; however, Bodhisattvas one lifetime away from Buddhahood are posited as illustrations of tenth-ground Bodhisattvas. Thus, through an inference based on the qualities, and so forth, of tenth-ground Bodhisattvas, it can be virtually decided that a Bodhisattva one lifetime away from Buddhahood is on the tenth ground.

---

[1] *srid pa mtha' ma'i byang sems.*

[2] Action, Performance, and Yoga Tantras.

[3] *sgyu lus, māyādeha.*

To what system does Asaṅga's *Grounds of Hearers* refer when, in speaking of persons who proceed by the mundane path, it gives as an example a Bodhisattva who is one lifetime away from Buddhahood? In the Mahāyāna sūtra system, this would be a tenth-ground Bodhisattva. Asaṅga, however, could be referring only to the system of Vasubandhu's *Treasury of Manifest Knowledge*, a Hīnayāna system.

According to Vasubandhu's *Treasury of Manifest Knowledge*, a Bodhisattva one lifetime away from Buddhahood is necessarily on the path of accumulation. The Teacher Shākyamuni Buddha or a rhinoceros-like Solitary Realizer[1] amasses the collections of merit and wisdom[2] over the path of accumulation and, in the next lifetime, passes from the path of preparation right through to the end in one meditative session. This is done in dependence on a final[3] fourth concentration. However, during the path of accumulation such practitioners separate from attachment to the afflictive emotions pertaining to the Desire Realm. This state of separation from attachment, therefore, occurs in dependence on a mundane path. Then, in dependence on the fourth concentration, one passes from the path of preparation through to the path of no more learning.

QUALMS WITH RESPECT TO "PATH"

Let us eliminate some qualms with respect to the "path" referred to in the term "progress in dependence on a mundane path." What are posited as the paths in dependence on which persons of the first two types—non-Buddhists and dull Buddhists—progress? Their path has the aspect of grossness/peacefulness.[4] For example, someone who is cultivating an actual absorption of the first concentration views the afflictive emotions pertaining to the Desire Realm as gross relative to the afflictive emotions of the Form Realm. The afflictive emotions of the Form Realm are also viewed as peaceful in comparison to those of the Desire Realm; other qualities of the Form Realm are seen as even more peaceful. Thus, to progress by means of a path in which one views the lower level as gross and the upper level as peaceful is to make use of a path that has the aspect of grossness/peacefulness. This is the type of mundane path in dependence on which persons of the first and second types progress.

On what kind of mundane path do persons of the third and fourth types

---

1 *bse ru lta bu rang sangs rgyas, khaḍgaviṣāṇakalpapratyekabuddha.*

2 *bsod nams dang ye shes kyi tshogs, puṇyajñānasaṃbhāra.*

3 *rab mtha'.*

4 *zhi rags rnam can gyi lam.*

progress? It is *not* a path that has as its aspect grossness/peacefulness. Such paths, used by persons of the first and second types, are designated by the name "mundane paths." However, the mundane path based on which persons of the third and fourth types progress does not have the aspect of grossness/peacefulness, for they have already realized the four noble truths. Therefore, they separate from attachment in dependence on a path of realizing selflessness.

Why is their path said to be mundane? The word "mundane" here refers to the path of a common being as opposed to that of a Superior. These are people who, by definition, cannot generate the path of a Superior; therefore they separate from attachment in dependence on a common being's path. Although Asaṅga's *Grounds of Hearers* contains no clear source for stating what *type* of mundane path it is by which these people progress, Jam-ȳang-shay-b̄a makes a great distinction here which I think is borne out in fact. This mundane path is called a path which has the uncontaminated truths as its aspect.[1] Here "that which has as its aspect" means "that which has as its object of observation"; the object of observation is the uncontaminated truths. This type of path is called a mundane path because the person is progressing in dependence on the path of a non-Superior—that is, of a common being. However, the person is not progressing in dependence on a path which has as its object of observation the grossness of a lower level and the peacefulness of an upper level.

If we think about this with reasoning, in dependence on viewing a lower level as gross and an upper level as peaceful, one can separate from attachment to the afflictive emotions pertaining to the lower level. Further, by viewing selflessness in dependence on a common being's path, one is able to undermine the ignorance which serves as the basis of both the lower and upper levels. Such a person is really seeing both the lower and upper levels as gross.

It is said that in dependence on a path that has as its object a viewing of the lower level as gross and the upper as peaceful one can separate from attachment to the level of Nothingness and below but not to the level of the Peak of Cyclic Existence. This is because a mind of the Peak of Cyclic Existence itself cannot separate from the afflictive emotions of that level and there is no mundane level above that. Thus, it cannot view some higher level as peaceful while seeing its own level as gross. This mind cannot separate from attachment to the afflictive emotions of its own level be-

[1] *zag med bden pa'i rnam can gyi lam.*

cause both mind and level are contaminated. Moreover, even if it were able to view its own level as gross and a hypothetical upper one as peaceful, this would be just an ordinary object, and if two things are similar in capacity, the first cannot cause the second to separate from attachment to the second. Thus, there are two reasons why a meditative equipoise of the peak of cyclic existence cannot serve as a cause of one's separating from attachment to the Peak of Cyclic Existence. One reason is that both the meditative equipoise and the level are contaminated; the other is that the object here—unlike the truths—is just an ordinary one. It is possible to separate from attachment to the Peak of Cyclic Existence in dependence on an uncontaminated first concentration because the latter is uncontaminated.

I have said that in dependence on a mundane path that has as its object the uncontaminated truths one can separate from attachment to the level of Nothingness and below. Can one also separate from the afflictive emotions of the Peak of Cyclic Existence through this path? There is no clear statement on this. My own guess is such a path can damage the afflictive emotions of the Peak of Cyclic Existence, but I do not think it can cause one to separate from attachment to—that is, to become devoid of—the afflictive emotions of the Peak of Cyclic Existence, for, in order to do that, it is necessary to have two factors, an uncontaminated object and an uncontaminated path—that is, an uncontaminated consciousness. Here the object is sufficient because this path has as its aspect the uncontaminated truths. The consciousness, however, is a mundane path and is affected by attachment; the moisture of attachment still permeates it. The mind of the Peak of Cyclic Existence is very subtle, and, therefore, a mundane consciousness probably cannot cause one to separate from the afflictive emotions of the Peak of Cyclic Existence. That is just my own estimation; you should examine it further. Separation from the afflictive emotions here means a temporary separation. It is necessary to have an uncontaminated path in order to separate, even temporarily, from the afflictive emotions of the Peak of Cyclic Existence.

We are essentially talking about three different degrees of undermining afflictive emotions. The first is to suppress them by means of calm abiding. The second is, further, to rely on a mundane path in order to become separated from attachment to afflictive emotions. The third is to abandon the afflictive emotions by means of a supramundane path. There are two types of abandonment, both of which are everlasting: abandonment forever of the artificial[1] afflictive emotions and abandonment forever of the innate[2] afflictive emotions. Actual abandonment can be accomplished only if one has achieved at least a Superior path—that is, a path of seeing. Even if the other types—suppression and separation from attachment—are called abandonments, they are not actual abandonments.

SOLITARY REALIZERS

I said earlier (p. 231) that in the system of Vasubandhu's *Treasury* the Teacher Shākyamuni Buddha and rhinoceros-like Solitary Realizers[3] accumulate merit, and so forth, over the path of accumulation and then, in one session, pass from the path of preparation through to the path of no more learning. Rhinoceros-like Solitary Realizers on the path of accumulation accumulate the collections of merit for at least one hundred eons—that is, one hundred great eons. Then, after completing the hundred eons of accumulation, they must engage in aspirational prayers within taking as the object of observation either a corpse in a cemetery or a skeleton. They reflect on the twelve links of dependent-arising in the forward and backward progressions, thinking with respect to the corpse or skeleton, "From what did this arise, and what will be its effect?" Their aspirational prayers are to be born in a particular social stratum[4]—in the royal,[5] brahmin,[6] or merchant[7] class—and that they may achieve enlightenment without depending on another teacher and, further, that if they teach students, they may do so without speaking. Such persons are rhinoceros-like Solitary Realizers.[8]

There is another type of Solitary Realizer known as a congregating[9] Solitary Realizer. Tibetan commentaries speak of two types here, greater and lesser congregating Solitary Realizers. The greater first passes through the paths of accumulation and preparation and goes through the three later paths in the next lifetime. The lesser congregating Solitary Realizer

---

[1] *kun btags, parikalpita.*

[2] *lhan skyes, sahaja.*

[3] *bse ru lta bu rang sangs rgyas, khaḍgaviṣāṇakalpapratyekabuddha.*

[4] *rigs, varṇa.*

[5] *rgyal rigs, kṣatriya.*

[6] *bram ze, brahmaṇa.*

[7] *rje'u rigs, vaiśya.*

[8] The rhinoceros is well-known for tending to remain alone.

[9] *tshogs dang spyod pa'i rang sangs rgyas, *vargacārinpratyekabuddha.*

achieves the first two fruits—Stream Enterer[1] and Once Returner[2]—in this lifetime and in the next lifetime achieves the last two fruits—Never Returner[3] and Foe Destroyer. Although Tibetan commentaries speak of these two types of congregating Solitary Realizer, Indian commentaries refer only to rhinoceros-like and congregating Solitary Realizers without further subdividing the latter.

1 *rgyun zhugs, śrotāpanna.*
2 *phyir 'ong, sakṛdāgāmin.*
3 *phyir mi 'ong, anāgāmin.*

17 MUNDANE PATH OF SPECIAL INSIGHT

SEVEN MENTAL CONTEMPLATIONS

It is said that an actual absorption of a concentration is achieved by way of seven mental contemplations. There are many types of mental contemplation; thus, it is necessary to get the count straight. I will first identify the seven mental contemplations mentioned by Asaṅga in the *Grounds of Hearers*, "One sets [the mind] in meditative equipoise by way of the seven mental contemplations." In that passage, the count begins with thorough, or individual, knowledge of the character. Asaṅga's *Grounds of Hearers* often mentions mental contemplations, sometimes speaking of seven and sometimes of six, four, or three. The last group is also mentioned in the *Sūtra Unraveling the Thought*. Thus, before considering the meaning of these we need to understand the distinctions of number.

The Seven Mental Contemplations

1 mental contemplation of individual knowledge of the character[1] (also known as thorough knowledge of the character[2])
2 mental contemplation arisen from belief[3]
3 mental contemplation of thorough isolation[4]
4 mental contemplation of joy-withdrawal[5]
5 mental contemplation of analysis[6]
6 mental contemplation of final training[7]
7 mental contemplation that is the fruit of final training.[8]

---

[1] *mtshan nyid so sor rig pa'i yid byed, lakṣaṇapratisaṃvedīmanaskāra.*

[2] *mtshan nyid rab tu rig pa.*

[3] *mos pa las byung ba'i yid byed, adhimokṣikamanaskāra.*

[4] *rab tu dben pa'i yid byed, prāvivekyamanaskāra.*

[5] *dga' ba sdud pai' yid byed, ratisaṃgrāhakamanaskāra.*

[6] *dpyod pa yid byed, mīmāṃsāmanaskāra.*

[7] *sbyor mtha'i yid byed, prayoganiṣṭhamanaskāra.*

[8] *sbyor mtha'i 'bras bu'i yid byed, prayoganiṣṭhaphalamanaskāra.*

These seven mental contemplations are abbreviated by Dzong-ka-ba into three groups:

three in terms of cause[1]: numbers 1, 2, and 5
three in terms of entity[2]: numbers 3, 4, and 6:
one in terms of effect[3]: number 7

The three in terms of cause consist of two that are posited in terms of cause in the sense of generating that which has not yet been generated and one that is designated from the viewpoint of increasing that which has already been generated. The texts contain no explicit statement of why the first two mental contemplations are posited in terms of generating what has not been generated because the reason is very clear, since the actual paths which serve as antidotes—uninterrupted paths or paths of release—cannot occur before the mental contemplation of thorough isolation. The first two mental contemplations are preparations for that and, thus, are cases of generating that which has not yet been generated.

The fifth mental contemplation is posited in terms of cause from the viewpoint of increasing that which has already been generated because, over the third and fourth mental contemplations, one is getting rid of most of the objects of abandonment,[4] and in the fifth, one analyzes to see whether or not they have all been abandoned. Therefore, the fifth is a technique for the increase of that which has already been generated. This is because, by this point, one has gotten rid of six of the nine divisions of objects of abandonment of the Desire Realm and, therefore, feels that they have probably all been abandoned. Because most of the manifest coarse afflictive emotions[5] have been suppressed, yogis even think that they have become like Foe Destroyers—as though all afflictive emotions have been overcome. Thus, yogis manifest the mental contemplation of analysis in order to investigate whether or not all the afflictive emotions pertaining to the Desire Realm have been abandoned and, thereby, understand that not all them have been abandoned. Therefore, they begin to cultivate the mental contemplation of final training for the sake of abandoning the afflictive emotions that remain. For this reason, the mental contemplation of analysis is a technique for increasing the antidotal consciousness which has

---

1 *rgyu'i dbang du byas pa gsum.*

2 *ngo bo'i dbang du byas pa gsum.*

3 *'bras bu dbang du byas pa gcig.*

4 *spang bya, prahātavya.*

5 *nyon mongs rags pa mngon gyur ba.*

already been generated. This is why it is known as an enhancer of the already generated. Although Tibetan commentaries give only brief mention to the mental contemplation of analysis, Asaṅga's *Grounds of Hearers* has a great deal on this topic. Thus, those are the three mental contemplations in terms of cause.

There are also three in terms of entity: the third, fourth, and sixth mental contemplations. Although it is not stated why these are called the three in terms of entity, there is no need for an explanation, as it is very clear. The reason is that in order to generate, for example, an actual first concentration, it is necessary to overcome the nine cycles of afflictive emotions pertaining to the Desire Realm. To do this, one needs an uninterrupted path and a path of release for each level of the afflictive emotions. Thus, at the time of the mental contemplation of thorough isolation, there are three uninterrupted paths and three paths of release for the sake of overcoming the first three levels of afflictive emotions pertaining to the Desire Realm. Similarly, there are two sets of three for the mental contemplation of joy-withdrawal for the sake of overcoming the fourth, fifth, and sixth cycles of the afflictive emotions pertaining to the Desire Realm, and two sets—one of three and one of two—at the point of the mental contemplation of final training, for the sake of overcoming the seventh, eighth, and ninth cycles of the afflictive emotions pertaining to the Desire Realm. (There are only one set of three and one set of two for the mental contemplation of final training because the last path of release is the seventh mental contemplation—the mental contemplation that is the fruit of final training.) These three mental contemplations are posited in terms of entity in the sense of being the entity of an antidote; they are the actual antidotal mental contemplations. The mental contemplation of analysis is not an actual antidotal consciousness because it cannot harm the afflictive emotions; it just analyzes to see whether or not they have all been abandoned.

With regard to the uninterrupted paths and paths of release of the mental contemplations of thorough isolation and of joy-withdrawal, every case of an uninterrupted path or path of release is, for instance, a mental contemplation of thorough isolation. With regard to those of the mental contemplation of final training, the three uninterrupted paths are mental contemplations of final training, but the third and last path of release is the actual mental contemplation that is the fruit of final training. Thus, there is a third path of release, even though it is not a mental contemplation of final training.

For example, the uninterrupted path of a path of seeing is itself a path of seeing. The path of release of a path of seeing is also a path of seeing. Similarly, an uninterrupted path of the eighth Bodhisattva ground is necessarily posited as in the continuum of someone on the eighth ground. The path of release of the eighth ground must also be posited as in an eighth-ground Bodhisattva's continuum. With regard to the tenth ground, however, there are two uninterrupted paths, one at the beginning and one at the end, but only one path of release. The initial uninterrupted path of the tenth ground is posited as being in the continuum of a Bodhisattva on the tenth ground; similarly, the final uninterrupted path of the tenth ground is also posited as being in the continuum of a tenth-ground Bodhisattva. However, the final path of release of the tenth ground is not posited as being in the continuum of a tenth-ground Bodhisattva. Rather, it is the first moment of an exalted knower of all aspects and thus is in the continuum of a Buddha. In the same way, the last of the three paths of release related to the sixth mental contemplation is not posited as being in the continuum of a person who has the mental contemplation of final training but, rather, as being in the continuum of a person who has the mental contemplation that is the fruit of final training.

The question whether this final path of release is a mental contemplation which is a first concentration is very complicated. What I am saying here is that it itself is the fruit of final training. The various tenet systems have different answers to the question whether this path of release is an actual first concentration, but there is no complication concerning its being the seventh mental contemplation. Everyone agrees that when one has the final path of release, one has attained the first concentration, but there is a great deal of complication regarding whether or not that final path of release itself is a first concentration.

The one mental contemplation that is posited in terms of effect is this last mental contemplation that is the fruit of final training. At this point the meditator has attained a true cessation which is a temporary abandonment of the ninth—the last—of the cycles of afflictive emotions pertaining to the Desire Realm; therefore, it is the fruit.

SIX MENTAL CONTEMPLATIONS

Asaṅga's *Grounds of Hearers* also mentions six mental contemplations. This reference to six is to mental contemplations in terms of being preparations; they are preparatory to the first concentration. These are the first six of the seven mental contemplations listed above. The first, then, is the mental contemplation of individual knowledge of the character.

Are there no more preparations than these six? It is not that there are no more, for before these there is another preparatory mental contemplation, that of a mere beginner—that is, calm abiding. This, however, is not explicitly mentioned as a preparatory mental contemplation in Asaṅga's *Grounds of Hearers.* It is not mentioned in any of these counts of mental contemplations, but it can be established by reasoning that simultaneous with the attainment of calm abiding is the attainment of a preparatory mental contemplation. Therefore, before one can attain the mental contemplation of individual knowledge of the character, one must attain calm abiding. Thus, there are seven preparatory mental contemplations.

Nevertheless, Asaṅga's *Grounds of Hearers* mentions six preparatory mental contemplations, although there are seven, because the attainment of the mental contemplation of a beginner at purifying afflictive emotions[1] begins with attainment of the mental contemplation of individual knowledge of the character. Here "purification"[2] refers, at minimum, to the beginning of the antidotal process of analysis that views the lower level as gross. It is said that, although the mental contemplation of individual knowledge of the character is not the beginning of the preparations, the mental contemplations which purify afflictive emotions begin with individual knowledge of the character, in the process of cultivating special insight. This is why Asaṅga posits six preparatory mental contemplations. The analysis of this is found in Ḏzong-ka-ḇa's *Great Exposition of the Stages of the Path.*

FOUR MENTAL CONTEMPLATIONS

Asaṅga's *Grounds of Hearers* also refers to four mental contemplations. These are:

concordant mental contemplation[3]: 1 and 2
antidotal mental contemplation[4]: 3 and 6 [also 4]
thoroughly clear mental contemplation[5]: 4
mental contemplation of individual investigation[6]: 5

---

1 *nyon mongs rnam par sbyong ba'i las dang po pa'i yid byed, kleśaviśuddhyādikarmikamanaskāra.*

2 *rnam par sbyong ba, viśuddhi.*

3 *rjes su mthun pa las byung ba'i yid byed.*

4 *gnyen po yid la byed pa.*

5 *rab tu dvang ba yid la byed pa.*

6 *so sor rtog pa yid la byed pa.*

The six preparatory mental contemplations mentioned in Asaṅga's *Grounds of Hearers* are included in these four, which are also set forth in terms of being preparatory mental contemplations. Among the six, the first two—the mental contemplation of individual knowledge of the character and the mental contemplation arisen from belief—are included in concordant mental contemplations. Included in the antidotal mental contemplations are the mental contemplations of thorough isolation and of final training. The mental contemplation of joy-withdrawal can also be considered an antidote, although it is included as a thoroughly clear mental contemplation as well. The mental contemplation of analysis is the mental contemplation of individual investigation.

Asaṅga explicitly sets forth why the mental contemplation of individual knowledge of the character and that arisen from belief are concordant mental contemplations. Although the actual antidote begins with the mental contemplation of thorough isolation, these two are similar to the actual antidotes; they accord with them and thus are concordant.

The mental contemplations of thorough isolation and final training are considered antidotal mental contemplations for the same reasons that they are considered to be in the category of those posited in terms of entity—namely, that they are actual entities of the antidote; they themselves are actual antidotes.

The mental contemplation of joy-withdrawal is both a thoroughly clear mental contemplation and an antidotal mental contemplation. It is the latter for the same reason given above—it is an actual antidote—and the former for reasons that are not set forth in either Asaṅga's *Grounds of Hearers* or Tibetan commentaries, where Asaṅga's statement is merely quoted without being analyzed. However, in my own estimation, according to some of the upper tenet systems' views on Manifest Knowledge, it is thought that, with the attainment of the mental contemplation of joy-withdrawal, one initially attains the feeling of bliss[1] that accompanies a preparation. When that is attained, a sense of great clarity is generated in the meditator's mind. This is a far greater sense of clarity than one has with calm abiding. In calm abiding, there is clarity with respect to the object of observation, but one has not abandoned any of the afflictive emotions, whereas here, internally, one is clarified, or purified, of afflictive emotions. The complications involved in deciding whether or not the final path of release can be posited as an actual first concentration (see p. 239)

---

[1] *tshor ba bde ba.*

are bound up with the complexities of this topic of the feeling that accompanies a preparation and whether or not it is blissful. Asaṅga's *Grounds of Hearers*, in a literal reading, refers to a lesser joy-withdrawal that is produced at the time of attaining the mental contemplation of thorough isolation. If the blissful feeling that accompanies a preparation is first attained with the mental contemplation of joy-withdrawal, it is the reason why this attainment is called the thoroughly clear mental contemplation.

It is easy to understand why the mental contemplation of analysis is called the mental contemplation of individual investigation.

THREE MENTAL CONTEMPLATIONS

There is also a reference to three mental contemplations. This is simply a list of three; the seven mental contemplations are not included in it. The three are:

1 a beginner at mental contemplation, *or, as an exception*, a beginning mental contemplation.[1] (The word "beginner"[2] usually refers to a person, but it does not necessarily refer to a person in this context.)
2 a mental contemplation of a mere beginner[3]
3 the mental contemplation of a beginner at purifying afflictive emotions[4]

A beginner at mental contemplation is posited as ranging from the attainment of the meditative stabilization of the ninth mind of the Desire Realm up to but not including calm abiding.[5] [The ninth mind of the Desire Realm is the ninth mental abiding.]

The mental contemplation of a mere beginner ranges from the attainment of calm abiding up to but not including the attainment of the mental contemplation of individual knowledge of the character.[6]

The mental contemplation of a beginner at purifying afflictive emotions ranges only over the mental contemplation of individual knowledge of the character.

In the first term "a beginner at mental contemplation," "mental contemplation"[7] refers to calm abiding. One is a beginner at mental contem-

[1] *yid la byed pa las dang po pa, manaskārādikarmika.*

[2] *las dang po pa, ādikarmika.*

[3] *las dang po pa tsam gyi yid byed.*

[4] *nyon mongs rnam par sbyong ba'i las dang po pa'i yid byed, kleśaviśuddhyādikarmikamanaskāra.*

[5] *'dod sems dgu pa'i ting nge 'dzin nas zhi gnas ma thob kyi bar la.*

[6] *zhi gnas thob pa nas mtshan nyid sor rig ma thob kyi bar la.*

[7] *yid la byed pa, manaskāra.*

plation—calm abiding—because one has not yet attained it. The term "beginner" here is unusual in that it refers to a consciousness, the ninth mind of the Desire Realm, rather than to a person, as it usually does.

Calm abiding itself is called the mental contemplation of a mere beginner. The meditator here is called a mere beginner because any actual path that can serve as an antidote to afflictive emotions begins with the mental contemplation of thorough isolation, and its direct inducer is special insight, the mental contemplation arisen from belief. Thus, the beginning work on it comes at the mental contemplation of individual knowledge of the character. Since calm abiding is achieved before that, calm abiding is called the mental contemplation of a mere beginner. Therefore, this term means that calm abiding is a mental contemplation of a person who is a mere beginner at purifying afflictive emotions.

Asaṅga's *Grounds of Hearers* uses the term "one-pointedness" in different ways. When Asaṅga says,[1] "A beginner at mental contemplation is in one-pointed activity," the term "one-pointed activity" is identified as the meditative stabilization of the ninth mind of the Desire Realm. He then states, "As long as one has not attained one-pointedness...," but here one-pointedness refers to calm abiding. A person who has not achieved calm abiding is called a beginner. Thus, a beginner at mental contemplation ranges from the attainment of the meditative stabilization of the ninth mind of the Desire Realm [that is, the ninth mental abiding] through to but not including the attainment of calm abiding.

Asaṅga's *Grounds of Hearers* then states, "After that, one has a mental contemplation." Next, there is a reference to the signs of the mental contemplation of a mere beginner, in which Asaṅga speaks of the signs of having achieved calm abiding. Therefore, it is clear that "mental contemplation of a mere beginner" refers to calm abiding. Similarly, the *Grounds of Hearers* frequently refers to the mental contemplation of individual knowledge of the character as the mental contemplation of a beginner at purifying afflictive emotions.

Question: In the term "beginner at mental contemplation," does the word "beginner" refer to a person or a consciousness?

Answer: In general, "beginner at mental contemplation" refers to a person, but, as used in Asaṅga's *Grounds of Hearers*, it does not refer to a person. This is because it occurs within a list of mental contemplations.

---

[1] The passage is cited with more context in *Meditative States*, 150.

In Tibetan commentaries a designation of eight mental contemplations is also used. There is nothing new in this. We first took as our basis the seven mental contemplations and then divided them from the viewpoint of cause, effect, and entity. The Tibetan commentaries add to these seven the mental contemplation of a mere beginner [that is, calm abiding] to get eight.

THREE YOGIS

As part of the general explanation of mental contemplations, we explained the seven, six, four, and three mental contemplations. There are also the three yogis mentioned in Asaṅga's *Grounds of Hearers.* Asaṅga in that text makes no distinction between mental contemplations and yogis. The two are different, but both categories refer to the same time span. The three yogis are:

1 a yogi who is a beginner[1]
   a. a beginner at mental contemplation[2]
   b. a person who possesses in his or her mental continuum the mental contemplation of a mere beginner[3]
   c. a beginner at purifying afflictive emotions[4]
2 a yogi who is purifying afflictive emotions[5]
3 a yogi who has passed beyond mental contemplation[6]

We have already identified the three beginner yogis: (a) a person who is a beginner at mental contemplation, (b) a person who possesses in her or his mental continuum the mental contemplation of a mere beginner, and (c) a beginner at purifying afflictive emotions. A yogi is the first type of beginner over the period of time ranging from the meditative stabilization of the ninth mind of the Desire Realm up to but not including the attainment of calm abiding. The second type of beginner yogi is a person who possesses in his or her continuum the mental contemplation of a mere beginner, which ranges from the time of achieving calm abiding up to but not including the attainment of the mental contemplation of individual knowledge of the character. The third beginner, a beginner at purifying afflictive

[1] *las dang po pa'i rnal 'byor pa.*
[2] *yid la byed pa las dang po pa.*
[3] *las dang po pa tsam gyi yid byed rgyud ldan gyi gang zag.*
[4] *nyon mongs rnam par sbyong ba'i las dang po pa.*
[5] *nyon mongs rnam par sbyong ba'i rnal 'byor pa.*
[6] *yid la byed pa las 'das pa'i rnal 'byor pa.*

emotions, is a person abiding in the mental contemplation of individual knowledge of the character. Thus, the three are generated in this order in the mental continuum of one person—that is, yogis become each of these, in turn, as they develop.

A person is the second type of yogi, one who is purifying afflictive emotions, from the attainment of the mental contemplation arisen from belief through to and including the mental contemplation of final training. Hence, there is a great difference between a beginner at purifying afflictive emotions—a person at the time of the mental contemplation of individual knowledge of the character—and a yogi who is purifying afflictive emotions, who is such from the point of the mental contemplation arisen from belief through the mental contemplation of final training. These two types of person are mutually exclusive. However, many scholars confuse the two. Some textbooks consider these two to be virtually the same, on the basis of a misreading of Asaṅga's *Grounds of Hearers*.

The third yogi is one who has passed beyond mental contemplation. This means that she or he has passed beyond preparation, not that he or she has no mental contemplation, for a yogi who has passed beyond mental contemplation is one who is abiding in, or has, the mental contemplation that is the fruit of final training, which is an actual first concentration and not a preparation for it.

Why are the mental contemplations from that arisen from belief through to that of final training given the name "mental contemplations purifying afflictive emotions," and why is the yogi who has them called a yogi who is purifying afflictive emotions? Except for the mental contemplation of analysis, those ranging from the mental contemplation of thorough isolation through the mental contemplation of final training are all actual antidotes. Even though the mental contemplation arisen from belief is not an actual antidote, it is the actual inducer of an antidote; it is the uncommon direct cause of an antidotal mental contemplation. For this reason, it is posited as a purifier. Similarly, the mental contemplation of analysis is not an actual purifier. However, through its analyzing whether or not all afflictive emotions have been abandoned, one realizes that they have not been. In this way, the mental contemplation of analysis directly induces the mental contemplation of final training. This is why all these are called mental contemplations purifying afflictive emotions.

This concludes the general explanation of mental contemplations. The purpose for giving it is to delineate the different sets of terminology, so that there will be no need to explain the context when these terms occur in a more detailed explanation. For listeners who have debated these topics previously, it is suitable to combine topics. For beginners, however, it is our custom in teaching to lay the basis by giving a general outline first and then to detail the topics individually.

Since I have already explained calm abiding, I will now begin a detailed explanation of the mental contemplation of individual knowledge of the character. Because of its difficulty, this topic should either be avoided entirely or explained fully. The other mental contemplations are easily understood.

18 INDIVIDUAL KNOWLEDGE OF THE CHARACTER

When yogic practitioners who have attained calm abiding are about to enter the mental contemplation of individual knowledge of the character, it is necessary for them to change the object of observation. If, for example, they have been meditating on the body of a Buddha in order to achieve calm abiding, once calm abiding has been achieved it is necessary to change the object of observation in order to pass on to the mental contemplation of individual knowledge of the character. That is why I mentioned earlier that in most cases a change must be made here. (See p. 217.) It cannot be said that in all cases the practitioner would have to change, for, if the object of observation for achieving calm abiding were the same as that for achieving the mental contemplation of individual knowledge of the character, it would not be necessary to change. For example, if the practitioner had taken emptiness as the object of observation for achieving calm abiding, it would not be necessary to change before attaining an actual absorption of the first concentration. However, such persons are extremely rare. I have already explained why this would be difficult from the point of view of both the object and the subject. (See p. 190.)

What would be the fault if one did not change the object at this time, if one continued to observe only the body of a Buddha? Indeed, in general it is very good to take as an object the body of a Buddha; one attains great merit by doing so. However, by continuing to meditate only on the body of a Buddha, one cannot have an actual antidote to afflictive emotions. At the least, if one wishes to progress by way of the mundane path, one must view the Desire Realm as faulty and the First Concentration as peaceful or advantageous. Just as the wisdom realizing emptiness is capable of acting as an antidote to the conception of true existence because it views such a conception as faulty, so here one must view the Desire Realm as faulty and the upper realm as advantageous for the process of the consciousness' acting as an actual antidote to take place.

For example, if one cultivates the altruistic mind of enlightenment of the Mahāyāna, that is very good. Yet, no matter how much one enhances or increases the altruistic mind of enlightenment, it cannot abandon even one type of afflictive emotion without the wisdom realizing emptiness. Similarly, if one wishes to progress by way of the mundane path, one must change the object of observation. If one is satisfied with just calm abiding and does not wish to go any higher, it is not necessary to change. According to Asaṅga's *Grounds of Hearers*, "If one wishes to progress further on the mundane or supramundane path, it is necessary to do the preparatory training." (See p. 220.) Because of the necessity for changing the object of observation, the fourfold preparatory training mentioned earlier (see p. 216ff.) must be done in order to see whether one can do this analysis.

Since it is necessary to change the object, one might wonder whether it is necessary to give up the mind of calm abiding which was observing, for example, the body of a Buddha, or whether, within retaining that, one would have a second object of observation. One would not use two objects of observation, keeping the former one and then, in addition, viewing the lower level as faulty, and so forth. One would also not completely give up the former object of observation. Rather, within the continuing presence of the calm abiding attained earlier, one generates a new mind either arisen from hearing or arisen from thinking. This is done for the sake of analysis.

Is analysis done from within the state of calm abiding, or is calm abiding left when analysis is done? This is a very important point. Some texts say that this is done within the state of the meditative equipoise of calm abiding whereas others say that it is done within the state of dwelling in calm abiding. My own opinion is that it should be the latter—within the state of dwelling in calm abiding.

The mental contemplation of individual knowledge of the character is a mind either arisen from hearing or arisen from thinking. Without actualizing such a mind, one cannot engage in analysis. Thus, because one has a mind of strong analysis, it must initially be manifest. If this were done within the state of the meditative equipoise of calm abiding, it would be necessary that the meditative equipoise be manifest. However, it would be impossible to manifest these two minds simultaneously—a manifest mind of meditative equipoise and a manifest mind of the mental contemplation of individual knowledge of the character. If these two were factors accompanying one main mind, it would be suitable, but these are two main minds.

When the mind of the mental contemplation of individual knowledge of the character is initially generated, it is necessary that it be manifest. The reason is that no one asserts that an inferential prime cognition[1] is not manifest. When it is generated, it is manifest; it cannot be non-manifest, or subliminal. This is because it is a mind newly induced by having engaged in analysis. For these same reasons, the mental contemplation of individual knowledge of the character must be manifest. Therefore, according to our own system, this analysis is done from within the state of dwelling in calm abiding.

How is this done? The previously attained mind of calm abiding becomes slightly hidden—that is, slightly subliminal. It serves as a concomitant[2] of the analysis; it does not serve as the actual mental basis for the analysis. However, when the mental contemplation of individual knowledge of the character turns into an entity of special insight, the meditative stabilization which accompanies it turns into a calm abiding; therefore, the earlier calm abiding serves as a mental basis in the sense of being a means of attainment.

The mental contemplation of individual knowledge of the character is mainly involved in analytical meditation. Why is analysis necessary? With respect to realizations that are states arisen from meditation,[3] there are two types:

1 realizational consciousnesses that are states arisen from stabilizing meditation[4]
2 realizational consciousnesses that are states arisen from analytical meditation[5]

The meditator has already attained a realizational consciousness that is a state arisen from stabilizing meditation inasmuch as she or he has already achieved calm abiding. The realizational consciousness that is a state arisen from analytical meditation is yet to be attained; it will be achieved with special insight. The attainment of special insight, the attainment of the meditative stabilization that is a union of calm abiding and special insight, and the realizational consciousness that is a state arisen from analytical meditation are simultaneous.

---

1 *rjes dpag tshad ma, anumānapramāṇa.*

2 *grogs, sahāya.*

3 *sgom byung gi rtogs pa.*

4 *'jog sgom gyi sgom byung gi rtogs pa.*

5 *dpyad sgom gyi sgom byung gi rtogs pa.*

Above (pp. 220-221) I referred to the alternation of stabilizing and analytical meditation even before the attainment of calm abiding—for example, when one does analytical meditation in order to bring about more clarity. Those occasions of analysis are minds of analytical meditation but not realizational consciousnesses that are states arisen from meditation. When one achieves calm abiding, one has developed, for the most part, the realizational consciousnesses of the stabilizing-meditation variety. However, one has not developed experience that is a state arisen from meditation with regard to analytical meditation. The reason for cultivating analysis at this time of the mental contemplation of individual knowledge of the character is to develop experience that is a state arisen from meditation with regard to analytical meditation. Thus, when one has developed, over the mental contemplation of individual knowledge of the character, this experience which is a state arisen from meditation with regard to analytical meditation, one attains special insight; when one has that type of experience, one has special insight.

We usually say that when one attains special insight one attains a union of calm abiding and special insight. The reason derives from this: one has already attained calm abiding; thus, when one develops experience that is a state arisen from meditation with regard to analytical meditation, since one already has experience of such a state with respect to stabilizing meditation, one then has these two in similar force and, thus, there is no need to have a further practice for developing a union of them.

At the time of the mental contemplation of individual knowledge of the character, calm abiding and special insight are not concomitants of a single consciousness. They do not become so until the attainment of special insight. When special insight is achieved, its uncommon feature is that these two are present at one time, accompanying one consciousness. When the meditative stabilization which is a union of calm abiding and special insight is achieved, the meditative stabilization which accompanies it is a calm abiding and the wisdom which accompanies it is a special insight. This is called a connecting together, or a connecting in unison, of calm abiding and special insight—a bringing together of equal concomitants. It is for this purpose that one cultivates the mental contemplation of individual knowledge of the character.

Question: What does it mean to say that calm abiding is present in a subliminal way, not manifestly?

Answer: It means that it has become weaker because the meditator has to generate another consciousness, which is analytical. If calm abiding were manifest, then, even though calm abiding and special insight are not in general contradictory, it is the nature of the person at that level that the one cannot operate manifestly while the other is manifest.

Question: It was said that it is not a case of completely giving up the previous object of observation. What should be understood by this?

Answer: To the subliminal mind of calm abiding, that previous object of observation continues to appear, but to the analytical mind—which is the main manifest one, the mental contemplation of individual knowledge of the character—the new object of observation appears. Previously the meditator had been concerned with only one thing—observing the body of a Buddha. Now, however, the meditator is concerned with two things; one is the object of a subliminal consciousness and the other, of a manifest consciousness. This is the same whether the path be mundane or supramundane. If it is the latter, one must change one's object of observation and begin to analyze emptiness while the mind of calm abiding retains its object of observation. It is said that "without stirring from meditative equipoise one should engage in the reasoning of the lack of being one or many."

Question: What is the difference between doing something from within a state of the meditative equipoise of calm abiding and doing it while dwelling within calm abiding?

Answer: An example of something similar is the generation of the ultimate mind of enlightenment—this being the wisdom consciousness of a Bodhisattva who is directly realizing emptiness. If one does not directly realize emptiness within a conventional altruistic mind generation,[1] one does not have an ultimate mind generation; the meditator has to realize emptiness directly while abiding in a conventional mind generation in order to have an ultimate one. Thus, Hearers and Solitary Realizers, even though they realize emptiness directly, do not have an ultimate mind generation. With regard to calm abiding, the distinction lies in the presence or absence of the term "meditative equipoise." The term "meditative equipoise of calm abiding" must refer to something that is manifest, whereas "calm abiding" need not indicate something that is manifest; it could be subliminal. "Meditative equipoise" is too strong a term to be used in the second case, although it occurs in this context in some texts.

---

1 *byang chub sems bskyed, bodhicittotpāda.*

For a sentient being—a non-Buddha—the state of meditative equipoise is necessarily different from the state subsequent to meditative equipoise. They are necessarily different entities. Consider even an ordinary activity. If it were possible to remain in a meditative equipoise of calm abiding and, at the same time, to manifest a mind of analysis, then a state of meditative equipoise and a state subsequent to meditative equipoise would be of one entity. If the mind of meditative equipoise itself does the analysis, that is a case of a mind of meditative equipoise and a mind of a state subsequent to meditative equipoise being of one entity. In this case, however, the mind of meditative equipoise is not the one that is analyzing.

Question: At the time of the attainment of special insight, are calm abiding and special insight of one entity?

Answer: Yes. The calm abiding and special insight which a person has in equal force upon attainment of special insight—which is at the point of the mental contemplation arisen from belief—are of one entity; they have one object of observation. That is the difference. With regard to the topic of dwelling in the state of calm abiding, the consciousness engaging in analysis has one object of observation and the calm abiding has a different one.

Question: If a person has special insight, and if that means that he or she has calm abiding and wisdom in equal force, and if they are of one entity, which is meditative equipoise?

Answer: All these factors are meditative equipoise. If one is, then all the others are. Similarly, the object of observation of the one must be the object of observation of the others. This is a very good question.

It is said that all phenomena are completely Buddhafied. This does not mean that a pot is completely Buddhafied but that, in relation to a pot, all phenomena are Buddhafied. This means that the mind which directly realizes the emptiness of the pot, within the state of directly realizing that emptiness, realizes the pot also. That is the meaning of meditative equipoise and the state subsequent to meditative equipoise being of one entity. Only a Buddha has this. The one consciousness has different objects of observation.

In our discussion here about analysis from within the state of dwelling in calm abiding, the consciousnesses are different. There are not two manifest minds existing simultaneously. If a person had such, she or he would be like a Buddha. There are no cases of simultaneous manifestation of two different mental consciousnesses,[1] except for Buddhas.

Question: Then special insight, which is a union of calm abiding and special insight and which one achieves upon attaining the mental contemplation arisen from belief, is not a case of having meditative equipoise and analytical wisdom present in one entity.

Answer: It is.

Question: But isn't that something only a Buddha can have—the two present in one entity?

Answer: No, because there is only one mental consciousness at any one time; there are different mental factors of meditative equipoise and wisdom accompanying that consciousness. Both have the same object. It would, in fact, be pathetic if you had to have two consciousnesses. This is a case of one consciousness' having these two factors in equal strength.

Question: Does this mean that when you achieve special insight you have to give up the previous object of calm abiding?

Answer: No. You have two calm abidings at this time, one manifest and the other subliminal. For example, compassion and the altruistic mind of enlightenment remain as a Bodhisattva progresses. They do not need to degenerate; they can remain subliminally. Why would the earlier calm abiding that has as its object of observation a Buddha's body have to deteriorate?

When one goes from the Hīnayāna to the Mahāyāna path, it is necessary to give up the Hīnayāna path—not because the Hīnayāna path is bad in general but because the Hīnayāna and Mahāyāna paths are posited by way of the motivation affecting the consciousness. Similarly, it is said that when one passes from the path of accumulation to the path of preparation, the path of accumulation no longer exists. Why does it become non-existent? Because one's state has advanced. The state of hearing and thinking is called a path of accumulation; when it changes into a state arisen from meditation, it is indicated by the name "path of preparation." The substantial continuum[2] is the same. If, however, in achieving special insight or an actual concentration you had to lose your previous calm abiding that was observing the body of a Buddha, it would be like a bear catching mice. He bends over, grabs one mouse, and sticks it between his buttocks; when he leans over again to catch a second mouse, the first

[1] *yid kyi rnam par shes pa, manovijñāna.*

[2] *rdzas rgyun.*

jumps free. Whenever he catches one, he loses one.

Calm abiding, and so forth, are posited in terms of qualities, whereas the paths of accumulation and preparation have to do with the boundaries of certain mental states. The five paths are posited in terms of the advancement of the factor of wisdom; they are levels within this mode of progress. Mahāyāna and Hīnayāna, on the other hand, are posited in terms of motivation.

Question: It was said (p. 146) that the state subsequent to meditative equipoise was something like analytical meditation. In what way is it different? Is it that in one case there are two mental factors and in the other, two main minds?

Answer: Yes. The mind of meditative equipoise and the mind of the state subsequent to meditative equipoise are different main minds. This is the case for both Buddhas and non-Buddhas, although for a Buddha they can occur simultaneously, whereas for non-Buddhas they cannot. The mode of perception, however, is not different for a Buddha. With regard to special insight, we are talking about two mental factors, that of wisdom and that of meditative stabilization.

Let us analyze further whether or not a person who has attained calm abiding and then attains the mental contemplation of individual knowledge of the character would give up the previous object of observation. The calm abiding already attained is a realizational consciousness that is a state arisen from meditation. The mental contemplation of individual knowledge of the character is a state arisen either from hearing or from thinking. Either of these is very different from the calm abiding that is a state arisen from meditation. However, the calm abiding must remain without deterioration when the mental contemplation of individual knowledge of the character is attained. Not only must it not deteriorate; that earlier calm abiding must act as the basis of the analysis, the basis from which the analysis is done. If that calm abiding remains without deterioration and is not given up, then, when the mental contemplation of individual knowledge of the character turns into the mental contemplation arisen from belief, does one not lose the mental contemplation of individual knowledge of the character?

At that point, the mental contemplation of individual knowledge of the character does not remain. It becomes non-existent. The mind of calm abiding does not turn into the mental contemplation of individual knowledge of the character when the latter is attained; rather, the mental contemplation of individual knowledge of the character is a new mind. However, when a person who has the mental contemplation of individual knowledge of the character attains the mental contemplation arisen from belief, the mental contemplation of individual knowledge of the character no longer exists. The reason is that "mental contemplation arisen from belief" is designated to that mind of the mental contemplation of individual knowledge of the character which originally was a state arisen from hearing and then, from thinking; when it turns into the entity of a state arisen from meditation, it is designated with the name "mental contemplation arisen from belief." Because the mental contemplation of individual knowledge of the character turns into the entity of the mental contemplation arisen from belief, the former no longer exists after it has changed into the latter.

As one progresses—for example, if one attains an actual first concentration and wants to achieve an actual second concentration—the latter must be achieved within the continued existence of the first concentration. Once the actual second concentration is attained, the actual first concentration must still exist. As the meditator attains all four concentrations and the four formless absorptions, he or she must have the continuation of the substantial entity of all eight of these.

It is the case with regard to some qualities that, as one progresses, the former qualities become non-existent. Some qualities, however, continue to exist as one progresses. In this case, one quality is manifest and the others are subliminal. At the time of attainment, there is only one agent manifest. I think that at the time of the path of preparation, all eight of the absorptions must be attained. However, most persons attain the path of seeing using the fourth concentration as their mental basis. This is because an actual fourth concentration is free from the eight faults,[1] such as the fluctuations of bliss, and also because one has an equal combination of calm abiding and special insight. Because this actual fourth concentration must serve as the mental basis for the consciousness that is directly realizing emptiness for the first time—and thus is for the first time acting as a direct antidote—it must be the best of mental bases. The fourth concentration is the best of mental bases.

When, with the fourth concentration acting as the mental basis, a person attains the uninterrupted path of the path of seeing, the other absorptions still remain. When the path's dexterity is more highly trained—when one

---

[1] *skyon, apakṣāla.*

progresses to higher levels of the path—it is no longer necessary for the fourth concentration to act as the mental basis. Any of the other absorptions or even a mind of the Desire Realm can serve as the mental basis. The fact that a mind of the Desire Realm can serve as the mental basis is set forth in Dzong-ka-ba's *Exposition of the Stages of the Path.* With the attainment of Buddhahood, one attains the twenty-one divisions of exalted wisdom. These are twenty-one different groups of, for example, the eight absorptions, the nine serial absorptions,[1] and so forth. These are not just one thing being designated by different names; they are continuations of different substantial entities.

Do all ten grounds exist in Buddhahood? No. This is because the names of the ten grounds are designated from the viewpoint of the progress of the mind directly realizing emptiness. Thus, there are some good qualities which must be given up as one progresses and some that need not be. This distinction has to be made. [For further discussion of these topics, see Chapter 14, p. 209ff.]

ENTITY

Is the entity of the mental contemplation of individual knowledge of the character suitable to be considered contaminated, uncontaminated, or both? The answer must be given according to the distinctions among the various schools of tenets. According to the system of Vasubandhu's *Treasury of Manifest Knowledge*—that is, the Vaibhāṣhika system—its entity is necessarily contaminated. In that system, only true paths[2] and true cessations are uncontaminated, and the Vaibhāṣhika interpretation of what true paths are is unlike that of the upper systems; the Vaibhāṣhikas consider very few things to be true paths.

In the Prāsaṅgika system, as well, the mental contemplation of individual knowledge of the character is necessarily contaminated, but the reason is a little different. In Prāsaṅgika system, whatever is uncontaminated is necessarily a meditative equipoise in the continuum of a learner. This means that whatever is uncontaminated in the continuum of a sentient being is necessarily a consciousness of meditative equipoise—although the Prāsaṅgikas do not say that all paths in the continuum of a Superior are necessarily uncontaminated. Their reason is that, according to their interpretation of "contaminated" and "uncontaminated," whatever has or in-

[1] *mthar gyis gnas pa'i snyoms 'jug, anupūrvavihārasamāpatti.*

[2] *lam bden, mārgasatya.*

volves the appearance of true existence[1] is necessarily contaminated. Therefore, there is no case of a mental contemplation of individual knowledge of the character that is uncontaminated because the uncontaminated is necessarily a consciousness of meditative equipoise, which is necessarily a realizational consciousness that is a state arisen from meditation. Because the mental contemplation of individual knowledge of the character is a state arisen from either hearing or thinking, there is no case of its being a state arisen from meditation; thus, it cannot be a meditative equipoise. Since it cannot be a meditative equipoise, it cannot be uncontaminated according to the Prāsaṅgika interpretation.

In the Chittamātra system and the other two Mādhyamika systems—Yogāchāra-Svātantrika and Sautrāntika-Svātantrika—there are some mental contemplations of individual knowledge of the character that are contaminated and some that are uncontaminated. This is easy to understand. Whether it is supramundane or mundane, the mental contemplation of individual knowledge of the character that is a preparation for the first concentration is necessarily contaminated. This is easily understood with regard to the mundane because the meditator has not attained any path. With regard to the supramundane path, it is contaminated because any mental contemplation of individual knowledge of the character that is attained before a first concentration necessarily occurs before the path of seeing has been attained.

How is the uncontaminated variety posited? In dependence on the first concentration, the meditator attains a Superior path. Then, through application, the second concentration is achieved. The second concentration, like the first, is achieved by way of the seven preparations. Since this person has already attained a Superior path and is seeking to achieve a higher concentration, all the preparations to that end are uncontaminated.

Thus, the senses in which these systems posit the mental contemplation of individual knowledge of the character as contaminated or uncontaminated are entirely different. According to these systems, any path in the continuum of a Superior is necessarily a Superior path—that is, a supramundane path. Further, whatever is a supramundane path is uncontaminated. What is contaminated according to them? The form aggregate—the body—in the continuum of a Foe Destroyer is contaminated because it arises from a contaminated cause. Even though the person has abandoned contaminants, she or he still has contaminated phenomena. This is because

---

[1] *bden par yod pa, satyasat.*

the body arose from contaminated causes.

There is another term to consider: "related to contaminants."[1] For instance, the main mind or mental factors that accompany an afflictive emotion are themselves not afflictive emotions but are related to afflictive emotions—to contaminants.

There are also phenomena said to be concordant with contaminants.[2] For example, the obstructions to omniscience[3] are themselves not afflictive emotions, nor are they related to afflictive emotions. However, their function is like that of afflictive emotions, and thus they are concordant with afflictive emotions. This is how "contaminated" and "uncontaminated" should be used within the context of Chittamātra, Yogāchāra-Svātantrika, and Sautrāntika-Svātantrika. The source here is Asaṅga's *Summary of Manifest Knowledge.*

The source for Prāsaṅgikas' assertion that a phenomenon polluted by ignorance or its latencies is contaminated is Chandrakīrti's *Clear Words.*[4] The reason Prāsaṅgikas hold this assertion is that Foe Destroyers, who have overcome ignorance, are not polluted by it but are polluted by the latencies of ignorance, which cause the appearance of true existence.

The source for Vaibhāṣhikas' assertion is the root text of Vasubandhu's *Treasury of Manifest Knowledge.*

DEFINITION

The definition of a mental contemplation of individual knowledge of the character is:

> a mental contemplation of a beginner at purifying afflictive emotions.[5]

This short definition is probably suitable, since I have already discussed the meaning of purification of afflictive emotions.

This definition has two parts which, together, apply only to the mental contemplation of individual knowledge of the character. If the definition said only, "the mental contemplation of a beginner," this could refer to calm abiding; it would not be enough to define a mental contemplation of individual knowledge of the character. If the definition said only, "a men-

---

1 *zag pa dang rjes su 'brel ba.*

2 *zag pa dang rjes su mthun pa.*

3 *shes bya'i sgrib pa, jñeyāvaraṇa.*

4 *tshig gsal ba, prasannapadā;* P5260, vol. 98.

5 *nyon mongs rnam par sbyong ba'i las dang po pa'i yid byed.*

tal contemplation that purifies afflictive emotions," this would also be unsuitable, for a mental contemplation arisen from belief could also be posited as an example of this; we stated earlier, in discussing the three yogis (p. 245), that a yogi who is purifying afflictive emotions ranges from the mental contemplation arisen from belief through the mental contemplation of final training. When these two elements are put together, however, the only preparation to which the definition can apply is the mental contemplation of individual knowledge of the character. This, then, is the general definition of that mental contemplation.

The definition of a mundane mental contemplation of individual knowledge of the character is:

> a mental contemplation of a beginner at purifying afflictive emotions which is individually analyzing the disadvantages and advantages—viewing any upper realm as peaceful or the lower realm as gross.[1]

"Any"[2] is used because this is a general definition of this mental contemplation; "any" means here that the definition has to be interpreted in terms of the context. If the definition referred to a specific level—for example, if one were giving the definition of a mundane mental contemplation of individual knowledge of the character which is a preparation for the first concentration, then it would specify that the Desire Realm was to be viewed as gross and the First Concentration, as peaceful. The specific definition would say, "viewing the Desire Realm as gross or viewing the First Concentration as peaceful." This would be added into the definition.

Would one consciousness perform both activities and view both the lower level as gross and the upper as peaceful? Yes.

Question: Would it do this within one period of time?

Answer: That depends on the length of the period intended. If the period of time is taken as a small instant, no. The uninterrupted path necessarily views the lower as gross, and the path of release views the upper as peaceful. Because they are one substantial continuum and there is a steady continuum, even though the consciousness cannot be viewing the upper as peaceful while it is viewing the lower as gross, and vice versa, there is one continuum.

---

[1] *khams gong 'og ci rigs pa zhi rags su ltas pa'i skyon yon so sor dpyad par byed pa'i nyon mongs rnam par sbyong ba'i las dang po pa'i yid byed.*

[2] *ci rigs pa.*

MODE OF ANALYSIS OF GROSSNESS/PEACEFULNESS

Now let me explain the mode of analysis mentioned in the definition. The lower level, such as the Desire Realm, is seen as faulty or disadvantageous, and the upper, such as the First Concentration, as advantageous.[1] Many different faults are perceived with regard to the Desire Realm. Asaṅga's *Grounds of Hearers*, however, speaks mainly of five faults related to the Desire Realm.

The Five Faults Related to the Desire Realm[2]

First fault

a. Desire Realm beings are of little import.[3]

b. They have many sufferings.[4]

c. They have many faulty objects of observation.[5]

Second fault

a. When one depends on phenomena of the Desire Realm, one does not experience auspiciousness.[6]

b. When one depends on phenomena of the Desire Realm, one does not know satisfaction.[7]

(1) not knowing satisfaction [8]

(2) having great desire [9]

c. With respect to Desire Realm phenomena, there is no end that satisfies the heart.[10]

Third fault

a. Excellent ones,[11]

b. Those who have become elevated,[12] and

c. Excellent beings deride the Desire Realm on many counts.[13]

---

[1] See also the description of these in *Meditative States*, 93-96.

[2] *'dod pa la brten pa'i nye dmigs lnga.*

[3] *'dod pa rnams ni gnog chung ba.*

[4] *sdug bsngal mang ba.*

[5] *nyes dmigs mang ba.*

[6] *'dod pa rnams la brten pa na ngoms mi myong.*

[7] *'dod pa rnams la chog mi shes.*

[8] *chog mi shes.*

[9] *'dod chen can.*

[10] *'dod pa rnams la snying tshim pa'i mtha' med pa.*

[11] *dam pa rnams.*

[12] *yang dag par song ba.*

[13] *skyes bu dam pa rnams kyis rnam grangs du ma'i sgo nas smad pa.*

Fourth fault

a. When one depends on [phenomena of] the Desire Realm, one will accumulate [one of the nine] thorough enwrapments.[1]

Fifth fault

a. When one depends on [phenomena of] the Desire Realm, there is not the least sinful non-virtue that one will not do.[2]

The first fault has three categories. The first is that beings of the Desire Realm are of little import. Even if they achieve some virtue, it brings little profit. This is because the mental basis is a mind of the Desire Realm. Until one arrives at a high Bodhisattva ground, one cannot use a mind of the Desire Realm with great profit.

The second category is that there are many sufferings. This means that no matter what conditions or circumstances one meets with, they mostly generate suffering. It is obvious that the feeling of pain is a case of suffering; feelings of pleasure and neutral feelings also induce suffering.

The third category means that there are many objects of observation which generate faulty states—that is, there are many objects capable of generating afflictive emotions, such as desire and hatred, in the perceiver. Usually, in texts, the word *nyes dmigs*,[3] which we often translate merely as "fault," applies to the afflictive emotions themselves. Here, however, the object of observation is designated with the name of the afflictive emotion. Usually, *nyes dmigs* refers to the internal, but here it refers to external objects of observation that serve as causes for generating afflictive emotions.

The second of the five faults related to the Desire Realm also has three categories. The first is that when one depends on phenomena of the Desire Realm—virtuous, non-virtuous, or neutral—one does not experience auspiciousness. There is no discussion of the first category in either Indian or Tibetan commentaries; however, there are phrases in other books in dependence on which it can be understood. The word *ngoms* is interpreted to mean *gya noms pa*, "auspiciousness,"[4] although it usually means "satisfaction." For instance, when one speaks of eating ordinary gross foods, one does not include the experiencing of the food of meditative stabilization, an experience of auspiciousness that is more elevated than just nourishing the body. Probably, the food of meditative stabilization is being contrasted

[1] *'dod pa rnams la brten pa na kun tu sbyor ba rnams nye bar gsog par 'gyur ba.*

[2] *'dod pa la brten pa na sdig pa mi dge ba mi bya ba cung zad kyang med pa.*

[3] *ādīnava.*

[4] *praṇīta.*

to the gross food of the Desire Realm.

The second category is that when one depends on phenomena of the Desire Realm one does not know satisfaction. No matter what one gets in terms of place, food, clothing, and so forth, more attachment is generated; something further is desired. This second category is divided into two parts: itself—that is, not knowing satisfaction—and another, having great desire. This latter means that within knowing you cannot get something, you force yourself to keep thinking about getting it. This fact is used as a reason for stopping afflictive emotions—because there is no end to them. The occurrence of this condition serves as a proof that they will increase limitlessly.

The third category is that with respect to Desire Realm phenomena there is no end that satisfies the heart. All three of these are basically similar; however, the afflictive emotions of sentient beings have many different forms. Even one afflictive emotion can occur in many different types. What is indicated here is that there would be no end which would fulfill the heart. I think there is probably a difference in strength among these three, the third being the worst. The first, that there is no auspiciousness in the Desire Realm, is general. The third, although much the same as the second, is a little stronger.

The third of the five faults of the Desire Realm, that great beings have derided the Desire Realm on many counts, also has three categories corresponding to three types of great beings who have done so. There are no clear Tibetan commentaries on this; thus, we cannot come to a very definite decision on these three categories.

In the first category, the word *dam pa,* which we generally translate as "excellent," can be posited in two ways, one in terms of good qualities and the other in terms of persons. For instance, Chandrakīrti's *Supplement to (Nāgārjuna's) "Treatise on the Middle"*[1] refers to engagement in the ten excellent paths of action, which are good qualities. Persons who have all ten of these excellent paths of actions are known as excellent persons. Thus, the first of the three categories related to the third fault of the Desire Realm concerns these excellent ones.

The second category, people who have become elevated, refers to people up to the point of being just about to attain a path. In the *Sitātapatrā Tantra,*[2] the term *yang dag par song ba* is applied to a person who is about

[1] *dbu ma la 'jug pa, madhyamkāvatāra;* P5261, P5262, vol. 98.

[2] *gdugs dkar.*

to enter a path but has not yet done so; however, there are also cases in which this term refers to people on the paths of accumulation and preparation. Thus, this category is more elevated than the first one.

The last category is an excellent being. This is almost the same as a valid person.[1] Such a person is one who, at the very least, has directly realized the four truths. Therefore, these excellent beings would be posited in terms of a Superior path, from the path of seeing on up. These three categories of people deride the Desire Realm. The latter part of the phrase, "deride on many counts,"[2] goes with all three categories.

Another text refers to seven transmigrators[3] who are excellent beings. They are all identified as Never Returners—seven types of Never Returners who will take rebirth in the Form Realm, become enlightened in the intermediate state, and so forth. These are special types of excellent beings, not the general type to which the above term refers. It is clear in sūtra that an excellent being is one who has attained the path of seeing, and so forth.

The fourth fault of the Desire Realm is that, when one depends on the phenomena of the Desire Realm, one will accumulate one of the nine thorough enwrapments.[4]

The Nine Thorough Enwrapments

1 thorough enwrapment of desire[5]
2 thorough enwrapment of anger[6]
3 thorough enwrapment of pride[7]
4 thorough enwrapment of doubt[8]
5 thorough enwrapment of ignorance[9]
6 thorough enwrapment of [bad] view,[10] view of the transitory collection [as real I and mine],[11] view holding to an extreme,[12] as well as wrong

[1] *tshad ma'i skyes bu.*
[2] *rnam grangs du ma'i sgo nas smad pa.*
[3] *'gro ba, gati.*
[4] *kun tu sbyor ba, saṃyojana.*
[5] *'dod chags kyi kun sbyor, *rāgasaṃyojana.*
[6] *khong khro'i kun sbyor, *pratighasaṃyojana.*
[7] *nga rgyal gyi kun sbyor, *mānasaṃyojana.*
[8] *the tshom gyi kun sbyor, *vicikitsāsaṃyojana.*
[9] *ma rig pa'i kun sbyor, *avidyāsaṃyojana.*
[10] *lta ba'i kun sbyor, *dṛṣṭisaṃyojana.*
[11] *'jig tshogs la lta ba, satkāyadṛṣṭi.*
[12] *mthar 'dzing pa'i lta ba, antagrāhadṛṣṭi.*

view[1]

7 thorough enwrapment of misapprehension of the supreme,[2] conception of a [bad] view as supreme,[3] and conception of ethics and systems of behavior as supreme[4]

8 thorough enwrapment of jealousy[5]

9 thorough enwrapment of miserliness[6]

The eighth and ninth, jealousy and miserliness, are chosen out of the long list of twenty secondary afflictive emotions because they are the two chief factors opposing altruism; helping others may be damaged through either jealousy or miserliness. Miserliness here does not refer only to resources; it means not using anything one might have—education, good qualities, and so forth—to help others.

The five [bad] views are separated into two groups as divisions of the sixth and seventh thorough enwrapments because the first three, the divisions of thorough enwrapments of [bad] views, are like objects and the divisions of thorough enwrapment of misapprehension of the supreme are like subjects, or apprehenders. The first three [bad] views are the objects of the two consciousnesses that misapprehend the supreme. It is these three that are viewed as marvelous.

What distinguishes the various misconceptions of being supreme? The misconception of [bad] views as supreme involves only the conceptions of the above three [bad] views as supreme; the conception of these as highly auspicious is the misconception that one has completely abandoned all afflictive emotions and that they will not return again.

How could one have this view with respect to ethics? The term "ethics" or "mode of conduct" here does not refer only to our usual modes of behavior. It refers to the abandonment of the afflictive emotions and not only to the abandonment of bad activities such as killing. If one conceived that the abandonment of the ten non-virtues was highly auspicious in the sense of considering it to be a complete abandonment of cyclic existence, then that would be a case of conceiving ethics and modes of conduct to be supreme, or better than they actually are. This thorough enwrapment

---

[1] *log lta, mithyādṛṣṭi.*

[2] *lta ba mchog 'dzin gyi kun sbyor, *dṛṣṭiparāmarśasaṃyojana.*

[3] *lta ba mchog 'dzin, dṛṣṭiparāmarśa.*

[4] *tshul khrims dang brdul zhugs mchog 'dzin, śīlavrataparāmarśa.*

[5] *phrag dog gi kun sbyor, *irṣyāsaṃyojana.*

[6] *ser sna'i kun sbyor, *mātsaryasaṃyojana.*

could exist only up to the path of seeing because someone who has attained a Superior path actually has something that is highly auspicious inasmuch as some afflictive emotions have been utterly abandoned. Before that, on the paths of accumulation and preparation, if one conceived one's attainments as some type of final abandonment, they would actually not be as auspicious as one conceived them to be.

The illustrations often used in texts for this are, for instance, the asceticisms of non-Buddhists which are mistakenly conceived to be sufficient cause for attaining liberation. Some non-Buddhists believe that, as a result of their engaging in severe asceticism, the body dries up and becomes thin, and one's sins diminish; thus, severe asceticism is included in this category. Buddhists might also have such a misapprehension of the supreme, however, if, for example, they felt that abandonment of the ten non-virtues was sufficient for liberation. This would also be a case of exaggerating their value. Some people say that a person who conceives the supreme mistakenly must be a non-Buddhist, but this is not the case. The ethics which are the object of this view do not necessarily have to be bad. They may be bad only in the sense that they are not highly auspicious and one is wrongly satisfied with them alone.

An illustration of a bad mode of conduct would be severe asceticism conceived as highly auspicious. A case of misconceiving ethics as highly auspicious would be to separate temporarily from attachment to afflictive emotions and to consider this as liberation. This does not mean whoever has any of these qualities is, as in the illustrations, a non-Buddhist.

The fifth fault of the Desire Realm is that, when one depends on phenomena of the Desire Realm, there is not the least sinful non-virtue that one would not do. Those who have attained actual concentrations and actual formless absorptions are able to take good measure of themselves, recognizing when their afflictive emotions are excessive. However, when one is engaged in the afflictive emotions of the Desire Realm, it is difficult to take one's own measure independently and to know what the limit should be.

Asaṅga's *Grounds of Hearers* makes many references to thorough entanglements,[1] such as the eight thorough entanglements:

1 non-shame[2]

---

[1] *kun dkris, paryavasthāna.*

[2] *ngo tsha med pa, āhrīkya.*

2 non-embarrassment[1]
3 excitement[2]
4 contrition[3]
5 sleep[4]
6 lethargy[5]
7 jealousy[6]
8 miserliness[7]

The first, non-shame, means not avoiding ill deeds from one's own point of view—one's own estimation of what one should be doing. It would be, for instance, not thinking about the future and not reflecting on what will happen if one engages in a certain ill-deed. Non-embarrassment is a case of not avoiding ill deeds from the viewpoint of considering others. It means that no matter what one does, there is no concern for others' estimation of oneself. The other thorough entanglements have already been explained.

These eight thorough entanglements are factors opposing the three trainings.[8] The first two are factors opposing proper ethics.[9] Excitement and contrition are factors opposing wisdom; sleep and lethargy are factors opposing meditative stabilization. Jealousy and miserliness are factors opposing all three trainings—ethics, wisdom, and meditative stabilization. This is because they are factors opposing altruism. Therefore, among these eight, the last two—jealousy and miserliness—are considered in the Mahāyāna to be very strong and very bad.

Question: Since both contrition and sleep are changeable mental factors[10] and can sometimes be considered virtuous, are even their virtuous forms considered thorough entanglements?

Answer: The sleep and contrition included within the eight thorough entanglements are only the non-virtuous forms, not the general ones. "Sleep" here is not merely sleepiness, but it could not include deep sleep. It is by

---

[1] *khrel med, anapatrāpya.*
[2] *rgod pa, auddhatya.*
[3] *'gyod pa, kaukṛtya.*
[4] *gnyid, middha.*
[5] *rmug pa, styāna.*
[6] *phrag dog, irṣyā.*
[7] *ser sna, mātsarya.*
[8] *bslab pa, śikṣā.*
[9] *tshul krims, śīla.*
[10] *sems byung gzhan 'gyur, *anyathābhāvacaitta.*

way of motivation that sleep becomes non-virtuous. (See p. 134.)

LEVEL

The most important topic with respect to the mental contemplation of individual knowledge of the character is probably the level in which it is included. It is necessary to have a basis for the discussion, and this is to be found in the presentation of hearing, thinking, and meditating.

1 There are states arisen from hearing and states arisen from thinking included within the level of the Desire Realm.
2 There are states arisen from hearing and states arisen from meditation included within the Form Realm; there is no state arisen from thinking included within the Form Realm.
3 There are only states arisen from meditation included within the levels of the Formless Realm.

These three are set forth in Vasubandhu's *Autocommentary on the "Treasury of Manifest Knowledge."* This type of differentiation of states arisen from hearing, thinking, and meditation in relation to the levels is done clearly only in that text, not in others. It is not that *everything* set forth in Vasubandhu's *Autocommentary on the "Treasury"* is either accepted or refuted by the higher systems of tenets. Although there are many points held in common with the higher systems of tenets, there are also points specific to the system of the *Treasury* itself—that is, the Kashmīri Vaibhāṣhika system. However, this point is asserted in common by both the lower and the higher systems of tenets.

The term "included within the level"[1] is frequently emphasized in Tibetan commentaries. Indian commentaries refer to something's being included within an equipoise level[2] or a non-equipoise level, or to a person who is of an equipoise level,[3] or who is not of that level. The Form and Formless Realms are described as those of an equipoise level, whereas the Desire Realm is described as that of a non-equipoise level.

With this as our basis for analysis, we need to investigate in what level the mental contemplation of individual knowledge of the character is included. For instance, if we take as our example the mental contemplation of individual knowledge of the character which is a preparation for the first concentration, in what level is it included? Tibetan commentaries give

---

1 *sas bsdus.*

2 *mnyam par bzhag pa'i sa.*

3 *mnyam par bzhag pa'i sa pa.*

two important and different interpretations.

The main interpretation is given by Ba-d̄rül Chö-ḡyi-gyel-tsen.[1] He, as well as Gyel-tsap,[2] Kay-drup,[3] and many monastic textbooks, say that this mental contemplation is included within an equipoise level—that is, within the level of an upper realm. The basis for their assertion is a passage from Asaṅga's *Grounds of Hearers.* There is a citation from a correct printing of this text that refers to this mental contemplation as a mental contemplation which is of an equipoise level; however, some incorrect printings of the same text say that it is a mental contemplation which is of a non-equipoise level—that is, in some corrupt texts there is a reference to it as a non-equipoise level but in other, correct, versions the negative is not there. It is the thought also of D̄zong-ka-b̄a's *Great Exposition of the Stages of the Path to Highest Enlightenment* that the mental contemplation of individual knowledge of the character is of an equipoise level. Almost all monastic textbooks follow this position—not just one or two, but most.

D̄zong-ka-b̄a's *Golden Rosary of Eloquence,* referring to the first mental contemplation as a preparation for the first concentration, states that this mental contemplation is included in the Desire Realm and is not included within an upper realm. He quotes Asaṅga's *Grounds of Hearers,* using the reading from the "corrupt" text, which has the negative—that is, which says that the mental contemplation of individual knowledge of the character is of a non-equipoise level. I do not think it is necessary here to make any reference to whether or not he was basing his assertion on a corrupt text; he had come to the decision that there should be a negative. It does not make any difference if all the texts lack a negative, for D̄zong-ka-b̄a was not thinking about whether or not the text was corrupt; he came to his decision through reasoning. D̄zong-ka-b̄a also says that this type of reasoning is to be applied to the rest of the preparations. If the person cultivating the preparatory mental contemplations is still of the Desire Realm, it is said that the first mental contemplation is included within the lower level. Thus, what D̄zong-ka-b̄a is saying is that if, with the life-basis of a Desire Realm being, one cultivates the preparations for the first concentration, then the mental contemplation of individual knowledge of the character is included within the lower level, and the same sort of reasoning is to be extended to the second of the preparatory contemplations leading

[1] This is likely Ba-so Chö-ḡyi-gyel-tsen (*ba so chos kyi rgyal mtshan,* 1402-1473).

[2] *rgyal tshab dar ma rin chen,* 1364-1432.

[3] *mkhas grub dge legs dpal bzang,* 1385-1438.

to any of the eight absorptions.

D̄zong-ka-b̄a's *Golden Rosary* is a very long and extensive text that quotes back and forth, right and left, from twenty-one different commentaries on Maitreya's *Ornament for Clear Realization;* thus, it is easy to confuse his own system with the other systems which he quotes but which are not his own. There are many cases in which he says, "Someone says,..." "Someone else says,..." and so forth. Thus, there are many different assertions. After that, he gives the opinion of someone else, and then of someone else again—that last "someone else" being D̄zong-ka-b̄a himself. There are many such cases; thus, it is easy to become confused.

D̄zong-ka-b̄a's own system is set forth in the very small text called *Notes on the Concentrations and Formless Absorptions,* in which it is asked, "What are the differences among the eight preparations?" "The eight preparations" means the eight sets of preparations leading to the concentrations and formless absorptions. If these are cultivated within the life-basis of a Desire Realm person, the mental contemplation of individual knowledge of the character can involve states arisen from either hearing or thinking. If the preparations are cultivated in a Form Realm basis [that is, by a person of the Form Realm], then the mental contemplation of individual knowledge of the character could be a state arisen from hearing, but there are no cases of that preparation's being a state arisen from thinking. If they are cultivated by a person having the life-support of a Formless Realm being—for instance by a person in Limitless Space—there would be no case of the mental contemplation of individual knowledge of the character's being a state arisen from hearing or thinking. It also cannot be a state arisen from meditation because it is a mental contemplation of individual knowledge of the character; therefore, it can be only a case of being produced by the power of one's birth. The statement in D̄zong-ka-b̄a's *Notes on the Concentrations and Formless Absorptions* that when the mental contemplation of individual knowledge of the character is cultivated by someone in the Formless Realm it is only produced by birth is a further elucidation of his *Golden Rosary.* He then concludes by giving a summary: Any preparation, when cultivated on the basis of the life-support of a lower level, is included in the lower level. This means that whatever the level of the person cultivating, that is the level of the first mental contemplation.

D̄zong-ka-b̄a's *Golden Rosary* does not give many reasons, but if one thinks about what is in the *Notes on the Concentrations and Formless Absorptions,* it makes no difference whether the text is corrupt or not, for

Dzong-ka-ba makes his point from the perspective of reasoning.

There are many monastic textbooks following Pa-tso, and so forth, which say that the mental contemplation of individual knowledge of the character is indeed of an equipoise level; these people attempt to explain away the presence of the negative in Asaṅga's *Grounds of Hearers* by saying that it was not in the original translation but added in below the line, with the result that when the translation was recopied the negative was inserted into the actual line. However, what is in Asaṅga's *Grounds of Hearers* itself is this:

> The individual analysis of the Desire Realm as gross and the First Concentration as peaceful by a mental contemplation of non-equipoise is called individual knowledge of the character.[1]

Following this is a statement which, although not an explicit reason, is an implicit one which, as it were, identifies the entity of the mental contemplation of individual knowledge of the character:

> Moreover, it is to be understood that this is a mixture of hearing and thinking.[2]

The explanation of the mental contemplation of individual knowledge of the character appears eight or nine times in Asaṅga's *Grounds of Hearers*. Of those, three are main, or more extensive, explanations. One of them occurs in the context of a general exposition of the mundane and supramundane paths, another at the time of explaining progress on the mundane path, and the third in the explanation of the mode of progress on the supramundane path. The explanation just cited occurs in the exposition of the mundane path. In the exposition of the supramundane path, it is explained that this mental contemplation is like the seeds of the doctrinal knowledge[3] and subsequent knowledge[4] of the path of seeing and is to be known as a mixture of hearing and thinking.[5]

We have seen that there is a system which one-pointedly says that the mental contemplation of individual knowledge of the character is included

---

1 *mnyam par ma bzhag pa'i sa pa yid la byed pa gang gis 'dod pa la rags pa dang bsam gtan dang por zhi bar so sor rtog par byed pa ni mtshan nyid so sor rig pa zhes bya ste.* For more on this passage, see *Meditative States,* 150 and 241-242, n. 6.

2 *de yang thos pa dang bsam pa 'dres pa rig par bya'o.*

3 *chos shes pa, dharmajñāna.*

4 *rjes su shes pa, anvayajñāna.*

5 *chos shes pa dang rjes su shes pa'i sa bon lta bu yin te de yang thos pa dang bsam pa 'dres pa rig par bya'o.*

within the upper level but that in Ḏzong-ka-ḇa's own text it is said to be included within the lower level. For example, if it is cultivated by a person of the Desire Realm, it is included within the Desire Realm. If a person of the Form Realm cultivates it as a preparation for an actual Formless Realm absorption, that mental contemplation of individual knowledge of the character is included within the Form Realm.

The reason this mental contemplation is asserted to be of the lower level is that, once Asaṅga's *Grounds of Hearers* says it is a mixture of hearing and thinking, then, since states arisen from thinking cannot be included within the Form Realm, it should be included in the lower level. Ḏzong-ka-ḇa's *Golden Rosary* and *Notes on the Concentrations and Formless Absorptions* both say that the mental contemplation of individual knowledge of the character, when cultivated by a person of a lower level, is included within that level. Thus, not only would the mental contemplation of individual knowledge of the character that is a preparation for the first concentration be included within the level of the Desire Realm, the mental contemplation of individual knowledge of the character would be the same for all eight concentrations and formless absorptions. For instance, when a person of the Desire Realm cultivates the second concentration, that mental contemplation of individual knowledge of the character would also be included within the Desire Realm. How many mental contemplations of individual knowledge of the character which are preparations could one cultivate as a person of the First Concentration? Seven; these would all be included within the level of the First Concentration. Similarly, if a person of the level of Nothingness were to cultivate the mental contemplation of individual knowledge of the character as a preparation for an actual absorption of the peak of cyclic existence, that mental contemplation would be included within the level of Nothingness.

Investigation is made of whether, when the mental contemplation of individual knowledge of the character that is a preparation for the first concentration is cultivated by a person of the Desire Realm, it is included within the Desire Realm or within the First Concentration. People feel that the only qualm rests there; that when a person of the Desire Realm cultivates the preparations for the second concentration, *that* mental contemplation of individual knowledge of the character—they feel—would be included within the Form Realm. This is not Ḏzong-ka-ḇa's opinion. He asserts that whatever mental contemplation of individual knowledge of the character is cultivated, whether as a preparation for the first concentration or as a preparation for the second, and so forth—if it is cultivated by a person of the Desire Realm, it is included within the Desire Realm level. I think that this is Ḏzong-ka-ḇa's own system.

In the works of any author there are often differences between those written earlier and later in that person's life. The *Golden Rosary* was written by Ḏzong-ka-ḇa early in his life and has very little on this point. The *Notes* provides profound proofs for points on the concentrations and formless absorptions; that text was written down later in his life.

Question: With regard to the mixture of hearing and thinking, if one who cultivates the mental contemplation of individual knowledge of the character is a person of the Form Realm, then that mental contemplation would have to be included within the Form Realm. In that case, how could it be explained as a mixture of hearing and thinking?

Answer: There are many different interpretations of the statement that this mental contemplation is a mixture of hearing and thinking. Some say that first it is an entity arisen from hearing and then it turns into an entity arisen from thinking. There is no clear statement on what "mixture" means here. The various texts on this topic have their own explanations, however.

From Ḏzong-ka-ḇa's viewpoint, "mixture" means that this mental contemplation is sometimes arisen from hearing and sometimes from thinking: there is no definiteness. Thus, it would first be a state arisen from hearing and then become a state arisen from thinking.

My own thought is that there certainly must be an instance of this mental contemplation's being included in the Desire Realm. I feel that it is difficult to prove directly that it would necessarily have to be included exclusively in either the Desire Realm or the Form Realm. I do not think either position can be proved on the basis of trying to decide which edition of Asaṅga's *Grounds of Hearers* is correct. You would only be left in a state of doubt without being able to state reasons for your position. This has been merely a brief, rough explanation at this point.

Question: Why are there no states arisen from thinking in the Form Realm?

Answer: The mental continuum is moistened with the meditative stabilization of the union of calm abiding and special insight, and the mind will not go into thought but immediately goes into a state arisen from meditation. This is stated in many texts.

MENTAL BASIS

Ḏzong-ka-ḇa's *Great Exposition of the Stages of the Path* says, "Within the state of the non-deterioration of a calm abiding that observes any of the varieties of phenomena...." On the basis of this, it can be shown that there would be a subliminal calm abiding that serves as the mental basis for the mental contemplation of individual knowledge of the character. Otherwise, this mental contemplation would have to be accompanied by a steady meditative stabilization. Jam-ȳang-shay-ḇa says that the consciousness serving as the mental basis is the subliminal calm abiding. It seems that Ḏzong-ka-ḇa's meaning, as well, is that there would be a subliminal calm abiding acting as the mental basis of this mental contemplation.

I have said that a consciousness arisen from meditation and a mind of an upper realm are simultaneous (see p. 105), but this does not mean that whatever is a state arisen from meditation is necessarily a mind of an upper realm. For example, when one arrives on a high Bodhisattva ground, it is possible for a mind of the Desire Realm to act as the mental basis for an uninterrupted path. This is a state arisen from meditation because it is an uninterrupted path. There are two such cases—one, very high on the path and the other, at the initial stages of the path. This is because, even if one has initially attained calm abiding, that mind of calm abiding cannot do everything and one must rely on a mind of the Desire Realm. When one arrives on the eighth ground, one has attained mastery with respect to the nine levels, whereby a mind of the Desire Realm can act as the mental basis. Such a Desire Realm mind would be very much like calm abiding; it would not be the usual type of Desire Realm mind.

DISCUSSION

Question: It is stated that pliancy is an antidote to laziness. It was also said that persons having the mental contemplation of individual knowledge of the character would have a steady meditative stabilization even if they did not have the subliminal calm abiding. Is it said that a person who has the subliminal calm abiding can use pliancy as an antidote to laziness or that one who has a steady meditative stabilization cannot apply this antidote?

Answer: There would be no such distinction made. In my own opinion, the meditator at this time would have both the subliminal calm abiding and the steady meditative stabilization that accompanies this mental contemplation. They are different entities, for one is subliminal and the other, manifest.

Your point is well taken. I think it would be good to have the subliminal calm abiding, for that would mean that one would have the pliancies, and so forth, which would act as the antidote to those factors which oppose the development of special insight. If one had only a steady factor of meditative stabilization, I think it would be difficult to have that opposition. Over the period of the mental contemplation of individual knowledge of the character, one must come to induce pliancy again in order to achieve a union of calm abiding and special insight. It would be very difficult to do that if one did not have a subliminal calm abiding during that time. Jam-ȳang-shay-b̄a is the first person who engaged in a great many analyses with respect to the mental basis of the mental contemplation of individual knowledge of the character. Others also analyzed regarding this, but not in such an extensive manner.

This is a very important point because the mental contemplation of individual knowledge of the character is a case of analytical meditation. Thus, it is very important to settle what its mental basis is. Nevertheless, even though so much analysis was done, it still does not appear very clearly to my mind. How a mental basis works, and so forth, can be explained in accordance with Jam-ȳang-shay-b̄a's and others' texts, but exactly how it performs this function and what the experience of this is would be difficult to explain.

Question: It would seem from what has been explained that the first state arisen from meditation would be the union of calm abiding and special insight, in which case calm abiding alone would not be a state arisen from meditation. I wonder if this is true and if there are different ways of explaining this because I have seen it said that calm abiding is a state arisen from meditation.

Answer: One does acquire a state arisen from meditation with the attainment of calm abiding. One simultaneously attains calm abiding, a mind of an upper realm, a mental contemplation of a mere beginner, and a state arisen from meditation. When I explained the reason for cultivating the mental contemplation of individual knowledge of the character, I explained that, although one had already attained a state arisen from stabilizing meditation, one had not yet attained a state arisen from analytical meditation and that, in order to attain it, one cultivates the mental contemplation of individual knowledge of the character.

Question: Does that mean that one has a mind of an upper realm when one achieves calm abiding and that one then loses it and returns to a mind of the Desire Realm during the cultivation of the mental contemplation of individual knowledge of the character?

Answer: No. Because of the distinction between the subliminal and the manifest, one does not lose it; it is within the state of calm abiding that the mental contemplation of individual knowledge of the character is generated. However, the manifest mind at that time is included within the level of the Desire Realm.

Question: Why is it that, although the mind of calm abiding is included within an upper realm, a mind that would seem to be higher than it—the mental contemplation of individual knowledge of the character—is said to be a mind of the Desire Realm?

Answer: The meditator is still of the Desire Realm and basically still has a mind of the Desire Realm. Even though he or she has attained a state arisen from meditation, this person has no strong power of mind with respect to analyzing objects. A person of the Form Realm would, by nature, have calm abiding; if such a person then manifested a Desire Realm mind, it would be a case of regression. Here, because the person is of the Desire Realm, her or his mind and body depend on the Desire Realm. We are speaking here of a person who has just attained calm abiding. Why is it that such a person can analyze only with a mind of the Desire Realm and cannot do so with a mind of the Form Realm? It is because the person has just attained calm abiding and is susceptible to its being disturbed. She or he does not have any capacity to view an upper level as peaceful and a lower one as gross but can analyze only with the coarse type of mind that he or she used to have. If the person were of the Form Realm, then manifestation of a Desire Realm mind would indeed be a case of regression.

Question: We usually think of the eight concentrations and formless absorptions as stacked up one on top of the other. I am wondering whether it would be suitable to think of these as concentric circles, in the sense that developing the concentrations, and so forth, and ascending the three realms is like peeling away coarser layers of the mind and approaching deeper and deeper levels of the mind.

Answer: Basically, as one ascends the levels one's meditation becomes deeper, more profound. There are two ways of progressing more deeply. One is as in the example of an onion—peeling off faults and going in deeper. The other is a case of the former mind's turning into the later mind without anything's being discarded.

Someone who attains the eighth absorption does not do so by discarding the others, as in the example of the onion. When one attains a second, the first remains. In that case, what is the difference between the first and the second? It is that the actuality of the absorption becomes stronger; the second is a different type of good quality from the first, and thus one's meditation becomes more powerful.

In these eight, it is not a case either of getting rid of the faulty elements *or* of the one turning into the other. Therefore, it is neither of these two types of progression, although the meditator attains higher realization. All these types of progression, however, are cases of the meditation's becoming more profound.

Question: Is there some sense, then, in which the Desire Realm could be considered as an outer fringe of consciousness?

Answer: Once persons of the Desire Realm achieve a mind of an upper realm—that is, when they achieve calm abiding—then, when they are able to use that mind for activities, the former mind is without capacity in relation to this new mind. It is not that the person no longer has a mind of the Desire Realm. Nevertheless, if the person can use a mind of an upper realm for a certain activity she or he will, of course, do so.

Question: Does this imply that purifying afflictive emotions does not mean obliteration of them but, rather, making them immobile or useless? In other words, if nothing is lost, what does it mean to say that the afflictive emotion is purified?

Answer: As one moves up, one indeed abandons the afflictive emotions—the non-virtuous minds of the lower level. However, there are many types of minds of the lower level—virtuous, neutral, and non-virtuous. When a person transmigrates and is born in an upper realm, that person does not have even the virtuous minds of the Desire Realm. This is not because there is any fault but because a boundary is made by karma. On the other hand, if a person of the Desire Realm achieves a mind of an upper realm, it is possible to have both; however, one has separated from attachment to the afflictive emotions of the Desire Realm.

Question: It was said that hell beings have the type of experience they have because of a factor of appearance, not actual external phenomena. Is this true for all six transmigrations?

Answer: The talk of an appearance factor of the mind[1] is probably much

[1] *sems kyi snang cha.*

the same for all six types of transmigrators. However, objects of experience are of two types, common and uncommon. There is no clear statement on this, but I think that when a person transmigrates from here to a hell, it is not a case of a person's going to a place that has burning iron and that already exists. Rather, simultaneous with that person's being reborn there, the whole situation is produced by the power of karma. This is how I consider it in connection with an uncommon appearance factor. One could misunderstand the term "mere appearance factor of the mind" as implying that the object does not exist, but this is something that actually does exist; it is produced by the power of a person's karma and harms that person. For example, when we experience the sufferings of heat, cold, and so forth, there is a factor which is common; however, I think that even if there is only one "heat" as on a hot day, that which I am experiencing and that which others experience are entirely different. Some people experience it as a great discomfort, and others, as a small one. Thus, the way in which feeling is produced is an uncommon proprietary effect.

Hell beings, beings in the intermediate state, and gods are in a different situation. They are spontaneously produced; when they are born, their environment is born with them, and their environment also expires with them. For instance, when a person is born as a god, that person makes use of his or her inestimable nature. When the person is born, the resources he or she uses are produced at that very time.

Question: The casual meditative absorptions[1] of the first concentration are divided into pure,[2] uncontaminated, and afflicted types. Are the resultant-birth meditative absorptions[3] also so divided?

Answer: No. An afflicted absorption is not an absorption. The effect of an uncontaminated absorption is, for example, to attain Foe Destroyerhood. The abandonment of that which is to be abandoned by the path of seeing can be posited as an effect of an uncontaminated absorption. With a contaminated absorption, there would be a temporary factor of having separated from attachment to some afflictive emotion. An afflicted absorption is a case of a person's becoming attached to the bliss of a contaminated absorption. Through tasting that bliss, the meditator becomes attached; this is designated as an afflicted absorption. Whatever is a casual absorption is necessarily a contaminated absorption; this is the only one that will pro-

---

1 *rgyu snyoms 'jug, *kāraṇasamāpatti.*

2 *dag pa, śuddha.*

3 *'bras bu skye ba'i snyoms 'jug, *kāryasamāpatti.*

duce a rebirth in the respective absorption. Whatever is a resultant-birth absorption is necessarily contaminated; both the casual absorption and resultant-birth absorption of any level are necessarily contaminated. The proper term for the latter is "resultant-birth meditative absorption."

Question: If someone is born in the level of Limitless Space, and so forth, can that meditative absorption become afflicted if one becomes attached to it?

Answer: Yes. There are afflictive emotions included within the level of Limitless Space. The person has separated from attachment to lower afflictive emotions but can generate afflictive emotions with respect to her or his own level. Thus, it is possible after rebirth at that level to generate an afflicted absorption.

Question: If, for example, one is born in the absorption of Limitless Space, can one fall from that absorption—since it was said that an afflicted meditative absorption is not an absorption?

Answer: An absorption arisen from application in this lifetime could deteriorate, but that absorption which one attains through rebirth cannot deteriorate. For instance, someone born in the First Concentration would always have calm abiding at least in a subliminal form; it would not necessarily be manifest. An afflicted absorption is merely designated as an absorption without actually being one, but all afflictive emotions of an upper realm are not called afflicted absorptions. There is a reason why an afflicted absorption is so called; it is because one has become attached to absorption; one has the taste of attachment to that meditative equipoise.

Question: It is said that one is born in one of the Five Pure Places[1] by cultivating alternating concentrations: one moment for contaminated, another moment for uncontaminated, and so forth. How long is a moment in this case?

Answer: Between two contaminated meditative equipoises, there is an uncontaminated one. These are of one continuum. The moment here is the length of the smallest period of time in which an action can be completed.

Question: How does what is studied in the topic of Awareness and Knowledge[2] relate to the nine mental abidings?

---

[1] *gnas gtsang lnga, pañcaśuddhāvāsakāyika.*

[2] *blo rig.* For a translation and commentary on a typical work of this genre, see Lati Rinbochay and Elizabeth Napper, *Mind in Tibetan Buddhism* (London: Rider and Company, 1980; Ithaca: Snow Lion, 1980).

Answer: It is very good to apply this study to the nine mental abidings or to other topics. For instance, there are the seven types of awareness.[1] Nowadays, people also insert the topic of minds and mental factors. The discussion of minds and mental factors is taken from a text of Chittamātrins Following Scripture [Asaṅga's *Summary of Manifest Knowledge*], whereas the topics of the seven divisions, and so forth, are taken from texts of the Sautrāntikas and Chittamātrins Following Reasoning [Dharmakīrti's *Commentary on (Dignāga's) "Compilation of [Teachings on] Valid Cognition,"* etc.] The first mental abiding is designated with the name of a mental factor of stability, but there are many other factors which accompany it. One could look into how many of the fifty-one mental factors could be present during any one mental abiding. One could also consider an inferential prime cognition: could that occur during any of the nine mental abidings, or could doubt, or a correctly assuming consciousness?[2] I think a correctly assuming consciousness could. The nine mental abidings can be understood in relation to the topic of minds and mental factors. During the nine mental abidings, one abandons the five faults by means of the eight applications, or antidotes, and without an explanation of mental factors one cannot understand this. If one puts these topics together, one can understand the reasons well.

---

[1] *blo, buddhi.*

[2] *yid dpyod.*

19 SUMMARY

Initially, I explained the six external causal prerequisites for calm abiding. Then I explained the physical posture, and then the three types of meditative stabilization on the inhalation and exhalation of breath—that of observing the inhalations and exhalations, that of the twenty-one cycles, and the nine-cycled dispelling of wind-corpses. At that time, I also explained the purification of impure motivation by way of the descent of ambrosia. I then set forth the reasons why one assumes the posture with the seven features of Vairochana and then the purposes for cultivating the meditative absorption on the inhalation and exhalation of the breath.

The next topics were the physical basis and mental basis for cultivating calm abiding. At that point, with respect to the mode of cultivation, I explained that it is not a case of viewing calm abiding but of actually cultivating and developing it. Six different kinds of meditation were set forth—for instance, [either] meditating on something within taking it as the object of apprehension of that mind or causing the mind to turn into a particular type of mind.

Next, the objects of observation of calm abiding were discussed. Two positions were refuted: that the object of observation of calm abiding is an object of the eye consciousness and that any object that appears easily to the mind is a suitable object of observation for achieving calm abiding. Methods of choosing an object of observation were discussed, and a brief, introductory, presentation of objects of observation for purifying behavior was given. The four categories of object of observation were then set forth, and the meaning of their names was given. The four subdivisions of the first category, pervasive objects of observation, were then discussed. Both Kamalashīla's and Asaṅga's presentations of the first two, non-analytical image and analytical image, were explained. Observing the limits of phenomena was not explained very clearly; I said that this would be explained more fully at the time of the discussion of the path of seeing, for which there was not time. There was also a brief discussion of thorough achievement of the purpose.

Next, I gave a more detailed presentation of the five objects of observation which purify behavior. First, I explained the mode of meditating on the unpleasant, for a person whose predominant afflictive emotion is desire. I explained the five ways of meditating on the unpleasant as presented in Asaṅga's *Grounds of Hearers* and the three yogas of meditating on the unpleasantness of the skeleton as presented in Vasubandhu's *Treasury of Manifest Knowledge.* I then explained that a person whose predominant afflictive emotion is hatred should cultivate love as an antidote. Here I explained Chandrakīrti's system: namely, that from among the three types of beings—friends, enemies, and neutral persons—one would first meditate on friends. I also explained his system of the three types of love observing mere sentient beings, phenomena, and the unapprehendable.

The next topic was the antidote needed by persons in whom obscuration predominates. I explained the importance of study concerning calm abiding, the four reasonings to be applied to the meaning of what one has heard, and ways of applying them to selflessness or dependent-arising. The meditation on the divisions of the constituents for those whose predominant afflictive emotion is pride was explained, and then, the meditation on inhalation and exhalation of the breath as an antidote to discursiveness. Although Asaṅga's *Grounds of Hearers* sets forth a great deal on this meditation, that system would have taken months to explain; therefore, I set it aside and, instead, explained the mode of meditation on the breath set forth in Vasubandhu's *Treasury of Manifest Knowledge.*

Objects of observation for developing skill were then explained—the aggregates, the constituents, the twelve sense-spheres; the fourth object of skill, the mode of traveling in cyclic existence by way of the twelve links of dependent-arising, was explained extensively in terms of two or three lifetimes. The twelve links were divided into parts: projectors and projected effects, or actualizers and actualized effects. The fifth of the objects of observation for developing skill, the appropriate and the inappropriate, was discussed briefly.

Just by way of pointing out the names of these topics, I mentioned the fourth category of objects of observation, those for purifying afflictive emotions, saying that they would be explained later in connection with viewing the lower level as gross and the upper level as peaceful at the time of the mundane path.

Other objects of observation of calm abiding were then explained: the auspicious marks of a Buddha's body, a divine body, hand symbols, observing certain places in the body—the place between the eyebrows, the heart, and so forth. A distinction was also made between objects of observation for persons newly achieving calm abiding and for persons who have already achieved it. Then I spoke on how to search for the object of observation of calm abiding and the measure of having found it, as well as the length of the session and when it is suitable to change the object of observation.

The next topic was the order of calm abiding and special insight. This topic had many subtopics—the actual and imputed calm abiding and special insight mentioned in Asaṅga's *Grounds of Hearers*, the reasons why, before special insight, one must achieve calm abiding; and the important points that before attaining special insight observing emptiness one has to achieve a calm abiding observing emptiness but that, in order to achieve a calm abiding observing emptiness, it is not necessary to achieve the nine mental abidings observing emptiness. I also pointed out that the attainment of special insight is preceded by the attainment of calm abiding according to the sūtra system and the three lower tantra sets but that, in Highest Yoga Tantra, there are cases of achieving calm abiding and special insight simultaneously. I then explained the benefits of calm abiding and special insight, and the reasons for cultivating them.

The next topic was the actual achievement of calm abiding of by way of the nine mental abidings. Two modes of achieving calm abiding were explained: (1) by way of abandoning the five faults by relying on the eight activities, or antidotes and (2) by way of progressing through the nine mental abidings. The individual sources for these were indicated. Mainly, the explanation of the achievement of calm abiding by means of the nine mental abidings was given as the basis, and the abandoning of the five faults by way of the eight antidotes was added to that. This way of combining the two was identified as a quintessential instruction from the textual lineage of the G̱a-dam-ḇas. In dependence on Jam-ȳang-shay-ḇa's text, qualms were eliminated with respect to laxity, slackness, lethargy, and so forth.

I then discussed the actual achievement of calm abiding and the order of the generation of pliancies, which occurs between the ninth mental abiding and the attainment of calm abiding. First, the names of the pliancies were given in the order of their generation; then, the definition of mental pliancy and the explanation of the assumption of bad mental and physical states were given; then, the definition of physical pliancy and the explanation of the blisses of physical and mental pliancy; then, the order of the generation of the pliancies and of their cessation; and then the mode of achieving calm abiding based on them, followed by the elimination of many qualms regarding this.

We then discussed the signs of having achieved calm abiding. At this point, I answered many of your questions regarding subliminal and manifest minds, the deterioration of their functioning, and so forth. Following this, I explained the mode of rising from meditative equipoise and the types of motivation that one is to contemplate during the state subsequent to meditative equipoise. I clarified at length the fact that this state subsequent to meditative equipoise is included within the meditative session. Thus, I want to make it clear now that the state subsequent to meditative equipoise is definitely included within the session. If you divide the session into the preparation, actual session, and conclusion, both meditative equipoise and the state subsequent to meditative equipoise are included within the actual session.

Next, I explained the mode of progress on the remaining paths based on calm abiding. I began the explanation of the mode of procedure of the mundane path. The four preparatory trainings were explained; then, the four persons who can progress on the mundane path. Presentation of the achievement of an actual absorption of the first concentration based on the seven mental contemplations was begun. In a general way, the presentation of the different numbers of mental contemplations was given. The first of the seven mental contemplations, that of individual knowledge of the character, was discussed in detail. The reason why it is necessary to generate the mental contemplation of individual knowledge of the character was given; also, how the mental contemplation of individual knowledge of the character engages in analysis, as well as its entity, definition, mental basis, and in what level it is included.

All these topics have been explained. What still remains to be explained is most of the mode of procedure of the mundane path and all of the mode of procedure of the supramundane path. Probably, in terms of percentage, the explanation of calm abiding is thirty percent of the whole.

Have I explained this from the viewpoint of my already having attained calm abiding or special insight? No. In the past I did a little study of the texts; at that time there were many scholars and adepts. I have explained this in dependence on my questioning of them, not in dependence on my own attainment of calm abiding and special insight. Nowadays, I have been a little sad that because of my youth at that time I did not ask questions fully. If I had been able to ask questions fully at that time, since there were so many scholars and adepts then—many who had achieved adepthood, even though one is not allowed to declare that one has done so—it probably would have made a difference. However, whatever I heard I have used in extending this explanation. Previously, I referred to instructions from experience, and so forth; I am saying now that I have not given an explanation from experience. There are some books written in terms of the practitioner's own experience and some based on other texts. I have gathered together many good explanations from texts written from both of these viewpoints, garnering explanations of how to sustain objects of observation in a meditative session. What I have done is to carry to you what these people have said.

With respect to the degree of error in what I have explained, what I did explain I explained carefully, and I worked hard at not making mistakes. Nevertheless, there may still be mistakes because sometimes, even if I am thinking one thing, I will say something else. There may also be cases in which I think something is right but it is not. Thus, you should examine this in the future. You do not have to accept what I say as being right. At the same time, if someone tells you that something I have said is wrong because no one else has ever said it, it does not necessarily follow. For instance, my own teachers have said that a direct realization of emptiness at the time of an uninterrupted path of a final path of seeing is emptiness. Most people are amazed at this teaching. If you investigate and debate the reasons for saying that this realization of emptiness is or is not emptiness, there are more reasons for saying that it is. Thus, you should examine carefully, and if something is indeed mistaken, you should leave it. If, when I explained topics, I inadvertently said things that you did not like, please be patient. From my own point of view, I have no sense that you disliked what I said. If something of the sort did occur, please be patient with it.

We are now separating physically, but we have great connection mentally. Good luck.

GLOSSARY

ENGLISH	TIBETAN	SANSKRIT
abandonment	spangs pa	prahāṇa
absorption	snyoms 'jug	samāpatti
achieving through engagement	'jug sgrub	prasthānapratipatti
action	las	karma
actual	dngos gzhi	maula
actual absorption	dngos gzhi'i snyoms 'jug	maulasamāpatti
aeon	bskal pa	kalpa
afflicted	nyon mongs can	kliṣṭa
affliction	nyon mongs	kleśa
afflictive obstructions	nyon mongs pa'i sgrib pa	kleśāvaraṇa
aggregate	phung po	skandha
aging and death	rga shi	jarāmaraṇa
altruistic aspiration to enlightenment	byang chub kyi sems	bodhicitta
altruistic mind generation	byang chub sems bskyed	bodhicittotpāda
altruistic mind of enlightenment	byang chub kyi sems	bodhicitta
analysis	dpyod pa	vicāra
analytical image	rnam par rtog pa dang bcas pa'i gzugs brnyan	savikalpakapratibimba
analytical meditation	dpyad sgom	
androgynous	mtshan gnyis pa	ubhayavyanjaña
anger	khong khro	pratigha
animal	dud 'gro	tiryañc
annihilation	chad pa	uccheda
antidotal mental contemplation	gnyen po yid la byed pa	
antidote	gnyen po	pratipakṣa
appearance factor	snang ngo	
appearance factor of the mind	sems kyi snang cha	
application	'du byed pa	abhisaṃskāra
apprehended object	bzung yul	grāhyaviṣaya
appropriate and inappropriate	gnas dang gnas ma yin pa	sthānāsthāna
arisen from hearing	thos byung	śrutamayī
arisen from meditation	sgom byung	bhāvanāmayī
arisen from thinking	bsam byung	cintāmayī
artificial	kun btags	parikalpita
ascertainment factor	nges ngo	
aspect	rnam pa	ākāra
aspiration	'dun pa	chanda

ENGLISH	TIBETAN	SANSKRIT
aspiration which is a wish to attain	'thob 'dod kyi 'dun pa	
aspiration which is an aspiration for that	de la 'dun pa'i 'dun pa	
aspirational prayer	smon lam	praṇidhāna
assumption of bad states	gnas ngan len	
atom	rdul phra rab	paramāṇu
attachment	sred pa	tṛṣṇā
auspiciousness	gya noms pa	praṇīta
authority	dbang thang che ba	
awareness	blo	buddhi
Awareness and Knowledge	blo rig	
bad transmigration	ngan 'gro	durgati
bare instruction	dmar khrid	
basis	rten	āśraya
basis of designation	gdags gzhi	
basis of the object of observation	dmigs pa'i rten	
beginner	las dang po pa	ādikarmika
beginner at mental contemplation	yid la byed pa las dang po pa	manaskārādikarmika
beginner at purifying afflictions	nyon mongs rnam par sbyong ba'i las dang po pa	
birth	skye ba	jāti
bliss	bde ba	sukha
Blissful Place	bde ba can	sukhāvatī
Bodhisattva	byang chub sems dpa'	bodhisattva
body	lus	kāya
body consciousness	lus kyi rnam shes	kāyavijñāna
brāhman	bram ze	brāhmaṇa
branch that is a benefit	phan yon gyi yan lag	*anuśaṃsāṅga
breath, exhalation and inhalation of	dbugs 'byung rngub	ānāpāna
Buddha	sangs rgyas	buddha
Buddha field	sangs rgyas kyi zhing	buddhakṣetra
Buddha Superior	sangs rgyas 'phags pa	
calm abiding	zhi gnas	śamatha
causal meditative absorption	rgyu snyoms 'jug	*kāraṇasamāpatti
causally concordant application	rgyu mthun pa'i sbyor ba	
cause	rgyu	hetu
central channel	rtsa dbu ma	avadhūtī
cessation	'gog pa	nirodha
change	yongs su sgyur ba	vivartanā

ENGLISH	TIBETAN	SANSKRIT
changeable mental factor	sems byung gzhan 'gyur	*anyathābhāvacaitta
channel	rtsa	nāḍi
Chittamātra	sems tsam pa	cittamātra
clairvoyance	mngon shes	abhijñā
clear appearance	gsal snang	
clear light	'od gsal	prabhāsvara
close setting	nye bar 'jog pa	upasthāpana
Cloudless	sprin med	anabhraka
coarse	rags pa	audārika
coarse pliancy	rags pa'i shin sbyangs	
collections of merit & wisdom	bsod nams dang ye shes kyi tshogs	puṇyajñānasaṃbhāra
color	kha dog	varṇa
common being	so so'i skye bo	pṛthagjana
compassion	snying rje	karuṇā
composed phenomenon	'dus byas	saṃskṛta
compositional factor	'du byed	saṃskāra
concentration	bsam gtan	dhyāna
conception of a [bad] view as supreme	lta ba mchog 'dzin	dṛṣṭiparāmarśa
conception of ethics & systems of behavior as supreme	tshul khrims dang brdul zhugs mchog 'dzin	śīlavrataparāmarśa
conception of true existence	bden 'dzin	
conceptuality	rnam rtog	vikalpa
concomitant	grogs	sahāya
concordant mental contemplation	rjes su mthun pa las byung ba'i yid byed	
condition	pratyaya	rkyen
confession	bshags pa	deśanā
congregating Solitary Realizer	tshogs dang spyod pa'i rang sangs rgyas	*vargacārinpratyekabuddha
consciousness	rnam par shes pa, rnam shes	vijñāna
constituent	khams	dhātu
contact	reg pa	sparśa
contaminated	zag bcas	sāsrava
continent	gling	dvīpa
continuous application	rtag sbyor	
continuous setting	rgyun du 'jog pa	saṃsthāpana
continuum	rgyud	saṃtāna
conventional truth	kun rdzob bden pa	saṃvṛtisatya
contrition	'gyod pa	kaukṛtya
cooperative condition	lhan cig byed rkyen	sahakāripratyaya
correctly assuming consciousness	yid dpyod	*manaḥ parīkṣā

ENGLISH	TIBETAN	SANSKRIT
counting	grangs pa	gaṇanā
cyclic existence	'khor ba	saṃsāra
definition	mtshan nyid	lakṣaṇa
demigod	lha ma yin	asura
dependent-arising	rten 'byung, rten cing 'brel bar 'byung ba	pratītyasamutpāda
descent of ambrosia	bdud rtsi 'bebs sbyang	
desire	'dod chags	rāga
Desire Realm	'dod khams	kāmadhātu
desisting from application	'du byed btang snyoms	upekṣā
Dialectician [Nihilist]	rtog ge pa	
direct perceiver/ direct perception	mngon sum	pratyakṣa
discipline	'dul ba	vinaya
disciplining	dul bar byed pa	damana
discrimination	'du shes	saṃjñā
discursiveness	rnam rtog	vikalpa
distraction	rnam par g.yeng ba	vikṣepa
division	dbye ba	
doctrinal knowledge	chos shes pa	dharmajñāna
doctrine	chos	dharma
doubt	the tshom	vicikitsā
drop	thig le	bindu
earth	sa	pṛthivī
effect	'bras bu	phala
effort	brtson 'grus	vīrya
effort arising from application	sbyor ba las byung ba'i brtson grus	
effort which is insatiable	chog ma shes pa'i brtson grus	
element	'byung ba	bhūta
emptiness	stong pa nyid	śūnyatā
entity	ngo bo	vastu
enumeration	grangs nges	
equanimity	btang snyoms	upekṣā
establishment in mindfulness	dran pa nye bar bzhag pa	smṛtyupasthāna
ethics	tshul krims	śīla
exalted knower	mkhyen pa	jñāta
exalted knower of all aspects	rnam pa thams cad mkhyen pa nyid	sarvākārajñatā
exalted wisdom	ye shes	jñāna
exalted wisdom of meditative equipoise	mnyam bzhag ye shes	samāhitajñāna

ENGLISH	TIBETAN	SANSKRIT
excitement	rgod pa	auddhatya
exertion	rtsol ba	vyāyāma
existence	srid pa	bhava
extreme	mtha'	anta
extreme of annihilation	chad mtha'	ucchedānta
extreme of cyclic existence	srid pa'i mtha'	bhavānta
extreme of permanence	rtag mtha'	śaśvatānta
extreme of solitary peace	zhi mtha'	*śāntānta
eye consciousness	mig gi rnam shes	cakṣurvijñāna
eye sense power	mig gi dbang po	cakṣurindriya
factor of clarity	gsal cha	
factor of stability	gnas cha	
factor of [subjective] clarity	dvang cha	
faith	dad pa	śraddhā
faith of conviction	yid ches pa'i dad pa	
faith which is a non-captivated clarity	mi 'phrog pa'i dvang pa'i dad pa	
familiarity	yongs su 'dris pa	paricaya
fault	nyes pa, nyes dmigs, skyon	ādīnava, apakṣāla
feeling	tshor ba	vedanā
final analysis (textbook)	mtha' dpyad	
final concentration	rab mtha'i bsam gtan	
fire	me	tejas
first concentration	bsam gtan dang po	prathamadhyāna
first [Bodhisattva] ground	sa dang po	prathamabhūmi
Five Pure Places	gnas gtsang lnga	pañcaśuddhāvāsakāyika
Foe Destroyer	dgra bcom pa	arhan
following	rjes su 'gro ba	anugama
forbearance	bzod pa	kṣānti
forcible engagement	sgrim ste 'jug pa	balavāhana
Forder	mu steg pa	tīrthika
forgetfulness	gdams ngag brjed pa	avavādasammoṣa
form	gzugs	rūpa
form aggregate	gzugs kyi phung po	rūpaskandha
form of one who has attained mastery	dbang 'byor ba'i gzugs	
Form Realm	gzugs khams	rūpadhātu
formless absorption	gzugs med kyi snyoms 'jug	ārūpyasamāpatti
Formless Realm	gzugs med khams	ārūpyadhātu
fortune	'byor ba	saṃpad
four noble truths	'phags pa'i bden pa bzhi	catvāryāryasatyāni
fourth concentration	bsam gtan bzhi pa	caturthadhyāna

ENGLISH	TIBETAN	SANSKRIT
fruit	'bras bu	phala
function	byed las	
Ḡa-dam-b̄a	dka' gdams pa	
general meaning (textbook)	spyi don	
generic image	don spyi	arthasāmānya
ge-s̄hay	dge bshes	
god	lha	deva
god of no discrimination	'du shes med pa'i sems can	asaṃjñisattva
going-as-a-hero meditative stabilization	dpa' bar 'gro ba zhes bya ba'i ting nge 'dzin	śūraṃgamo nāma samādhi
grasping	len pa	upadāna
great compassion	snying rje chen po	mahākaruṇā
great love	byams pa chen po	mahāmaitrī
gross	rags pa	audārika
ground	sa	bhūmi
hand symbol	phyag mtshan	
happiness	bde ba	sukha
happy transmigration	bde 'gro	sugati
harmful intent	gnod sems	vyāpāda
hatred	zhe sdang	dveṣa
haughtiness	rgyags pa	mada
Hearer	nyan thos	śrāvaka
hearing	thos pa	śruta
heat	drod	uṣmagata
hell	dmyal ba	naraka
hell-being	dmyal ba	nāraka
higher ethics	lhag pa'i tshul khrims	adhiśīla
higher meditative stabilization	lhag pa'i sems	adhicitta
higher wisdom	lhag pa'i shes rab	adhiprajñā
Highest Yoga Tantra	bla med kyi rgyud	anuttarayogatantra
human	mi	manuṣya
hungry ghost	yi dvags	preta
I	nga	ahaṃ
ignorance	ma rig pa	avidyā
illusory body	sgyu lus	māyādeha
illusory-like state subsequent to meditative equipoise	rjes thob sgyu ma lta bu	
immeasurable	tshad med	apramāṇa
immeasurable equanimity	btang snyoms tshad med	
immediately preceding condition	de ma dag rkyen	samanantarapratyaya
impermanence	mi rtag pa	anitya
impermanence of sound	sgra mi rtag pa	

ENGLISH	TIBETAN	SANSKRIT
individual emancipation	so sor thar pa	pratimokṣa
inference, inferential cognition	rjes dpag	anumāna
inferential prime cognition	rjes dpag tshad ma	anumānapramāṇa
inherent existence	rang bzhin gyis grub pa	svabhāvasiddhi
innate	lhan skyes	sahaja
instruction from experience	myong khrid	
intense application	gus sbyor	
intensity	ngar	
intention	sems pa	cetanā
intermediate state	bar do	antarābhāva
interrupted engagement	bar du chad cing 'jug pa	sacchidravāhana
introspection	shes bzhin	saṃprajanya
investigation	nye bar rtog pa	upalakṣaṇā
jealousy	phrag dog	irṣyā
joy	dga' ba	prīti
Joyous Place	dga' ldan	tuṣita
knower of bases	gzhi shes	vastujñatā
knower of paths	lam shes	mārgajñatā
lacking "normative" maleness	ma ning	paṇḍaka
lama	bla ma	guru
laxity	bying ba	laya
laziness	le lo	kausīdya
laziness of inadequacy	sgyid lugs pa'i le lo	
laziness of neutral activities	snyoms las kyi le lo	
laziness which is an attachment to bad activities	bya ba ngan zhen gyi le lo	
leapover	thod rgal	
leg of manifestation	rdzu 'phrul gyi rkang pa	ṛddhipāda
leisure	dal ba	kṣaṇa
lethargy	rmugs pa	styāna
liberation	thar pa	vimokṣa
life-faculty	srog gi dbang po	jivitendriya
limitless consciousness	rnam shes mtha' yas	vijñānānantya
Limitless Space	nam mkha' mtha' yas	ākāśānantya
lineage	rigs	gotra
logical reasoning	'thad sgrub kyi rigs pa	upapattisādhanayukti
love	byams pa	maitrī
love observing mere sentient beings	sems can tsam la dmigs pa'i byams pa	
love observing phenomena	chos la dmigs pa'i byams pa	
love observing the unapprehend-able	dmigs med la dmigs pa'i byams pa	

ENGLISH	TIBETAN	SANSKRIT
Mādhyamika	dbu ma pa	mādhyamika
main mind	gtso sems	
making one-pointed	rtse gcig tu byed pa	ekotīkaraṇa
mandala	dkhyil 'khor	maṇḍala
manifest coarse affliction	nyon mongs rags pa mngon gyur ba	
matter	bem po	kanthā
meditating, meditation	sgom pa	bhāvanā
meditative absorption	snyoms 'jug	samāpatti
meditative absorption of cessation	'gog pa'i snyoms 'jug	nirodhasamāpatti
meditative equipoise	mnyam bzhag	samāhita
meditative stabilization	ting nge 'dzin	samādhi
meditative stabilization of counting	grangs pa'i ting nge 'dzin	
meditative stabilization of ninth mind of Desire Realm	'dod sems dgu pa'i ting nge 'dzin	
Meditator [Nihilist]	snyoms 'jug pa	
mental abiding	sems gnas	cittasthiti
mental basis	sems rten	
mental bliss	yid bde	saumanasya
mental body	yid lus	
mental consciousness	yid kyi rnam par shes pa	manovijñāna
mental contemplation	yid la byed pa	manaskāra
mental contemplation arisen from belief	mos pa las byung ba'i yid byed	adhimokṣikamanaskāra
mental contemplation of a beginner at purifying afflictions	nyon mongs rnam par sbyong ba'i las dang po pa'i yid byed	kleśaviśuddhyādikarmikamanaskāra
mental contemplation of a mere beginner	las dang po pa tsam gyi yid byed	
mental contemplation of analysis	dpyod pa yid byed	mīmāṃsāmanaskāra
mental contemplation of final training	sbyor mtha'i yid byed	prayoganiṣṭhamanaskāra
mental contemplation of individual investigation	so sor rtog pa yid la byed pa	
mental contemplation of individual knowledge of the character	mtshan nyid so sor rig pa'i yid byed	lakṣaṇapratisaṃvedīmanaskāra
mental contemplation of joy-withdrawal	dga' ba sdud pa'i yid byed	ratisaṃgrāhakamanaskāra
mental contemplation of thorough isolation	rab tu dben pa'i yid byed	prāvivekyamanaskāra
mental contemplation that is the fruit of final training	sbyor mtha'i 'bras bu'i yid byed	prayoganiṣṭhaphalamanaskāra

ENGLISH	TIBETAN	SANSKRIT
mental discomfort	yid mi bde	daurmanasya
mental engagement	yid la byed pa	manaskāra
mental factor	sems byung	caitta
mental image	don spyi	arthasāmānya
mental pleasure	yid bde	saumanasya
merchant class	rje'u rigs	vaiśya
merit	bsod nams	puṇya
method	thabs	upāya
mind	sems	citta
mind-basis-of-all	kun gzhi rnam shes	ālayavijñāna
mindfulness	dran pa	smṛti
miserliness	ser sna	mātsarya
mode	ji lta ba	
mode of being	yin lugs	
mode of production	skyed tshul	
mode of subsistence	gnas lugs	
monk	dge slong	bhikṣu
mount	bzhon pa	
mundane path	'jig rten pa'i lam	laukikamārga
mutually exclusive	'gal ba	virodha
nāga	klu	nāga
naked instruction	dmar khrid	
name and form	ming gzugs	nāmarūpa
name basis	ming gzhi	
nature	rang bzhin	svābhāva
Nature Body	ngo bo nyid sku	svabhāvikakāya
neither pleasure nor suffering	sdug bsngal ma yin bde ba yang ma yin	aduḥkhāsukha
neuter	za ma	ṣaṇḍha
neutral	lung du ma bstan pa	avyākṛta
neutral feeling	btang snyoms	upekṣā
Never Returner	phyir mi 'ong	anāgāmin
Nihilist	rgyang 'phen pa	āyata
nine mental abidings	sems gnas dgu	navākārācittasthiti
non-abiding nirvāṇa	mi gnas pa'i mya ngan las 'das pa	apratiṣṭhanirvāṇa
non-affirming negative	med dgag	prasajyapratiṣedha
non-analytical image	rnam par mi rtog pa'i gzugs brnyan	nirvikalpakapratibimba
non-application	'du mi byed pa	anabhisaṃskāra
non-associated compositional factor	ldan min 'du byed	viprayuktasaṃskāra
non-conceptual exalted wisdom	rnam par mi rtog pa'i ye shes	

ENGLISH	TIBETAN	SANSKRIT
non-discrimination	'du shes me pa	asaṃjñā
non-disturbed effort	mi 'thugs pa'i brtson grus	
non-embarrassment	khrel med	anapatrāpya
non-revelatory form	rnam par rig byed ma yin pa'i gzugs	avijñaptirūpa
non-shame	ngo tsha med pa	āhrīkya
non-virtue, non-virtuous	mi dge ba	akuśala
not-unable	mi lcog med	anāgamya
nothingness	ci yang med	ākiṃcanya
novice	dge tshul	śramaṇera
object	yul	viṣaya
object of abandonment	spang bya	prahātavya
object of knowledge	shes bya	jñeya
object of negation	dgag bya	pratiṣedhya
object of observation	dmigs pa	ālaṃbana
object-of-observation condition	dmigs rkyen	ālambanapratyaya
object-of-observation support	dmigs rten	
objects of observation for purifying afflictions	nyon mongs rnams sbyong gi dmigs pa	kleśaviśodanaālambana
objects of observation for purifying behavior	spyad pa rnam sbyong gi dmigs pa	caritaviśodanaālambana
objects of observation for [developing] skill	mkhas pa'i dmigs pa, mkhas par byed pa'i dmigs pa	kauśalyālambana
obscuration	gti mug	moha
observed-object condition	dmigs rkyen	ālambanapratyaya
observing the fruit	'bras bu la dmigs pa	
observing the limits of phenomena	dngos po'i mtha' la dmigs pa	vastvantālambana
obstructions to liberation	nyon mongs pa'i sgrib pa	kleśāvaraṇa
obstructions to omniscience	shes bya'i sgrib pa	jñeyāvaraṇa
offer realization, to	rtogs pa phul ba	
omen of pliancy	shin sbyangs skye ba'i snga bltas	
Once Returner	phyir 'ong	sakṛdāgāmin
operative consciousness	'jug shes	
ordinary being	'jig rten rang 'ga' ba	
Outsider	phyi rol pa	
overapplication	'du byed pa	abhisaṃskāra
pacifying	zhi bar byed pa	śamana
pain	sdug bsngal	duḥkha
particle	rdul phra rab	paramāṇu
path	lam	mārga

ENGLISH	TIBETAN	SANSKRIT
path having the aspect of grossness/peacefulness	zhi rags rnam can gyi lam	
path having the uncontaminated truths as its aspect	zag med bden pa'i rnam can gyi lam	
path of accumulation	tshogs lam	saṃbhāramārga
path of meditation	sgom lam	bhāvanāmārga
path of no more learning	mi slob lam	aśaikṣamārga
path of preparation	sbyor lam	prayogamārga
path of release	nam grol lam	vimuktimārga
path of seeing	mthong lam	darśanamārga
peaceful	zhi ba	śānta
peak	rtse mo	mūrdhan
peak of cyclic existence	srid rtse	bhavāgra
perfection	pha rol tu phyin pa, phar phyin	pāramitā
Perfection of Wisdom	shes rab kyi pha rol tu phyin pa, sher phyin	prajñāpāramitā
Perfection Vehicle	phar phyin gyi theg pa	pāramitāyāna
permanence	rtag pa	śaśvatā
person	gang zag	pudgala
pervasive objects of observation	khyab pa'i dmigs pa	vyāpyālambana
physical basis	lus rten	
physical sense power	lus kyi dbang po	kāyendriya
placement	'jog pa	sthāna
pleasure	bde ba	sukha
pliancy	shin tu sbyangs pa	praśrabdhi
pliancy difficult to analyze	brtags par dka' ba'i shin sbyangs	
pliancy easy to analyze	brtags par sla ba'i shin sbyangs	
possibility	mu	
pot	bum pa	ghaṭa
potency	nus pa	
power	stobs	bala
practical instruction	nyams khrid	
preceptual [Ga-dam-ba]	gdams ngag pa	
preceptual instruction	gdams ngag	avavāda
predisposition	bags chags	vāsanā
preparation	nyer bsdogs	samāntaka
preparatory training	ngon 'gro'i sbyor ba	
prerequisites	tshogs bsten pa	
• staying in an agreeable place	mthun pa'i yul na gnas pa	
• having few desires	'dod pa chung ba	
• knowing satisfaction	chog shes pa	
• not having many activities	bya ba mang po'i 'du 'dzi yong su spang ba	

ENGLISH	TIBETAN	SANSKRIT
• pure ethics	tshul khrims dag pa	
• thoroughly abandoning thoughts	rnam rtog yong su spang ba	
pride	nga rgyal	māna
prime cognition	tshad ma	pramāṇa
product	'dus byas	saṃskṛta
projected effect	'phangs 'bras	
proprietary effect	bdag po'i 'bras bu	adhipatiphala
proof statement	sgrub ngag	
pure	dag pa	śuddha
pure land	dag zhing	kṣetraśuddhi
purifying	yongs su dag pa	pariśuddhi
quintessential instruction	man ngag	upadeśa
reality	de kho na nyid	tathatā.
reasoning	rigs pa	yukti
reasoning of dependence	ltos pa'i rigs pa	apekṣāyukti
reasoning of nature	chos nyid kyi rigs pa	dharmatāyukti
reasoning of performance of function	bya ba byed pa'i rigs pa	kāryakāraṇayukti
reflective meditation	shar sgom	
refuge	skyabs	śaraṇa
resetting	slan te 'jog pa	avasthāpana
resultant-birth meditative absorption	'bras bu skye ba'i snyoms 'jug	*kāryasamāpatti
revelatory form	rnam par rig par byed pa'i gzugs	vijñaptirūpa
rhinoceros-like Solitary Realizer	bse ru lta bu rang sangs rgyas	khaḍgaviṣāṇakalpapratyekabuddha
root affliction	rtsa nyon	mūlakleśa
royal class	rgyal rigs	kṣatriya
scattering	'phro ba	
seal	phyag rgya	mudrā
second concentration	bsam gtan gnyis pa	dvitīyadhyāna
secondary affliction	nye ba'i nyon mongs	upakleśa
self	bdag	ātman
selflessness	bdag med pa	nairātmya
selflessness of persons	gang zag gi bdag med	pudgalanairātmya
sense consciousness	dbang shes	indriyajñāna
sense power	dbang po	indriya
sentient being	sems can	sattva
separation from attachment	chags bral	kāmād virakta
serial absorption	mthar gyis gnas pa'i snyoms 'jug	anupūrvavihārasamāpatti

ENGLISH	TIBETAN	SANSKRIT
setting in equipoise	mnyam par 'jog pa	samādhāna
setting the mind	sems 'jog pa	cittasthāpana
seven cause-and-effect quintessential instructions	rgyu 'bras man ngag bdun	
shape	dbyibs	saṃstāna
sign	mtshan ma	nimitta
similar association	mtshung ldan	saṃprayukta
simultaneous	gcig car	sakṛt
slackness	zhum ba	
sleep	gnyid	middha
slightly hidden phenomenon-	cung zad lkog gyur	
social stratum	rigs	varṇa
Solitary Realizer	rang sangs rgyas	pratyekabuddha
sound generality	sgra spyi	śabdasāmānya
space-like meditative equipoise	mnyam bzhag nam mkha' lta bu	
special insight	lhag mthong	vipaśyanā
sphere	skye mched	āyatana
spiritual community	dge 'dun	saṃgha
spiritual friend	dge ba'i bshes gnyen	kalyāṇamitra
spiritual guide	dge ba'i bshes gnyen	kalyāṇamitra
spontaneous	lhun gyis grub pa	anābhoga
spontaneous engagement	lhun grub tu 'jug pa	anābhogavāhana
stabilization	ting nge 'dzin	samādhi
stabilizing meditation	'jog sgom	
stage of completion	rdzogs rim	niṣpannakrama
stage of generation	bskyed rim	utpattikrama
stages of the path	lam rim	
state subsequent to meditative equipoise	rjes thob	pṛṣṭhalabdha
Stream Enterer	rgyun zhugs	śrotāpanna
subsequent cognition	bcad shes	
subsequent knowledge	rjes su shes pa	anvayajñāna
subsequent realization of phenomena as illusory	rjes thob sgyu ma lta bu	
substantial cause	nyer len	upādāna
substantial continuum	rdzas rgyun	
substantial entity	rdzas	dravya
subtle	phra mo	sūkṣma
subtle pliancy	phra ba'i shin sbyangs	
suffering	sdug bsngal	duḥkha
Superior	'phags pa	ārya
support	rten	āśraya

ENGLISH	TIBETAN	SANSKRIT
support which is the object of observation	dmigs pa'i rten	
supported	brten pa	
supramundane path	'jig rten las 'das pa'i lam	lokottaramārga
supreme mundane qualities	'jig rten pa'i chos kyi mchog	laukikāgryadharma
tangible object	reg bya	spraṣṭavya
tantra set	rgyud sde	tantrapiṭaka
tenets	grub mtha'	siddhānta
textbook, monastic	yig cha	
textual [Ga-dam-bas]	gzhung pa pa	
textual instruction	gzhung khrid	
thing	dngos po	bhāva
thinking	bsam pa	cintā
third concentration	bsam gtan gsum pa	tritīyadhyāna
thorough achievement of the purpose	dgos pa yongs su grub pa	kṛtyānuṣṭāna
thorough entanglement	kun dkris	paryavasthāna
thorough enwrapment	kun tu sbyor ba	saṃyojana
thorough knowledge of the character	mtshan nyid rab tu rig pa	
thorough pacifying	nye bar zhi bar byed pa	vyupaśamana
thoroughly clear mental contemplation	rab tu dvang ba yid la byed pa	
thought definitely to leave cyclic existence	nges 'byung	niḥsaraṇa
three realms and nine levels	khams gsum sa dgu	
training	bslab pa	śikṣā
transmigrator	'gro ba	gati
treatise	bstan bcos	śāstra
true cessations	'gog pa'i bden pa	nirodhasatya
true existence	bden par yod pa	satyasat
true origins	kun 'byung bden pa	samudayasatya
true paths	lam bden pa	mārgasatya
true sufferings	sdug bsngal bden pa	duḥkhasatya
ultimate truth	don dam bden pa	paramārthasatya
uncommon dominant condition	thun mong ma yin pa'i bdag rkyen	samānantarapratyaya
uncontaminated	zag med	anāsrava
unfluctuating	mi g.yo ba	āniñjya
unimpeded mental body	yid lus thogs pa med pa	
uninterrupted engagement	chad pa med par 'jug pa	nischidravāhana
uninterrupted path	bar chad med lam	ānantaryamārga

ENGLISH	TIBETAN	SANSKRIT
union of calm abiding and special insight	zhi lhag zung 'brel	
unpleasant	mi sdug pa	aśubha
Unpleasant Sound	sgra mi nyan	kuru
upper realm	khams gong ma	
Vairochana	rnam par snang mdzad	vairocana
valid cognition	tshad ma	pramāṇa
valid person	tshad ma'i skyes bu	
varieties	ji snyed pa	
vibrant	thu re	
view	lta ba	dṛṣṭi
view holding to extreme	mthar 'dzing pa'i lta ba	antagrāhadṛṣṭi
view of transitory collection [as real] I & mine	'jig tshogs la lta ba	satkāyadṛṣṭi
virtue, virtuous	dge ba	kuśala
virtuous root	dge ba'i rtsa ba	kuśalamūla
vow	sdom pa	saṃvara
water	chu	āp
welfare	don	artha
wind	rlung	prāṇa, vāyu
wisdom	shes rab	prajñā
wisdom realizing emptiness	stong nyid rtogs pa'i shes rab	
wisdom subsequent to meditative equipoise	rjes thob ye shes	pṛṣṭhalabdhajñāna
Wisdom Truth Body	ye shes chos sku	jñānadharmakāya
world system	'jig rten gyi khams	lokadhātu
wrong view	log lta	mithyādṛṣṭi
yoga	rnal 'byor	yoga
yoga of a beginner at mental contemplation	yid la byed pa las dang po pa'i rnal 'byor	manaskārādikarmika-[yoga]
yoga of someone who is practiced	yongs su sbyangs pa byas pa'i rnal 'byor	kṛtaparicaya-[yoga]
yoga of one whose mental contemplation is perfected	yid la byed pa yongs su rdzogs pa'i rnal 'byor	atikrāntamanaskāra-[yoga]
yogi	rnal 'byor pa	yogi
yogi who has passed beyond mental contemplation	yid la byed pa las 'das pa'i rnal 'byor pa	
yogi who is a beginner	las dang po pa'i rnal 'byor pa	
yogi who is purifying afflictions	nyon mongs rnam par sbyong ba'i rnal 'byor pa	
youth	lang 'tsho	

BIBLIOGRAPHY

Note: Sūtras and tantras are listed alphabetically by English title in the first section. Indian and Tibetan treatises are listed alphabetically by author in the second section. Other works are listed alphabetically by author in the third section.

"P," standing for "Peking edition," refers to the Tibetan Tripiṭaka (Tokyo-Kyoto: Tibetan Tripiṭaka Research Foundation, 1956).

1. SŪTRAS AND TANTRAS

Compendium of the Principles of All Ones Gone Thus (root Yoga Tantra)
sarvatathāgatatattvasaṃgrahanāmamahāyānasūtra
de bzhin gshegs pa thams cad kyi de kho na nyid bsdus pa zhes bya ba theg pa chen po'i mdo
P112, vol. 4 (Toh. 479)
Sanskrit: *Sarva-tathāgata-tattva-saṅgraha*, reproduced by Lokesh Chandra and David L. Snellgrove. Śata-piṭaka Series, vol. 269. New Delhi: 1981.

Guhyasamāja Tantra (root Highest Yoga Tantra)
sarvatathāgatakāyavākcittarahasyaguhyasamājanāmamahākalparāja
de bzhin gshegs pa thams cad kyi sku gsung thugs kyi gsang chen gsang ba 'dus pa zhes bya ba brtag pa'i rgyal po chen po
P81, vol. 3
Sanskrit: Benoytosh Bhattacharya, ed. *Guhyasamāja Tantra or Tathāgataguhyaka.* Gaekwad's Oriental Series No. 53. Baroda: Oriental Institute, 1967.

Kāraṇḍavyūha Sūtra
āryakāraṇḍavyūhanāmamahāyānasūtra
'phags pa za ma rtog bkod pa zhes bya ba theg pa chen po'i mdo
P784, vol. 30

Perfection of Wisdom Sūtras
prajñāpāramitāsūtra
shes rab kyi pha rol tu phyin pa'i mdo
P vols. 12-21
See: E. Conze. *The Large Sūtra on Perfect Wisdom.* Berkeley: U. Cal., 1975

Sūtra of Teaching to Nanda on Entry to the Womb
āyuṣmannandagarbhāvakrāntinirdeśa
tshe dang ldan pa dga' bo mngal du 'jug pa bstan pa
P760.13, vol. 23

Sūtra on the Ten Grounds
daśabhūmikasūtra
mdo sde sa bcu pa
P761.31, vol. 25
Sanskrit: P. L. Vaidya, ed. *Daśabhūmikasūtram.* Buddhist Sanskrit Texts No. 7. Darbhanga: Mithila Institute, 1967.
English translation: M. Honda. 'An Annotated Translation of the "Daśabhūmika."' in D. Si-

nor, ed., *Studies in Southeast and Central Asia*, Śatapiṭaka Series 74. New Delhi: 1968, 115-276.

Sūtra Unraveling the Thought
saṃdhinirmocanasūtra
dgongs pa nges par 'grel pa'i mdo
P774, vol. 29
Edited Tibetan text and French translation: Étienne Lamotte, *Saṃdhinirmocanasūtra: l'Explication des mystères*. Louvain: Université de Louvain, 1935.

Vajra Garland Tantra
vajramālā/ śrīvajramālābhidhānamahāyogatantrasarvatantrahṛdayarahasyavibhaṅga
rdo rje phreng ba/ rnal 'byor chen po'i rgyud dpal rdo rje phreng ba mngon par brjod pa rgyud thams cad kyi snying po gsang ba rnam par phye ba
P82, vol. 3

2. SANSKRIT AND TIBETAN WORKS

Āryadeva (*'phags pa lha*, second to third century C.E.)

Four Hundred/ Treatise of Four Hundred Stanzas
catuḥśatakaśāstrakārikā
bstan bcos bzhi brgya pa zhes bya ba'i tshig le'ur byas pa
P5246, vol. 95
Edited Tibetan and Sanskrit fragments along with English translation: Karen Lang. "Āryadeva on the Bodhisattva's Cultivation of Merit and Knowledge." Ann Arbor: University Microfilms, 1983.
English translation: *Yogic Deeds of Bodhisattvas: Gyel-tsap on Āryadeva's Four Hundred*. Commentary by Geshe Sonam Rinchen, translated and edited by Ruth Sonam. Ithaca: Snow Lion Publications: 1994.
Italian translation of the last half from the Chinese: Giuseppe Tucci, "La versione cinese del Catuḥśataka di Āryadeva, confronta col testo sanscrito et la traduzione tibetana." *Rivista degli Studi Orientalia* 10 (1925), 521-567.

Asaṅga (*thogs med*, fourth century)

Summary of Manifest Knowledge
abhidharmasamuccaya
chos mngon pa kun btus
P5550, vol. 112
Sanskrit: *Abhidharma Samuccaya of Asaṅga*. Edited and reconstructed by Pralhad Pradhan, in Visva-Bharati Series, No.12. Santiniktan: Visva-Bharati, (Santiniketan Press), 1950.
French translation: Walpola Rahula. *La compendium de la super-doctrine (philosophie) (Abhidharmasamuccaya) d'Asaṅga*. Paris: École Française d'Extrême-Orient, 1971.

Five Treatises on the Grounds

1 Grounds of Yogic Practice
yogācārabhūmi
rnal 'byor spyod pa'i sa
P5536-5538, vol. 109-110

Grounds of Bodhisattvas
bodhisattvabhūmi
byang chub sems pa'i sa
P5538, vol. 110
Sanskrit edition: *Bodhisattvabhumi (being the XVth Section of Asangapada's Yogacarabhumi)*. Edited by Nalinaksha Dutt, in Tibetan Sanskrit Works Series, vol. 7. Patna: K.P. Jayaswal Research Institute, 1966. Also: Wogihara, Unrai, ed. *Bodhi-*

sattvabhūmi: A Statement of the Whole Course of the Bodhisattva (Being the Fifteenth Section of Yogācārabhūmi). Tokyo: 1930-1936.

Translation of the Chapter on Suchness, the fourth chapter of Part I which is the fifteenth volume of the *Grounds of Yogic Practice:* Janice D. Willis. *On Knowing Reality.* Delhi: Motilal, 1979.

2 Compendium of Ascertainments
nirṇayasaṃgraha/ viniścayasaṃgrahaṇī
rnam par gtan la dbab pa bsdu ba
P5539, vol. 110-111

3 Compendium of Bases
vastusaṃgraha
gzhi bsdu ba
P5540, vol. 111

4 Compendium of Enumerations
paryāyasaṃgraha
rnam grang bsdu ba
P5543, vol. 111

5 Compendium of Explanations
vivaraṇasaṃgraha
rnam par bshad pa bsdu ba
P5543, vol. 111

Grounds of Hearers
nyan sa
śrāvakabhūmi
P5537, vol. 110
Sanskrit edition: Tibetan Sanskrit Works Series, vol. 14, *Śrāvakabhūmi.* Edited by Karunesha Shukla. Patna: K.P. Jayaswal Research Institute, 1973

Two Summaries

1 *Summary of Manifest Knowledge*
abhidharmasamuccaya
chos mngon pa kun btus
P5550, vol. 112
Sanskrit: *Abhidharma Samuccaya of Asaṅga.* Edited and reconstructed by Pralhad Pradhan, in Visva-Bharati Series, No.12. Santiniktan: Visva-Bharati, (Santiniketan Press), 1950
French translation: Walpola Rahula. *La compendium de la super-doctrine (philosophie) (Abhidharmasamuccaya) d'Asaṅga.* Paris: École Française d'Extrême-Orient, 1971.

2 *Summary of the Great Vehicle*
mahāyānasaṃgraha
theg pa chen po bsdus pa
P5549, vol. 112
French translation and edited Chinese and Tibetan texts: Étienne Lamotte, *La somme du grand véhicule d'Asaṅga,* rpt. 2 vol. Publications de l'Institute Orientaliste de Louvain, vol.8. Louvain: Université de Louvain, 1973.
English translation: John P. Keenan. *The Summary of the Great Vehicle by Bodhisattva Asaṅga: Translated from the Chinese of Paramārtha.* Berkeley: Numata Center for Buddhist Translation and Research, 1992.

Atisha (*atiśa/ atīśa,* 982-1054)
Lamp for the Path to Enlightenment
bodhipathapradīpa

byang chub lam gyi sgron ma
P5343, vol.103
English translation with Atisha's autocommentary: Richard Sherbourne, S.J., *A Lamp for the Path and Commentary*. London: George Allen & Unwin, 1983.

Bhāvaviveka (*legs ldan 'byed*, c. 500-570?)

Blaze of Reasoning/ Commentary on the "Heart of the Middle Way": Blaze of Reasoning
madhyamakahṛdayavṛttitarkajvālā
dbu ma'i snying po'i 'grel pa rtog ge 'bar ba
P5256, vol. 96
Partial English translation (chap. III. 1-136): S. Iida. *Reason and Emptiness*. Tokyo: Hokuseido, 1980

Heart of the Middle Way
madhyamakahṛdayakārikā
dbu ma'i snying po'i tshig le'ur byas pa
P5255, vol. 96
Partial English translation (chap. III. 1-136): S. Iida. *Reason and Emptiness*. Tokyo: Hokuseido, 1980

Chandrakīrti (*zla ba grags pa*, seventh century)

[Auto]commentary on the "Supplement to (Nāgārjuna's) 'Treatise on the Middle'"
madhaymakāvatārabhāṣya
dbu ma la 'jug pa'i bshad pa/ dbu ma la 'jug pa'i rang 'grel
P5263, vol. 98. Also: Dharamsala: Council of Religious and Cultural Affairs, 1968.
Edited Tibetan: Louis de la Vallée Poussin. *Madhyamakāvatāra par Candrakīrti*. Bibliotheca Buddhica IX. Osnabrück: Biblio Verlag, 1970.
French translation (up to VI.165): Louis de la Vallée Poussin. *Muséon* 8 (1907), 249-317; *Muséon* 11 (1910), 271-358; and *Muséon* 12 (1911), 235-328.
German translation (VI.166-226): Helmut Tauscher. *Candrakīrti-Madhyamakāvatāraḥ und Madhyamakāvatārabhāṣyam*. Wien: Wiener Studien zur Tibetologie und Buddhismuskunde, 1981.

Clear Words, Commentary on (Nāgārjuna's) "Treatise on the Middle"
mūlamadhyamakavṛttiprasannapadā
dbu ma rtsa ba'i 'grel pa tshig gsal ba
P5260, vol. 98. Also: Dharamsala: Tibetan Publishing House, 1968.
Sanskrit: *Mūlamadhyamakakārikās de Nāgārjuna avec la Prasannapadā Commentaire de Candrakīrti*. Louis de la Vallée Poussin, ed. Bibliotheca Buddhica IV. Osnabrück: Biblio Verlag, 1970.
English translation (Ch. I, XXV): T. Stcherbatsky. *Conception of Buddhist Nirvāṇa*. Leningrad: Office of the Academy of Sciences of the USSR, 1927; revised rpt. Delhi: Motilal Banarsidass, 1978, 77-222.
English translation (Ch. II): Jeffrey Hopkins. "Analysis of Coming and Going." Dharamsala: Library of Tibetan Works and Archives, 1974.
Partial English translation: Mervyn Sprung. *Lucid Exposition of the Middle Way, the Essential Chapters from the Prasannapadā of Candrakīrti translated from the Sanskrit*. London: Routledge, 1979 and Boulder: Prajñā Press, 1979.
French translation (Ch. II-IV, VI-IX, XI, XXIII, XXIV, XXVI, XXVII): Jacques May. *Prasannapadā Madhyamaka-vṛtti, douze chapitres traduits du sanscrit et du tibétain*. Paris: Adrien-Maisonneuve, 1959.
French translation (Ch. XVIII-XXII): J. W. de Jong. *Cinq chapitres de la Prasannapadā*. Paris: Geuthner, 1949.
French translation (Ch. XVII): É. Lamotte. "Le Traité de l'acte de Vasubandhu, Karmasid-

dhiprakaraṇa," *MCB* 4 (1936), 265-288.

German translation (Ch. V and XII-XVI): St. Schayer. *Ausgewahlte Kapitel aus der Prasannapadā.* Krakow: Naktadem Polskiej Akademji Umiejetnosci, 1931.

Supplement to (Nāgārjuna's) "Treatise on the Middle"

madhyamakāvatāra

dbu ma la 'jug pa

P5261, P5262, vol. 98

Edited Tibetan: Louis de la Vallée Poussin. *Madhyamakāvatāra par Candrakīrti.* Bibliotheca Buddhica IX. Osnabrück: Biblio Verlag, 1970.

English translation (Ch. I-V): Jeffrey Hopkins. In *Compassion in Tibetan Buddhism.* Valois, NY: Gabriel Snow Lion, 1980.

English translation (Ch. VI): Stephen Batchelor, trans. In Geshé Rabten's *Echoes of Voidness.* London: Wisdom, 1983, 47-92. *See also* references under Chandrakīrti's *[Auto]-Commentary on the "Supplement."*

Dharmakīrti (*chos kyi grags pa,* seventh century)

Seven Treatises on Valid Cognition

Analysis of Relations

sambandhaparīkṣā

'brel pa brtag pa

P5713, vol. 130

Ascertainment of Prime Cognition

pramāṇaviniścaya

tshad ma rnam par nges pa

P5710, vol. 130

Commentary on (Dignāga's) "Compilation of [Teachings on] Valid Cognition"

pramāṇavārttikakārikā

tshad ma rnam 'grel gyi tshig le'ur byas pa

P5709, vol. 130

Also: Sarnath, India: Pleasure of Elegant Sayings Press, 1974.

Sanskrit: Swami Dwarikadas Shastri, ed. *Pramāṇavarttika of Āchārya Dharmakīrtti.* Varanasi: Bauddha Bharati, 1968.

English translation (Ch. II): Masatoshi Nagatomi, *A Study of Dharmakīrti's Pramāṇavarttika: An English Translation and Annotation of the Pramāṇavarttika, Book I.* Ph.D. dissert., Harvard Univ., 1957.

Drop of Reasoning

nyāyabinduprakaraṇa

rigs pa'i thigs pa zhes bya ba'i rab tu byed pa

P5711, vol.130

English translation: Th. Stcherbatsky. *Buddhist Logic.* New York: Dover Publications, 1962.

Drop of Reasons

hetubindunāmaprakaraṇa

gtan tshigs kyi thigs pa zhes bya ba rab tu byed pa

P5712, vol. 130

English translation: Th. Stcherbatsky. *Buddhist Logic.* New York: Dover Publications, 1962.

Principles of Debate

vādanyāya

rtsod pa'i rigs pa

P5715, vol. 130

Proof of Other Continuums

saṃtānāntarasiddhināmaprakaraṇa

rgyud gzhan grub pa zhes bya ba'i rab tu byed pa
P5716, vol. 130
Dharmamitra (*chos kyi bshes gnyen*)
Clear Words, a Commentary on (Maitreya's) 'Ornament for Clear Realization'
abhisamayālaṃkārakārikāprajñāpāramitopadeśaśāstraṭīkāprasphuṭapadā
shes rab kyi pha rol tu phyin pa'i man ngag gi bstan bcos mngon par rtogs pa'i rgyan gyi tshig le'ur byas pa'i 'grel bshad tshig rab tu gsal ba
P5194, vol. 91
D̄zong-ka-b̄a L̄o-sang-drak-b̄a (*tsong kha pa blo bzang grags pa*, 1357-1419)
Golden Rosary of Eloquence/ Extensive Explanation of (Maitreya's) "Ornament for Clear Realization, Treatise of Quintessential Instructions on the Perfection of Wisdom," As Well As Its Commentaries
legs bshad gser gyi phreng ba/shes rab kyi pha rol tu phyin pa'i man ngag gi bstan bcos mngon par rtogs pa'i rgyan 'grel pa dang bcas pa'i rgya cher bshad pa
P6150, vol. 154
Also: Sarnath: Pleasure of Elegant Sayings Press, 1970.
Also: The Collected Works of Rje Tsoṅ-kha-pa Blo-bzaṅ-grags-pa, vol. tsa. New Delhi: Ngawang Gelek Demo, 1975ff.
Great Exposition of the Stages of the Path/ Stages of the Path to Enlightenment Thoroughly Teaching All the Stages of Practice of the Three Types of Beings
lam rim chen mo/ skyes bu gsum gyi rnyams su blang ba'i rim pa thams cad tshang bar ston pa'i byang chub lam gyi rim pa
P6001, vol. 152
English translation of the part on the object of negation: Elizabeth Napper. In *Dependent-Arising and Emptiness*. London: Wisdom Publications, 1989.
English translation of the parts on calm abiding and special insight: Alex Wayman. In *Calming the Mind and Discerning the Real*. New York: Columbia University Press, 1978; reprint New Delhi, Motilal Banarsidass, 1979.
Illumination of the Thought, Extensive Explanation of (Chandrakīrti's) "Supplement to (Nāgārjuna's) 'Treatise on the Middle"
dbu ma la 'jug pa'i rgya cher bshad pa dgongs pa rab gsal
P6143, vol. 154. Also: Sarnath, India: Pleasure of Elegant Sayings Press, 1973. Also: Delhi: Ngawang Gelek, 1975. Also: Delhi: Guru Deva, 1979.
English translation (Ch. I-V): Jeffrey Hopkins. In *Compassion in Tibetan Buddhism*. Valois, New York: Snow Lion, 1980.
English translation (Ch. VI: stanzas 1-7): Jeffrey Hopkins and Anne C. Klein. In Anne C. Klein *Path to the Middle: Madhyamaka Philosophy in Tibet: The Oral Scholarship of Kensur Yeshay Tupden*. Albany: SUNY Press, 1994. 147-183 and 252-271.
Medium Exposition of the Stages of the Path/ Small Exposition of the Stages of the Path to Enlightenment
lam rim 'bring/ lam rim chung ngu/ skyes bu gsum gyi nyams su blang ba'i byang chub lam gyi rim pa
P6002, vol. 152-153. Also: Dharamsala: Shes rig par khang, 1968. Also: Mundgod: dga' ldan shar rtse, n.d., (edition including outline of topics by Trijang Rinbochay). Also: Delhi: Ngawang Gelek, 1975. Also: Delhi: Guru Deva, 1979.
English translation of the section on special insight: Robert Thurman. "The Middle Transcendent Insight" in *Life and Teachings of Tsong Khapa*. Dharamsala: Library of Tibetan Works and Archives, 1982, 108-85.
English translation of the section on special insight: Jeffrey Hopkins. "Special Insight: From D̄zong-ka-b̄a's *Middling Exposition of the Stages of the Path to Enlightenment Practiced by*

Persons of Three Capacities with supplementary headings by Trijang Rinbochay." Unpublished manuscript

Notes on the Concentrations and Formless Absorptions

bsam gzugs zin bris

P6148, vol. 154

Haribhadra (*seng ge bzang po*, late eighth century)

Clear Meaning Commentary/ Commentary on (Maitreya's) "Ornament for Clear Realization, Treatise of Quintessential Instructions on the Perfection of Wisdom"

spuṭhārtha/ abhisamayālaṃkāranāmaprajñāpāramitopadeśaśāstravṛtti

'grel pa don gsal/ shes rab kyi pha rol tu phyin pa'i man ngag gi bstan bcos mngon par rtogs pa'i rgyan ces bya ba'i 'grel pa

P5191, vol. 90

Sanskrit: Unrai Wogihara, ed., *Abhisamayālaṃkārālokā Prajñā-pāramitā-vyākhyā, The Work of Haribhadra.* Tokyo: The Toyo Bunko, 1932-5; reprinted., Tokyo: Sankibo Buddhist Book Store, 1973.

Illumination of (Maitreya's) "Ornament for Clear Realization"

abhisamayālaṃkārnāmaprajñāpāramitopadeśasāstravṛtti

shes rab kyi pha rol tu phyin pa'i man ngag gi bstan bcos mngon par rtogs pa'i rgyan ces bya ba'i 'grel pa

P5191 vol. 90

Jam-ȳang-shay-b̄a (*'jam dbyangs bzhad pa*, 1648-1721)

Great Exposition of Tenets/ Explanation of 'Tenets,' Sun of the Land of Samantabhadra Brilliantly Illuminating All of Our Own and Others' Tenets and the Meaning of the Profound [Emptiness], Ocean of Scripture and Reasoning Fulfilling All Hopes of All Beings

grub mtha' chen mo/ grub mtha'i rnam bshad rang gzhan grub mtha' kun dang zab don mchog tu gsal ba kun bzang zhing gi nyi ma lung rigs rgya mtsho skye dgu'i re ba kun skong

Musoorie: Dalama, 1962

English translation (beginning of the chapter on the Consequence School): Jeffrey Hopkins. In *Meditation on Emptiness.* London: Wisdom Publications, 1983.

Great Exposition of the Concentrations and Formless Absorptions/ Treatise on the Presentations of the Concentrations and Formless Absorptions, Adornment Beautifying the Subduer's Teaching, Ocean of Scripture and Reasoning, Delighting the Fortunate

bsam gzugs chen mo/ bsam gzugs kyi snyoms 'jug rnams kyi rnam par bzhag pa'i bstan bcos thub bstan mdzes rgyan lung dang rigs pa'i rgya mtsho skal bzang dga' byed

Folio printing in India; no publication data.

Kamalashīla (c. 740-795)

Stages of Meditation

bhāvanākrama

sgom pa'i rim pa

Sanskrit: *First Bhāvanākrama.* G. Tucci, ed. Minor Buddhist texts, II, Serie Orientale Roma IX, 2. Rome: IS.M.E.O., 1958, 185-229. *Third Bhāvanākrama.* G. Tucci, ed. Minor Buddhist texts, III, Serie Orientale Roma XLIII. Rome: IS.M.E.O., 1971.

P5310-12, vol. 102; Toh 3915-17, Dharma vol. 73, Tokyo *sde dge* vol. 15

Maitreya (*byams pa*)

Five Doctrines of Maitreya

1 *Great Vehicle Treatise on the Sublime Continuum/ Treatise on the Later Scriptures of the Great Vehicle*

mahāyānottaratantraśāstra

theg pa chen po rgyud bla ma'i bstan bcos
P5525, vol. 108
Sanskrit: E. H. Johnston (and T. Chowdhury) ed. *The Ratnagotravibhāga Mahāyānottara-tantraśāstra.* Patna: Bihar Research Society, 1950.
English translation: E. Obermiller. "Sublime Science of the Great Vehicle to Salvation." *Acta Orientalia,* 9 (1931), 81-306. Also: J. Takasaki. *A Study on the Ratnagotravibhāga.* Rome: IS. M.E.O., 1966.
2 *Differentiation of Phenomena and the Final Nature of Phenomena*
dharmadharmatāvibhaṅga
chos dang chos nyid rnam par 'byed pa
P5523, vol. 108
3 *Differentiation of the Middle and the Extremes*
madhyāntavibhaṅga
dbus dang mtha' rnam par 'byed pa
P5522, vol. 108
Sanskrit text: *Madhyānta-vibhāga-śāstra.* Ramchandra Pandeya ed. (Delhi: Motilal Banarsidass, 1971). Also: *Madhyāntavibhāga-bhāṣya.* Gadjin M. Nagao, ed. (Tokyo: Suzuki Research Foundation, 1964).
Translation: Stefan Anacker, *Seven Works of Vasubandhu* (Delhi: Motilal Banarsidass, 1984). Also, of chapter one: Thomas A. Kochumuttom, *A Buddhist Doctrine of Experience* (Delhi: Motilal Banarsidass, 1982). Also, of chapter one: F. Th. Stcherbatsky, *Madhyāntavibhāga, Discourse on Discrimination between Middle and Extremes ascribed to Bodhisattva Maitreya and Commented by Vasubandhu and Sthiramati,* Bibliotheca Buddhica XXX (1936), (Osnabrück: Biblio Verlag, 1970); reprint: (Calacutta: Indian Studies Past and Present, 1971). Also, of chapter one: David Lasar Friedmann, *Sthiramati, Madhyāntavibhāgaṭīkā: Analysis of the Middle Path and the Extremes* (Utrecht: 1937).
4 *Ornament for Clear Realization*
abhisamayālaṃkāra
mngon par rtogs pa'i rgyan
P5184, vol. 88
Sanskrit text: Th. Stcherbatsky and E. Obermiller, ed. *Abhisamayālaṃkāra-Prajñāpāramitā-Updeśa-Śāstra.* Bibliotheca Buddhica XXIII. Osnabrück: Biblio Verlag, 1970.
English translation: Edward Conze. *Abhisamayālaṃkāra.* Serie Orientale Roma. Rome: Is.M.E.0., 1954.
5 *Ornament for the Great Vehicle Sūtras*
mahāyānasūtrālaṃkāra
theg pa chen po'i mdo sde rgyan gyi tshig le'ur byas pa
P5521, vol. 108
Sanskrit text: Sitansusekhar Bagchi, ed. *Mahāyāna-Sūtrālaṃkāraḥ of Asaṅga* [with Vasubandhu's commentary]. Buddhist Sanskrit Texts, No.13. Darbhanga: Mithila Institute, 1970.
Sanskrit text and translation into French: Sylvain Lévi. *Mahāyānasūtrālaṃkāra, exposé de la doctrine du grand véhicule selon le système Yogācāra.* 2 vols. Paris: 1907, 1911.
Sanskrit text and translation into English: Surekha Vijay Limaye. *Mahāyānasūtrālaṃkāra by Asaṅga.* Bibliotheca Indo-Buddhica Series No. 94 Delhi: Sri Satguru Publications, 1992.
Nāgārjuna (*klu sgrub,* first to second century C.E.)
Friendly Letter
bshes pa'i spring yig
suhṛllekha
P5682, vol. 129

English translation: Geshe Lobsang Tharchin and Artemus B. Engle, *Nāgārjuna's Letter.* Dharamsala: Library of Tibetan Works and Archives, 1979.

Shāntideva (*zhi ba lha,* eighth century)

Engaging in the Bodhisattva Deeds

bodhi[sattva]caryāvatāra

byang chub sems dpa'i spyod pa la 'jug pa

P5272, vol. 99.

Sanskrit text: P. L. Vaidya, ed. *Bodhicaryāvatāra.* Buddhist Sanskrit Texts, no. 12. Darbhanga: The Mithila Institute, 1988.

Sanskrit and Tibetan texts: Vidhushekara Bhattacharya, ed. *Bodhicaryāvatāra.* Bibliotheca Indica, vol. 280. Calcutta: The Asiatic Society, 1960.

Sanskrit and Tibetan texts with Hindi translation: Rāmaśaṁkara Tripāthī, ed. *Bodhicaryāvatār.* Bauddha-Himālaya-Granthamālā, vol. 8. Leh, Ladākh: Central Institute of Buddhist Studies, 1989.

English translation: Stephen Batchelor. *A Guide to the Bodhisattva's Way of Life.* Dharamsala: Library of Tibetan Works and Archives, 1979. Also: Marion Matics. *Entering the Path of Enlightenment.* New York: Macmillan Co, 1970. Also: Kate Crosby and Andrew Skilton. *The Bodhicaryāvatāra.* Oxford: Oxford Univ. Pr., 1996. Also: Padmakara Translation Group. *The Way of the Bodhisattva.* Boston: Shambhala, 1997. Also: Vesna A. Wallace and B. Alan Wallace. *A Guide to the Bodhisattva Way of Life.* Ithaca: Snow Lion, 1997.

Contemporary commentary by H.H. the Dalai Lama, Tenzin Gyatso. *Transcendent Wisdom.* Ithaca: Snow Lion, 1988. Also: H.H. the Dalai Lama, Tenzin Gyatso. *A Flash of Lightning in the Dark of the Night.* Boston: Shambhala, 1994.

Vasubandhu (*dbyig gnyen,* fl. 360)

Treasury of Manifest Knowledge

abhidharmakośakārikā

chos mngon pa'i mdzod kyi tshig le'ur byas pa

P5590, vol. 115

Sanskrit text: P. Pradhan, ed. *Abhidharmakośabhāṣyam of Vasubandhu.* Patna: Jayaswal Research Institute, 1975. Also: *Abhidharmakośa & Bhāṣya of Ācārya Vasubandhu with Sphuṭārtha Commentary of Ācārya Yaśomitra,* Swami Dwarikadas Shastri, ed., Bauddha Bharati Series no. 5 (Banaras: Bauddha Bharati, 1970).

French translation: Louis de la Vallée Poussin. *L'Abhidharmakośa de Vasubandhu.* 6 vols. Bruxelles: Institut Belge des Hautes Études Chinoises, 1971.

English translation of the French: Leo M. Pruden, *Abhidharmakośabhāṣyam.* Berkeley: Asian Humanities Press, 1988.

Wonch'uk (Tib. *rdzogs gsal/ wen tshig/ wen tshegs/ wanydzeg,* Chin. *Yüan-ts'e;* 613-696)

Extensive Commentary on the "Sūtra Unraveling the Thought"

'phags pa dgongs pa nges par 'grel pa'i mdo'i rgya cher 'grel pa

P5517, vol. 116.

Chinese edition: *Dai-nihon Zokuzōkyō, hsü tsang ching* (Hong Kong Reprint, 1922, 134.d-535.a). Also: *Da Zang Jing* (Taipei: Xin Wen Fong Publishing Co., Ltd.), 1977, vol. 34, 581-952, and vol. 35, 1-100. Reconstruction of the first portion of the eighth fascicle and all of the tenth fascicle: Inaba Shōju: *Enjiki Gejinmikkyōsho Sanitsububan no kanbunyaku* (Kyoto: Hōzōkan, 1949).

3. OTHER WORKS

Gyatso, Tenzin, Dalai Lama XIV. *Opening the Eye of New Awareness.* Translated by Donald Lopez Jr. with Jeffrey Hopkins. London: Wisdom Publications, 1985.

Hopkins, Jeffrey. *Meditation on Emptiness.* London: Wisdom Publications, 1983.

Joshi, L.M. "Facets of Jaina Religiousness in Comparative Light," L.D. Series 85. Ahmedabad: L.D. Institute of Indology, May 1981. 53-8.

Klein, Anne C. "Mental Concentration and the Unconditioned" in *Paths to Liberation: The Marga and Its Transformations in Buddhist Thought,* ed. by Robert E. Buswell, Jr., and Robert M Gimello. Honolulu: University of Hawaii Press, 269-308.

Lang, Karen. *Āryadeva's Catuḥśataka: On the Bodhisattva's Cultivation of Merit and Knowledge.* Indiske Studier VII. Copenhagen: Akademisk Forlag, 1986.

Lati Rinbochay, Denma Lochö Rinbochay, Leah Zahler, Jeffrey Hopkins. *Meditative States in Tibetan Buddhism.* London: Wisdom Publications, 1983.

Lati Rinbochay and Elizabeth Napper. *Mind in Tibetan Buddhism.* London: Rider and Company, 1980; Ithaca: Snow Lion Publications, 1980.

Lati Rinbochay and Jeffrey Hopkins. *Death, Intermediate State and Rebirth in Tibetan Buddhism.* London: Rider and Co., 1979; Ithaca: Snow Lion Publications, 1980.

Poussin, Louis de la Vallée. *L'Abhidharmakośa de Vasubandhu.* 6 vols. Bruxelles: Institut Belge des Hautes Études Chinoises, 1971.

Sherbourne, Richard, S.J. *A Lamp for the Path and Commentary.* London: George Allen & Unwin, 1983.

Tharchin, Geshe Lobsang and Artemus B. Engle. *Nāgārjuna's Letter.* Dharamsala: Library of Tibetan Works and Archives, 1979.

Wogihara, Unrai, ed. *Abhisamayālaṃkārālokā Prajñā-pāramitā-vyākhyā. The Work of Haribhadra.* Tokyo: The Toyo Bunko, 1932-5; reprint ed., Tokyo: Sankibo Buddhist Book Store, 1973.

INDEX

C

D

E

earth (element), 62
earth wind, 26
effect
proprietary, 45
effort
arising from application, 88, 89
perfection of, 194
power of, 88-89
relationship to exertion, 73
which is insatiable, 88, 89
eighth mental abiding, 32, 89, 90, 91, 163, 165
elements
four, 62, 120, 121
emanated beings, 170
emptiness, 112, 137, 145, 187, 189, 218, 247, 251. (*see also* mode)
as a slightly hidden phenomenon, 190
as apprehended object, 179
as limit of phenomena, 187
as mode of phenomena, 64, 184, 192
as object of observation, 192
as object of observation for calm abiding, 63, 64-65, 68, 161-62, 165-66, 167-68, 190-91, 212
as object of observation for special insight, 167
as object of observation for special insight, 64, 166, 191
Bodhisattva Superior's meditation on, 179
direct cognition/ realization of, 41, 130, 131, 156, 181-82, 188, 228, 229, 252, 255
by a Bodhisattva, 60
generally not an object of observation for beginners, 186
generic image of, 165-66, 181
in relation to causality, 195
in state subsequent to meditative equipoise, 36-37
manifestation of, 229
meditative equipoise on, 138
object of negation, 170-71
realization of
as cause of unimpededness, 120, 170
seeking calm abiding from within the view, 118, 168
seeking the view within a meditative state, 168
subsequent realization of, 182
understanding of, 145, 147, 228
union of calm abiding and special insight realizing, 147
emptinesses, eighteen, 68
Engaging in the Bodhisattva Deeds, 193
enlightenment
attainment of, 228, 229
manifesting or actualizing, 229
equanimity. (*see also* feeling, neutral; even-mindedness; *and* desisting from application
equanimity, immeasurable, 90
equipoise level, 205-6, 267, 201, 270, 271, 272
establishments in mindfulness, four, 69
ethics, 266
perfection of, 194
eunuchs, 175
even-mindedness, 55
exalted knower of all aspects, 118, 180, 218, 239
exalted knowers, three, 181
meditation on, 180-81
mental basis of, 182
exalted wisdom, 46, 229
actualization of, 229
directly realizing the truth, 229
of meditative equipoise, 129, 130, 131
twenty-one divisions of, 59-63
excellent paths of action, ten, 262
exchange of self and other, 154
excitement, 34, 35, 54, 77, 80, 82, 83-86, 87, 88, 89, 90, 91, 92, 96, 127, 164
antidotes to, 87
definition of, 83
during training in special insight, 220, 221, 223, 43
subtle, 83
thorough entanglement of, 266
exertion, 120

G